Meinhard von Gerkan

Architecture 1997-1999

von Gerkan, Marg und Partner

Birkhäuser – Verlag für Architektur
Birkhäuser – Publishers for Architecture
Basel · Boston · Berlin

A CIP catalogue record for this book is available from the Library of Congress, Washington D. C., USA.

Deutsche Bibliothek – CIP-Einheitsaufnahme
Von Gerkan, Marg und Partner <Hamburg>:
Architecture 1995 - 1997 / Von Gerkan, Marg und Partner /
Meinhard von Gerkan.
- Basel ; Boston ; Berlin : Birkhäuser, 1998
ISBN 3 - 7643 - 5844 - 0 (Basel...)
ISBN 0 - 8176 - 5844 - 0 (Boston)
NE: Gerkan, Meinhard von [Mitarb. Pastuschka, Bernd]; HST

All project descriptions were written by gmp with the exeption of the press releases. All rights reserved by the publisher or author.

© 2000 Meinhard von Gerkan
Birkhäuser – Publishers for Architecture,
P.O. Box 133, CH-4010 Basel, Switzerland

Chefredakteur Chief Editor: Bernd Pastuschka
Übersetzung Translation: Bianca Murphy, Martin Murphy,
Ursula Perry, Stephen Perry
Buchgestaltung, Umschlaggestaltung Layout, Cover layout:
Dominique Oechsle, Hamburg
Lektor Lector: Bettina Ahrens
Dokumentation Documentation: Irina Gheorghiu

Reproduktion Reproduction: Heiner Leiska, Hamburg
Nina Fulde, Beatrix Hansen
Druck Print: Druckerei zu Altenburg

Titelmotiv Front cover: Bahnhof Berlin-Spandau (Foto Photo: Hans Bach)

Gedruckt auf säurefreiem Papier, hergestellt aus chlorfrei gebleichtem
Zellstoff. TCF ∞
Printed on acid-free paper produced from chlorine-free pulp. TCF ∞
Printed in Germany
ISBN 3 - 7643 - 6232 - 4

9 8 7 6 5 4 3 2 1

INHALT

EDITORIAL
PRESSESPIEGEL

LEHRE UND FORSCHUNG

Hörsaalzentrum der TU Chemnitz
Hörsaalzentrum der Universität Oldenburg
Neubau Geisteswissenschaften, Universität Leipzig
Mensa Fachhochschule Regensburg
Physikalische Institute, Berlin-Adlershof
Landesgymnasium St. Afra, Meißen
Gymnasium Waltersdorfer Chaussee, Berlin
Lehrbauhof II, Berlin-Marzahn
Deutsche Schule und Dienstwohnungen in Peking
Vortragspult

KULTUR

„Christus-Pavillon", Expo 2000, Hannover
Kunsthalle Bremen - „Weserbahnhof II"
Museum Constantini, Buenos Aires
Industriemuseum Chemnitz
Gemeindezentrum Johnsallee, Hamburg
Gorée Memorial, Dakar, Senegal
Musiktheater Graz, Österreich
Bürgerhaus Saulgau
Rhodarium Bremen

VERWALTUNG UND ARBEIT

Dresdner Bank am Pariser Platz, Berlin
Bayerische Rückversicherung, München
Telekom-Zentrale, Suhl
Generaldirektion Deutsche Post AG, Bonn
Telekom-Zentrale, Holzhauser Straße, Berlin
Bertrandt AG Technologie-Zentrum, Ehningen

CONTENTS

EDITORIAL
PRESS COMMENTARIES

8   EDITORIAL
9   PRESS COMMENTARIES

RESEARCH AND TEACHING

22   Chemnitz Technical University - Auditoria
42   Oldenburg University - Auditoria
54   Leipzig University - Humanities Faculty
55   College Refectory, Regensburg
56   Institutes of Physics, Berlin-Adlershof
62   St. Afra Grammar-School, Meißen
63   Waltersdorfer Chaussee Grammar-School, Berlin
64   Lehrbauhof II, Berlin-Marzahn
66   German School and Service Housing, Peking
74   Lectern

CULTURE

80   "Christian Pavilion", Expo 2000, Hanover
92   Bremen Art Gallery - "Weserbahnhof II"
94   Museum Constantini, Buenos Aires
98   Chemnitz Industrial Museum
99   Community Centre Johnsallee, Hamburg
100 Gorée Memorial, Dakar, Senegal
104 Music Theatre, Graz, Austria
105 Citizens' Hall, Saulgau
106 Rhodarium Bremen

ADMINISTRATION AND WORK

110 Dresdner Bank, Pariser Platz, Berlin
128 Bayerische Rückversicherung, Munich
130 Telekom Headquarters, Suhl
136 Deutsche Post AG Headquarters, Bonn
138 Telekom Headquarters, Holzhauser Straße, Berlin
150 Bertrandt AG Technology Centre, Ehningen

MESSE UND KONSUM

Philips Messestand   156
Messe Rimini, Italien   166
Messe Düsseldorf   168
Geschäftshaus Neuer Wall, Hamburg   170
Forum Köpenick, Berlin   172

VERKEHR

Bahnhof Berlin-Spandau   178
Transrapid Station, Schwerin   190
Lehrter Bahnhof, Berlin   194
S-Bahn Stationen Hannover   198
Flughafen Teneriffa   200
Flughafen München - Terminal 2   204
Flughafen Stuttgart - Terminal 3   210
Flughafen Berlin-Brandenburg International   212
Faltbrücke Kiel-Hörn   220
Eisenbahnbrücke über die Havel, Berlin-Spandau   224
Brücke über die Wublitz, Potsdam   227
Innengestaltung Transrapid   228
Interieur Metropolitan Express Train   232

STAAT UND KOMMUNE

Parlament und Kongreßzentrum Hanoi, Vietnam   244
Gerichtshof Antwerpen, Belgien   250
Rathaus Bramsche   252
Zentrale Polizeitechnische Dienste, Duisburg   254
Spielbank Bad Steben   256
Heckscherklinik, München   262
Kinder- und Frauenklinik Universität Dresden   263
Vertretung der Bundesländer Niedersachsen   264
und Schleswig-Holstein in Berlin
Vertretung der Bundesländer Brandenburg   268
und Mecklenburg-Vorpommern in Berlin
Botschaftsresidenz der Vereinigten Arabischen Emirate, Berlin   272

EXHIBITION AND CONSUMERISM

Philips Exhibition Stand
Rimini Exhibition Grounds, Italy
Düsseldorf Exhibition Grounds
Commercial Premises Neuer Wall, Hamburg
Köpenick Forum, Berlin

TRANSPORT

Berlin-Spandau Train Station
Transrapid Station, Schwerin
"Lehrter Bahnhof" New Train Station, Berlin
Suburban Line Stations, Hanover
Tenerife Airport
Munich Airport - Terminal 2
Stuttgart Airport - Terminal 3
Berlin-Brandenburg International Airport
Folding Bridge, Kiel-Hörn
Railway Bridge across the River Havel, Berlin-Spandau
Bridge across the River Wublitz, Potsdam
Interior Design Transrapid
Interior Design Metropolitan Express Train

STATE AND COMMUNITY

Parliament und Congress Centre, Hanoi, Vietnam
Law Courts, Antwerp, Belgium
Town Hall, Bramsche
Police Headquarters, Technical Depot, Duisburg
Bad Steben Casino
Heckscher Clinic, Munich
Children's and Gynaecological Hospital, Dresden University
Federal Offices of Lower Saxony
and Schleswig-Holstein in Berlin
Federal Offices of Brandenburg
and Mecklenburg-Vorpommern in Berlin
United Arab Emirates Embassy, Berlin

STÄDTEBAU

„Brauerei Ottakring", Wien - Städtebauliche Neustrukturierung 276
Messeplatz Basel, Schweiz 280
Teerhof, Bremen 281
Calenberger Esplanade, Hannover 282
Wohnbebauung, Berlin-Friedrichshain 292
„Das Städtische Haus", Berlin 296
Alsterfleet Bebauung, Hamburg 298
„Haus der Architekten", Düsseldorf 300
Wohn- und Geschäftshaus am Benediktsplatz, Erfurt 301
Interimsbebauung - Expo 2000, Hannover 302
„HafenCity", Hamburg 310
Lärmschutzwand in Regensburg 314
Ortszentrum Schöneiche 318

RESTAURIERUNG UND INTERIEUR

Restaurierung des Thalia Theaters, Hamburg 324
Umbau und Restaurierung Hapag Lloyd AG
am Ballindamm, Hamburg 328
Hamburgische Staatsoper 334
– Neugestaltung Foyer und Garderobe

ANHANG

Curricula Vitae 336
Erfolgreiche Wettbewerbe und Gutachten 339
Fertiggestellte Bauten 341
Im Bau befindliche Projekte
In Planung befindliche Projekte
Auszeichnungen 342
Ausstellungen 343
Bücher 344
Werkverzeichnis 1965-1999 345
Bildnachweis 356

URBAN DESIGN

276 "Brewery Ottakring", Vienna - Urban Restructuring
280 Basle Exhibition Grounds, Switzerland
281 Teerhof, Bremen
282 Calenberger Esplanade, Hanover
292 Housing Development, Berlin-Friedrichshain
296 "The Urban House", Berlin
298 Alsterfleet Development, Hamburg
300 "Institute of Architects", Düsseldorf
301 Residential and Commercial Building, Benediktsplatz, Erfurt
302 Temporary Development - Expo 2000, Hanover
310 "HafenCity", Hamburg
314 Acoustic Barrier, Regensburg
318 Schöneiche Town Centre

RESTORATION AND INTERIOR DESIGN

324 Restoration Thalia Theatre, Hamburg
328 Conversion and Restoration Hapag Lloyd AG,
Ballindamm, Hamburg
334 State Opera House Hamburg
– Redesign of Foyer and Cloakroom

APPENDIX

336 Curricula Vitae
339 Successful Competition Entries
341 Completed Projects
Projects under Construction
Projects at Planning Stage
342 Awards
343 Exhibitions
344 Books
345 Comprehensive List of Works 1965-1999
356 Photo Credits

MEINHARD VON GERKAN
Editorial

Architektur 1966 - 78, gmp I
Architektur 1978 - 83, gmp II
Architektur 1983 - 88, gmp III
Architektur 1988 - 91, gmp IV
Architecture 1991 - 95, gmp V
Architecture 1995 - 97, gmp VI

Der vorliegende Band Architektur 1997 bis 1999 - gmp VII, schließt an die Reihe der vorangegangenen Publikationen an. Damit sind die Arbeitsergebnisse unserer Architektensozietät, die seit 1965 besteht, fortlaufend dokumentiert worden. Nahezu alle Arbeiten, die in dem Zeitraum von 1997 bis 1999 entstanden sind, werden in diesem Band vorgestellt. Projekte, die bereits in einer früheren Ausgabe vorgestellt wurden und sich noch in der Realisierungs- und Planungsphase befinden, sollen als fertiggestelltes Ergebnis im nächsten Band gezeigt werden. Trotz dieser Auslassungen sind 48 Projekte und 20 Realisierungen für den zweijährigen Zeitraum zur Berichterstattung verblieben.

Die Fortsetzungsreihe der Monographien dient mehreren Zielsetzungen:
- Als Nachweis dessen, was wir entwerfen, wie wir entwerfen und inwieweit die realisierten Ergebnisse der konzeptionellen Absicht entsprechen.
- Der Sicherung des konzeptionellen und inhaltlichen Gleichklangs aller Hervorbringungen unserer Sozietät.
- Der Orientierung für Bauherren, Berater und Mitarbeiter.
- Der Überprüfung, wie sich die realisierte Wirklichkeit zum theoretischen Anspruch verhält.

Die Paradigmen unserer theoretischen Position sind in den Vorworten der vorausgegangenen Bände nachzulesen und haben bis heute ihren Bestand behalten.
Durch die Beschreibung unserer Entwurfsmethode als "dialogisch" soll herausgestellt werden, daß nach unserem Verständnis im Prozeß des Entwerfens Frage und Anwort in inniger Wechselwirkung stehen, jede spezifische Aufgabenstellung induziert eine oder mehrere Lösungen, deren Analyse und Bewertung wirkt aber zurück auf die Aufgabe und verändert deren Wertigkeiten und Forderungen.
Diese unsere architekturtheoretische Position des Entwerfens im Dialog ist somit keine abstrakte Plattform des Geistes, sondern eine konkrete Philosophie unseres Handelns. Deswegen bedarf sie nicht nur der permanenten Überprüfung ihrer Glaubwürdigkeit, sondern zugleich der Sicherung, daß ein kreatives Atelier mit weit mehr als 250 Mitarbeitern diesem Leitbild gleichsinnig folgt. Dies vermag eine Sammlung konkreter Entwürfe und Bauten anschaulicher zu vermitteln als abstrakte Thesen. In diesem Sinne sind die Monographien vornehmlich ein Fundus zur Information und Orientierung in der eigenen Sozietät. Entgegen der Praxis in den vorangegangenen Bänden, in denen jeweils ein namhafter Architekturkritiker bzw. Bauhistoriker zu unserer Arbeit und dem jeweiligen Band Stellung bezogen hat, haben wir uns dieses Mal entschlossen, völlig unabhängige Kritiken, die in der Fach- und Tagespresse erschienen sind, dem Buch voranzustellen. Es wurde eine Auswahl getroffen, die sich auf Bauten und Projekt bezieht, die in diesem Band vorgestellt werden.
Für die Genehmigung der Autoren und Verlage zum Abdruck der Publikationen in unserem Buch bedanken wir uns sehr herzlich.

MEINHARD VON GERKAN
Editorial

Architektur 1966 - 78, gmp I
Architektur 1978 - 83, gmp II
Architektur 1983 - 88, gmp III
Architektur 1988 - 91, gmp IV
Architecture 1991 - 95, gmp V
Architecture 1995 - 97, gmp VI

The present volume, Architecture 1997 - 99, gmp VII, contributes to the sequence of previous publications. The realized works from our architectural practice, which was founded in 1965, have thus been continuously documented. Almost all projects, which have been realized over the period 1997 to 1999, are presented in this volume. Projects, which have been illustrated in previous volumes and which are still under construction or in the planning phase, will be presented as completed buildings in the next publication. Despite these omissions 48 projects and 20 realizations are illustrated over this two-years-period.

The serialized monographs serve several purposes:
- As a record of what we design, how we design and to what extent the results are in accordance with the conceptional intention.
- As a safeguard for the continuity of all our works regarding concept and content.
- As orientation for clients, consultants and employees.
- As verification for the relation between built reality and theoretical demand.

The paradigms of our theoretical position can be found in the prefaces of the previous volumes and are still valid.

The description of our design method as "dialogical" emphasizes that according to our understanding, question and answer are in a close correlation during the design process. Each specific task induces one or several solutions, their analysis and evaluation however reacts towards the task, changing its value and demands.
Our theoretical design standpoint is therefore no abstract mental platform, but a definite philosophy of our behaviour.
Therefore the continuous examination of its credibility is as necessary as simultaneously maintaining a creative practice of more than 250 employees adhering to this guideline. This can be clearly illustrated via a collection of definite designs and buildings, rather than an abstract thesis. In this respect, the monographs are primarily an information bank for orientation within our own office.
Contrary to the practice in previous volumes, where a renowned architectural critic or historian has made commentary to our works and the volume in hand, we decided this time to select independent critics, which have been published in the architectural and daily press. A selection has been made, which corresponds to buildings and projects presented in this book. We cordially thank the authors and publishers for their approval to reproduce these publications in this volume.

DIE WOCHENSCHAU
(BAUWELT 1998, HEFT 3)

Nach der "Ummantelung" des Kröpcke-Centers und der Halle 8/9 (Heft 33/1997, Seite 1791) haben sich gmp (v. Gerkan, Marg und Partner), Hamburg, mit dem Pavillon der christlichen Kirchen Deutschlands bereits ihr drittes Hannoveraner Bauprojekt im Rahmen der Expo 2000 gesichert. In einem beschränkten Wettbewerb setzten sich gmp gegen Kleine - Ripken - Teicher aus Hannover, Peter Kulka aus Köln, die Planungsgruppe Stieldorf, Hornschuh - Pollich - Türler aus Königswinter und das Architekturbüro 3L-Plan aus Menden durch.
Der Entwurf sieht die räumliche Schließung der Platzwände der Expo - Plaza (die ebenfalls auf ein Konzept von gmp zurückgeht, siehe Heft 21/1996) vor. Die beiden Baukörper des Pavillons sollen mit einer 75 m langen, 16 m hohen und 4 m tiefen Kolonnadenwand umgeben werden, die einen Übergang vom Freiraum zu den Bauflächen schafft. Auf dem nördlichen Teil des Areals planen die Architekten einen Veranstaltungssaal mit Foyer und Bücherladen, auf dem südlichen Teil einen Feierraum (Grundfläche: 21 x 21 m; Höhe: 18 m). Um einen kontemplativen Gegenpart zu den "architektonischen Aufgeregtheiten" einer Weltausstellung zu setzen, beschränken sich gmp auf wenige Materialien: Sichtbeton, verzinkter Stahl; die zweischalige Fassade des großen Zentralraums besteht außen aus Glas und innen aus dünn geschnittenem, lichtdurchlässigem Marmor und Alabaster. Der Feierraum erhält ein Oberlicht.
Alle Baukörper – mit Ausnahme der unter dem Feierraum liegenden unterirdischen "Krypta" – beruhen auf einem modularen Baukasten (Rastermaß: 3,60 m), so daß sie nach dem Ende der Expo zerlegt und in anderer Kombination wieder aufgebaut werden können; für den Saalkomplex schlagen gmp eine Nachnutzung als Gemeindezentrum vor.

AM PARISER PLATZ
BEI DEM VERSUCH, DER DRESDNER BANK EINE FORMALE FASSADE AM PARISER PLATZ, BERLINS SCHICKSTEM PIAZZA, ZU GEBEN, HAT VOLKWIN MARG DEN NEO-KLASSI-ZISMUS EIN WENIG ZU HEFTIG IN DIE ARME GESCHLOSSEN. ABER DIE INNENGESTALTUNG IST EIN UNERWARTETES, ERFINDUNGSREICHES VERGNÜGEN.
(THE ARCHITECTURAL REVIEW, 1/99)

Der Pariser Platz liegt direkt hinter dem Brandenburger Tor, wenn man sich dem Zentrum Berlins vom Tiergarten aus nähert. Das neo-klassizistische Tor war das bedeutendste auf der westlichen Seite der Zollmauer, die die Stadt im 18. Jahrhundert umgab. Der Platz eröffnet sich am westlichen Ende der Straße Unter den Linden, der prunkvollen Stadtachse, entlang der die siegreichen Truppen aller Regime von den Hohenzollern bis hin zur DDR im Triumph marschierten.
Vor dem Krieg war dies der prächtigste Platz Berlins, eingerahmt von der Amerikanischen und Französischen Botschaft, dem besten Hotel (Adlon), der Akademie der Künste und einigen pikfeinen Wohn- und Büroblocks. Nach dem Krieg und dem Mauerbau wurde der Platz verwüstet und Teil der Todeszone. Nach der Wiedervereinigung der Stadt bestand die allgemeine Übereinkunft, den Pariser Platz erneut zur ersten Adresse der Stadt zu machen. Die Botschaften sollten zurückkehren, das Hotel und die Kunstakademie wiedererrichtet und angesehene Firmen dazu ermuntert werden, rund um den Platz zu bauen. Aber es gab einige Auseinandersetzungen über das Erscheinungsbild der Gebäude. Nach den Bestimmungen einer kritischen Rekonstruktion (S. 30) mußte die Traufhöhe 22 Meter betragen und die Gebäude eine klare Abschlußkante gegen den Himmel aufweisen. Steinverkleidungen waren weitestgehend anzubringen. Die Auslegungsbandbreite dieser Beschränkungen war enorm. Das Adlon ist uneingeschränkt repro (S. 25); J.P. Kleihues entwarf rationalistische Gebäude beiderseits des Propylaeums, die Vorgänger aus der Vorkriegszeit widerspiegeln, ohne jedoch ins Kitschige abzugleiten; Moore Ruble Yudell gaben der riesigen Amerikanischen Botschaft, die soeben in der Süd-West-Ecke des Platzes fertiggestellt wird, ein gedämpftes postmodernes Äußeres; Günther Behnisch (zusammen mit Manfred Sabatke und Werner Durth) haben einen Vorschlag für eine neue Akademie der Künste zwischen der Botschaft und

DIE WOCHENSCHAU
(BAUWELT 1998, ISSUE 3)

After the "enveloping" of the Kröpcke-Center and Hall 8/9 (issue 33/1997, p. 1791), gmp, Hamburg, secured their third Hanover EXPO 2000 project with the German Pavilion of Christian Churches. In a limited competition gmp succeeded against Kleine, Ripken, Teicher from Hanover, Peter Kulka from

Cologne, Planungsgruppe Stieldorf, Hornschuh, Pollich, Türler from Königswinter and 3L-Plan from Menden.
The concept proposes the spatial enclosure of the EXPO-Plaza walls (which are also based on a gmp concept; issue 21/1996). Both Pavilion buildings are to be framed by a 75 m long, 16 m high and 4 m deep colonnade, creating a transition from the open spaces to built areas. The architects propose an multi-purpose hall with foyer and book-shop on the northern part of the site and a solemnity hall (21 metres square and 18 metres high) on the southern section.
In order to pose a contemplative counterpart to the "architectural highlights" of a world exhibition, gmp confined themselves to few materials: fair-faced concrete and galvanized steel. The double facade of the large central hall is externally constructed from glass and internally made from thinly cut, light-transmissive marble and alabaster, the solemnity hall is illuminated via a top-light.
All buildings, with the exception of the underground "Crypt", which is located below the solemnity hall, are based on a modular construction system (grid dimension: 3,60 m), so they can be dismantled after the EXPO and rebuilt in a different composition elsewhere. Gmp proposed a community centre as the future use for the hall complex.

IN PARISER PLATZ
IN ATTEMPTING TO MAKE A FORMAL FRONT FOR THE DRESDNER BANK ON PARISER PLATZ, BERLIN'S POSHEST PIAZZA, VOLKWIN MARG MAY HAVE EMBRACED NEO-CLASSICISM A LITTLE TOO FERVENTLY. BUT THE INTERIOR IS AN UNEXPECTED, INGENIOUS PLEASURE.
(THE ARCHITECTURAL REVIEW, 1/99)

Pariser Platz is the square immediately behind the Brandenburg Gate as you approach the centre of Berlin from the Tiergarten. The Neo Classical Gate was the main one in the western side of the customs wall that surrounded the city in the eighteenth century, and the Platz is at the west end of Unter den Linden, the ceremonial axis of the city, down which the victorious troops of all regimes from the Hohenzollerns to the DDR have marched in triumph.
Before the War, the square was the grandest in Berlin, walled by the American and French embassies, the best hotel (the Adlon), the Akademie der Künste, and several very posh blocks of flats and offices. After the War and the Wall, the square was laid waste and became part of the death zone. When the city was reunited, everyone was in favour of Pariser Platz being made into a fine urban space again. The embassies would move back; the hotel and arts academy would be reinstated, and prestigious firms would be encouraged to build round the square. But there was a good deal of disagreement about what the new buildings should look like. Under the rules of critical reconstruction (p30), eaves heights had to be 22 metres, and buildings had to have a proper termination against the sky. Stone cladding was to be used as far as possible. Interpretations of these constraints have varied enormously. The Adlon is in undiluted repro (p25); J.P. Kleihues has made Rationalist buildings that echo preWar predecessors on each side of the propylaeum, but without quite descending into kitsch; Moore Ruble Yudell have made the huge US embassy now finishing in the south-west corner of the piazza in muted PoMo; Günther Behnisch (with Manfred Sabatke and Werner Durth) proposed a new arts academy between the embassy and the

dem Adlon an der Südseite des Platzes eingereicht. Aber der Fortgang ist aufgrund der Einwände gegen die freie, abstrakte Glasfassade zögerlich. Gegenüber dem Behnisch-Grundstück befindet sich auf der Nordseite eines der wenigen Gebäude, die bislang fertiggestellt wurden, die Berliner Zentrale der Dresdner Bank von gmp, von Gerkan, Marg & Partner. Stilistisch etwa in der Mitte aller Stilrichtungen angesiedelt, ist die cremefarbene Kalkstein-Ansicht nüchtern und beinahe symmetrisch, der doppelhohe Eingang wird in fast klassischen Proportionen umgeben von paarweise angeordneten Fenstern. An sonnigen Tagen sorgen bewegliche bronzefarbene Sonnenblenden für eine gewisse Abwechslung auf der Fassade, die bronzene Zierde belebt zurückhaltend die schlichten Steinplatten. Das Dach wurde, gleich dem Adlon, in dem vom Architekten bevorzugten patinierten Kupfer ausgeführt.
Nach Durchschreiten der bronze-gerahmten Türen eröffnet sich ein vollkommen unerwarteter Raum. Ein kreisförmiges Atrium erhebt sich durch die gesamte Gebäudehöhe bis hin zu dem flach gewölbten Glasdach. Auf den meisten Etagen blicken die in deutschen Geschäftsgebäuden so innig geliebten kleinen Büros über den Luftraum hinweg, durch Fenster, die sich nun aufgrund einer bindenden Vorschrift öffnen lassen. Da das Grundstück von benachbarten Brandwänden eingeschlossen ist, war eine solche Anordnung erforderlich (die Ausnahme bildet natürlich die Frontfassade, von der aus kleine Büros zum Platz hin ausgerichtet sind). Die innenliegenden Büros waren mit Tageslicht zu versorgen, welches über das Dach eindringen mußte. Was sich als Nachteil andeutete, wurde geschickt zum Vorteil umgewandelt: die dunkelgraue Struktur wurde bis ins kleinste Detail geschliffen und mit detaillierten Verbindungselementen versehen. Eine sorgsame Farbwahl belebt einzelne Räume und den zentralen Bereich. Am bedeutendsten ist die Art, in der die Auftritte der Wendeltreppe und Böden der inneren Putzbalkone aus transluzentem Glas hergestellt wurden. Was sich normalerweise als stimmungsloses Detail zeigt, wurde in ein leuchtendes Gestaltungselement verwandelt. Das trifft besonders auf die Balkone zu, die durch am äußeren Rand befestigte Strahler beleuchtet werden.
Analog zur Außenseite werden Eleganz und bankgemäßes Dekor durch sorgsame Abstimmung der Proportionen und edle Materialen sichergestellt. Der kreisförmige Raum mit seinen harten Oberflächen erzeugt ebenfalls eine gewisse Zurückhaltung und Ruhe: es ist mit Sicherheit kein Ort für kleine Kinder, aber gleichzeitig ist dies keine Bank, in der man einen Scheck einlöst oder die Kontoüberziehung zurückführt. Dieser Ort ist dem ruhigen Streben nach und der Manipulation von Großem Geld gewidmet und ist damit ein durch und durch angemessenes Mitglied im Reigen um den neuen Pariser Platz.

Anne Vyne

AUFS DACH GEPACKT

DIE NEUEN EINKAUFSCENTER IN KÖPENICK UND AM GESUNDBRUNNEN. (ARCHITEKTUR IN BERLIN / JAHRBUCH 1998)

Grundsätzlich stellt sich die Frage, ob Einkaufszentren eine kritische Besprechung lohnen. Kennst Du eines, kennst Du sie alle, lautet in Anlehnung an Thomas Morus' Utopia das Urteil. Sie brauchen einen "Magneten", einen anchor-shop: Super-, Hobby- oder Freizeitmarkt, der heute meist ein Elektronikshop für allerlei Video- und Computermaschinen ist, sowie einen ausgeklügelten Branchenmix. Dunkle Ecken darf es nicht geben; Verdreckungsgefahr. Sonderläden für, sagen wir, die Reparatur eines ererbten Regenschirms oder mit weißem Marzipan aus Königsberg - sucht man vergeblich. Solche Liebhaberecken der Stadt sind im Mahlstrom des Konsummittelmaßes der Center untergegangen. Der allgemeine Tenor, daß Einkaufszentren daher durch Ausbluten des Einzelhandels in "Streulage" eine Gefahr für die Stadt darstellen, ist sowohl richtig als auch bekannt. Aber er erinnert mittlerweile auch an die argumentative Schlacht um die Tante-Emma-Läden, die dadurch ebenfalls nicht zu erhalten waren. Daran (allein) ist die Stadt bisher nicht gestorben. Folgerichtig gibt es heute schon vereinzelte Stimmen, die etwa das Centro in Oberhausen als "Überwintergarten der Urbanität" (Michael Mönninger in der Berliner Zeitung) ansprechen.

Adlon on the south side of the square, but progress has been slow because of objections to its free, abstracted glass facade.
Opposite the Behnisch site is one

of the few buildings to be fully completed so far, the Berlin headquarters of the Dresdner Bank by gmp, von Gerkan Marg & Partner, which takes up the middle of the north side of the square. Falling somewhere in the middle of the spectrum of styles, its creamy limestone elevation is sober and nearly symmetrical, with paired vertical windows arranged roughly in Classical proportions round a central double-height entrance.
Adjustable bronze shades provide a degree of variation in the elevation on sunny days, and bronze trim sombrely relieves the plain stone wall slabs. The roof, like that of the Adlon, is in the planners' preferred patinated copper.
Once through the bronze framed doors, a completely unexpected space is revealed. A circular atrium rises through the whole height of the building to a shallowly domed rooflight. On most of the upper floors, the small offices so beloved by German business look over the void, through (the now virtually mandatory) openable windows. The site necessitated some such arrangement, for it is surrounded by party (fire) walls (except of course at the front, where little offices look out over the piazza). If inner offices were to have daylight, it had to be brought in from the top. What could have been a grim well is transformed by deft touches: the dark grey steel inner structure is honed to the smallest sections and has finely detailed joints. Colours are carefully chosen to enliven individual rooms and (by borrowing) the central space. Most important of all is the way in which the treads of the spiral staircase and the floors of the inner window-cleaning galleries are made of translucent glass. What might have been deadening elements have become luminous, particularly in the latter case, for lamps at the edge of the galleries make them glow in their own right.
As with the outside, elegance and bankerly decorum is provided by very careful control of proportions and good materials. The circular space with all those hard surfaces also engenders a degree of modesty and quietness in behaviour: it is certainly no place to bring a small child, but then this is not the sort of bank you visit to cash a cheque or reduce your overdraft. It is devoted to the quiet pursuit and manipulation of Big Money, and so of course it is a most appropriate inhabitant of the new Pariser Platz.

Anne Vyne

ROOF EXTENSION

THE NEW SHOPPING CENTRES IN KÖPENICK AND AT GESUNDBRUNNEN. (YEAR BOOK 1998/ ARCHITEKTUR IN BERLIN)

Principally the question should be asked if a shopping centre is worth debating. "If you know one, you know them all", is the conclusion derived from Thomas Moore's Utopia. They require a "magnet", an "anchor-shop": supermarkets, d-i-y shops or leisure outlets, which are now primarily electronic shops offering video games and computers, as well as a clever business mix; dark areas must be avoided. Specialized shops for example, for the repair of an inherited umbrella or selling delicatessen from Königsberg, do not exist. Such eccentric corners of a city, disappeared in the grindstone of mediocre shopping-centre consumerism.
The general tenor, that shopping centres pose a danger for the city due to the draining of retailers in distributed locations, is well-known and substantiated. But this is reminiscent of the debate concerning self-sufficient corner shops, which also did not survive. This however, did not lead to the city's destruction. Consequently, there are single voices, which refer to the

Das Forum Köpenick

Das Forum Köpenick der Hamburger Architekten gmp (von Gerkan, Marg und Partner) verlohnt Überlegungen zum Typus. Zumal nach dem Mauerfall hat er in Berlin und Umgebung eine Reihe scheußlicher, schnell aus Stahl, Glas und Aluminium zusammengeschraubter Exemplare gefunden; Hinterlassenschaften eines (Handels-)Blitzkrieges in der Terra incognita des Einzelhandels, der DDR. Eiche, Havelpark, Lindenpark, Ring- und Stern-Center - wer nennt die Namen alle! Sie schwimmen grundsätzlich in einem Asphalt- oder Knochensteinteich, auf dem für Konsumenten das Parken kostenlos ist. Die Center-Managements lieben das Wort »Verweilqualität«, da es sich gut macht im Marketing. Wie das Wort klingt, sehen die Center meist auch aus: mit Kübeln und Pflanzen aus Tunesien oder Wilhelmsruh lieblos bestückt, Halogenstrahlerchen verbreiten gleißenden Ersatzsonnenschein. Anders das Forum Köpenick. Man erkennt es natürlich schon bei der Anfahrt, da es riesig ist. Eben noch rumpelt die S-Bahn durch die stadtflüchtige Seele, bleiben die Augen in Karlshorst, dem östlichen Zehlendorf, und der Wuhlheide hängen, da taucht südlich des Bahndamms das Forum Köpenick auf; kantig, gradlinig, blockhaft, physiognomisch eine Mischung aus alter industrieller Produktionshalle und neuer elektronischer Eleganz. Wer will, kann sowohl in der Entwurfsfigur wie in der Ausführung des Baukörpers die Metapher des Mikrochips wiederfinden. Die Farbe ist sonderbar altrosa und changiert ins Lila. In der Baubeschreibung des Büros wird sie »lavaroter Werkstein« genannt. Dazu viel silberfarbenes Aluminium um die Fenster, an Gebäudeecken und -kanten. Dank der Kantenfassungen mit den (für gmp) typischen eingezogenen Ecken wirkt der Riesenbau fürs Auge ins Erträgliche gedämpft. Es ist nicht nur die klare Rationalität des Entwurfs, sondern auch dieses Stilmittel im Detail, das ihm die monumentale Schwere und lastende Größe nimmt.

Das Herzstück des Forums ist die Halle. Unter großen Dächern lautet der Titel eines gmp-Bürobuchs. Es ist ihre Spezialität, eine Obsession für die Rechen- und Konstruktionskunst der Ingenieure, die sie bauästhetisch einzusetzen wissen. Hier in Köpenick ist die Halle 18 Meter breit, 25 Meter hoch und 150 Meter lang, eine ungewöhnlich klare und demonstrative Größe. Sie verbindet den Haupteingang an der Bahnhofstraße mit dem Wuhletal auf der Rückseite. Letztere ist vorhanden nur flüchtig angelegt, wird aber demnächst eine eingreifende landschaftsgärtnerische Gestaltung erfahren; formidabel, hoffentlich. Die Wuhle ist schmal, aber ein hübsches Flüßchen.

Konstruktiv ist das Dach ein Tonnengewölbe aus Glas und Stahl, das durch filigrane Zugstreben stabilisiert wird. Brücken durchqueren die Halle; manche sind etwas breit geraten, um Stellfläche (für Eiskaffees u.ä.) zu erhalten und nähern sich dann schon fast Etagen an. Die Rentabilitätsforderung des Bauherren setzte sich hier gegen den Wunsch der Architekten durch. Im übrigen ist die Ausstattung wie die einer Straße behandelt, Granit auf den Böden, der lavarote Werkstein von der Außenfassade an den Wänden und Blindfenster in den oberen Etagen. Durchaus stattliche Bäume sowie erwähnenswert hübsches, wenn auch einfaches Buchenholz-Mobiliar sind eingestellt; Rundbänke und Pflanzkübel. Da das Forum mitten in der Stadt steht, wurden die Autos nicht rundum, sondern in zwei Etagen aufs Dach gepackt. Mit einem Trick kaschierte der zuständige Projektleiter Joachim Rind von gmp (aus dem Aachener Büro) die nötige Autodurchfahrt durch die Halle: Die Tunnelbrücken sind in der Halle verspiegelt und reflektieren das Glasdach; nicht gerade hochwertigste Spiegel, aber immerhin.

Das Forum vermittelt nun bei aller Robustheit der ästhetischen Mittel durchaus keine unangenehme Atmosphäre, sondern wirklich die eines Stadtplatzes, einer Piazetta, wenn man so will. Das liegt nicht nur an der stilistischen Geschlossenheit (der "einen Handschrift"), sondern vor allem an der Robustheit selbst. Sie bewirkt, daß sich das Gebäude höchstwahrscheinlich wie eine Ladenzeile in der Stadt gegen wechselnde Moden der Drapierung zur Wehr setzen kann. Es muß nicht alle drei, vier Jahre neu tapeziert werden. Zweitens machen sich Breite und Freizügigkeit der großen Halle bemerkbar. Beide mußten dem Bauherrn mit argumen-

Oberhausen "Centro" as the "green-house for urbanity" (Michael Mönninger in Berliner Zeitung).

Köpenick Forum

The Köpenick Forum by the Hamburg architects gmp (von Gerkan, Marg und Partner) is worth while debating this typology. After the fall of the wall the architect found a series of dreadful, quickly contrived specimens, erected from steel, glass and aluminium; legacies of a (trade) blitzkrieg in the terra incognita of the GDR retail trade. Eiche, Havelpark, Lindenpark, Ring- and Stern-Center: too many to mention! They all swim in a concrete pond, where parking is free for consumers. The shopping-centre management promote the phrase "quality of stay", extremely applicable for marketing campaigns. This terminology corresponds to the physical appearance of the centres: banal decoration with pots and plants from Tunisia or Wilhelmsruh, halogen spot lights emit blurring substitute sunshine. The Köpenick Forum is different. Due to its enormous scale it can be distinguished, when approaching. Momentarily, the suburban train makes its way through the urban quarters, the eyes glance at Karlshorst, the eastern Zehlendorf, and Wuhlheide, when suddenly in a southerly direction the Köpenick Forum appears: squared, regular, block-like, a mixture of an old industrial factory and modern electronic elegance. If desired, the metaphor of a microchip can be seen in the design stage through to the building's completion. The colour is similar to an old rose and is iridescent to purple, the architects´ project description refers to the colour as "lava red stone". Silver-coloured aluminium is applied around the windows, corners and edges. Thanks to the framed edges with the (for gmp) characteristic recessing corners, the building mass is optically reduced to an endurable volume. It is not only the clear design rationality, but this stylistic device in detail, which reduces the monumental heaviness and oppressive size.

The Forum's core is the hall. Under extensive roofs is the title of a gmp publication. It is their speciality, an obsession in the art of calculation and construction of engineers, who know how to apply these rules in an aesthetic building fashion. In Köpenick the hall is 18 metres wide, 25 metres high and 150 metres long, an unusually clear and demonstrative volume. The hall connects the main entrance along Bahnhofstraße with Wuhletal to its rear, which has hardly been considered, but will be treated with a comprehensive landscape design. The Wuhle is a small but picturesque stream.

The vaulted roof, constructed from glass and steel, is stabilized by delicate tensile cables. Bridges span the hall, some being designed a little wider than normal to create floor area (e.g. ice-cream stands), and resemble complete floors. In this respect, the client's profit requirements were carried through against the architects´ wishes. The remaining interior is treated like a streetscape: granite floors and the lava red stone as used on the external facade repeated on walls and blank windows on the upper levels. Quite magnificent trees and remarkably effective furniture made from beech-wood are erected as circular benches and plant tubs. As the Forum is located in the city centre, parking lots were not situated around but as tow levels on top of the Forum. The project architect Joachim Rind of gmp (Aachen office) wittingly concealed the required car thoroughfare through the hall: the tunnels are cladded with mirrors and reflect the glass roof.

Despite the robust application of aesthetic means, the Forum conveys no unpleasant atmosphere, but the feeling of an urban piazza space. This is the result of a stylistic unity ("one signature") and of the robustness itself. It effects, that the building is likely to resist the changing shop-window fashions just like a row of shops in the city, it does not have to be re-decorated every three to four years. Furthermore, the width and openness of the hall have their qualities. Both

tativen (Sicherheits-)Tricks abge-
schlenzt werden, der soviel semiöf-
fentliche Fläche nur widerwillig her-
gab. Aber man fühlt sich dadurch
nicht in einer Konsumentenreuse.
Die Akustik ist Raunen und Murmeln,
keine akustische Umweltverschmut-
zung. Die Temperatur: temperiert,
nicht wohnzimmerwarm. Winters
kann man den Mantel anbehalten.
Und wegen ihrer Höhe kann die Halle nicht verhängt werden durch allerlei Sonderangebotsfahnen zum
WSV oder SSV oder überhaupt SV.
Klar und rational in der Form, solide
bis gut im Material, so könnte die
Formel für das Forum Köpenick lau-
ten. Wenn denn eine historische
Typologie vom Basar über das Kauf-
und Warenhaus zu den Einkaufscen-
tern unserer Tage skizziert werden
soll, dann würde sich das Forum
Köpenick darin als eigenständiges
und durchaus stadtfähiges Exemplar
gut behaupten können.
Schließlich aber zeigt auch der direkte Vergleich zum beinahe innerstäd-
tisch gelegenen Gesundbrunnen-
Center am bisherigen S- und U-,
fürderhin auch ICE-Bahnhof Gesundbrunnen im Wedding das architektonische Niveau des Forums Köpenick.
Beide, Köpenick und Wedding, gin-
gen im Herbst 1997 fast zeitgleich
ans Konsumentennetz.

Gerwin Zohlen

DARF DENN KLAPPEN
TEUER SEIN?
**WENN ÄSTHETIK TRIFFT: EIN
KIELER BRÜCKENSCHLAG MIT
HINDERNISSEN.
(FRANKFURTER ALLGEMEINE
ZEITUNG 28.05.1998)**

Kiel liegt, wie man weiß, an der
gleichnamigen Förde, deren äußers-
tes Ende „Hörn" genannt wird. Auf
dessen einer Seite liegt die wohlan-
ständige Stadt, auf der anderen, der
Ostseite, die Industrie mit den Werf-
ten. Das ist die „schäle Siek" von Kiel,
der Stadtteil Gaarden ist immer noch
Arbeiter- und Kleineleuteviertel und
liegt „auf der falschen Seite". Der
Werftstandort aber verliert, wie überall in Deutschland, zunehmend an
Bedeutung. So gab der größte Betrieb, die HDW Howaldtswerke Deutsche Werft, riesige stadtnahe Flächen
für neue Nutzungen frei. Wie in allen
Hafenstädten der Welt bot dies die
Chance für neue urbane Entwick-
lungen.

Schon Anfang der neunziger Jahre
wurde in Kiel ein neues Stadtviertel
mit der üblichen Mischung aus Wohnen, Büros und wassernahen Freizeit-
einrichtungen geplant. Eine der
großen Skandinavien-Fährlinien war
bereit, mit ihrem Terminal auf die
andere Fördeseite zu ziehen und damit die Initialzündung zu geben. Ein-
zige Bedingung: Der umständliche
Weg um die Hörn herum mußte
durch eine Brückenverbindung zwischen Hauptbahnhof und Innenstadt
einerseits, dem neuen Terminal und
Gaarden andererseits verbessert werden. Diese Brücke aber mußte
beweglich sein, weil am Ende der
Förde die Liegeplätze der Ausflugs-
und Fördelinienschiffe liegen.
Soweit war alles klar und unstrittig.
Dann zog der - selbst bei der regie-
renden SPD, die ihn seinerzeit geholt
hatte - umstrittene Stadtbaurat Otto
Flagge ein Kaninchen aus dem Hut:
Den Brückenentwurf der Hamburger
Architekten von Gerkan, Marg & Partner und des weltweit für seine filigranen, innovativen Konstruktionen be-
kannten Stuttgarter Ingenieurbüros
Schlaich, Bergermann und Partner.
Zusammen hatten sie eine wirkliche
Sensation entwickelt, die zunächst
auch als solche von der Presse ge-
würdigt wurde, eine Weltneuheit,
eine mittels Stahlseilen auf- und zu-
klappbare „Dreifeld-Klappbrücke".
Die stellt man sich am besten so vor
wie den Arm einer Gliederpuppe,
nur daß die drei Teile Ober-, Unter-
arm und Handfläche bei der Brücke
gleich groß sind. Auf- und zuge-
klappt wird sie, wie wenn man den
Arm, der ja auch mir am Schulterge-
lenk festsitzt, zu einem Ende hin
ineinander faltet. Bei hydraulisch be-
triebenen Ladebrücken von Schiffen
gibt es das schon. Und Brücken, die
aus zwei Feldern bestehen, können
auch problemlos mit Hilfe von Stahlseilen bedient werden. Bei drei Feldern allerdings potenzieren sich die
Schwierigkeiten, zumal wenn man
den Anspruch stellt, die Mechanik
auch noch sichtbar zu lassen - funk-
tionierend nicht nur im Sommer,
sondern auch bei Windstärke neun,
Eisgang und extremer Kälte.
Der Stadtbaurat und die Entwerfer
sahen in der Brücke mehr als nur
einen Funktionsträger für Fußgänger
und Radfahrer, nämlich ein Signal für
den Technologiestandort Kiel und
seinen Aufbruch „zu neuen Ufern".
Doch nur der „Beirat für Stadtgestal-
tung" begrüßte die Neuerung, die

had to be drawn from the client
with mischievous (security) argu-
ments, who was hesitant and un-
willing to give away so much semi-
public floor-space. The feeling of a
consumer cage is not apparent,
where the acoustic is a whisper and
murmur with no noise pollution.
The temperature is conditioned,
however not excessively warm,
coats can be kept on in winter. Due
to its height, the hall does not
allow for excessive advertising ban-
ners during sales. Clear and rational
forms, solid and quality materials:
this could be the winning formula
of the Köpenick Forum. If a historic
typology from bazaars via department stores through to modern
shopping centres were to be
sketched out, the Köpenick Forum
would stand out as an independent
and truly urban specimen.
In conclusion, the direct comparison to the centrally located
Gesundbrunnen-Center at the previous underground and future
InterCityExpress-station Gesundbrunnen in Wedding, clarifies the
architectural quality of the
Köpenick Forum. Both, Köpenick
and Wedding, entered the
consumer market almost simultaneously in autumn 1997.

Gerwin Zohlen

SHOULD FOLDING BE
EXPENSIVE?
**WHEN AESTHETICS STRIKES: THE
PROBLEMS WITH THE KIEL
CONNECTION.
(FRANKFURTER ALLGEMEINE
ZEITUNG 28.05.1998)**

Kiel is located on the Kieler Förde,
with its furthest point called
"Hörn". The respectable city is located on one side, whilst industrial
sites and shipyards are located on
the east side. This side of Kiel is
disparagingly viewed, the quarter
"Gaarden" still being the home of a
working class majority and located
"on the wrong side". The significance as an industrial shipbuilding
location is decreasing, as elsewhere
in Germany. The largest enterprise,
HDW Howaldtswerke Deutsche
Werft, released large site areas with
close proximity to the city for fresh
utilization, offering the opportunity
for new urban developments.

In the early nineties, a new urban
quarter with the usual mix of housing, offices and leisure institutions
on the water-front had been
planned in Kiel. One of the mayor
Scandinavian ferry links was
prepared to move its ferry terminal
to the other side of the "Förde",
thereby initiating the project. The
only pre-condition: The detour
around the Hörn had to be im-
proved by a bridge link between
the inner city and the main train
station on one side, and the new
terminal and Gaarden on the other.
This bridge however had to be re-
tractable, because the moorings of
excursion and local ferry boats are
located at the end of the Förde.
The issue was so far clear, then the
chief planning officer, Otto Flagge,
proposed a surprising concept: The
bridge design of Hamburg architects von Gerkan, Marg & Partner
and the Stuttgart engineering
office Schlaich, Bergermann und
Partner, internationally renowned
for their delicate, inventive constructions. Together, they had
developed an innovative sensation,
as initially described in the media; a
world first, a three-sectional bridge
opened and closed by a steel rod
mechanism.
It is appropriate to imagine the
bridge construction as the arm of a
puppet, with the exception that
the upper and lower arm and hand
are of equal length. Its opening
and closing mechanism is comparable to folding the arm, being
attached only the shoulder joint,
towards one side. This mechanism
already exists for hydraulically
powered loading bridges from

ships. Two sectional bridges can
also be easily operated with steel
cables, three sections however
multiply the difficulties, especially
when the aim is to visualize the
mechanics. An undisturbed operation had to be guaranteed in
summer, as well as with gale force
winds, ice flows and extreme cold
in the winter.

Gaardener Bevölkerung dagegen sah in jeder Brücke „nur Nachteile", die CDU fühlte sich als Oppositionspartei zum Nein verpflichtet, Bauverwaltung, Tiefbauamt und Hafendirektor waren unisono dagegen, die SPD war gespalten. Nicht weil man die Brücke ablehnte oder mochte, sondern je nachdem, wie man Otto Flagges hochfliegende Pläne zur Stadtentwicklung schätzte oder ihnen mißtraute.

Dann schien die Entwicklung allen Bedenkenträgern recht zu geben: Es gab ernsthafte Probleme beim Bau der Brücke. Als man auf der Neptunwerft in Rostock, die den Bauauftrag bekommen hatte, die Erprobung in der Halle begann, erwies sich die Konstruktion als zu schwer. Alle, die es schon immer gewußt hatten, waren begeistert, auch die Presse schwenkte auf die Seite der Brückengegner. Der Rechnungshof stellte fest, man könne in Holland in jedem Kaufhaus eine billigere und bessere Brücke bekommen, die Losung von der „Luxusbrücke statt Schulen oder Kindergärten" ging um. Selbst die Fährlinie drohte mit Regreßforderungen, weil die versprochene Verbindung zur Stadt auf sich warten ließ. Niemand wollte wissen, daß eine Erprobung dazu dient, Fehler zu finden und auszubessern. Es gab kein Pardon, zumal alles auch noch mitten im Kommunalwahlkampf geschah, an dessen Ende Norbert Gansel als haushoher Sieger zum Bürgermeister von Kiel gewählt wurde. Der durchschlug erst einmal den gordischen Knoten: Für knapp eine Million Mark wurde ein Ersatzsteg gebaut; das Brücken-Kunststück jedoch wurde weiter erprobt, weil schon zu viel investiert worden war.

Inzwischen, ein halbes Jahr später als ursprünglich geplant und tatsächlich um rund ein Drittel teurer als vorgesehen, steht die neue Brücke in leuchtendem Rot und Gelb vor dem selten blauen Himmel, und nicht nur das: Sie bewegt sich auch und hat knapp 3,5 Millionen Mark gekostet. Das, was trotz aller Querelen entstanden ist, ist staunenswert schön, und macht richtig Spaß; ein Riesenspielzeug für Erwachsene, ein Mobile wie von Tinguely, nur mit einem praktischen Zweck.

Wenn zuweilen ein großes Segelschiff durch die Öffnung fährt, merkt man, wie sehr diese Brücke Kiel gefehlt hat: Sie ist ein Sinnbild der neuen Hafennutzung, die in den nächsten Jahren noch wachsen wird, ist die Verbindung eines zukünftigen Stadtteils mit dem traditionellen Wohnen am Wasser und den Freizeitaktivitäten, die sich aus der traumhaften Lage ergeben, bildet das Zeichen eines High-Tech-Standorts, der seine Kompetenz aus den Erfahrungen mit dem Bau großer Schiffe gewonnen hat. Ein fröhliches Mobile aus Seilen, Winden und Gegengewichten, das zweieinhalb Minuten lang bei jeder Öffnung oder Schließung zeigt, daß es mehr gibt als nur den nackten Zweck.

Kiel hätte schon früher stolz sein können, wenn es statt auf die „Brückenkaufhäuser" Hollands auf dessen neue Brücken geschaut hätte: Nach dem Bau der neuesten Maas-Brücke in Rotterdam, die zuvor auch öffentlich wegen Mehrkosten kritisiert worden war, erhielten dort die Stadtverordneten einen Design-Preis. Sie hätten „der Kunst Vorrang vor allen finanziellen Zwecken eingeräumt", lautete die Begründung der Jury.

Gert Kähler

L'IDIOSINCRASIA DI EIFFEL
LEHRTER STATION, BERLIN PROGETTO:
VON GERKAN, MARG + PARTNER
(L'ARCA LUGLIO/AGOSTO 1999, No 139)

Una fra le più importanti stazioni ferroviarie progettate di recente è quella situata nello storico luogo della Lehrter Station, a est di Humboldthafen, a Berlino che verrà realizzata entro il 2002 dallo studio GMP formato dagli architetti von Gerkan, Marg + Partner.

Lo studio di progettazione di von Gerkan ha avuto modo, in passato, di dimostrare una capacità specifica a progettare interventi di grande impatto territoriale e, soprattutto, è sempre stato in grado di generare, sul territorio, segni di uno specifico significato „strutturale".

Strutturale inteso in due modi, sia come strutturazione del tessuto urbano tramite impianti nodali sia per il modo sapiente con cui viene ingegnerizzata la struttura portante dell'edificio. Ecco i due „numeri" fondamentali che regolano la geometria e la distribuzione della materia portante.

The municipal building authority and the designers considered this bridge more than a functional device for pedestrians and cyclists, but as a symbol for Kiel as a location for new technology and the opening of new boundaries. But only the advisory board for urban design welcomed the innovation, while the population of Gaarden found nothing but negativity, the opposing Christian Democratic Party felt obliged to refuse the project, planning authorities and Harbour Director were in unison against the design. The Social Democratic Party was split, not due to the bridge design itself, but to the controversial standing and partial distrust towards Otto Flagge. Finally the development seemed to justify all doubts, serious problems during the bridge construction occurred. When testing began in the Neptun shipyard in Rostock, which won the contract, the construction proved too heavy. Everyone with doubts was agitated, even the media changed its side to being opponents of the bridge. The audit office stated, a cheaper and better bridge was on offer of the shelf in the Netherlands. The keyword "luxury bridge instead of schools and nurseries" circulated. Even the ferry link threatened recourse, after the promised connection to the city centre was delayed.

Nobody was interested in the fact, that experiments are undertaken to discover and solve mistakes. No excuse was accepted, especially due to the ongoing local elections. The newly elected mayor, Norbert Gansel, cut the Gordian knot: A substitute bridge-link was erected for about a million marks, while the actual bridge was tested further, because high amounts had been invested already.

Meanwhile, six months later than originally planned and thirty per cent over budget, the new bridge has been erected in signal red and yellow, at a cost of almost 3.5 million marks. That the bridge has been realized despite all the problems is remarkable and a joy: a huge toy for adults, like a mobile by Tinguely, but with a more practical use.

When a large sailing vessel passes through the opening it is obvious, how much this bridge was necessary for Kiel: as the symbol of the new harbour utilization, which will grow in the next couple of years; as the connection of a future urban quarter with traditional housing at the water-front and leisure activities in a wonderful location; as the sign of a high-tech site, which has gained its competence and experience in the ship-building industry. A joyful mobile of cables, winches and counter-weights, in motion for two-and-a-half minutes during each opening and closure, illustration more than pure function.

Kiel could have been proud earlier, had it drawn reference from the latest Dutch bridge instead of standard ready made concepts: After the construction of the latest bridge across the River Maas in Rotterdam (which had also been publicly criticized for excess costs) the town councillors received a design award. The jury's reasoning was that art had been given priority over financial constraints.

Gert Kähler

L'IDIOSINCRASIA DI EIFFEL
LEHRTER STATION, BERLIN
(L'ARCA JULY/AUGUST 1999, No 139)

One of the most important railway stations to be built over recent times is located where Lehrter Station used to stand, to the east of Humboldthafen in Berlin.
The station was designed by the GMP team of architects comprised of von Gerkan, Marg + Partner.
The von Gerkan practice has already proven its worth at designing works of great territorial impact and, most notably, has always shown great skill at leaving traces of notable "structural" significance on the landscape. Structural is here to be taken as meaning both the structuring of the urban fabric through nodal constructions and the clever way in which the bearing structure of a building is engineered. These are the two key features governing the geometric form and distribution of bearing material.
Von Gerkan's projects almost

Queste sono principalmente le caratteristiche dei progetti di von Gerkan che spiccano, quasi sempre, per le caratteristiche dei numeri sapienti che contengono. Sono numeri di progetto che possiedono essenzialmente due valenze significative: la prima è la capacità di esprimere strutture di una raffinata avanguardia e, la seconda, di generare una distribuzione innovativa della materia. Così, per esempio, l'arco a quattro cerniere dell'impalcato ferroviario superiore è una soluzione di avanguardia progettuale sia per calcolo che per estensione.

Vediamo innanzitutto i numeri geometrici, cioè le dimensioni di questo progetto.

Il complesso è formato da 164.000 metri quadrati di superficie coperta di cui 75.000 metri quadrati destinati alle attività commerciali; 4.300 metri quadrati sono per i servizi ferroviari, 19.500 metri quadrati comprendono i trasporti e le zone di distribuzione e, infine, 35.000 metri quadrati destinati alle piattaforme ferroviarie vere e proprie. Numeri apparentemente astronomici per una stazione ferroviaria impostata su semplici regole ma, se si osserva la sua articolazione, appare in realtà una complessa distribuzione tridimensionale dello spazio. Una vera e propia implosione dello spazio urbano e un'articolata aggregazione di molteplici funzioni, anche cittadine.

Proprio nel punto baricentrico della stazione si sviluppano, su due livelli, un tunnel inferiore, a 15 metri di profondità, rispetto al piano della stazione, che contiene il piano del ferro dell'ICE – treno ad alta velocità, treno, fra l'altro, che corre sul territorio tedesco da est a ovest; inoltre un impalcato ferroviario, disposto normalmente al precedente, destinato alla linea ferroviaria U-Bahn, anche questa ad alta velocità, che corre da nord a Sud, disposta a 10 metri dal livello stradale.

Insomma un vero e proprio „incrocio" ferroviario di importanza internazionale che von Gerkan è stato capace di trasformare in un articolato centro urbano di grande risonanza. Sono questi „mega" progetti che, non più in relazione con le dimensioni tradizionali della città, sono destinati a trasformare la città stessa in una articolata aggregazione territoriale.

Ai progettisti non è sfuggita l'importanza di un uso appropriato del progetto, cioè delle capacità del proget-

to che, se trattato con intelligenza e maestria, è in grando di programmare e di comprendere tutti i significati del costruire. Primo fra tutti è capire che la struttura portante è lo scheletro di un „corpo", come tale è l'ultimo a „morire" ed è l'ultimo ad abbandonare il significato della „forma".

Lo scheletro è, inoltre, il solo in grado di definire le caratteristiche di un „corpo".

Il divenire dell'architettura, la trasformazione dello spazio dell'uomo deve passare di qui. E' impensabile continuare a credere che possa passare dallo scimmiottamento delle architetture del passato.

Lo sforzo delle nuove generazioni di progettisti deve essere teso per lo più allo studio approfondito delle scienze strutturali dei numeri capaci di distribuire la struttura portante secondo le nuove regole dei calcolatori, secondo le regole tridimensionali degli „algoritmi" che vedono e prevedono le nuove articolazioni spaziali nel rispetto degli equilibri della materia. E' inutile bendare gli occhi ai giovani con la cantilena della tradizione e della storia dell'architettura, pensando di ottenere una blanda copiatura di un passato ormai morto. Gustave-Alexandre Eiffel, con la sua idiosincrasia per la filosofia e per la storia, ci ha dimostrato, da tempo, che è la tecnica quella che organizza la vita.

Mario Antonio Arnaboldi

GROSSER BAHNHOF
DER GRÖSSTE BAHNHOF BERLINS WIRD AN DER STELLE ERRICHTET, AN DER SICH DIE HAUPTBAHNSTRECKEN AUS DEM NORDEN UND SÜDEN, DEM OSTEN UND WESTEN KREUZEN. EINE ENTSPRECHEND AUSDRUCKSVOLLE GESTE IST NOTWENDIG, UM DEN ZENTRALPUNKT DES EUROPÄISCHEN SCHIENENSYSTEM ZU FEIERN.
LEHRTER BAHNHOF, BERLIN
ARCHITEKT:
GMP VON GERKAN, MARG & PARTNER
(THE ARCHITECTURAL REVIEW 1/99)

Der Lehrter Bahnhof ist darauf ausgerichtet, Berlins Hauptbahnhof zu werden. Vor dem Krieg befand sich auf dem Grundstück ebenfalls ein Bahnhof, der allerdings zerstört wurde. Heute ist dort eine unbedeutende S-Bahn-Haltestelle in Hochlage. Aber Arbeiten sind bereits eingeleitet für den neuen Komplex, der an

always stand out for the clever numerical foundations underpinning their design. Their main characteristics might be described as: first and foremost, the ability to create cutting-edge structures and, secondly, the way material is put to such innovative use. This is epitomised, for instance, by the four-hinged arch of the upper framework of the railway, which is at the cutting-edge of design in terms of both engineering and extension. So let's begin by taking a look at the geometric proportions or, in other words, the sheer scale of this project. The complex features 164,000 square metres of covered surface. 75,000 square metres are designed for commercial activities, 4,300 for railway services, 19,500

for transport and distribution purposes, and the remaining 35,000 for the railway platforms themselves. Seemingly astronomical figures for a railway station designed along quite simple lines, but, analysing its complete layout, actually featuring an elaborate three-dimensional arrangement of space. A genuine implosion of urban space and intricate combination of multiple functions (including inner-city services). The barycentre of the station develops over two levels into a 15-metre-deep lower tunnel beneath the station level, where the ICE lines are located (a high–speed train running east–west across Germany) and a railway framework designed for the U–Bahn railway line (another high–speed line) that runs north-south 10 metres below road level. Von Gerkan has shown great skill in converting this international railway junction into an intricate urban centre of striking impact. These "mega" projects are quite out-of-step with the traditional scale of cities, managing to transform the city into an elaborate combination of territorial events. The architects realized just how it important it was to use this project

properly, or in other words to draw on the qualities of a design capable, if handled with skill and intelligence, of planning for and incorporating every aspect of building. First and foremost, an awareness that a bearing structure is the skeleton of a "body" and as such it is the last to "die" and the last to give up the idea of "form". A skeleton is also the only thing truly capable of shaping the features of a "body". The future of architecture, the transformation of human space must not lose sight of this. There is no sense in pretending that the way ahead lies in copying the architecture of the past. Our architects of the future must study the structural sciences in-depth, working out the calculations allowing bearing structure to be arranged as stipulated by the latest laws of computer science, based on the three-dimensional rules of algorithms that open up the way to and actually envisage new spatial arrangements carefully geared to matter.

There is no use in blindfolding youngsters eyes by telling that same old story about the history and heritage of architecture, in the hope that they will end up blandly imitating a past that no longer exists. Gustave Alexandre Eiffel's philosophical-historical leanings taught us, long ago, that life is actually organised around technology.

Mario Antonio Arnaboldi

GRAND CENTRAL
THE BIGGEST STATION IN BERLIN WILL BE THE POINT AT WHICH THE GREAT ROUTES FROM NORTH TO SOUTH AND EAST TO WEST CROSS. AN APPROPRIATLY DRAMATIC GESTURE WAS NEEDED TO CELEBRATE THE FOCUS OF THE EUROPEAN RAIL SYSTEM.
LEHRTER BAHNHOF, BERLIN
ARCHITECT:
GMP VON GERKAN, MARG & PARTNER
(THE ARCHITECTURAL REVIEW 1/99)

The Lehrter Bahnhof is set to become Berlin's main railway station. Before the War, there was a station on the site, but it was destroyed, and now there is only a rather dingy S-Bahn (district railway) halt there, high up on the raised tracks. But work is already

der Kreuzung von zwei ICE-Haupt-verbindungslinien des euro-asiatischen Festlandes liegt: In Nord-Süd-Richtung von Skandinavien nach Sizilien und in West-Ost-Richtung von London nach Moskau und weiter nach Asien.

Zudem wird eine neue U-Bahn-Linie in Nord-Süd-Richtung errichtet, und die S-Bahn zwischen Ost und West grundlegend renoviert. Der Bahnhof ist für die Nutzung durch die gesamte Stadt vorgesehen, wobei die meisten anderen Bahnhöfe (z.B. der Bahnhof Zoo) weiterhin in Betrieb bleiben. Somit wird der Lehrter Bahnhof insbesondere das Regierungsviertel mit Tausenden von Beamten bedienen sowie Moabit, das gemischte Stadtviertel im Norden. Beabsichtigt ist eine Katalysatorfunktion für einen Stadtteil, der über viele Jahre hinweg vernachlässigt wurde. Der Verfall wurde im übrigen durch Speer eingeleitet: Der Bahnhof war geplant als nördlicher Endpunkt der glorreichen Nord-Süd-Achse der Nazis und seine Zerstörung wurde bis 1942 betrieben, unterstützt von britischen Bomben.

Die Ordnung des Bahnhofes ist einfach und zugleich gewagt: Die Gleise des Ost-West-ICE und der S-Bahn werden sich auf gleicher Höhe befinden, nämlich 10 Meter über dem Straßenniveau. Die Nord-Süd-Linie wird zusammen mit der U-Bahn etwa 15 Meter unterirdisch in zwei der zahlreichen Tunnel verlaufen, die durch das sandige Erdreich unterhalb des Stadtzentrums gegraben werden (es kam zu keinerlei Beeinträchtigungen der Infrastruktur während der Wiederherstellung eines neuerlichen Hauptstadtstatus für Berlin). Autos, Busse, Taxis und Fußgänger erhalten Zugang auf Straßenebene. Oberhalb des hochgelegenen Bahnsteigs wird sich ein elegantes Glasdach von 430 m Länge spannen. Dach und Bahnsteiganlage werden zwei parallele Gebäuderiegel (50 m breit und 170 m lang) durchdringen, um exakt oberhalb der unterirdischen ICE-Strecke positioniert zu werden, folglich etwas abgewinkelt der gekrümmt verlaufenden Achse der langen Bahnhofshalle folgend.

Zwischen den Riegeln (in denen Geschäfte, Serviceeinrichtungen und ein Hotel untergebracht sein werden) wird sich die mehrgeschossige Bahnhofshalle befinden, welche ebenfalls von einem Glasdach überspannt wird. Durch alle Hallenebenen ver-

laufende Lufträume lassen Tageslicht bis zu den untersten Bahnsteigen des ICE in Nord-Süd-Richtung und der U-Bahn eindringen.

Sowohl Gebäuderiegel als auch Glasdach werden als prägnante Stahlstruktur konstruiert, die Riegel mit einem externen gerasterten Rahmen: direkt, Rationalist und Preuße (wenngleich sich das Hauptbüro des Architekten in Hamburg befindet). Die Dächer sind raffiniert als leichte Schalen konzipiert, die aus einem nahezu rhomboidförmigen Rasterformat von 1,2 m x 1,2 m gefügt werden. Jede Einheit wird durch diagonale Kabel umklammert, während die gesamte Struktur von Stützen getragen wird. Die Konstruktion verspricht, so etwas wie eine doppelseitige Version von Grimshaws Bahnsteighalle von Waterloo (AR September 1993) zu werden. Es wird interessant sein zu sehen, wie diese beiden Strukturtypen zusammenwirken und ob, trotz der Nüchternheit der Glasscheiben, der Bahnhof wirklich so einladend wirken wird wie der Architekt erhofft. Dieser spricht vom Lehrter Bahnhof als Brückenschlag zur City und mit der richtigen Handhabung könnte der Bahnhof ein überaus eindrucksvoller, dynamischer und aufregender Ort werden. Wie dem auch sei, das langgestreckte Glasdach oberhalb der hochgelegenen Bahnsteige sollte dem Kanzler einen prächtigen Ausblick bescheren, wenn er nach Norden aus dem Fenster sieht: ein doppeltes Symbol der Wiedergeburt - der Stadt und des europäischen Schienenverkehrssystems.

Anne Vyne

QUATTRO TORRI PER LA FIERA DEL FUTURO
PRESENTATO IL PROGETTO DELLA NUOVA SEDE:
IL PIANO GREGOTTI NEL CESTINO LA PROPOSTA DELLO STUDIO DI AMBURGO PREVEDE 95MILA MQ DI FABBRICATO. LAVORI AL VIA NEL '98.
(IL RESTO DEL CARLINO 15.11.1997)

Sarà suddiviso in aree espositive anche autonome l'una dall'altra. Eccolo, arriva dalla Germania, è il nuovo progetto della nuova Fiera alle Celle. Che, parola del presidente Lorenzo Cagnoni, „sarà pronta nell'autunno del 2000".
Il progetto, affidato dopo una gara europea, allo studio GMP, von Gerkan, Marg + Partner, che ha la sede

under way on the new complex, which will be the junction of two of the main ICE (high-speed train) lines of the Continent: north-south from Scandinavia to Sicily and east-west from London to Moscow and on to Asia.

There will also be a new north-south underground (U-Bahn) track, and the east-west S-Bahn will be thoroughly renovated. The station is for the whole capital, but most of the other stations (for instance the Zoo Bahnhof will remain in use, and the Lehrter-Bahnhof will serve particularly the government quarter with its thousands of commuting civil servants and Moabit, the mixed area to the north. It is intended to act as catalyst for a part of the city that has been derelict for many years. The dereliction was incidentally started by Speer: the station was to be the northern termination of the grandiose Nazi north-south axis and demolition for it went on until 1942, assisted by British bombs. Station organization is simple and bold: the east-west ICE track will be at the same level as the S-Bahn, 10 metres above the streets. The north-south line will be down with the U-Bahn some 15 metres below ground level in two of the many tunnels being driven through the sandy soil under the centre of the city (there has been no stinting on infrastructure in making Berlin the capital once more). Cars, buses, taxis and pedestrians will be catered for at street level. Over the upper level platforms will be a delicate glass roof 430m long. Roof and platforms will penetrate two parallel slabs of building, 50m wide and 170m long, to be set exactly on the line of the underground ICE track, and hence slightly skewed to the curved axis of the long train shed. Between the slabs (which will contain shops, service facilities and a hotel) will be the many levelled station hall, again covered with a glass roof. Voids cut through all levels of the hall will bring daylight right down to the lowest platforms for the north-south ICE trains and the U-Bahn.

Both slabs and glass roofs will have expressed steel structures, the slabs with gridded external frames: direct, Rationalist and Prussian (though the architects' main office

is in Hamburg). The roofs will be ingenious light-weight shells built up on slightly rhomboidal 1.2m x 1.2m grids, each unit braced by diagonal cables, with the whole carried by trussed supports. It promises to be rather like a double-sided version of Grimshaw's train shed at Waterloo (AR September 1993). It will be interesting to see how the two kinds of structure work together, and whether, for all the austerity of the slabs, the station really will be as welcoming as the architects hope. They talk of the Lehrter-Bahnhof as a gateway to the city, and with the right handling, the station hall could be a most impressive, dynamic and exciting place. Whatever else, the long glass roof over the upper platforms should provide the Chancellor with a magnificent view when he looks north from his offices: a double symbol of rebirth: of the city and of the European railway system.

Anne Vyne

FOUR TOWERS FOR THE EXHIBITION OF THE FUTURE
PLANNING PRESENTATION OF THE NEW EXHIBITION AREA: DESIGN BY GREGOTTI IGNORED
THE HAMBURG PRACTICE PROPOSES 95,000 M² FLOOR AREA, CONSTRUCTION START 1998
(IL RESTO DEL CARLINO 15.11.1997)

The exhibition area will be separated into exhibition sections, which also can be used independently. The planning for the new exhibition grounds near Celle is from Germany. "The completion date will be autumn 2000," exclaimed president Lorenzo Cagnoni. The planning, which has been confided to the architectural practice gmp, von Gerkan, Marg und Partner, after a European-wide competition, was presented yesterday. Gmp's headquarters are located in Hamburg and the office is renowned for the Stuttgart and Hamburg airports and exhibition grounds in Leipzig and Hanover. The German design resembles in no way the original concept, which was previously designed by Gregotti, this design proposed parking on the roof area. The struc-

principale a Amburgo e che ha già firmato gli aeroporti di Berlino, Stoccarda e Amburgo, la nuova fiera di Lipsia e di Hannover, è stato presentato ieri.

Il progetto tedesco non tiene per nulla conto del piano di massima firmato un paio d'anni fa da Vittorio Gregotti: quello che prevedeva i parcheggi sul tetto die padiglioni. La struttura del nuovo quartiere fieristico riminese è stata concepita come una moderna ripresa della tradizione dell'architettura classica italiana.

Il nuovo quartiere avrà 95mila metri quadrati di edificato e superficie utile, suddiviso in aree esposive, tecniche e per servizi. Sarà organizzato su di un unico livello con ingresso principale sul lato sud collegato con la viabilitá ordinaria e servito, in futuro, da una fermata della metropolitana Rimini-Riccione. Altri ingressi si troveranno sui lati est e ovest. I parcheggi copriranno fino a 5.500 posti auto e saranno collocati nelle adiacenze die tre ingressi.

Quattro torri luninose alte circa 30 metri caratterizzeranno l'entrata principale, la cui area antistante sarà una vera e propia „Piazza degli eventi", all'occorrenza copribile, illuminabile e sonorizzabile. A centro del quartiere un' ampia hall di smistamento die flussi con una grande rotonda coperta da una cupola di 50 metri di diametro: qui sorgeranno gli uffici dell' ente, un' area congressi finalizzata all' attività fieristica, zone riservate ai più vari servizi, punti ristorazione. I dieci padiglioni espositivi, con dimensione trasversale di 62 metri, saranno privi di pilastri interni per consentire una ottimale distribuzione degli spazi.

Grande cupola di vetro ospiterà gli uffici dell'ente e i servizi.

I porticati posti su entrambi i lati dell' area centrale permetteranno l' accesso ai singoli padiglioni espositivi. La conformazione del quartiere fieristico e la dislocazione die suoi ingressi renderanno possibile lo svolgimento contemporaneo di più menifestazioni, anche con diverse peculiarità. Il progetto globale prevede futuri ampliamenti, fino al raggiungimento di 125mila metri quadrati di edificato con 16 padiglioni. Il presidente Cagnoni ha spiegato che il progetto, dopo il pronunciamento del consiglio generale della Fiera, approderà a

fine marzo in Comune per ottere la concessione edilizia. Gara d'appalto subito dopo e apertura die cantieri entro l'autunno del '98. L'investimento complessivo risulterà di 179 miliardi (153 per le opere in muratura e il resto per gli impianti, allacciamenti e cosi via). Due anni fa l'investimento era stato stimato intorno ai 157 miliardi. La differenza è sostanzialmente dovuta alle spese (da 6 a 13 miliardi) per l'acquisizione delle aree alle Celle.

BEGEHRENSWERT WIE DAS GLÜCK UND BEWEGT WIE DAS SPIEL

HEUTE IST SPATENSTICH FÜR DIE SPIELBANK IN BAD STEBEN: DER ENTWURF EINES STARARCHITEKTEN. (FRANKENPOST VOM 10.06.1999)

Nach jahrelanger Vorbereitungszeit beginnt heute mit dem ersten Spatenstich der Bau für ein in der Region einzigartiges Gebäude: die Spielbank Bad Steben. Der Entwurf stammt von dem Hamburger Meinhard von Gerkan, der als der führende Architekt in Deutschland gilt. BAD STEBEN.

- Für Meinhard von Gerkan ist es eine Premiere. Der Stararchitekt, dessen Name weltweit für zahlreiche prägende öffentliche Gebäude steht und der bei Wettbewerben weit über hundert erste Preise gewonnen hat, wird in Bad Steben seine erste Spielbank bauen. „Alle außergewöhnlichen Bauaufgaben sind für einen Architekten ein gestalterischer Leckerbissen", antwortete er auf die Frage unserer Zeitung, warum er sich am Architekturwettbewerb für Bad Steben beteiligt habe. Gerade bei einer Spielbank bestehe die Möglichkeit, neue Wege zu gehen und experimentell eine neue Architektur zu entwickeln.

Meinhard von Gerkan macht in dem Gebäude zahlreiche Anspielungen auf das Glücksspiel und die umgebende Landschaft. Da ist zum einen das Wellendach - ein Auf und Ab wie beim Glücksspiel oder so bewegt wie das Wasser im Stebenbach, der an der Spielbank vorbeifließt; da ist zum anderen die Glasfassade - zerbrechlich wie das Glück und aus einem Material, das in den fränkischen und thüringischen Mittelgebirgen seit dem Mittelalter in verschieden-

ture of the new exhibition area in Rimini was designed as a photograph from traditional Italian architecture.

The new exhibition grounds will provide a built floor area of 95,000 m², comprising of exhibition, technical and service areas. The concept is planned on a single level, with its main entrance from the south side and connections to the local traffic network and train station for the new link Rimini-Riccione. Further entrances are located on the east and west side. The parking area provides 5,500 spaces and are in close proximity to the three entrances.

Four illuminated towers, approximately 30 m high, are the symbol of the main entrance, its forecourt intended as an open activity square, which can be covered and illuminated if required. A generous circulation hall with a large rotund, covered by a 50 m diameter domed roof, is located in the centre of the exhibition area.

Exhibition administrational offices, a congress centre, various service facilities and restaurants are situated here.

Ten exhibition halls with a width of 62 m are designed without columns in order to achieve an optimum usage of the floor space.

Exhibition offices and service areas are placed around a large glass dome.

The colonnades on both sides of the main area offer access to the single exhibition halls.

The design of the exhibition area and the positioning of the entrances, allows for the implementation of events of various scales. The planning also considers a future extension of up to 125,000 m² built area spread over sixteen halls. President Cagnoni declared, that the design will be handed in

for planning permission in March, after consultations with the exhibition board. Construction will start in autumn 1998, directly after the completion of the tender bids. The investment accounts for 179 billion Lira (153 billion for the building, the remainder for connections, secondary installations, etc.). Two years ago, the investment was estimated at 157 billion. The difference in costs (from 6 to 13 billion) being the results of site purchase.

DESIRABLE AS GOOD FORTUNE AND FLUCTUANT AS GAMBLING

TODAY IS THE INITIATION CEREMONY FOR THE CASINO IN BAD STEBEN: THE DESIGN OF A RENOWNED ARCHITECT. (FRANKENPOST VOM 10.06.1999)

After many years of preparation the construction of an unique building in the region started today with an initiation ceremony: the Casino Bad Steben. The design has been developed by the Hamburg architect Meinhard von Gerkan, who is regarded as the leading architect in Germany. BAD STEBEN.

- For Meinhard von Gerkan this is a first. The renowned architect, whose name is connected with numerous outstanding international buildings and who has won more than a hundred competitions, will build his first casino in Bad Steben. "All specialized design tasks are of great interest and importance to the architect," he responded to our question, as to why he had taken part in the Bad Steben competition. The casino typology offers the opportunity to experiment and develop a new architecture.

Meinhard von Gerkan introduced numerous references to the fortunes of gambling and the surrounding landscape. For example the corrugated steel roof: turbulent like gambling or the water of Steben stream, flowing past the casino; or the glass facade: fragile as good fortune and made from a material, which has been produced in the lower mountain ranges of Franken and Thüringen since the Middle Ages.

ster Form hergestellt wird.

Das Gebäude werde einen sehr hohen Stellenwert haben, sagte der Architekt Rudolf Unglaub vom Nailaer Ingenieurbüro Unglaub, Sachs und Seuß, der die Bauleitung vor Ort übernommen hat. Sowohl von der Gestaltung als auch von der Funktion her sei es ein hochwertiger Sonderbau, von dem eine große Werbewirkung ausgehen werde.

Meinhard von Gerkan unterhält mit seinem Partner Volkwin Marg das erfolgreichste Architekturbüro Deutschlands mit über 300 Mitarbeitern. Zu seinen großen Projekten zählen die klassisch-schöne Musikhalle in Lübeck, der hochgelobte Lehrter Bahnhof in der Nähe des Reichstags in Berlin und die luftigleichte Neue Messe in Leipzig, von der Meinhard von Gerkan schreibt, hier habe er sich als Entwerfer in einem Grenzbereich zwischen Realität und Utopie bewegt. Beim Wettbewerb für den Umbau des Berliner Reichstags belegte er hinter dem Briten Sir Norman Foster den zweiten Platz.

Die Süddeutsche Zeitung zählte kürzlich in einem Artikel Meinhard von Gerkan zu der „kleinen Handvoll global führender Architekten": zusammen mit seinem Partner Volkwin Marg, dem Kalifornier Frank O. Gehry, dem Italiener Renzo Piano, dem Engländer Sir Richard Rogers und natürlich Norman Foster. Gerkan wurde 1935 im lettländischen Riga geboren und verlor durch den Krieg Vater und Mutter. 1945 kam er nach Hamburg, wo er seitdem lebt und arbeitet. Er hat mehrere Lehraufträge an Universitäten, unter anderem in Braunschweig, Tokio und Pretoria. In Büchern und Aufsätzen setzt er sich immer wieder mit der Theorie des Gestaltens auseinander. Der Architekt bekennt sich ausdrücklich dazu, daß die einfachste Lösung im Zweifelsfall die beste sei. Architektur sei eine Kunst in der sozialen Anwendung; sie habe den Menschen als Lebensraum zu dienen. „Deswegen ist der gut gestalteten Normalität gegenüber einer mittelmäßigen Außergewöhnlichkeit immer der Vorzug zu geben." Welches seiner vielen Projekte ist für ihn persönlich das liebste? Auf diese Frage unserer Zeitung antwortete der Architekt, die öffentlichen Bau-

ten seien ihm am wichtigsten, „weil sie neben der Funktionserfüllung auch einen urbanen und gesellschaftliche" Beitrag zu leisten haben. Zu Bauten dieser Art gehören die Flughäfen in Hamburg und Stuttgart, die Konzerthalle in Lübeck sowie der große Zentralbahnhof in Berlin. Im übrigen sei es mit den eigenen Projekten wie mit den eigenen Kindern: „Die Frage, welches einem am liebsten ist, kann man nicht beantworten."

Elfriede Schneider

KEINE ANGST MEHR VOR BLAU, GELB UND ROTBRAUN
BUNTES WISSEN IST EIN FARBIGES RUHEKISSEN: ZWEI NEUE HÖRSAALZENTREN IN OLDENBURG UND CHEMNITZ WIDER DIE GRAUEN VERHÄLTNISSE.
(FRANKFURTER ALLGEMEINE ZEITUNG, 25.01.1999)

„Egal welche Farbe, Hauptsache grau!" gilt als die häufigste Antwort von Architekten auf die Frage des Bauherrn, wie denn die neuen Wände, Stützen und Decken gestrichen werden sollen. Auf das vielbeschäftigte Hamburger Architekturbüro von Gerkan, Marg & Partner traf das in den letzten Jahren zumindest insofern zu, als ihre Bauten farblich immer hanseatisch distinguiert Farbe zeigten. Das hat sich nun geändert: Ein mächtiger Kubus in kräftig ockerfarbenem grobem Putz, der auf einer gelben Betonkonstruktion aufliegt, die entfernt an einen Portikus erinnert - so empfängt das neue Hörsaalzentrum der Technischen Universität in Chemnitz den überraschten Besucher. Im Inneren werden die einzelnen Bauteile blau, gelb und braunrot voneinander abgesetzt und doch aufeinander bezogen - eine völlig neue Facette in der Arbeit der Architekten.

Aber eine, die sinnvoll ist. Denn die Hochschule in Chemnitz liegt am südlichen Rand der Stadt inmitten von Plattenbauten der siebziger Jahre. Nicht deren Bauweise ist das Problem, sondern ihre Anordnung zu einem abstrakten Muster, das mit einem ablesbaren, geordneten Stadtraum nichts zu tun hat - die leeren Flächen zwischen den Bauten fran-

The building will play an important role, explained the architect Rudolf Unglaub from the engineering practice Unglaub, Sachs und Seuß, Naila, who carried out site supervision. Regarding design as well as function the casino is a high-quality building, which will result in positive advertising.

Together with his partner Volkwin Marg, Meinhard von Gerkan runs Germany's most successful architectural practice with over 300 employees. His major projects include the Lübeck's classical music hall, the highly praised Lehrter Bahnhof close to Berlin's Reichstag and Leipzig's light-weight "Neue Messe", where Meinhard von Gerkan himself commented on designing in a border zone between reality and utopia. In the competition for the renovation of Berlin's Reichstag, he received a second place after the British architect Sir Norman Foster. The Süddeutsche Zeitung recently included Meinhard von Gerkan in the small circle of globally leading architects: "Together with his partner Volkwin Marg, the Californian Frank O. Gehry, the Italian Renzo Piano, the

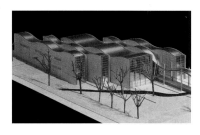

Briton Sir Richard Rogers and of course Norman Foster.

Gerkan was born in 1935 in the Lettish Riga and lost his mother and father in the war. In 1945 he arrived in Hamburg, where he has lived and worked ever since. Von Gerkan gives lectures at several universities, amongst them Braunschweig, Tokyo and Pretoria. Repeatedly, he discusses the theory of design in books and essays. Von Gerkan expressly supports his conviction, that in case of doubt the simplest solution is the best. Architecture is an art in social application, which has to serve mankind as a living space. "Therefore

well designed normality is always to be preferred to mediocre extravaganza."

Which one of his numerous projects is personally his favourite? The answer to this questions was, that public buildings were of primary importance to him, because they have to meet urban and social requirements besides solely fulfilling their function. Buildings of this kind are the Hamburg and Stuttgart airports, Lübeck's concert hall as well as Berlin's central train station. Besides that, your own projects are comparable to your own children: "One cannot say, which one is your favourite."

Elfriede Schneider

NO FEAR FOR COLOUR BLUE, YELLOW AND REDDISH BROWN
COLOURFUL KNOWLEDGE IS A COLOURED CUSHION: TWO NEW AUDITORIA COMPLEXES IN OLDENBURG AND CHEMNITZ AGAINST A GREY BACKDROP.
(FRANKFURTER ALLGEMEINE ZEITUNG, 25.01.1999)

"It does not matter which colour, but it must be grey!," was known as the common answer from architects to the client's question, how walls, columns and ceilings were to be painted. This was accurate for the active von Gerkan, Marg & Partner practice in Hamburg, as their buildings always show hanseatic colours. The approach is somewhat different now, a massive cube with strongly ochre-coloured plaster, resting on a yellow concrete construction is the welcome of the new auditoria complex of the Chemnitz Technical University to the surprised visitor. Interior building elements contrast and refer to each other with blue, yellow and reddish brown. This is a completely new aspect in the architects' work.

However this makes sense, because the Chemnitz University is located on the southern edge of the city amongst tower blocks of the seventies. Their construction typology is not the problem, but their abstract

sen aus. Deshalb wohl gewannen von Gerkan, Marg und Partner mit ihrem prägnanten Entwurf 1994 den Städtebaulichen Wettbewerb zur Neuordnung und Erweiterung der Technischen Universität. Sie hatten eine kräftige, neue Struktur vorgeschlagen, deren wichtigste Bestandteile blockhafte Reihen von Bauten, ein neuer Grünzug und eine nord-südlich verlaufende Allee bildeten. Das Hörsaalzentrum und eine künftige gegenüberliegende Bibliothek sollen ein Universitätsforum als Bindeglied zwischen Hauptstraße und Grünzug bilden. Das Vorlesungsgebäude als Vorhut setzt nun schon einen starken Akzent gegen die Tristesse der Umgebung. Demselben Ziel dient die kräftige, schwere Gliederung der Baukörper: Ein Winkel aus Seminar- und Hörräumen faßt ein großes Foyer, das unter der aufgeständerten Masse zweier großer Hörsäle liegt. Deren schräger Boden, der den ansteigenden Sitzreihen entspricht, ist im Inneren sichtbar, so daß der Besucher durch die immer näher rückende Baumasse fast bedrängt wird.

Der gewinkelte niedrige Baukörper ist außen mit silbergrauem Wellblech verkleidet, die stählernen Fluchttreppen zwischen den Sälen liegen offen - die dienenden Funktionen stellen sich als „technisches Gerät" dar. Doch dem zentralen Bereich mit seiner ganzen Schwere verleiht das durchgehende Farbkonzept Vielfalt - der Hörsaalbaukörper in hellem Gelb schwebt förmlich in der zweigeschossigen Eingangshalle mit ihrem rötlichen Erd- und dem kräftig blauen Obergeschoß.

Das nimmt zuweilen den Charakter eines abstrakten Tafelbildes an. Denn die Farbe sondert nicht einzelne Baukörper voneinander, sondern betont den Zusammenstoß verschiedener Wand- oder Deckenteile, mit frappanten Überschneidungen. Das geht nicht immer gut: Wenn die gewohnte Materialdisziplin der Architekten mit dem neuen Mut zur Farbe kollidiert - helles Naturholz als Geländerhandlauf vor einer gelben Wand, dann kann das schon mal dem Auge weh tun. Aber im ganzen stimmt das Konzept, weil die kubische, von der Farbe gesteigerte Wirkung der Baukörper den Kern eines

neuen unverwechselbaren Orts schafft.

Ein halbes Jahr zuvor wurde die gleiche Bauaufgabe in Oldenburg von denselben Architekten fertiggestellt. Trotz seines ganz anderen Charakters diente das Oldenburger Gebäude als eine Art Experimentierfeld für Farbwirkungen. Allerdings werden sie hier nur als Aperçu im Foyer und an einem Teil der Fassade verwendet. Ansonsten dominieren die naturgegebenen Farben von Holz, Stahl und Sichtbeton.

Ansonsten lassen sich die beiden Hörsaalzentren aber kaum vergleichen: In Oldenburg war nur das Auditorium Maximum der bestehenden Carl-von-Ossietzky-Universität zu planen und in eine Umgebung zu setzen, in der kleinteilige und kleinkarierte Bauten dominieren. Folgerichtig hat die Architektur dort auch ein ganz anderes Gestaltungskonzept verfolgt: An einer belebten Straßenkreuzung im Westen der Stadt wurde mit dem zylindrischen Baukörper eine Markierung gesetzt, die der Bedeutung einer fakultätsübergreifenden Einrichtung gerecht wird. Die geometrisch reine Form wird aufgebrochen durch Vor- und Rücksprünge in der Fassade und durch die unterschiedliche Behandlung der Fronten zwischen der offenen Foyerseite und der weitgehend geschlossenen Bühnenseite. Ein Gang, der an der Kreuzung in einem langgestreckten Baukörper mit Seminarräumen endet, bindet den Zylinder in die vorhandene Bebauung ein. Der Abstraktheit der reinen geometrischen Lehre - Zylinder und Rechteck - entspricht das Weiß der geputzten Fassade.

Nur eine Fläche der Außenwand ist farblich in zartem Ocker abgesetzt und wirkt wie eine Kulisse vor dem weißen Hintergrund. Innen wiederum läßt ein leuchtendes Blau den Behindertenaufzug als frei stehenden Baukörper mitten im Foyer gegen die dezenten Farben von Holz, Gußasphaltboden und Sichtbetonstützen abstechen.

Ein Architekt - denn Meinhard von Gerkan steht in der Bürogemeischaft für diese neue Entwicklung - entdeckt die Farbe. Das könnte mehr werden als eine Erscheinung unter vielen. Schließlich ist das Hamburger Büro

pattern arrangement, which has little to do with a definable urban space, where the empty spaces between the blocks become frayed. That may be the reason for the competition winning proposal by von Gerkan, Marg und Partner in 1994 for the re-arrangement and extension of the Institute of Technology. They proposed a strong new structure, based on block-like lines of buildings, a new landscaped stripe and an avenue in

a north-south direction.

The auditoria centre and a future library opposite will form a university forum as the connecting element between main road and landscaped stripe. The centre as the vanguard already forms strong contrast against the dismal surrounding context. The strong, heavy arrangement of the buildings follows the same aim: A line of seminar rooms and a large foyer are located underneath the volume of two large auditoria, with their inclined floors, which follow the ascending seating arrangement, being internally visible, almost suppressing the visitor with their narrowing building mass.

The low buildings arranged at an angle are externally cladded with silver-grey corrugated steel sheets. The steel escape stairs are located externally between the lecture rooms: the serving functions are designed as "technical appliances". On the contrary, the central space with its heaviness is given variety with continuous colour concept: the lecture hall unit in bright yellow almost hovers in the two-storey entrance hall, painted red on the ground floor and its powerful blue on the upper level.

This sometimes gives the impression of an abstract panel, because the colours do not separate single build-

ing parts, but emphasize the connection of different wall and ceiling elements with surprising intersections. That does not always work: when the architect's usual material discipline collides with the new courage for using colour (light wood used for handrails in front of a yellow wall) it could be an eye-sore. But overall, the concept is correct, because the cubic effect of the buildings, which are intensified by colour, generate the core of a new characteristic space.

Six months earlier, the same design task had been completed in Oldenburg by the same architects. Despite its completely different character, the Oldenburg university served as an experimental field for effects of colour, although it was only applied as a witty effect in the foyer and on parts of the facade. Otherwise the naturally given colours of wood, steel and fair-faced concrete prevailed.

Besides that, these two auditoria centres cannot be compared: In Oldenburg, only the main auditorium for the existing Carl-von-Ossietzky University had to be designed and arranged in a context, where small-scale and provincial buildings dominate. Consequently, the architecture pursued a completely different design concept: a cylindrical building mass poses a mark next to a busy street junction in the western part of the city, acknowledging the significance of an institution serving different faculties. The geometrically pure form is broken up in the facade with projections and recesses and by the varied elevational treatment between the open foyer side and the primarily closed stage side. A corridor, ending in an elongated building with lecture rooms, integrates the cylinder into the existing building.

The abstraction of the pure geometric application, cylinder and rectangle, corresponds to the white colour of the plastered facade. Only one exterior surface is painted with light ochre and appears like a stage-set in front of the white background. Internally, a bright blue disabled lift contrasts as a free-standing element in the centre of

mit Großaufträgen beschäftigt, die künftig, vom zentralen neuen Lehrter Bahnhof über den Umbau des Olympiastadions bis zum Neubau des Flughafens Schönefeld, das Erscheinungsbild und die Wahrnehmung des öffentlichen Raums in Berlin und damit auch der Bundesrepublik mitprägen werden. Jetzt gilt nicht mehr die vornehme Zurückhaltung natürlicher Materialien. Mit der Farbe kommt eine zusätzliche Komponente ins Spiel, die das architektonische Repertoire erweitert.

Gert Kähler

STÄDTEBAULICHE RÜCKEROBERUNG DES ALTEN EUROPAHAFENS VIA KUNSTHALLE

KUNSTSAMMLER UND INVESTOR HANS GROTHE PLANT KUNSTHALLE UND DIENSTLEISTUNGSZENTRUM AUF DEM GELÄNDE DES WESERBAHNHOFES II.
(A & W, NO. 70, 11/98)

Archaische Assoziationen und Formen der klassischen Moderne summieren sich zur Kunsthalle Weserbahnhof II. Der in einem Gutachterverfahren erfolgreiche Entwurf der Hamburger Architekten von Gerkan, Marg und Partner (gmp) für die Kunsthalle auf dem Gelände Weserbahnhof II soll neuen Werken des deutschen Malers und Objektkünstlers Anselm Kiefer Raum geben. Die vom Sammler Hans Grothe initiierte und finanzierte Kunsthalle wird zugleich Auftakt für eine Neunutzung des Areals zwischen Stephanitorsbollwerk und Weserkaje für Büro- und Diestleistungszwecke.

Kreuzfahrtterminal vis-à-vis?
Die städtebauliche Rückeroberung des alten Europahafens beginnt mit einem Kulturbauwerk. Während der Teerhof auf sein versprochenes Kulturdrittel wartet (siehe Artikel in diesem Journal), plant der Kunstsammler und Investor Hans Grothe für das von ihm 1996 erworbene 16.500 m² große Grundstück konkret. Nach der Errichtung der etwa 420 m² großen Ausstellungshalle ist in einer zweiten Stufe ein Dienstleistungsbereich mit einer Bruttogeschoßfläche von ca. 30.000 m² vorgesehen. Die

Realisierung der gewerblichen Bauten ist beim aktuellen Überangebot an Büroflächen jedoch eher mittelfristig zu sehen. Mit einem entsprechenden Zeithorizont sind auch die infrastrukturellen Bemühungen der Kommune zu betrachten. So ist angedacht, die Lloydstraße als Allee bis zur Weser auszubauen, mit einem Durchstich unterhalb der trennenden Bahn- und Straßentrassen für Straßenbahn, Fußgänger und Radfahrer eine Verbindung zur Innenstadt zu schaffen und für den „Weser Shuttle" sowie die „Weiße Flotte" einen Anleger Weserbahnhof II zu etablieren und ggfs. einen Fahrgastterminal für Kreuzfahrtschiffe einzurichten.

Oberflächen mit Bleiplatten verkleidet.
Konkret sind hingegen die Planungen für die basilikal konzipierte Kunsthalle. Sie wird ausschließlich neue Werke Anselm Kiefers aufnehmen. Das Mittelschiff bietet einen neun Meter hohen, 20 Meter tiefen und acht Meter breiten Ausstellungsraum, der nur durch Lichtbänder in der Decke belichtet wird. Die schmalen Seitenschiffe mit geneigten Dachflächen bleiben gänzlich ohne Tageslicht zugunsten eines „introvertierten Charakters" (gmp-Projekterläuterung). Diesen Charakter unterstreichen die Bleiplatten, die alle Oberflächen verkleiden sollen. Sollte ein zur Zeit in Madrid ausgestelltes Werk Anselm Kiefers für die Kunsthalle in Frage kommen, könnte, so Grothe, mit den Bauarbeiten im Herbst 1998 begonnen werden. Fällt die Entscheidung Grothes gegen dieses Kunstwerk, „könnte es noch ein Jahr dauern." Der Kunsthallenentwurf wird dem auszustellenden Objekt angepaßt.

Friedhelm Feldhaus

the foyer against the modest colours of wood, screed floor and fair-faced concrete columns.
The architect Meinhard von Gerkan, who promotes this new development within the partnership, discovers colour for himself. This could develop into more than one phenomenon amongst many. After all, the Hamburg office is busy with large-scale projects (Lehrter Bahnhof, the Olympic Stadium renovation and the newly constructed Schönefeld airport), which will in the future characterize the appearance and perception of public space in Berlin and therefore Germany. The noble restraint of natural materials holds limited merit. Colour contributes an additional component, expanding the architectural repertoire.

Gert Kähler

URBAN RENEWAL OF THE OLD "EUROPAHAFEN" WITH ART GALLERY

ART COLLECTOR AND INVESTOR HANS GROTHE PLANS A GALLERY AND SERVICE CENTRE ON THE WESERBAHNHOF II SITE.
(A & W, NO. 70, 11/98)

Archaic associations and attributes of classical modernism characterize the "Kunsthalle Weserbahnhof II". The successful design in form of a feasibility study by the Hamburg architects von Gerkan, Marg und Partner (gmp) for an art gallery on the Weserbahnhof II site will provide space for works by the German painter and sculptor Anselm Kiefer. The art gallery, initiated and financed by the collector Hans Grothe, is simultaneously the prelude for a new usage of the site between "Stephanitorsbollwerk" and "Weserkaje" for office and service functions.

Future Ferry Terminal?
The urban renewal of the old Europahafen is initiated with a cultural building. While the "Teerhof" is waiting for the promised cultural development (refer to Journal article), the art collector and investor Hans Grothe has definite intentions for the 16,500 m² site, purchased in 1996. After the

erection of the 420 m² exhibition hall, a service centre with 30,000 m² gross floor space is intended for the second phase. Due to the recent surplus of office space, the realization of the commercial buildings are to be regarded as a medium-term project. The infrastructural developments from the community have a corresponding time-horizon. An extension of the Lloyd-allee as an avenue down to the River Weser has been proposed, with an underpass for trams, pedestrians and cyclists

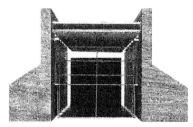

below the street and train level. This new connection will create a link to the city centre and establish a landing-stage "Weserbahnhof II" for the "Weser Shuttle" and the "White Line". The realization of a passenger terminal may also be feasible.

Cladded Lead Surfaces.
Plans for the basilica-like art gallery are completed, which will solely provide space for new works by Anselm Kiefer. The nave provides a 9 metre high, 20 metre deep and 8 metre wide exhibition hall, lit only by light stripes in the ceiling. The narrow aisles with inclined roof surfaces have limited lighting in favour of a "solemn character" (gmp-project explanation). This atmosphere is enforced with lead panels, which will clad all surfaces. If a piece of art by Anselm Kiefer, presently exhibited in Madrid, is considered for the art gallery, the construction works could be initiated in autumn 1998, explains Grothe. If Grothe decides against this art piece, "it could take another year". The design of the art gallery will be adjusted to the objects exhibited.

Friedhelm Feldhaus

FORSCHUNG UND LEHRE

RESEARCH AND TEACHING

HÖRSAALZENTRUM DER TU CHEMNITZ

WETTBEWERB: 1994 - 1. Preis
ENTWURF: Meinhard v. Gerkan
PROJEKTLEITUNG: Dirk Heller,
Astrid Lapp
MITARBEITER: Angelika Juppien,
Knut Maass, Ralf Schmitz,
Michele Watenphul
BAUHERR: Staatshochbauamt
Chemnitz
BAUZEIT: 1996 - 1998
BGF: 8.856 m²
BRI: 51.766 m³

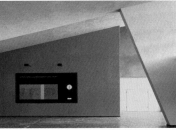

2

In der ersten Euphorie von Freiheit und Expansion nach der deutschen Wiedervereinigung machte die TU Chemnitz eine ehrgeizige Erweiterung des Universitäts-Campus zum Gegenstand eines städtebaulichen Wettbewerbes. Als erstes sollten ein sehr großes Hörsaal- und Seminargebäude faßt ein großes Foyer, das unter dem aufgeständerten Volumen der beiden großen Hörsäle liegt. Deren schräger Boden, den ansteigenden Sitzreihen folgend, ist als Decke sichtbar. Die Baukörperfügung sorgt trotz großer Tiefe des Bauwerks für Tageslicht in den innenliegenden Foyerzonen, in

3

sowie ein Institut realisiert werden, danach die Bibliothek folgen. Der ausgewählte Entwurf von gmp sah eine flexible Linearstruktur als langfristiges Entwicklungsmodell und ein Eingangsforum vor, das von Hörsaalkomplex und Bibliothek baulich gefaßt werden sollte. Von allem ist nur das Hörsaalgebäude als reale Baumaßnahme übrig geblieben und dieses auch um ein Drittel verkleinert. Die Euphorie ist einer Ernüchterung gewichen, das Entwicklungsgelände scheint dem Wildwuchs von Gewerbeflächen geopfert zu werden. Damit bildet das Hörsaalgebäude vorerst den Schluß - und nicht den ersten Baustein einer zukünftigen Erweiterung. Dem wird die kräftige Gliederung der Baukörper gleichwohl gerecht. Ein Winkel aus Seminarräumen dem vertikal durchgehende Lufträume mit Dachoberlichtern versehen wurden. Dadurch wird das Milieu im Gegensatz zur Dunkelzonenstimmung vieler großer Universitätsbauten hell und heiter stimuliert. Auch die beiden großen Hörsäle sind keine „black boxes". Die Lichtstimmungen des Himmels versorgen die Zuhörer mit mentalem Stimulanz. Der andere dominante Gestaltungsparameter ist die intensive Farbigkeit von Wänden und Decken. Dies entspricht nicht dem ursprünglichen Entwurfskonzept, sondern wurde während der Bauzeit aus der Not eines radikalen Sparzwangs und den Eindrücken einer Mexikoreise des Architekten geboren. Das preisgünstigste Material großer Wand- und Deckenflächen ist Putz, die Farbe gibt es fast gratis dazu.

1 RAUHER INDUSTRIEPUTZ FÜR DIE VIELEN GROSSEN WANDFLÄCHEN FOLGTEN DEM GEBOT GRÖSSTER SPARSAMKEIT. EIN MEXIKO-BESUCH MIT BAUTEN VON BARAGAN UND LEGORETTO WAR DER ANSTOSS, EINE FARBINSZENIERUNG ZU UNTERNEHMEN.
2 STÄDTEBAULICHER LAGEPLAN MIT GEPLANTER ERWEITERUNG DER TU.
3 DER NEUBAU IM BESTAND AUS DER VOGELPERSPEKTIVE.
4 TRAGENDE WANDSCHEIBEN UNTERHALB DES GROSSEN HÖRSAALES BEGRENZEN DAS EINGANGSFOYER.

1 ROUGH PLASTER FOR MANY LARGE WALL SURFACES FOLLOWED ECONOMIC REQUIREMENT. A VISIT TO MEXICO AND BUILDINGS OF BARAGAN AND LEGORETTO INSPIRED THE COLOUR CONCEPT.
2 SITE PLAN IN URBAN CONTEXT WITH PROPOSED EXTENSION OF THE INSTITUTE OF TECHNOLOGY.
3 AERIAL VIEW OF PROPOSAL IN EXISTING CONTEXT.
4 SUPPORTING WALL PANELS UNDERNEATH THE LARGE AUDITORIUM FRAME THE ENTRANCE FOYER.

1

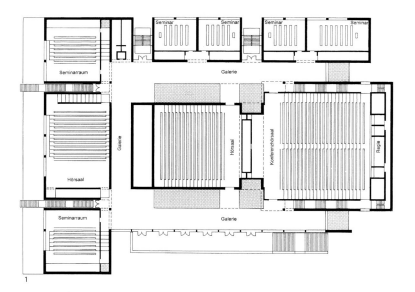

1

2

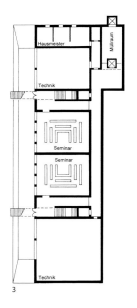

3

Der Besuch von Bauten Baragans und Legorettos lieferte die Anregung, mit einfachsten Mitteln prägnante Gestaltkraft zu gewinnen. Der sehr mutige Griff in Farbtöpfe war nicht zuletzt auch eine Reaktion auf die graue Tristesse des Ortes mit seinen sehr kargen Großtafelbauten. Der Bau bekennt sich zu seiner Bescheidenheit und zeigt das Prinzip der Einfachheit auch in der Reduktion und Disziplinierung der Details. Die Farbwahl selbst sowie die Disposition, nicht mit Körpern sondern mit Flächen die Räume zu gestalten, ging aus einem intensiven experimentellen Prozess hervor, der in dem Oeuvre von gmp ein neues Kapitel aufschlägt. Das Prinzip sparsamster Einfachheit - der Bau wurde weit unter dem ursprünglichen Budget realisiert - dominierte auch alle anderen Entscheidungen zur Gestaltung:
- Industrieestrich für die Fußböden.
- Streckmetall für die Decken.
- Wellblech an der Fassade.
- Stählerne Fluchttreppen, die zwischen den Sälen im Freien liegen.

In the initial euphoria of freedom and expansion after the German reunification, the Chemnitz Institute of Technology initiated a town-planning competition for the ambitious extension of the university campus. First of all a large auditoria and seminar building as well as an institute should be built, followed by a library. Gmp's winning concept suggested a linear structure, offering flexibility for long-term development, and an entrance forum to be framed by auditoria and libraries. Of all the proposed buildings, the auditoria complex was the only to be constructed, which was considerably reduced in scale from its original dimension. Euphoria gave way to disillusionment, with the development site being sacrificed to the uncontrolled expansion of commercial sites. Presently the auditoria are the final and not as originally conceived the first phase of future extension, this fact is reflected in the strong building structure. A line of seminar rooms frames a foyer volume, located underneath two large auditoria, with their inclined floors, which follow the ascending seating arrangement, being visible from the underside. The building arrangement allows for natural lighting into the inner foyer zones, despite the large depth of the buildings, where vertical voids with top lights were intended. This renders a light and cheerful

1 OBERGESCHOSS.

2 ERDGESCHOSS.

3 GRUNDRISS EBENE -1.

4 HAUPTZUGANG VON OSTEN. WANDSCHEIBEN TRAGEN DEN GROSSEN HÖRSAAL UND GLIEDERN DIE EINGANGS-FRONT.

1 UPPER LEVEL.

2 GROUND LEVEL.

3 PLAN LEVEL -1.

4 MAIN ENTRANCE FROM THE EAST. WALL PANELS SUPPORT THE LARGE AUDITORIUM AND DEFINE THE ENTRANCE ELEVATION.

4

ambience in contrast to the darkness reminiscent in many large universities. The two large auditoria are also not classified as "black boxes"; the sky panorama provides mental stimulation for the students. The other dominant design characteristic is the intense colouring of walls and ceilings. This does not correspond to the initial design concept, but has been developed during the realization phase due to radical financial restrictions and from the architect's impressions gained during a journey to Mexico. The most economic material for extensive wall and ceiling surfaces is plaster, applying colour thereafter is reasonable. The visit to buildings of Baragan and Legoretto offered the stimulation to gain outstanding design results via simple means. The daring use of colour has also been a response to the otherwise grey dullness of the town with sparse tower blocks. The building declares its modesty and shows the principle of simplicity also in the reduction and discipline of details. The colour choice and the design of rooms with surfaces instead of volumes is the result of an intensive experimental process, opening a new chapter in the oeuvre of gmp. The principle of economic simplicity, were the building was complete far below the initial budget, has ramifications on all other design decisions:
- industrial screed for floors
- perforated metal sheets for ceilings
- corrugated sheet steel on the facade
- steel escape stairs, located externally between the auditoria.

1

2

3

1-3 DIE FLUCHT-
TREPPEN SIND IN
GEBÄUDESCHLITZEN
ZWISCHEN DEN
HÖRSÄLEN ANGE-
ORDNET. SIE FÜHREN
OHNE WETTER-
SCHUTZ DIREKT
INS FREIE.
1-3 ESCAPE STAIRS
WITHOUT WEATHER
PROTECTION ARE
LOCATED IN NICHES
BETWEEN THE
AUDITORIA AND
LEAD DIRECTLY
OUTSIDE.

2

3

1 DEM FOYER IM OBERGE-
SCHOSS IST EINE GROSSE
TERRASSE NACH SÜDEN
VORGELAGERT, VON DER
EINE BREITE FREITREPPE
AUF DAS GELÄNDENIVEAU
FÜHRT. AUCH DIE GESTAL-
TUNG DER FASSADE FOLG-
TE DEM DIKTAT GRÖSSTER
SPARSAMKEIT.
RAUHPUTZ UND ALUMINI-
UMWELLBLECH SIND
PREISLICH NICHT ZU
UNTERBIETEN.
2 ZWEILÄUFIGE FLUCHT-
TREPPE AUF DER NORD-
SEITE ZWISCHEN DEN
HÖRSÄLEN.
3 UNTERHALB DER SÜD-
TERRASSE ÖFFNET SICH
DAS FOYER AUCH ZUM
ZUM FREIRAUM.
NÄCHSTE DOPPELSEITE:
EINE KLARE GEO-
METRISCHE GLIEDERUNG
MACHT DIE FUNKTIONELLE
ANORDNUNG DER
VERKEHRSZONEN UND
HÖRSÄLE ABLESBAR UND
UNTERSTÜTZT DURCH VER-
TIKALE SICHTBEZIEHUN-
GEN DIE ORIENTIERUNG.

1 ADJACENT TO THE
FOYER ON THE FIRST LEVEL
EXTENDS A LARGE, SOUTH-
FACING TERRACE, FROM
WHICH A FLIGHT OF STEPS
DESCENTS TO THE GROUND
LEVEL.
THE FACADE DESIGN
FOLLOWED ECONOMICAL
RESTRICTIONS.
PLASTER AND CORRUGATED
ALUMINIUM SHEETS ARE
INCOMPARABLE IN PRICE-
WORTHINESS.
2 ESCAPE STAIRS ON THE
NORTH SIDE BETWEEN THE
AUDITORIA.
3 THE FOYER OPENS UP
TOWARDS THE LANDSCAPE
ON GROUND LEVEL
UNDERNEATH THE
SOUTH TERRACE.
NEXT PAGE:
A CLEAR GEOMETRICAL
ORDER CLARIFIES THE
ARRANGEMENT OF CIRCU-
LATION AREAS AND
AUDITORIA THEREBY
CLARIFYING VERTICAL
CIRCULATION.

1

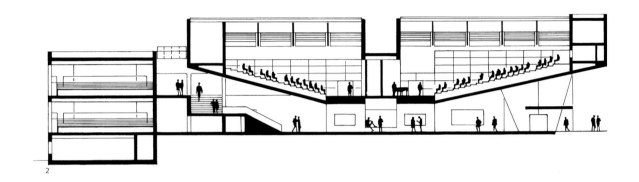

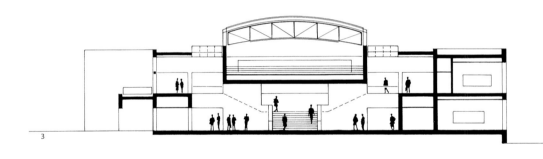

1 FOYERZONE AUF
DER SÜDSEITE IM
OBERGESCHOSS.
OBERLICHTER UND
OFFENE LUFTRÄUME
SORGEN FÜR TAGES-
LICHT AUCH IM
INNEREN DES TIEFEN
BAUKÖRPERS.
ABGEHÄNGTE DECKE
AUS STRECKMETALL,
FUSSBÖDEN IN
INDUSTRIEESTRICH.
2 LÄNGSSCHNITT.
3 QUERSCHNITT.
1 FOYER AREA ON
THE SOUTH SIDE ON
THE UPPER LEVEL.
TOPLIGHTS AND
VOIDS ALLOW DAY-
LIGHT TO ENTER THE
DEPTH OF THE
BUILDING. SUSPEND-
ED CEILING MADE
FROM STEEL MESH,
SCREED FLOORS.
2 LONGITUDINAL
SECTION.
3 CROSS SECTION.

1

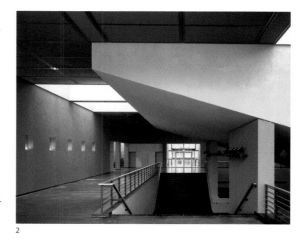

2

3

4

1 DEM SPARSAM REDUZIERTEN MATE-RIALEINSATZ ENTSPRICHT DIE KARGHEIT DES DETAILS = REDUK-TION AUF DIE DIS-POSITION VON FLÄCHEN UND FARBEN.
2 HAUPTAUFGANG AUF DER WESTSEITE.
3 OBERES FOYER AUF DER NORDSEITE.
4 DIE NUR VON DER DIMENSION GROSS-ARTIGE HAUPT-TREPPE FOLGT DER AXIALSYMMETRIE.

1 THE SCARCITY OF DETAIL CORRESPONDS THE ECONOMIC MATERIAL USE = REDUCTION TO ARRANGEMENT OF WALLS AND COLOURS.
2 MAIN STAIRCASE ON THE WEST SIDE.
3 UPPER FOYER ON THE NORTH SIDE.
4 THE DIMENSION-ALLY IMPRESSIVE MAIN STAIRCASE FOLLOWS THE AXIAL SYMMETRY.

1

1+2 DER GROSSE
HÖRSAAL BIETET
1000 SITZPLÄTZE;
SEITLICHE OBER-
LICHTER GEWÄHREN
OPTIMALE TAGESLICHT-
STIMMUNG UND
LASSEN SICH GLEICH-
WOHL VERDUNKELN.
1+2 THE LARGE
AUDITORIUM OFFERS
1000 SEATS;
TOPLIGHTS ALLOW
FOR OPTIMAL NATU-
RAL LIGHTING AND
CAN BE DARKENED.

2

1 AUFGANG ZUR
OBEREN EBENE EINES
DER MITTLEREN
HÖRSÄLE MIT
ABGETREPPTER SITZ-
ANORDNUNG.
2 BESTUHLUNG UND
WANDBEKLEIDUNG
SIND AUS AHORN-
HOLZ.
1 STAIRCASE TO
UPPER LEVEL OF AN
AUDITORIUM WITH
SEPARATED SEAT
ARRANGEMENT.
2 SEATING FURNI-
TURE AND WALL
CLADDING MADE
FROM MAPLE WOOD.

2

IN DER ACHSE DES
TREPPENAUFGANGES
GESTIKULIERT DIE
INTERAKTIVE FIGUR
„DER HALBLEITER
VON CHEMNITZ"
DES KÜNSTLERS
STEPHAN VON HUENE.
THE INTERACTIVE
SCULPTURE "THE
SEMICONDUCTOR
OF CHEMNITZ" BY
STEPHAN VON
HUENE SIGNIFIES
THE STAIRCASE AXIS.

HÖRSAALZENTRUM DER UNIVERSITÄT OLDENBURG

WETTBEWERB: 1990/1992 - 1. Preis
ENTWURF: Meinhard v. Gerkan
PROJEKTLEITUNG: Klaus Lenz
MITARBEITER: Karl-Heinz Behrendt,
Bettina Groß, Susan Krause,
Bernd Kottsieper, Jens Reichert,
Dagmar Winter
BAUHERR: Staatshochbauamt
Oldenburg
BAUZEIT: 1996 - 1998
BGF: 5.163 m²
BRI: 29.135 m³

Das Auditorium Maximum der Carl-von-Ossietzky-Universität liegt in einer durch kleinteilige Bauten und einige maßstabsprengende Groß-bauten der 60er Jahre gekennzeich-neten Umgebung an einer belebten Straßenkreuzung im Westen der Stadt. Der Entwurf reagiert auf die disparate Situation durch einen kraftvollen, zweigeschossigen, zylindrischen Baukörper, der markant der Bedeutung einer fakultätsübergreifenden Einrichtung gerecht wird. Die geometrisch reine Form wird aufgebrochen durch Vor- und Rücksprünge und durch die unterschiedliche Behandlung der Fassaden zwischen der offenen Foyer- und der Bühnenseite. An die vorhandenen Bauten der Universität wird der Zylinder durch eine Brücke angebunden, die auf seiner anderen Seite, an der Straßenkreuzung, in einem langgestreckten Baukörper mit den Seminarräumen endet.

Der Abstraktheit der reinen geometrischen Form entspricht das Weiß der geputzten Fassade. Nur zwei Flächen der Außenwand werden farblich differenziert und wirken wie eine Kulisse vor dem weißen Hintergrund. Innen ist es der Behinder-

1

1 DIE „BÜHNENSEITE" DES GROSSEN DREITEILBAREN HÖRSAALES.
2 GEOMETRIE UND DURCHDRINGUNG WERDEN IN DER LUFTAUFSICHT ABLESBAR.
3 DETAILS DER BESCHATTER VOR DEM PANORAMAFENSTER DES GROSSEN HÖRSAALES.

1 "STAGE SIDE" OF THE LARGE AUDITORIUM, SEPARABLE IN THREE PARTS.
2 GEOMETRY AND FILTRATION ARE PERCEIVABLE IN THE AERIAL VIEW.
3 DETAILS OF SHADING DEVICE IN FRONT OF PANORAMIC AUDITORIUM WINDOWS.

2

3

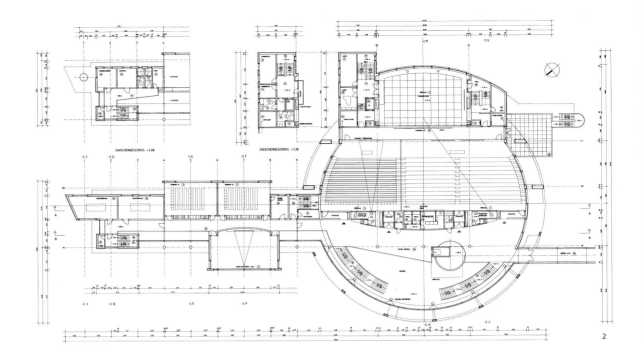

1 DURCHDRINGUNG
DES ZYLINDRISCHEN
BAUKÖRPERS MIT
DEM RIEGEL.
2 ERDGESCHOSS-
GRUNDRISS.
3 OBERGESCHOSS-
GRUNDRISS.

1 BAR FORM
INTERSECTING
CYLINDRICAL
BUILDING VOLUME.
2 GROUND
LEVEL PLAN.
3 UPPER
LEVEL PLAN.

tenaufzug als frei stehender Baukörper mitten im Foyer, der mit einem kräftigen Blau gegen die Farben natürlicher Materialien von Holz, Gußaphaltboden und Sichtbetonstützen besteht.

Der Veranstaltungssaal im Obergeschoß ist mit allen notwendigen technischen Einrichtungen ausgestattet, um für Theater, Kongresse und Kulturereignisse dienen zu können. Er ist in drei Raumabschnitte unterteilbar, in denen gleichzeitig Veranstaltungen stattfinden können.

The main lecture hall in the Carl-von-Ossietzky-University is situated on a busy street junction, in an area defined by a mix of small-scale buildings and town blocks from the sixties. The concept reacts against this disparity with a strong, cylindrical two-storey form, which fulfils the significance of an institution used by various faculties. The pure geometry is fragmented with projecting and recessing elements and through various facade aesthetics between the open foyer and stage side. A bridge links the cylinder to existing university buildings, which is terminated by a longitudinal building comprising of lecture rooms. The white plastered facade corresponds to the clear building geometry. Two areas on the external facade are emphasized with colour and appear to be scenery in front of the white background. Internally, the disabled lift designed as a free standing element in the foyer, is painted with a powerful blue, contrasting against the natural materials like wood, the poured asphalt floor and fair-faced columns. The function hall on the upper floor is equipped with the required technology to serve for theatre, congress and cultural events. It is subdivided in three sections, where events can take place simultaneously.

FÜGUNG UND
DURCHDRINGUNG
DES BAUKÖRPERS.
COMPOSITION AND
FILTRATION OF THE
BUILDING.

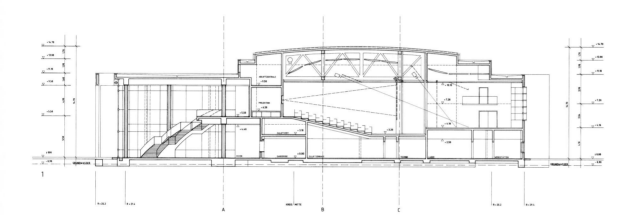

1

2

3

1 DIE GEOMETRIE
VON KREIS UND
GERADE, NATURMA-
TERIALIEN UND
WENIGE FARBAKZEN-
TE BESTIMMEN
DIE ARCHITEKTUR-
SPRACHE.
2 DIE GESCHWUNGE-
NE GARDEROBEN-
WAND WIRD VON
EINER BEPLANKUNG
MIT HOLZLEISTEN
GEGLIEDERT.
1 THE GEOMETRY
OF CIRCLE AND
STRAIGHT LINE,
NATURAL MATERIALS
AND LIMITED
COLOURED ACCENTS
CHARACTERIZE
THE ARCHITECTURAL
LANGUAGE.
2 THE CURVED
CLOAKROOM WALL
IS STRUCTURED BY
WOOD PLANKING.

1

2

DER GROSSE
HÖRSAAL MIT 1000
SITZPLÄTZEN.
1 SCHALLREFLEK-
TOREN ÜBER DER
BÜHNE.
2 BESTUHLUNG
MIT BUCHENHOLZ-
MÖBELN.
3 BLICK ÜBER DAS
PODIUM DURCH DAS
PANORAMAFENSTER
INS GRÜNE MIT
OPTIONALER
VERDUNKELUNG.
THE LARGE
AUDITORIUM HOLDS
1.000 SEATS.
1 SOUND REFLECTORS
ABOVE THE STAGE.
2 SEATING MADE
FROM BEECH WOOD.
3 VIEW ABOVE THE
PODIUM THROUGH
THE PANORAMIC
WINDOW - WITH OP-
TIONAL DARKENING.

1

2

3

NEUBAU GEISTES-WISSENSCHAFTEN, UNIVERSITÄT LEIPZIG

WETTBEWERB: 1997
ENTWURF: Meinhard v. Gerkan mit Stephan Rewolle

Der Neubau muß sich neben der Universitätsbibliothek und dem Dimitroffmuseum behaupten und sich in eine vorhandene gründerzeitliche Straßen- und Baustruktur einfügen. Diese wird in Höhe und Blockhaftigkeit aufgenommen, gegenüber der Bibliothek wird deren Symmetrieachse weitergeführt. Innerhalb dieser Vorgaben besteht das strukturelle Gerüst aus einer festen „Schale" von Büroräumen und einem weichen, d.h. flexibel nutzbaren „Kern" von Räumen. Eine Längsachse im Erdgeschoß öffnet die Innenhöfe nach außen, zur Stadt hin.

1 AXONOMETRIE.
2 NORMALGESCHOSS.
3 LAGEPLAN.
4 SÜDANSICHT.

1 AXONOMETRIC.
2 STANDARD LEVEL.
3 SITE PLAN.
4 SOUTH ELEVATION.

This new faculty building is to "stand its ground" next to the university library and the Dimitroff Museum, and to integrate in an existing turn-of-the-century street and urban structure. This is taken into account with the new building's height and block character, whilst the library's symmetry axis is continued. The structural skeleton consists of a firm "shell" of offices, and a "soft" (i.e. flexibly usable) "core" of other spaces. A corridor at groundfloor level forms the longitudinal main axis and opens the inner courtyard towards the city.

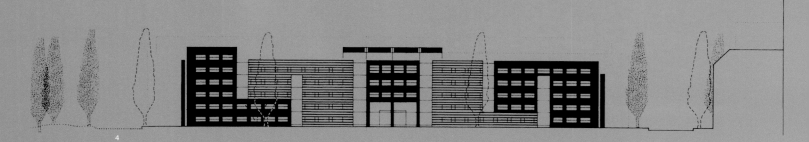

1

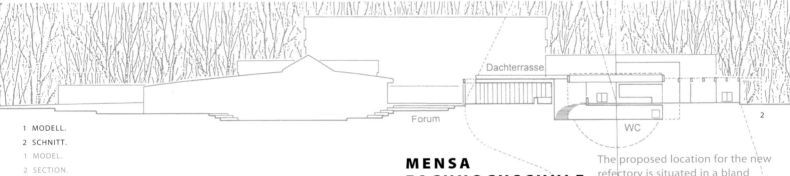

Dachterrasse

Forum

WC

2

1 MODELL.
2 SCHNITT.
1 MODEL.
2 SECTION.

MENSA FACHHOCHSCHULE REGENSBURG

WETTBEWERB: 1998
ENTWURF: Meinhard v. Gerkan mit Stephan Rewolle

Eine höchst indifferente städtebauliche Situation an einem freiräumlichen Verbindungsweg wurde als Standort für eine neue Mensa vorgesehen. Der Entwurf wurde aus dem Dialog zweier Elemente heraus entwickelt: Zum einen dem Wirtschaftstrakt, in dem die Speisen zubereitet werden, zum anderen einem in freier Form in die Landschaft sich einschmiegenden Gebäudeteil, der die Speisesäle aufnimmt und durch seinen fließenden Raumcharakter trotz der großen Zahl von Tischen eine Atmosphäre bieten möchte, die zum Verweilen einlädt.

The proposed location for the new refectory is situated in a bland urban context adjacent to a main road. The design has been developed from the dialogue between two elements: firstly, the service wing, were meals are prepared and secondly, the dining hall section, which nestles into the landscape. The open character of the space offers an inviting atmosphere despite the large number of tables.

1+2 MASSENMODELL.
3 NUTZUNGS-
VERTEILUNG.
4 LAGEPLAN.
1+2 MASSING
MODEL.
3 DISTRIBUTION
OF USE.
4 SITE PLAN.

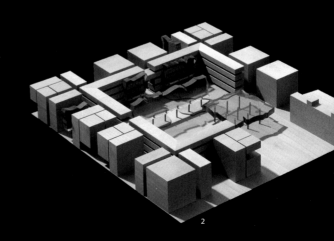

PHYSIKALISCHE INSTITUTE, BERLIN-ADLERSHOF

WETTBEWERB: 1998 - 2. Preis
ENTWURF: Meinhard v. Gerkan mit Sona Kazemi

In Analogie zu einer Molekular-struktur werden einzelne, je nach funktionaler Erfordernis unter-schiedlich große, aber als Quadrat auf einer gleichen Grundform beruhende Einheiten zu einem großen Grundriß-Quadrat geordnet. Es besetzt als blockhaft wirkender Gesamtbaukörper das Grundstück. Eine innere, alle Einzelbauteile verbindende Spange schließt die Form um die quadratische Frei-fläche im Inneren. Die Figur des Konzeptes verbindet eine städte-bauliche Ordnungsfunktion mit klar gegliederter Nutzungsstruktur.

In analogy to a molecular structure, various square units are composed to form a large square plan, their size varying with functional requirements. The plan occupies the site as a monolithic form. An internal brace connects the single built elements and completes the square around the open spaces. The concept combines a structural urban order with a clearly defined plan of use.

3

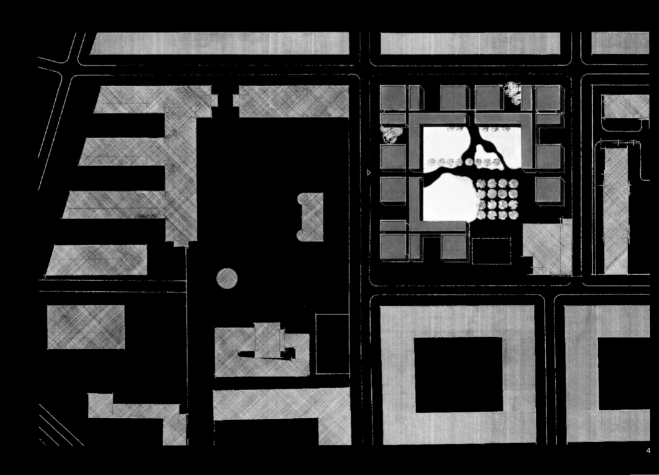

4

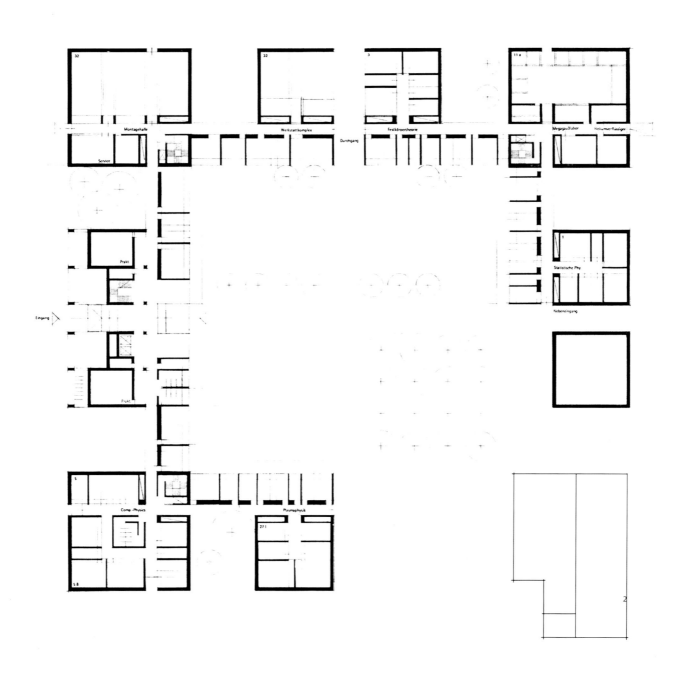

3

1 ANSICHT SÜD-WESTEN.

2 ERDGESCHOSS.

3 SCHNITT ANSICHT.

4 1. OBERGESCHOSS.

1 SOUTH-WEST
ELEVATION.

2 GROUND LEVEL.

3 SECTION ELEVATION.

4 FIRST LEVEL.

4

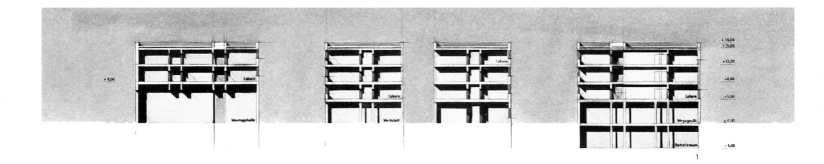

1

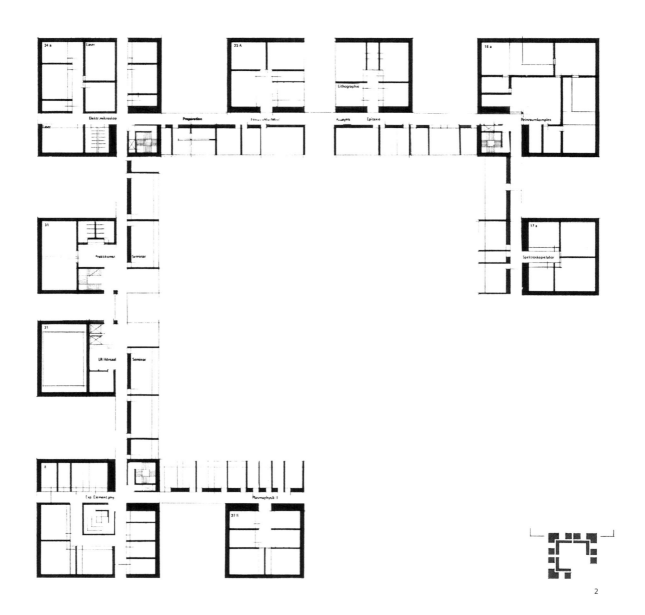

2

1 SCHNITT.

2 2. OBERGESCHOSS.

3 ANSICHT
NORD-OSTEN.

4 3. OBERGESCHOSS.

1 SECTION.

2 SECOND LEVEL.

3 NORTH-EAST
ELEVATION.

4 THIRD LEVEL.

4

LANDES-GYMNASIUM ST. AFRA, MEISSEN

WETTBEWERB: 1997
ENTWURF: Meinhard v. Gerkan
mit Nicolai Pix

Das topografisch bewegte, durch
alten Baubestand vorgeprägte
und intensiv übergrünte Grundstück
fordert zu einem Dialog zwischen
Architektur und Landschaft heraus.
Typologisch sind die Bauelemente
gleich. Die Unterkunftshäuser haben
einen zentralen Gemeinschafts-
bereich, der winkelförmig von den
Wohnzellen eingefaßt wird. Die neu-
en Elemente liegen an der Stelle der
zum Abriß bestimmten Altbauten.
Damit werden vorhandene Grünflächen geschont und die überkom-
mene Räumlichkeit der Bauten neu
interpretiert.

The varying topography on the
site, characterized by the old trees
and vast green areas, challenges a
dialogue between architecture and
landscape. Typologically the buildings are identical, the housing units
have a central communal area,
embraced by the accommodation
facilities. The proposed structures
will occupy the site of the old buildings, which are to be demolished.
Therefore the existing green areas
are protected and out-of-date
premises are newly interpreted.

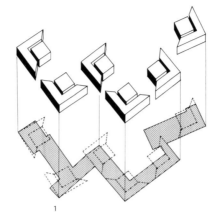

1

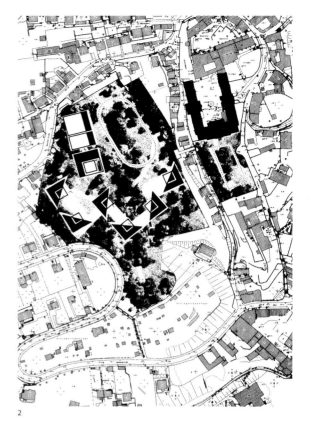

2

3

1 ANORDNUNG DER
WOHNHÄUSER.
2 LAGEPLAN.
3 WOHNHAUS
MITTELSTUFE.
1. OBERGESCHOSS.
2. OBERGESCHOSS.
ERDGESCHOSS.
4 QUERSCHNITT.
1 ARRANGEMENT
OF RESIDENTIAL
BUILDINGS.
2 SITE PLAN.
3 RESIDENTIAL
BUILDING - MEDIUM
SCALE .
FIRST LEVEL.
SECOND LEVEL.
GROUND LEVEL.
4 CROSS SECTION.

4

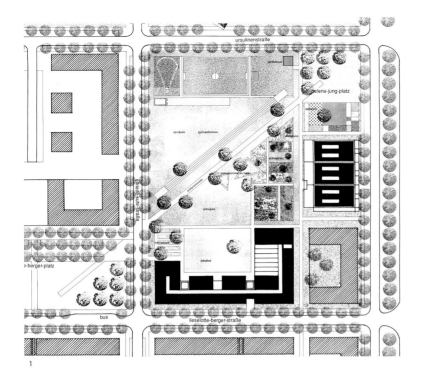

1

GYMNASIUM WALTERSDORFER CHAUSSEE, BERLIN

WETTBEWERB: 1997 - 4. Preis
ENTWURF: Meinhard v. Gerkan
MITARBEITER: Michael Biwer, Nicolai Pix

Die Baukörper vervollständigen das bestehende städtebauliche Ensemble und bilden eine sich zum Park hin öffnende, U-förmige Figur, die den Schulhof umschließt; das Prinzip wiederholt sich im Inneren, wo die Klassenräume Fach- und Sonderräume umfassen, die durch Aufweitungen der Flure gegliedert und als „Schulbausteine" ablesbar sind. Die Aula erhält einen Zugang von innen wie von außen, um auch für externe Veranstaltungen genutzt werden zu können; der angrenzende Musiksaal bildet dafür eine flexible Bühne.

These building volumes complete an existing urban development and are arranged in a U-shape which encloses the school yard. The U is repeated inside where normal classrooms surround the special subject teaching and ancillary spaces. These units are legible from the plan as "school building blocks" because they are separated by wide corridors. Access to the main assembly hall is from the inside and outside so that it can also be used for public events, for which the adjoining music hall offers a flexible stage.

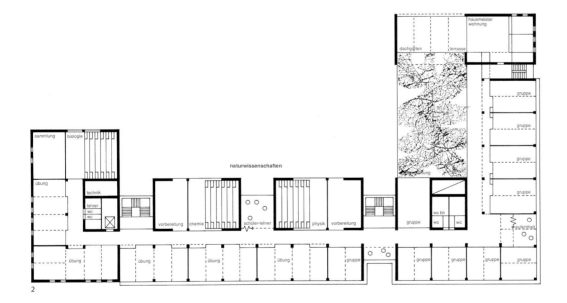

2

3

1 LAGEPLAN.
2 OBERGESCHOSS.
3 SÜDANSICHT.

1 SITE PLAN.
2 UPPER LEVEL.
3 SOUTH ELEVATION.

1

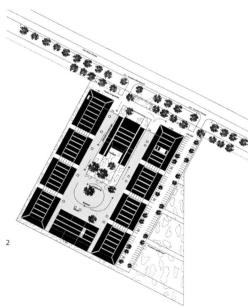

2

LEHRBAUHOF II, BERLIN-MARZAHN

WETTBEWERB: 1997 - 1. Rang
ENTWURF: Meinhard v. Gerkan mit Johann v. Mansberg

Eine einfache, einprägsame Bauform, die mit geneigten Dachformen mittige, hohe Hallenräume mit Sheds ebenso integriert wie die niedrigeren Randzonen für Nebenräume: So soll ein Ort geschaffen werden, der der Gesichtslosigkeit üblicher Gewerbegebiete an den Stadträndern widersteht. Die gesamte Anlage wird daher als Umfassung eines „Innenhofes" entwickelt, der als Werkhof für die Anlieferung wie auch als Pausenhof dient, und als zentrale Fläche alle Aktivitäten des Lehrbauhofes sichtbar aufeinander bezieht.

A simple, memoriable building form which integrates both central high halls with sloping roofs and sheds as well as lower peripheral ancillary spaces. It is meant to create a place which resists the usual anonymity of urban peripheral business and industrial areas. The entire complex is therefore conceived as the enclosure of an "inner court": a shop floor which also serves as a delivery yard and leisure space between classes. It is also the focus for everything that goes on in this trainee builders' yard.

1 MODELL.
2 LAGEPLAN.
3 SÜDOSTANSICHT.
4+5 DETAILS ZUR BAUKÖRPER- UND DACHAUSBILDUNG.
6 ERDGESCHOSS.
7 NORDOSTANSICHT.

1 MODEL.
2 SITE PLAN.
3 SOUTH-EAST ELEVATION.
4+5 DETAILS OF BUILDING AND ROOF STRUCTURE.
6 GROUND LEVEL.
7 NORTH-EAST ELEVATION.

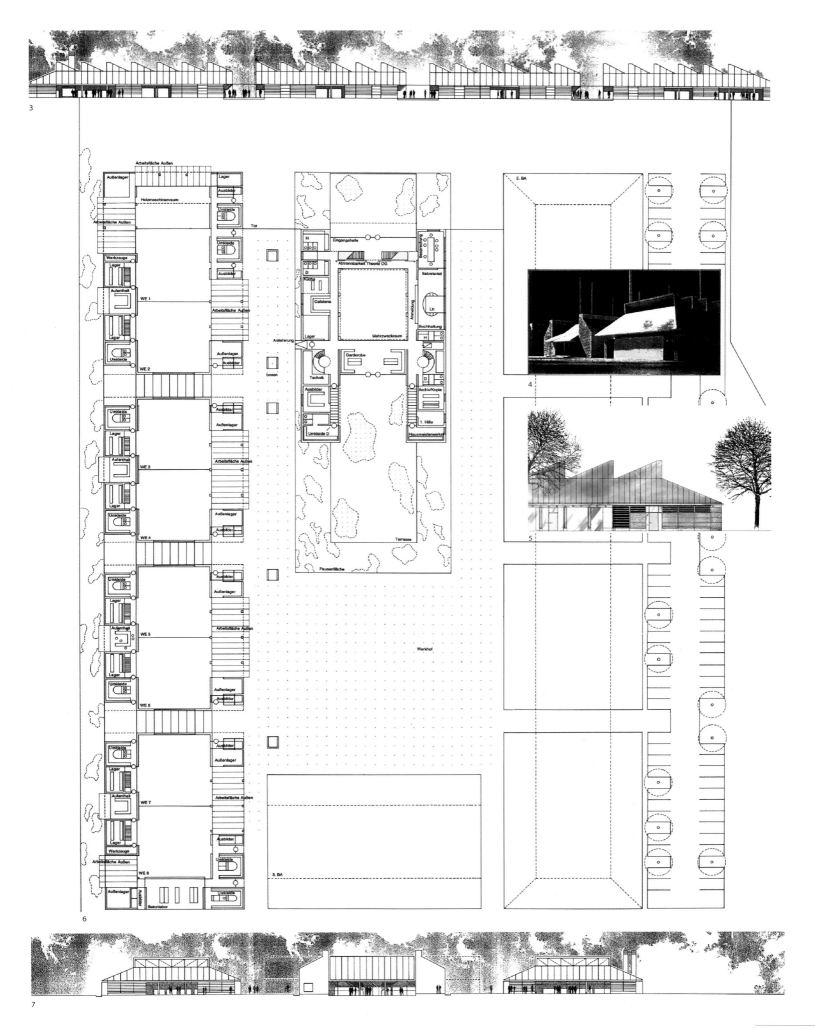

DEUTSCHE SCHULE UND DIENSTWOHNUNGEN IN PEKING

WETTBEWERB: 1998 - 1. Preis
ENTWURF: Meinhard v. Gerkan
mit Michael Biwer
MITARBEITER: Bettina Groß,
Elke Hoffmeister
LEITUNG DER AUSFÜHRUNG:
Klaus Staratzke, Michael Biwer,
Sibylle Kramer
MITARBEITER: Michèle Watenphul,
Knut Maass, Uli Rösler,
Diana Heinrich, Jörn Bohlmann,
Rüdiger v. Helmolt
BAUHERR: Bundesrepublik
Deutschland, BRR
BAUZEIT: 1999 - 2000
BGF: Schule 9.658 m²
Dienstwohnungen 9.657 m²
BRI: Schule 33.534 m³
Dienstwohnungen 30.923 m³

Eine deutsche Schule in China ist
ein Aushängeschild des Landes. Andererseits muß sich der Bau mit den
Bindungen des Ortes auseinandersetzen: dem traditionellen Wunsch
nach Umfassung eines Hauses, den
komplizierten Abstandsregeln, dem
Verbot einer Grenzbebauung.
Da auf dem Grundstück auch ein
Sportplatz mit einer 100 m-Bahn unterzubringen war, entstand der Entwurf als „Puzzle" dieser Bedingungen: Ein einfach gefügter Baukörper,
der Schule, Kindergarten und Sporthalle in einem Gebäude vereinigt,
mit einem differenzierten Freiflächenangebot und einer „Grünen
Mitte" auf dem Dach der Sporthalle.
Zwei neungeschossige Wohntrakte
ergänzen den flacheren Schulbaukörper kontrapunktisch zu einem
geschlossenen Ensemble und nutzen das in der 20-Millionen-Stadt
knappe Bauland voll aus.

A German School in China is a positive advertisement for the country.
Nevertheless, the building must
meet requirements set by the location: The traditional request for an
enclosure, the complex regulations
of building clearance and the prohibitive construction on the site
boundary. The required sports-field
with a 100-metre-track on site led
to the design idea of a "puzzle" solution with the following functions:
A simple building containing a
school, nursery and sports hall

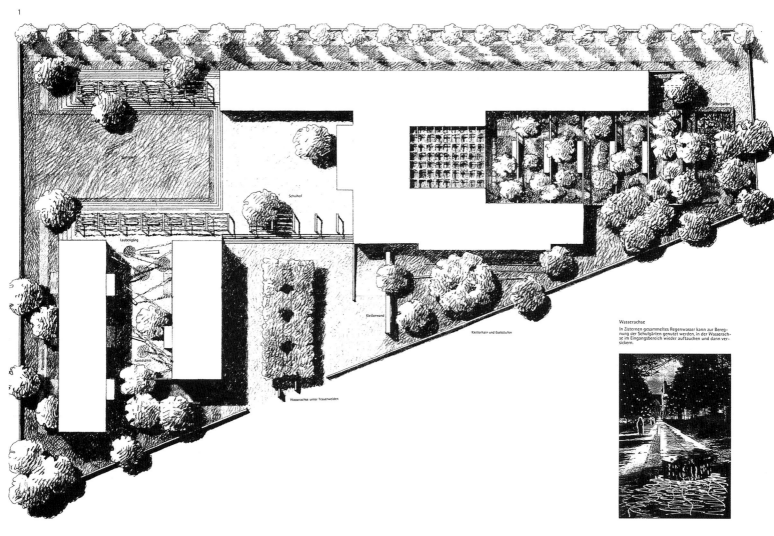

Wasserachse
In Zisternen gesammeltes Regenwasser kann zur Beregnung der Schulgärten genutzt werden, in der Wasserachse im Eingangsbereich wieder auftauchen und dann versickern.

Stufen
dienen als verbindendes Element zwischen den Ebenen Schulhof/Wohnhof und
Sportanlagen/Vorfahrtsbereich. Gleichzeitig fungieren sie als Zuschauertribüne
und Sitzgelegenheit.

Wandelgarten
Auf dem Dach der Sporthalle winden sich schmale Gartenwege durch eine üppige Vegetation aus Stauden, Blütensträuchern und kleinkronigen Gehölzen,
die an den "Fernen Westen" erinnern soll. Denkbar sind Fliederbüsche, Heidekräuter und Bauernrosen.
Hier können Schüler ihre botanischen Kenntnisse erweitern oder durch die
Oberlichter der Turnhalle ein Handballspiel verfolgen.

Laubengänge und hängende Gärten
Im heißen Pekinger Sommer sind schattige Bereiche im Grünen begehrte Zufluchtsorte. Über dem Lesegarten im 2. OG bilden Rankseile und -pflanzen ein
Blätterdach, unter dem auch Unterricht im Freien stattfinden kann.
In den Laubengängen beidseitig des Sportplatzes spendet ein Dach aus Blauregen (Wisteria sinensis) Schatten.
Auch im Hofraum zwischen den Wohngebäuden winden sich Rankgewächse an
Drähten oder Stangen in die Höhe.

Kindergarten mit Kletterhain
Der Kinder-Garten bietet vielfältige Spielmöglichkeiten: An der hohen Wand,
die den belebten Vorfahrtsbereich von der Spielzone abgrenzt, können Klettergerüste, Rutschen und Stangen befestigt werden. In den Obstbaumhain vor der
Eselsstufen sind Kletterseile und Schaukeln gehängt. Auf Holzstegen und
Drahtseilen können die Kinder von Baum zu Baum balancieren.

deutsche schule peking

combined with a differentiated use of open spaces and a "Green Centre" on the roof of the sports hall. Two nine-storey housing blocks together with the low-rise school building form a closed ensemble and comprehensively use the valuable space in a capital with a population of 20 million.

1 LANDSCAPE PLAN.
2 COMPETITION MODEL.
3 SITE PLAN.
EXTENSION CONCEPT.
ENTRANCE ELEVATION.
FACADE DETAIL.

2

3

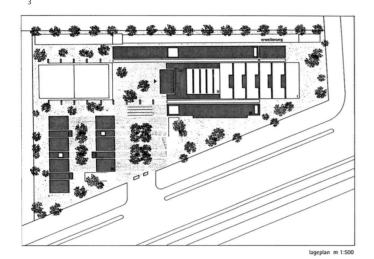

lageplan m 1:500

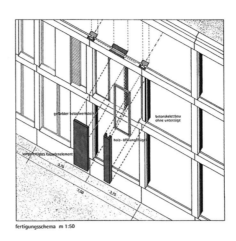

fertigungsschema m 1:50

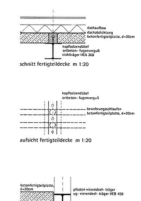

schnitt fertigteildecke m 1:20

aufsicht fertigteildecke m 1:20

verbindung vierendeel- träger mit nebenträgern m 1:20

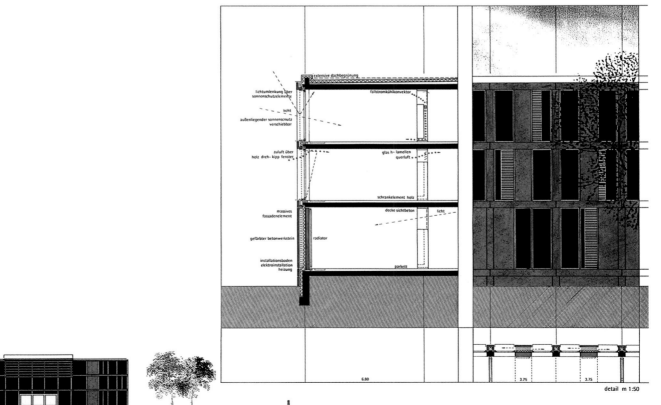

ansicht eingang m 1:200

deutsche schule peking

detail m 1:50

1 GROUND
LEVEL PLAN.
VARIOUS USES.
LONGITUDINAL
SECTION OF SCHOOL.
2 SUPPORTING
STRUCTURE ABOVE
SPORTS HALL.
3 FIRST LEVEL PLAN.
VIEW INTO SPORTS
HALL.
CROSS SECTION OF
SPORTS HALL.
CROSS SECTION OF
HALL.

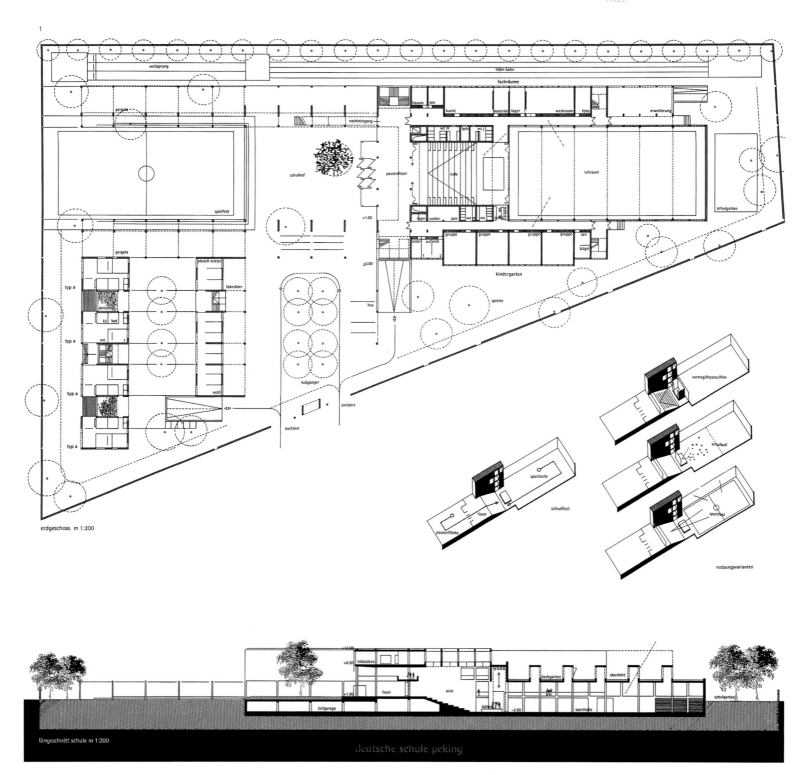

erdgeschoss m 1:200

längsschnitt schule m 1:200

deutsche schule peking

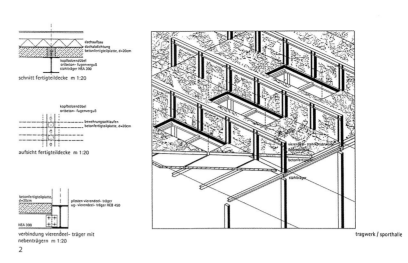

schnitt fertigteildecke m 1:20

dachaufbau
dachabdichtung
betonfertigteilplatte, d=20cm
kopfbolzendübel
ortbeton- fugenverguß
stahlträger HEA 300

aufsicht fertigteildecke m 1:20

kopfbolzendübel
ortbeton- fugenverguß
bewehrungsschlaufen
betonfertigteilplatte, d=20cm

verbindung vierendeel- träger mit
nebenträgern m 1:20

betonfertigteilplatte
d=20cm
pfosten vierendeel- träger
ug- vierendeel- träger HEB 450
HEA 300

vierendeel- stahlkonstruktion
bodenplatte
betonfertigteile
stahlträger

tragwerk / sporthalle

2

3

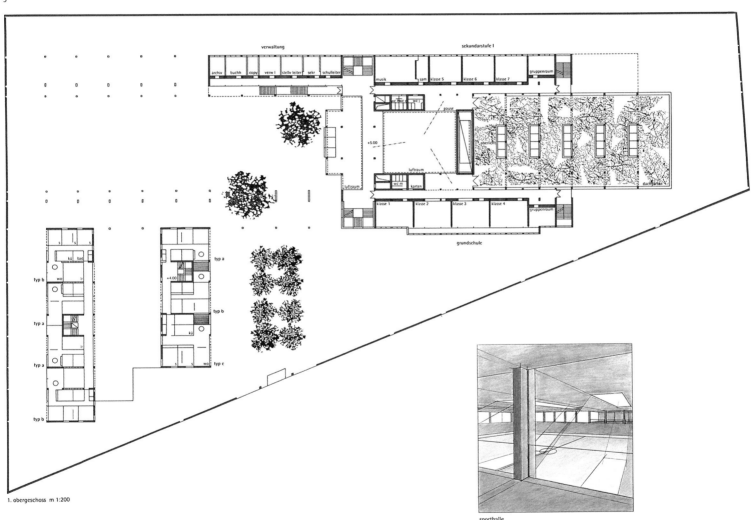

verwaltung

archiv | buchh | copy | verw I | stellv leiter | sekr | schulleiter

sekundarstufe I

musik | sam | klasse 5 | klasse 6 | klasse 7 | gruppenraum

wc h | wc d | wc j

pause

+5.00

oberlicht

luftraum

luftraum | wc m | karten

klasse 1 | klasse 2 | klasse 3 | klasse 4 | gruppenraum

dachgarten

grundschule

typ b

kü | bad

wo

typ a

typ a

typ b

+4.00

typ a

typ b

typ c

kü

wo

s | s

1. obergeschoss m 1:200

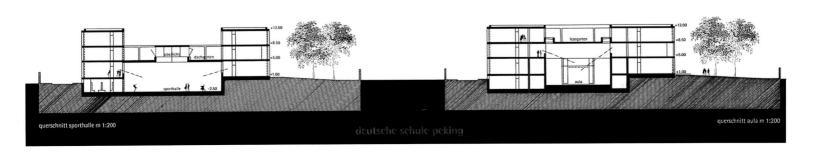

sporthalle

querschnitt sporthalle m 1:200

+12.00
+8.50
+5.00
+1.00

oberlicht | dachgarten

sporthalle | -2.50

querschnitt aula m 1:200

+12.00
+8.50
+5.00
+1.00

lesegarten

aula

deutsche schule peking

1 BASEMENT
LEVEL OF SCHOOL.
ROOF TERRACE
ABOVE SPORTS HALL.
VIEW INTO HALL.
NORTH ELEVATION.
2 SECOND LEVEL.
CORRIDOR.
SOUTH SECTION-
ELEVATION.

1

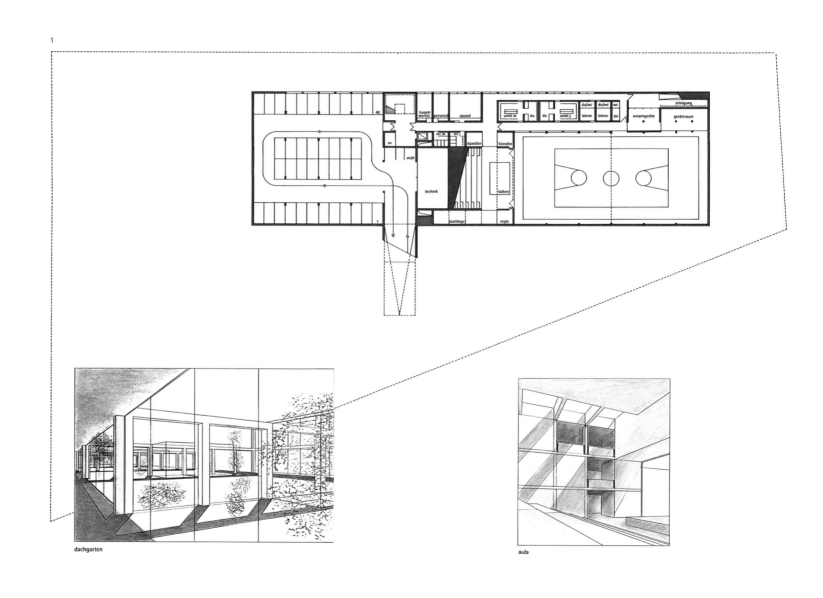

dachgarten

aula

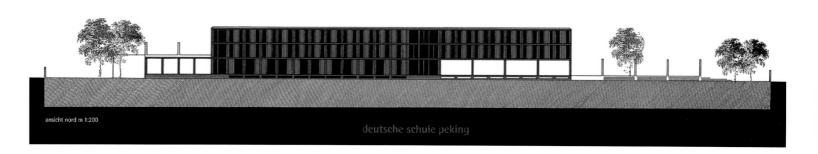

ansicht nord m 1:200

deutsche schule peking

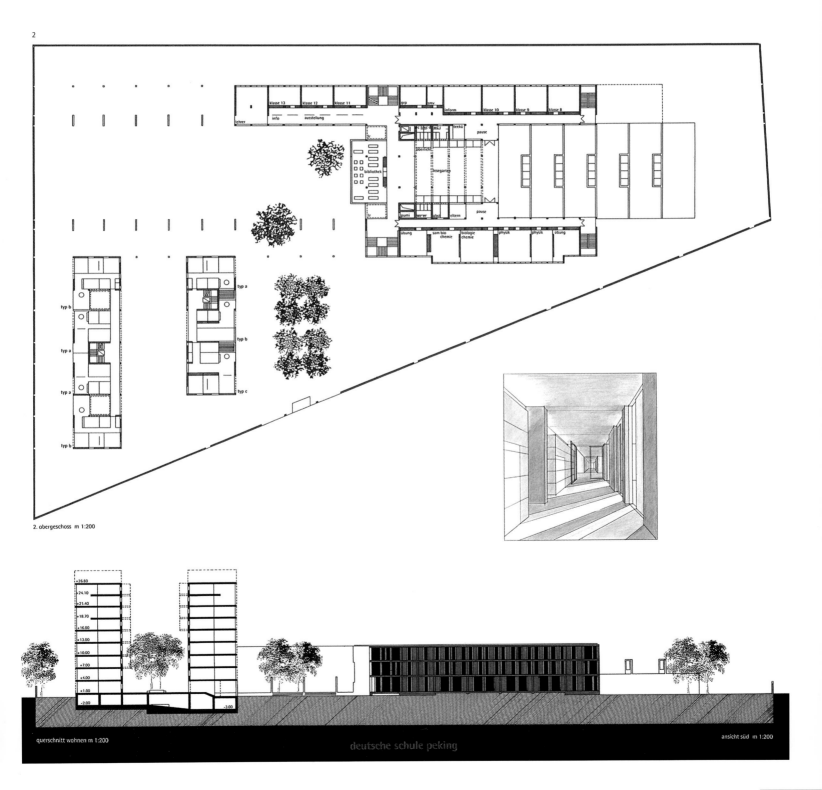

2

2. obergeschoss m 1:200

querschnitt wohnen m 1:200

ansicht süd m 1:200

deutsche schule peking

北京

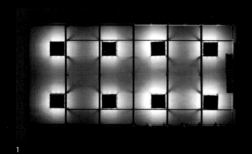

1

2

3

4

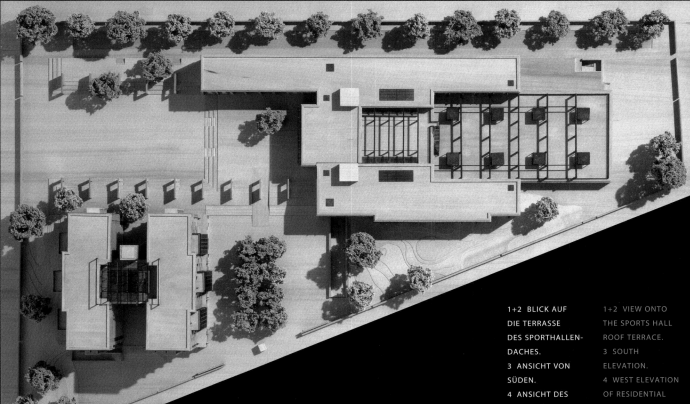

1+2 BLICK AUF
DIE TERRASSE
DES SPORTHALLEN-
DACHES.
3 ANSICHT VON
SÜDEN.
4 ANSICHT DES
WOHNHAUSES VON
WESTEN.
5 LAGEPLAN IM MO-
DELL. DIE ABSTÄNDE
VON DEN GRUND-
STÜCKSGRENZEN
FOLGEN DEN BAU-
REGELN PEKINGS.
6 BLICK AUF
DEN EINGANG ZUR
SCHULE.
7 ANSICHT VON
OSTEN.

1+2 VIEW ONTO
THE SPORTS HALL
ROOF TERRACE.
3 SOUTH
ELEVATION.
4 WEST ELEVATION
OF RESIDENTIAL
BUILDING.
5 MODEL OF SITE
PLAN. SITE BOUND-
ARY CLEARANCES
ARE IN ACCORDANCE
WITH BEIJING PLAN-
NING REGULATIONS.
6 VIEW TO THE
SCHOOL ENTRANCE.
7 EAST ELEVATION.

5

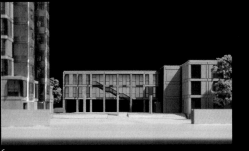

6

7

VORTRAGSPULT

ENTWURF: Meinhard v. Gerkan, 1990
AUSFÜHRUNG: 1998
MITARBEITER: Volkmar Sievers

Was im Ruhezustand flach und bescheiden an einer Wand steht, entpuppt sich als überraschend differenziertes Möbelstück. Durch Ausklappen der Beine und Hochklappen der Pultfläche entsteht ein klassisches Rednerpult mit schräger Ablage, integrierter Beleuchtung und einer weiteren Ablagefläche für Wasserglas und Flasche. Das Möbelstück wird in Schweizer Birne gefertigt und hat eine sichtbare Verzinkung an den Holzstößen - der handwerklichen Ablesbarkeit entspricht die Logik des Auf- und Abbauens.

This piece of folding furniture, when propped up flat against a wall, appears rather modest, but reveals a surprisingly differentiated design when its legs are drawn apart and the desk top is lifted. This makes a classic lectern with slightly inclined top, integrated light and a further tray for a glass of water etc. It is made of Swiss pearwood and has visible zink-coated metal joints. The design logic corresponds to the functional logic of folding and unfolding.

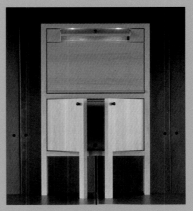

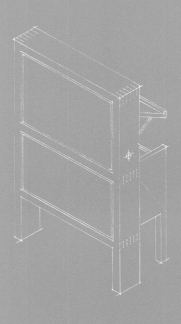

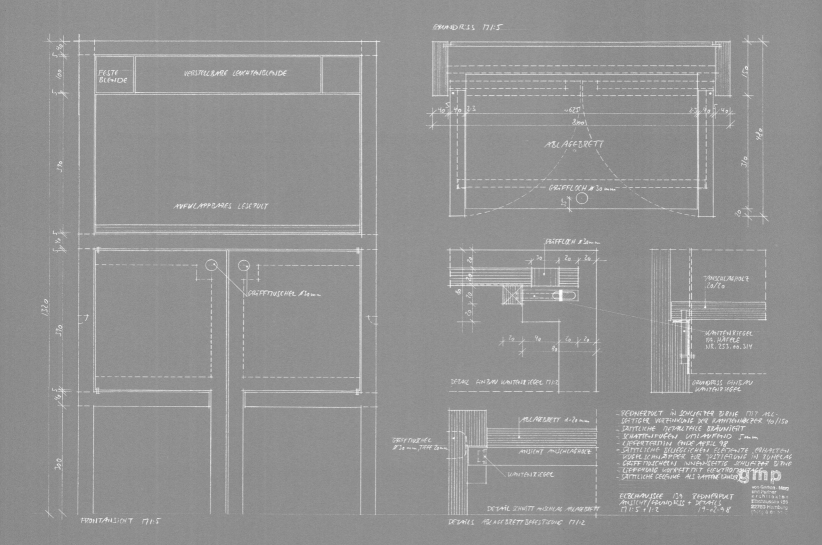

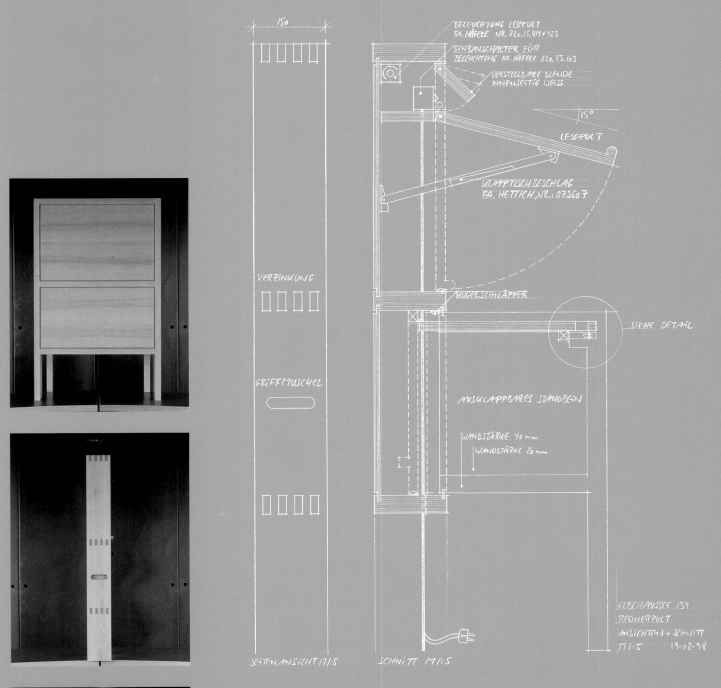

150

BELEUCHTUNG LESEPULT
FA. HÄFELE NR. 820.15.414+423

EINBAUSCHALTER FÜR
BELEUCHTUNG FA. HÄFELE 820.23.103

VERSTELLBARE BLENDE
INNENSEITIG WEISS

15°

LESEPULT

KLAPPTISCHBESCHLAG
FA. HETTICH, NR.: 073607

VERZINKUNG

GRIFFMUSCHEL

KUGELSCHNÄPPER

SIEHE DETAIL

AUSKLAPPBARES STANDBEIN

WANDSTÄRKE 40 mm

WANDSTÄRKE 20 mm

ELBCHAUSSEE 139
REDNERPULT
ANSICHTEN + SCHNITT
1:5   19-02-98

SEITENANSICHT 1:5

SCHNITT M1:5

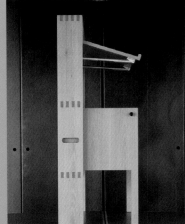

KULTUR

CULTURE

"CHRISTUS-PAVILLON", EXPO 2000, HANNOVER

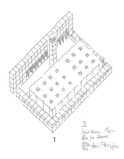

1

WETTBEWERB: 1997 - 1. Preis
ENTWURF: Meinhard v. Gerkan, Joachim Zais
MITARBEITER: Gregor Hoheisel, Sona Kazemi, Stephan Rewolle
LEITUNG DER AUSFÜHRUNG: Joachim Zais, Jörn Orthmann
MITARBEITER: Ulf Düsterhöft, Matias Otto, Olaf Schlüter, Horst-Werner Warias, Andreas Hahn, Thomas Dreusicke, Helge Reimer
AUSSTELLUNG: Monika van Vught, Magdalene Weiß
AUFTRAGGEBER: Evangelisches Büro für die Weltausstellung Expo 2000
BAUZEIT: 1999 - 2000
BGF: 2.004 m²
BRI: 18.548 m³

Der Pavillon der christlichen Religionen - ein gemeinsamer Beitrag der evangelischen und katholischen Kirche zur EXPO 2000 - soll ein kontemplatives Gegenstück zum Jahrmarkt der Eitelkeiten mit seinen architektonischen Aufgeregtheiten sein: strukturell einfach und sinnfällig, reduziert auf wenige Materialien, präzise im Detail, unverwechselbar in der Anmutung und Raumstimmung. Die Pavillonarchitektur beschränkt sich darauf, das konstruktive Gefüge des modularen Systems mit seinen Details exakt zu zeigen. Die sehr zurückhaltende und einfache Materialität - Stahl, Glas, Kies und Wasserflächen werden nur durch einen großen Baum „geschmückt". Ein umlaufender Kreuzgang von 3,6 m Breite und 7,20 m Höhe umgrenzt den Gesamtkomplex und dient zugleich als Wandelhalle und Ausstellungsinszenierung. Im nördlichen Teil umfaßt der „Kreuzgang" einen großvolumigen Raum von 21 m auf 21 m Grundfläche und 18 m Raumhöhe, dessen Dach von neun schlanken kreuzförmigen Stahlstützen getragen wird. Dieser durch Lichtführung und betonte Vertikalität mit besonderer Feierlichkeit und Würde akzentuierte Raum kann sowohl direkt vom Platz betreten werden als auch über Mehrfachverbindungen zum umlaufenden Kreuzgang. Im Übergang zwischen dem Christusraum und dem Kreuzgang sind auf einer jeweiligen Grundfläche von 3,6 m x 3,6 m mit einer einer Höhe von ebenfalls 3,6 m räumliche „Enklaven" angeordnet, kleine Räume der Stille, in denen Themen des Christentums und der Kirche in einer semantischen Interpretation den Besuchern vermittelt werden sollen. Treppenverbindungen führen in die unterirdische „Krypta", der eine frei konturierte, weich ausgebildete Raumfassung aus Sichtbetonwänden erhält, in denen gleichwohl drei der kreuzförmigen Stahlstützen in Fortsetzung des großen Daches eindringen. Die Rauminszenierung erfolgt in allen Bereichen mittels einer Modulation des Lichtes. Der Christusraum empfängt mittig über den Säulenköpfen Oberlicht, das die Vertikalität der schlanken Säulen betont.
Die umhüllende Fläche aus dünngeschnittenem Marmor bildet eine lichtdurchlässige Schale, deren lebendige Farbigkeit die Raumstimmung erzeugen wird. Entgegengesetzt die Akzentuierung des Lichtes in der „Krypta". Schmale Lichtschlitze im Verlauf der Stützenachsen sowie ein umlaufendes, in den Boden eingelassenes

1 ENTWURFSSKIZZE.
2 AUSFUHRUNGS-MODELL.
3 DACHAUFSICHT IN DER DARSTELLUNG DES ENTWURFS-MODELLS.
1 CONCEPT SKETCH.
2 CONSTRUCTION MODEL.
3 ROOF PLAN IN CONCEPT MODEL.

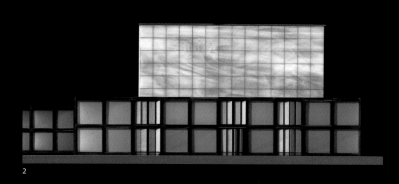

2

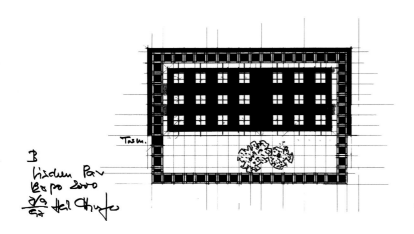

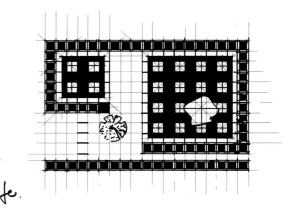

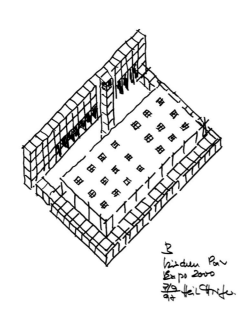

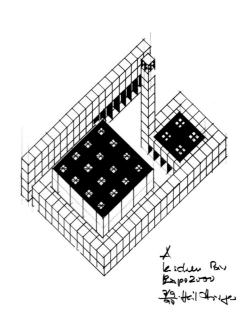

ALTERNATIVE SKIZZEN ZUM WETTBEWERBSENTWURF.
ALTERNATIVE SKETCHES FROM COMPETITION DESIGN.

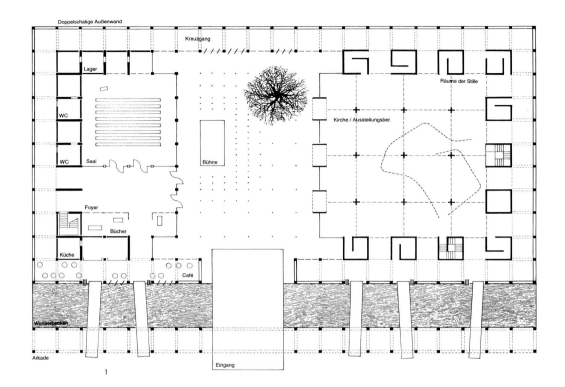

1

1 GRUNDRISS
ERDGESCHOSS.
2 ANSICHT VON
DER PLAZA.
3 HOFANSICHT
DER KIRCHE.
4 LÄNGSSCHNITT.

1 GROUND
LEVEL PLAN.
2 PLAZA ELEVATION.
3 COURTYARD
ELEVATION OF THE
CHURCH.
4 LONGITUDINAL
SECTION.

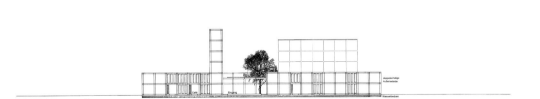

2

3

4

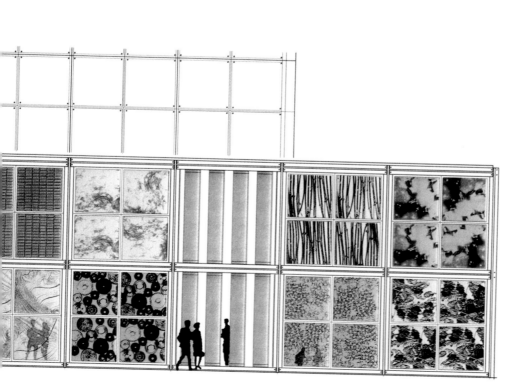

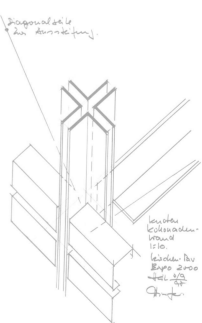

DIE KONSTRUKTION
DES KREUZGANGES.
VON DEMONTABLEN
STAHLRAHMEN EIN-
GEFASSTE GLASFEN-
STER IN DER GRÖSSE
VON 3,6 X 3,6 M
THEMATISIEREN
DURCH MATERIAL-
FÜLLUNGEN
„NATUR" UND
„TECHNIK".
DAS GENERALTHEMA
DER EXPO 2000
LAUTET „MENSCH,
NATUR, TECHNIK".
THE CONSTRUCTION
OF THE CLOISTER.
STEEL FRAMED
GLASS WINDOWS
3,6 X 3,6 M
ILLUSTRATE THE
THEMES "NATURE"
AND "TECHNOLOGY"
BY PRESENTING
VARIOUS MATERIALS.
THE OVERALL THEME
OF THE EXPO 2000
IS "MAN, NATURE,
TECHNOLOGY".

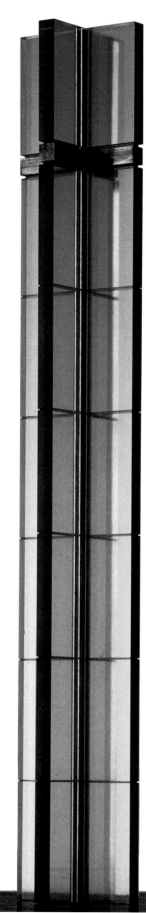

Lichtband sorgen für Streiflicht, das die Materialität des Betons betont und durch die Intensität der Lichtschatten dem Raum mystische Dramatik gibt. Der umlaufende „Kreuzgang" erhält eine zweischalige Glasfassade, die in ihren Zwischenräumen großformatige Glasvitrinen darstellt. Diese Zwischenräume werden mit Materialien verschiedenster Art aus dem Bereich der Natur sowie aus dem Bereich der Technik als Bestandteil einer Gesamtdramaturgie gefüllt. In Abhängigkeit von der jeweiligen Füllung werden diese Wände partiell mehr oder weniger transluzent, partiell auch transparent sein. Der gesamte Baukomplex wird nach Ende der Weltausstellung in Hannover zerlegt und in einer modifizierten Kombination als Klosteranlage in Volkenroda in Thüringen wiedererrichtet.

The Pavilion of Christian religions, a combined contribution of the Catholic and Protestant Churches for the EXPO 2000, is intended to be a contemplative counterpart to the vanity fair with architectural highlights: Simple in structure, reduced to a few materials, precise in detail, unmistakable in its appearance and spatial atmosphere. The architecture of the pavilion is restricted to the clear presentation of the modular construction and its details. The modest and simple choice of materials, steel, glass, gravel and water, are "decorated" with the addition of one large tree. The surrounding cloister, 3.60 m wide and 7.20 m high, frames the overall complex and simultaneously functions as an exhibitions space. In the north the cloister comprises a voluminous hall 21 m square and 18 m high, with its roof supported by nine slender cross-formed steel columns. This hall, its dignity and solemnity emphasized by lighting and strong verticality, can be approached directly from the main square as well as from several connections from the surrounding cloister. Spatial "enclaves", 3.60 m high, deep and wide, are located in the transmission between "Christ Hall" and the cloister as "Rooms of Silence", where themes of Christianity and the Church are communicated to the visitor in a semantic interpretation. Staircases lead to the underground "crypt". The walls are freely contoured with fair-faced concrete and three of the large cross-formed steel columns are continued through from the expansive ceiling. The spatial atmosphere of all areas is created by a modulation of light. The "Christ Hall" receives light from top-lights centrally located above the column heads, emphasizing the vertical quality of the slender columns. The surrounding surfaces of thinly cut marble form a light-transmissive envelope, its lively colours creating a spatial atmosphere. In contrast to this the lighting emphasis in the "crypt" is solemn: Thin light slots along the column axis and a surrounding strip of light in the floor create a focus, which emphasizes the character of concrete and renders a mystical intensity through the effects of shadows. The surrounding "cloister" is equipped with a double glass facade, used as large-scale showcases. The space between is filled with various materials from nature and technology as part of the overall presentation. Depending on the respective content, the glass walls are more or less translucent or partially transparent. The whole complex will be dismantled after the EXPO in Hanover and re-erected in a modified form as a monastery in Volkenroda, Thüringen.

1

2

1 KIRCHTURM! KREUZ! WEGWEISER! DER 25 M HOHE TURM AUS GLAS UND STAHL DIENT ALS SYMBOL FÜR DIE EXPO 2000. 2 DER „CHRISTUS-RAUM". NEUN KREUZFÖRMIGE SCHLANKE STAHL-SÄULEN VON 18 M HÖHE BESTIMMEN DEN CHARAKTER DES FEIERRAUMES, DES-SEN UMFASSUNGS-WÄNDE AUS TRANS-LUZENTEM MARMOR GEFERTIGT SIND. 3 WETTBEWERBS-MODELL.

1 CHURCH TOWER! CROSS! SIGNPOST! THE 25 M HIGH TOWER MADE FROM GLASS AND STEEL IS THE SYMBOL OF THE EXPO 2000. 2 THE "CHRIST ROOM". NINE CROSS-FORMED SLENDER STEEL COLUMNS 18 M HIGH DEFINE THE CHARACTER OF THE SOLEMNITY HALL, WITH FRAMING WALLS MADE FROM TRANS-LUCENT MARBLE. 3 COMPETITION MODEL.

3

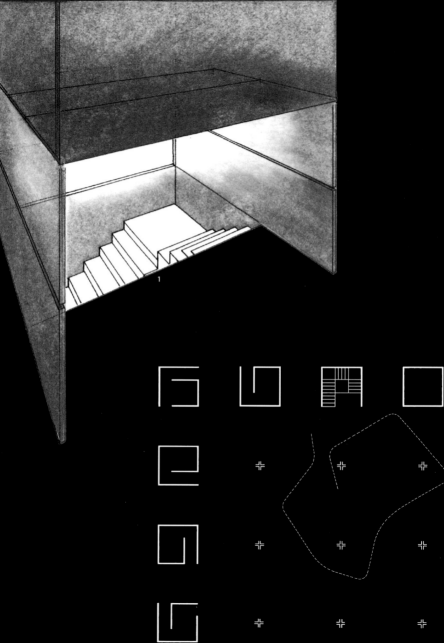

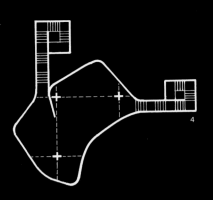

4

5

1-3 ENKLAVEN ALS
„RÄUME DER STILLE"
BILDEN DEN ÜBER-
GANG ZWISCHEN
DEM UMFASSENDEN
„KREUZGANG UND
DEM CHRISTUS-
RAUM". DIE WÄNDE
SIND AUS CORTEEN-
STAHL.
4-5 IM UNTERGE-
SCHOSS LIEGT DIE
VON BETONWÄNDEN
UMFASSTE KRYPTA.
DREI KREUZSTÜTZEN
DES DARÜBER LIE-
GENDEN CHRISTUS-
RAUMES DRINGEN
DURCH DIE DECKE.
DIE ACHSEN
WERDEN DURCH
LICHT BETONT.

1-3 ENCLAVES AS
"ROOMS OF SILENCE"
FORM THE TRANS-
MISSION BETWEEN
THE SURROUNDING
"CLOISTER AND THE
CHRIST ROOM".
THE WALLS ARE CON-
STRUCTED FROM
CORTEEN STEEL.
4-5 THE CRYPT IS
LOCATED IN THE
BASEMENT AND IS
FRAMED BY CON-
CRETE WALLS. THREE
CROSS-FORMED
COLUMNS OF THE
CHRIST ROOM ABOVE
PENETRATE THROUGH
THE CEILING. THE
AXES ARE EMPHASI-
ZED WITH LIGHT.

DER AKTUELLE PLANUNGSSTAND – ZUR REALISIERUNG VORGESEHEN

THE LATEST PLANNING STATUS – INTENDED FOR REALIZATION

DAS BEENGTE GRUNDSTÜCK AN DER EXPOPLAZA SOWIE DER SEHR BEGRENZTE KOSTENRAHMEN HABEN DAS PROJEKT REDUZIERT, OHNE DIE KONZEPTIONELLE IDEE ZU BEEINTRÄCHTIGEN.
1 HOFANSICHT DER KIRCHE.
2 HOFANSICHT SERVICEBEREICH.
3 QUERSCHNITT DER KIRCHE.
4 GRUNDRISS ERDGESCHOSS UND SCHNITTANSICHT VON DER PLAZA.
5 GRUNDRISS UNTERGESCHOSS UND ANSICHT VON NORDEN.

THE RESTRICTED SITE AT THE EXPO PLAZA AS WELL AS THE TIGHT BUDGET REDUCED THE PROJECT, WITHOUT IMPAIRING THE CONCEPTIONAL IDEA.
1 CHURCH ELEVATION FROM COURTYARD.
2 SERVICE AREA ELEVATION FROM COURTYARD.
3 CROSS SECTION OF CHURCH.
4 GROUND LEVEL PLAN AND SECTIONAL ELEVATION FROM THE PLAZA.
5 BASEMENT LEVEL PLAN AND NORTH ELEVATION.

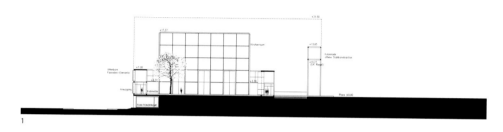

1

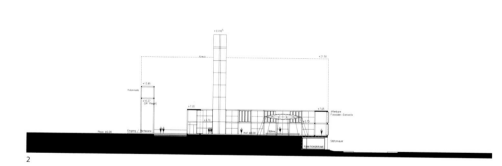

2

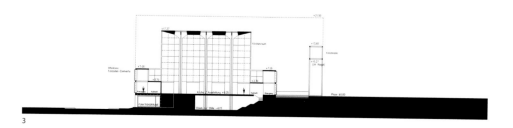

3

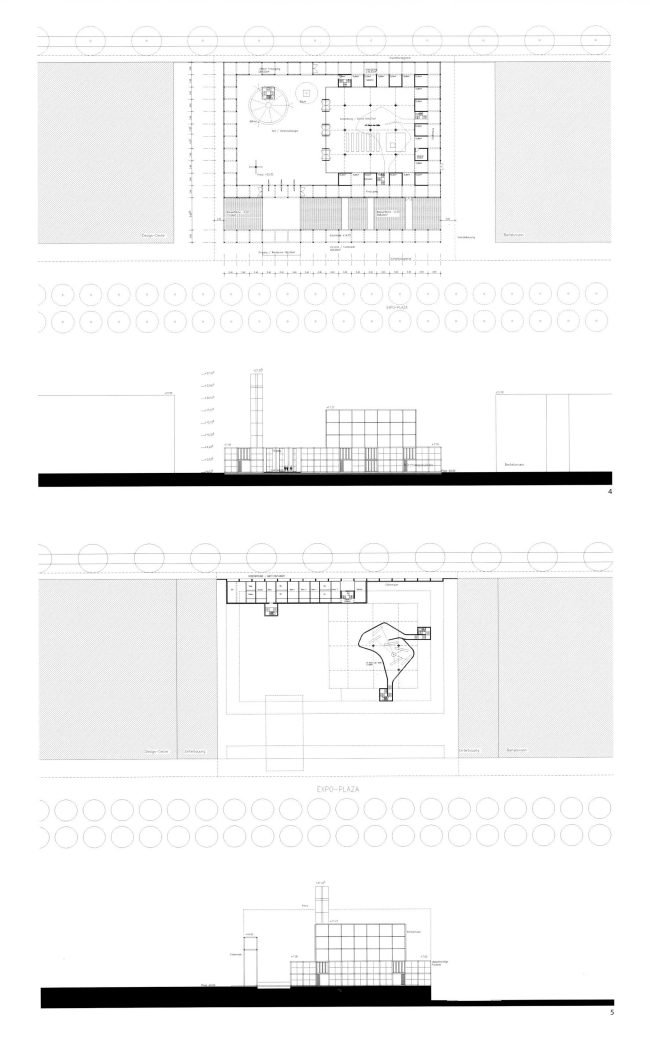

4

5

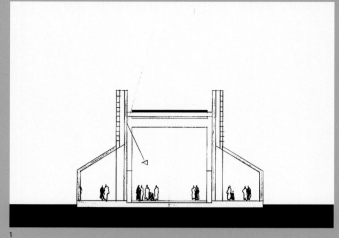

1

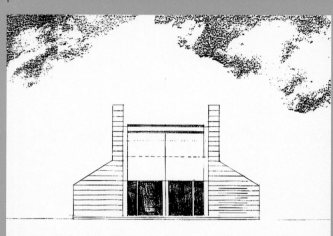

2

1 SCHNITT.
2 ANSICHT.
3 GRUNDRISS.
4 MODELL IN
DER FRONTANSICHT.
5 LAGEPLAN.
1 SECTION.
2 ELEVATION.
3 PLAN.
4 FRONT ELEVATION
OF MODEL.
5 SITE PLAN.

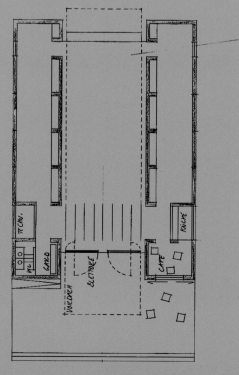

3

4

KUNSTHALLE BREMEN - "WESER-BAHNHOF II"

WETTBEWERB: 1997 - 1. Preis
ENTWURF: Meinhard v. Gerkan
MITARBEITER:
Johann v. Mansberg,
Stephan Rewolle

Die Kunsthalle bildet den Kern eines neuen Stadtquartiers auf dem Gelände des Weserbahnhofs II. Dessen basilikaler Querschnitt bietet im Mittelschiff einen 9 m hohen, 20 m tiefen und 8 m breiten Ausstellungsraum, der Streifenoberlicht von der Decke empfängt. Die schmalen Seitenschiffe sind dagegen sehr introvertiert. In dem differenzierten Raumangebot sollen zeitgenössische Künstler sich mit wenigen Exponaten der Öffentlichkeit präsentieren.

The Art Gallery is the focus of a new urban quarter on the site of the "Weserbahnhof II". The basilica-formed section provides a central exhibition hall, 9 m high, 20 m long and 8 m wide, with linear top lights. Contrary to this openness the narrow aisles are very secluded. Contemporary artists will present their works to the public in these diversified volumes.

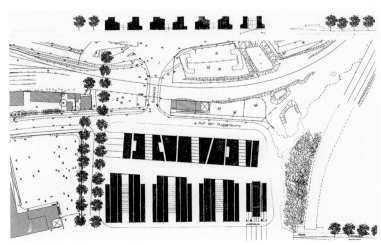

5

MUSEUM CONSTANTINI, BUENOS AIRES

WETTBEWERB: 1997
ENTWURF: Meinhard v. Gerkan
MITARBEITER: Sigrid Müller,
Michael Biwer, Stefanie Driessen,
Anja Knobloch-Meding, Nicolai Pix

Ein Kunstmuseum ist innerhalb
einer Stadt ein Gebäude mit besonderer Bedeutung. Sein Funktionieren
hängt von der optimalen Belichtung
der Exponate ab. Der Entwurf faßt
beide Anforderungen in eine architektonische Lösung zusammen:
Eine doppelschalige, über das Dach
gebogene Glaswand mit integriertem
Blendraster filtert das von Süden
einfallende Licht - die Sonne steht

im Norden - und bildet zugleich eine
markante Form für das Museum.
Sie umschließt eine dreigeschossige
Halle, an der die über Rolltreppen
erschlossenen Ausstellungsebenen
liegen. Sie sind zum Park hin orientiert, in dem sich die Museumsinsze-
nierung im Freien fortsetzt.

A museum of arts is a building with
special status in a city. Its operation
depends on optimal light conditions
for the exhibits. This proposal combines both requirements within one
architectural solution: A double-
glazed facade curves across the
roof, integrated with louvers, filtering
the light entering from the south -
whilst the sun is in the north.
Simultaneously it characterizes the
powerful form of the museum. The
facade encloses a three-level hall,
which leads to corresponding exhi-

bition levels via escalators. These
levels are orientated towards
the park, where the exhibition is
continued.

1+2 ARBEITSMODELL.
3 LAGEPLAN.
4 DIE GENERIERUNG
DES MUSEUMS-
BAUKÖRPERS.
1+2 WORKING
MODEL.
3 SITE PLAN.
4 GENERATION
OF THE MUSEUM
BUILDING.

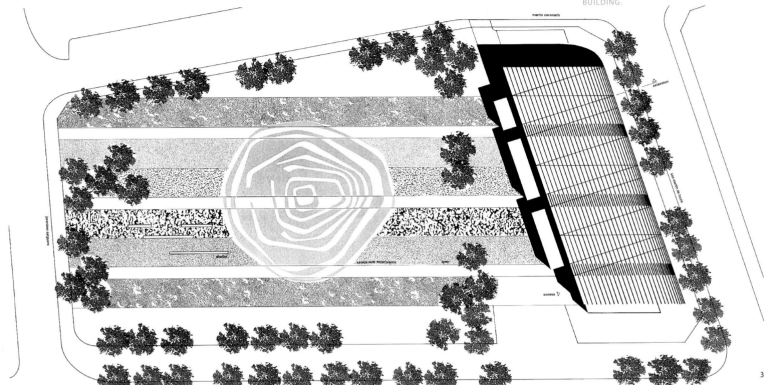

3

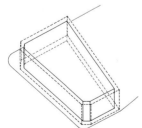
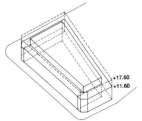
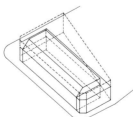
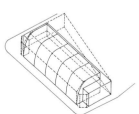
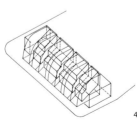

4

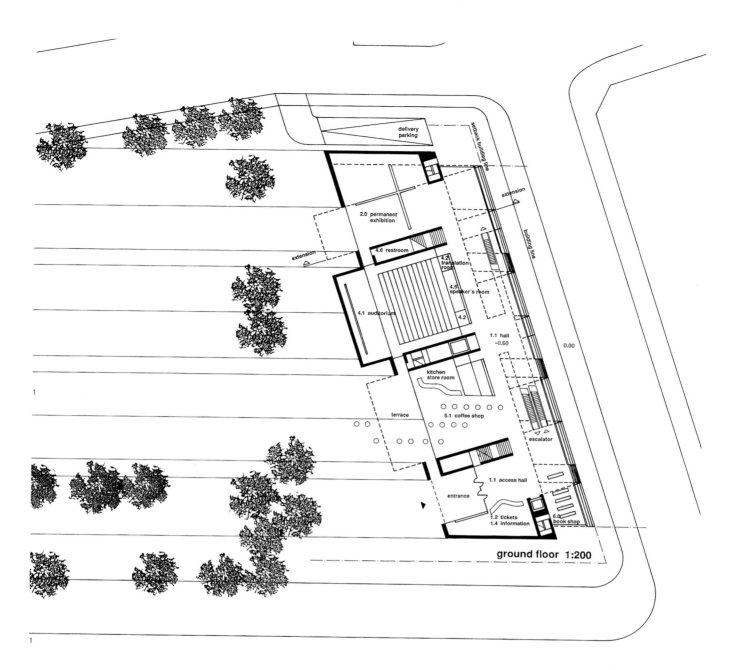

delivery parking

setback building line

extension

building line

2.0 permanent exhibition

extension

4.6 restroom

4.2 translation room

4.5 speaker's room

4.1 auditorium

4.2

1.1 hall
−0.60

0.00

kitchen store room

terrace

5.1 coffee shop

escalator

1.1 access hall

entrance

1.2 tickets
1.4 information

6.0 book shop

ground floor 1:200

1

1

1 ERDGESCHOSS.

2 OBERGESCHOSSE.

3 QUERSCHNITT,

ANSICHTEN.

5 GROUND LEVEL.

6 UPPER LEVEL.

7 CROSS SECTION,

ELEVATIONS.

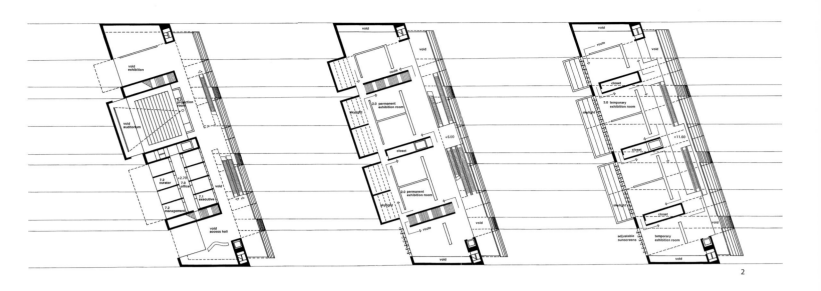

2

3

INDUSTRIEMUSEUM CHEMNITZ

WETTBEWERB: 1997
ENTWURF: Meinhard v. Gerkan
mit Philipp Kamps

Die Integration einer Museumsnutzung in vorhandene, brachliegende Industriebauten sowie deren Erweiterung und Ergänzung ist eine Frage des Dialogs zwischen Alt und Neu. Der Entwurf greift die strukturellen Merkmale der Situation auf und schafft durch eine sukzessive Überlagerung ein bauliches und städtebauliches Ordnungsgerüst, welches in dieser Situation keine solitäre Architekturaussage zuläßt. Flexibilität und die Realisierung in mehreren Schritten sind gleichermaßen bestimmende Parameter des aus strukturelle Prinzipien reduzierten Entwurfsgedankens.

The integration of a museum in disused industrial buildings and their proposed extension creates a dialogue between old and new. The design corresponds to existing structural patterns and via a gradual layering an urban framework develops, rejecting solitaire architecture. Flexibility and the building realization over several phases are the defining parameters of the concept, which is founded upon structural principles.

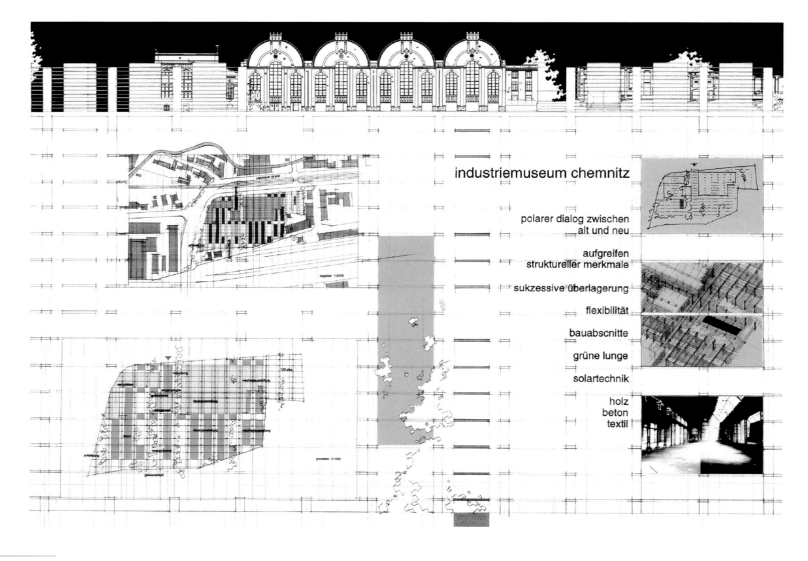

industriemuseum chemnitz

polarer dialog zwischen alt und neu

aufgreifen struktureller merkmale

sukzessive überlagerung

flexibilität

bauabscnitte

grüne lunge

solartechnik

holz
beton
textil

GEMEINDEZENTRUM JOHNSALLEE, HAMBURG

WETTBEWERB: 1997
ENTWURF: Meinhard v. Gerkan mit Philipp Kamps

Für das in einer Villenstraße in Hamburg-Harvestehude gelegene Gemeindehaus der Christenge-meinschaft ist eine Erweiterung im rückwärtigen Grundstücksteil vor-gesehen. Hier soll ein Kirchenraum gebaut werden. Der Entwurf dazu fügt sich in den schiefwinkligen Zu-schnitt der umfassenden Grund-stücksgrenzen zu den nachbarlichen Flächen ein und bildet in Verbin-dung mit einem polygonalen Sattel-dach einen Feierraum, der die Aus-richtung auf den Altar mit einer „gebrochenen Raumgeste" vereint. Die Konstruktion des Gebäudes ist als Holzfachwerk konzipiert.

An extension to the Christian Community Centre in the form of a prayer room is proposed for the rear of the existing site, which is located amongst traditional city villas in Hamburg-Harvestehude. The con-cept follows the irregular bounda-ries towards the neighbouring sites. In connection with the saddle roof the plan creates a space that unites a concentration towards the altar, creating a "divided spatial gesture". The building construction method is timber frame.

3

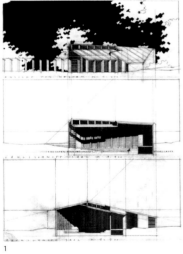

1

2

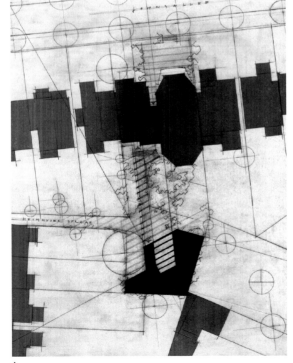

4

1 ANSICHT,
SCHNITTE.
2 ANSICHT,
GRUNDRISS.
3 FASSADENDETAIL.
4 LAGEPLAN.
1 SECTIONS,
ELEVATION.
2 ELEVATION, PLAN.
3 FACADE DETAIL.
4 SITE PLAN.

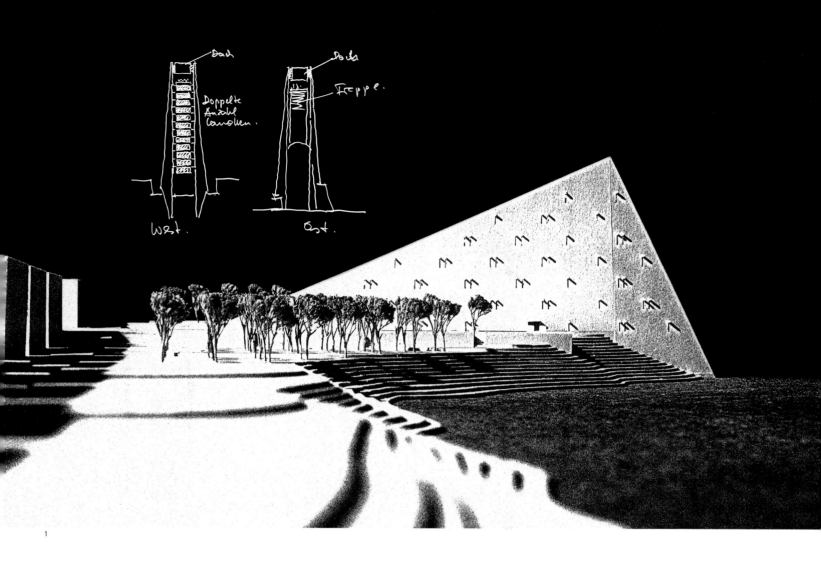

1

GOREE MEMORIAL, DAKAR, SENEGAL

WETTBEWERB: 1997
ENTWURF: Meinhard v. Gerkan
mit Michael Biwer

Ein Monument als Denkmal für die als Sklaven verschleppten Afrikaner, ein Symbol, dessen Wurzeln in der Geschichte des Kontinents liegen und dessen Ausdruck Aufstieg und Hoffnung verheißt. Das Memorial dominiert als kraftvoller Solitär. Die Räume des Kulturkomplexes verschwinden in einem Sockelbau, zugleich Symbol der Unterdrückung und baulicher Ausdruck des Leidens und des Schweigens, der Verbundenheit mit der Erde Afrikas. Auf dieser Basis erhebt sich das Monument: der dramatisch ansteigende, schmale Hallenraum zelebriert die Erinnerung an das Vergangene. Seine äußere Symbolik ist dem entgegengesetzt: der Sonne ausgesetzt, führt eine „Himmelsleiter" zu einer Plattform, die einen weiten Ausblick auf den Atlantik bietet.

A memorial for Africans abducted as slaves, as a symbol with its roots founded in the history of the continent and with its expression promising prosperity and hope. The memorial is a powerful solitaire. The rooms of the cultural complex are located at plinth level, which is simultaneously a symbol of suppression and a built expression of suffering and concealment and an attachment to African soil. The monument emerges from the plinth: The dramatically ascending, narrow hall celebrates the recollection of the past. Its external symbolic is contradictive: Exposed to sun-light, a "gateway to heaven" leads to a platform, offering a wide view across the Atlantic.

1+4 MODELLSTUDIE
UND ERSTE
ENTWURFSSKIZZEN.
2 LAGEPLAN.
3 KONZEPTIONELLE
METAPHER.
1+4 MODEL STUDY
AND INITIAL DESIGN
SKETCHES.
2 SITE PLAN.
3 CONCEPTIONAL
METAPHOR.

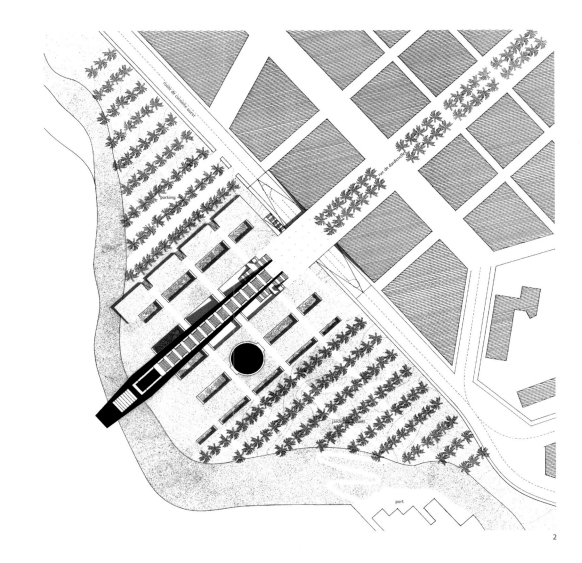

2

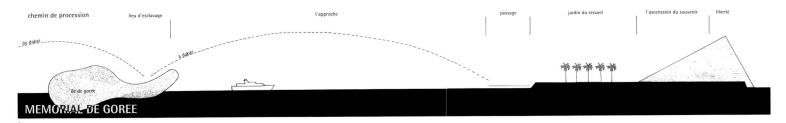

chemin de procession   lieu d'esclavage   l'approche   passage   jardin du recueil   l'ascenssion du souvenir   liberté

de dakar

à dakar

île de gorée

MEMORIAL DE GOREE

3

4

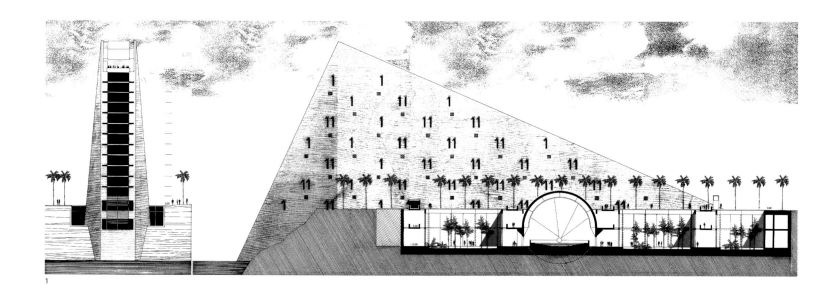

1

2

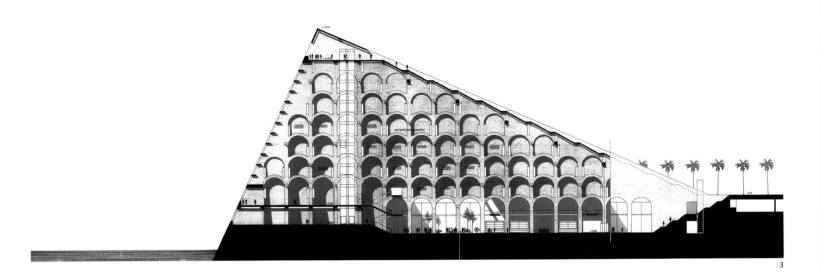

3

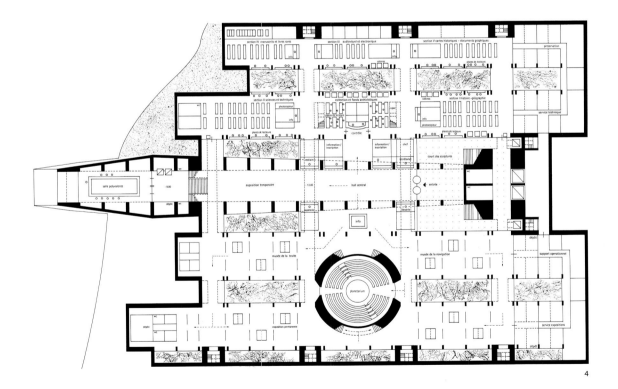

4

MUSIKTHEATER
GRAZ, ÖSTERREICH

WETTBEWERB: 1998
ENTWURF: Meinhard v. Gerkan
mit Sona Kazemi

Eine im Kern geometrische Komposition: Entlang der Grundstücks- und Straßenkante entsteht ein langgestreckter Baukörper, der in der Mitte in Höhe und Breite versetzt ist, so daß der Mittelpunkt des Gebäudes im Schnittpunkt eines Achsenkreuzes liegt. Der Zweiteilung entspricht die Nutzung von öffentlichen Bereichen und solchen, die nur intern gebraucht werden; hinzu kommt ein Kern (Montagehalle), der beide Teile verbindet. Der multifunktionale Saal schiebt sich südlich zum Palais Meran und einer Remise vor, wo auch der öffentliche Eingang liegt. This is a basically geometric composition: an elongated building along the border line between site and street with a middle part offset in both height and length so that the core of this centre forms a cross axis. This division in two matches the requirement of spaces to be used publicly and others which are for internal use only. The core is a large multi-purpose hall which joins the two wings and pushes southward towards the Palais Meran and the coach house (Remise), where the public entrance is situated.

1

2

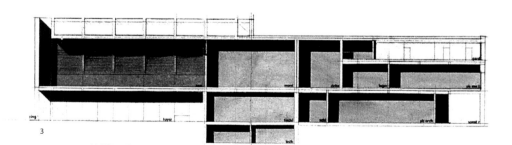

3

4

1 LAGEPLAN.
2 2. OBERGESCHOSS.
1. OBERGESCHOSS.
ERDGESCHOSS.
UNTERGESCHOSS.
3 LÄNGSSCHNITT.
4 MODELL.
1 SITE PLAN.
2 SECOND LEVEL.
FIRST LEVEL.
GROUND LEVEL.
LOWER LEVEL.
3 LONGITUDINAL
SECTION.
4 MODEL.

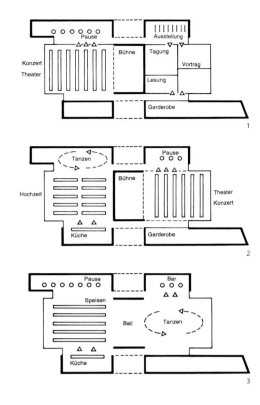

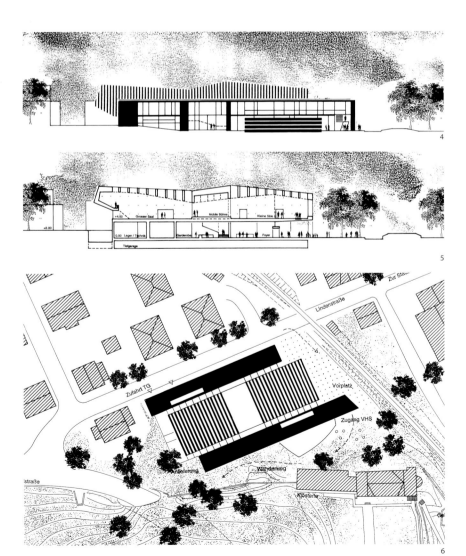

BÜRGERHAUS SAULGAU

WETTBEWERB: 1997
ENTWURF: Meinhard v. Gerkan
MITARBEITER: Anja Knobloch-Meding,
Sigrid Müller

Das neue Bürgerhaus mit Kulturamt, Tanzcafé, Volkshochschule und Veranstaltungssälen für vielfältige Nutzungen ist für den Ort ein wichtiger Identifikationspunkt und definiert wegen dieser Bedeutung wie auch architektonisch den Bereich um die Lindenstraße neu. Der Baukörper ist in eine dominierende Mittelzone und zwei außenliegende schmale Streifen gegliedert, deren Versatz einen Platz zur Lindenstraße hin öffnet. Dieser setzt sich im Foyer fort. Die Säle im Mittelbereich gewährleisten größtmögliche Flexibilität und bieten Ausblick auf die Stadt und den Grünzug.

The new community centre with department of culture and various social and educational facilities is an important new identifying feature within its environment and defines through its significance and architecture the area around Lindenstrasse. The building form is divided into a dominant middle zone and two external narrow strips, which stagger to form a new open square towards Lindenstrasse, which carries on into the foyer area. The new halls in the middle zone create the greatest possible flexibility and offer views on to the city and the open landscape.

1-3 NUTZUNGS-
VARIANTEN.
4 NORDANSICHT.
5 LÄNGSSCHNITT.
6 LAGEPLAN.
7 MASSENMODELL.
1-3 VARIOUS USES.
4 NORTH
ELEVATION.
5 LONGITUDINAL
SECTION.
6 SITE PLAN.
7 MASSING MODEL.

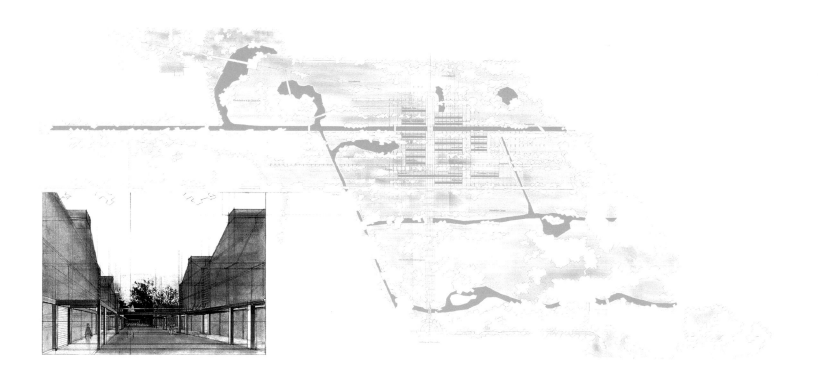

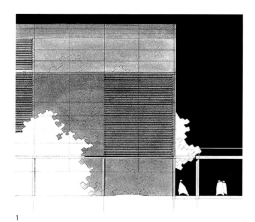

1

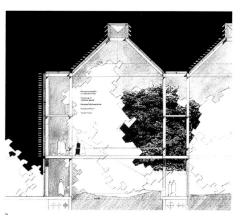

2

RHODARIUM
BREMEN

WETTBEWERB: 1998
ENTWURF: Meinhard v. Gerkan
MITARBEITER: Philipp Kamps,
Pinar Gönul-Cinar

Rückgrat der gesamten Anlage ist
eine Rhododendronallee, die an die
Haupterschließung des Parks anknüpft und den Besuch sämtlicher
unterschiedlicher Gewächshäuser
erlaubt. Das Ensemble unterschiedlich großer Gewächshäuser verzahnt
sich bei immer gleicher, strenger
Struktur mit dem Park. Durch die
bandartig lineare Anordnung quer
zur Haupterschließung ergeben
sich ständig wechselnde Aus- und
Durchblicke bei immer gleich
bleibender, prinzipieller Strenge
der Bauten selbst. Die Schauhäuser
interpretieren den historischen
Typus neu durch eine einfache
Stahlkonstruktion mit "structural
glazing" und außenliegenden,
verstellbaren Verschattungs-
elementen.

The rhododendron alley forms a
major spine connecting the central
axis route through the park and
allows access to a variety of different green houses. The grouping
of differing sized green houses are
tied together with a continuous
rigorous structure within the park.
Due to the ribbon-like nature of
the arrangement set across the
major axis, continuously changing
views and glimpses are created
through the simple unchanging
clarity of the buildings themselves.
Simple steel framed structures with
structural glazing and externally
mounted adjustable shading
devices re-interpret this historic
building type.

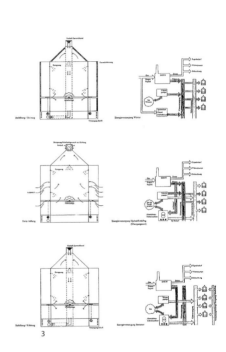

3

1 TEILANSICHT.
2 DETAILSCHNITT.
3 KLIMASTEUERUNG
DER HALLEN.
4+5 DAS MODELL
VERDEUTLICHT
DAS STRUKTURELLE
PRINZIP.
1 PARTIAL ELEVATION.
2 DETAILED SECTION.
3 CLIMATIC CONTROL
OF THE HALLS.
4+5 STRUCTURAL
MODEL.

VERWALTUNG UND ARBEIT

ADMINISTRATION AND WORK

1

DRESDNER BANK, PARISER PLATZ, BERLIN

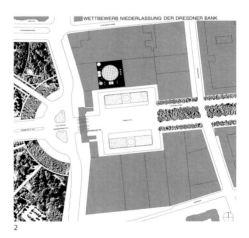

2

WETTBEWERB NIEDERLASSUNG DER DRESDNER BANK

1 DIE „GUTE STUBE"
BERLINS AM PARISER
PLATZ IM WIEDERAUFBAU.
2 LAGEPLAN.
DIE SEITEN DES GRUND-
STÜCKES BILDEN BRAND-
WÄNDE.
3 VERTIKAL FALTBARE
FENSTERLÄDEN DIENEN
ALS BESCHATTER UND
GEBEN - BEWEGLICHEN
AUGENLIDERN GLEICH -
DEM HAUS EIN CHARAK-
TERISTISCHES ANTLITZ.
1 THE PARLOUR OF
BERLIN AT PARISER
PLATZ UNDER RECON-
STRUCTION.
2 SITE PLAN.
FIRE WALLS FORM THE
LONGITUDINAL BOUND-
ARIES OF THE SITE.
3 VERTICALLY FOLDABLE
SHUTTERS SERVE AS
BLINDS AND LIKE MOV-
ING EYE-LIDS ADD
A CHARACTERISTIC
COUNTENANCE TO THE
BUILDING.

WETTBEWERB: 1995 - 1. Preis
ENTWURF: Meinhard v. Gerkan
PROJEKTLEITUNG: Volkmar Sievers
MITARBEITER: Claudia Abt, Kerstin
Dwertmann, Peter Kropp, Brigitte
Queck, Werner Schmidt
BAUHERR: Schweitzer Grundbesitz-
und Verwaltungs GmbH & Co. KG
BAUZEIT: 1996 - 1997
BGF: 11.600 m²
BRI: 59.912 m³

Die repräsentative „Gute Stube" Berlins, der traditionsreiche Pariser Platz
am Brandenburger Tor soll im Sinne
der „kritischen Rekonstruktion" wiederhergestellt werden. Einen Teil
der umschließenden Platzwand bildet der Neubau der Dresdner Bank;
er fügt sich in Höhe und Grundriß
zurückhaltend in das Konzept der
Neubebauung ein.
Die schwach ockerfarben getönte
Sandsteinfassade mit den senkrecht
betonten Fensteröffnungen vermittelt zusammen mit den Bronzeprofi-
len der Fenster und den verstellbaren
Verschattern sowie den patinierten
Kupferplatten des Staffelgeschosses
einen Gesamteindruck von vorneh-
mer, verhaltener Repräsentanz, der
an diesem Ort angemessen ist.

Im Grundriß bildet das Haus ein weiteres Glied in der bauhistorischen
Kette des Zusammenspiels von Kreis
und Rechteck, wie es beim Schinkel-
schen Alten Museum bereits begonnen wurde. Der Kreis bildet hier die
Grundform einer sich hinter dem
Foyer öffnenden Halle mit 31 m im
Durchmesser und einem linsenförmi-
gen, gläsernen Dach. Eine frei ausla-
dende Spiraltreppe und zwei Aufzüge erschließen die Geschosse, deren
Büros zur Halle hin orientiert sind.
Die Halle selbst ist um einige Stufen
gegenüber dem Eingangsniveau ab-
gesenkt; die Stufen laufen arenaartig
um und betonen die geometrische
Grundform. Inzwischen hat sich die
Halle als ein hervorragender und
sehr begehrter Ort für Veranstaltungen aller Art erwiesen. Den Büros
sind gläserne Galerien vorgelagert,
die der inneren Hülle eine filigrane
Gliederung verleihen. Eingeschnitte-
ne Lufträume mit Besprechungsinseln führen das Tageslicht an den
Fluren entlang in das Erdgeschoß.
Representative "front parlour" for
Berlin, the historically rich Pariser
Platz by Brandenburg Tor has to
be re-established with an eye to
"critical re-construction". Dresdner
Bank´s new building forms one
segment of the new enclosed square,
whilst complying to the restrictive height and plan regulations,
set for the overall concept of the

3

development.
The slightly ochre toned sandstone
façade with its vertically accen-
tuated window openings and bronze
profiles, adjustable shading and
patinated copper panels to the
staggered floors, communicate a
general impression of nobility and
restrained presence, appropriate
to the location.
The building develops in its plan
form a further link in the historical
chain of the interplay of circle and
rectangle, as introduced in Schin-
kels Altes Museum. The circle forms
the main hall with a 31 metre
diameter lens-like glazed roof
which opens up behind the foyer
space. The offices are orientated
towards the hall void and are approached through a free-standing
spiral stair and two lifts. The hall
itself has been lowered by a few
steps from entrance level; these
steps rotate in layout to form an
arena, thereby emphasizing the basic geometric form. The hall has
proved to be an excellent and
much sought after place for all
sorts of events. Glazed galleries are
located in front of the offices which
give the interior fassade a delicate
quality. Voids have been sliced into
the space with meeting "islands"
directing daylight along the corridor spaces and onto the ground
floor level.

1

2

1 DIE SYMMETRIE
DES ZWEIGESCHOS-
SIGEN EINGANGS-
PORTALS WIRD
DURCH DIE AUS DER
KOMBINATION MIT
EINER BEHINDERTEN-
RAMPE ASYMME-
TRISCH GESTALTETEN
EMPFANGSTREPPE
KONTRASTIERT.
2 DETAILANSICHT
DES PORTALS MIT
AUSSENLAMPEN
BEI NACHT.

1 THE SYMMETRY OF
THE TWO-STORY
ENTRANCE PORTAL IS
CONTRASTED WITH
THE ASYMMETRY OF
THE MAIN STAIRCASE
AND THE DISABLED
RAMP.
2 DETAILED ELEVA-
TION OF THE PORTAL
WITH ILLUMINATION.

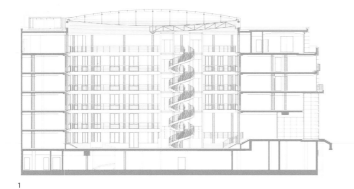

1

1 QUERSCHNITT.
2 FASSADEN-
DETAILS IN SCHNITT
UND TEILANSICHT.
3 VERTIKAL
VERFAHRBARE
FALTKLAPPLÄDEN
DIENEN ALS
BESCHATTER UND
ELEMENTE
LEBENDIGER DIFFE-
RENZIERUNG.
1 SECTION.
2 FACADE DETAILS
IN SECTION AND
PARTIAL ELEVATION.
3 VERTICALLY
FOLDING LOUVERS
SERVE AS SUN
PROTECTION,
CREATING A FACADE
DYNAMIC.

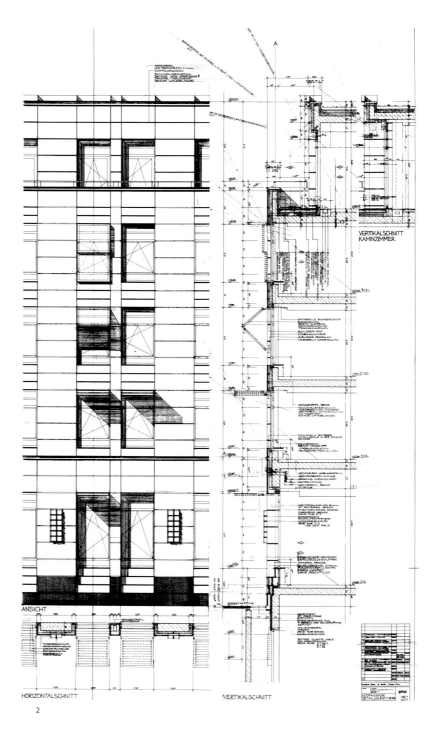

2

3

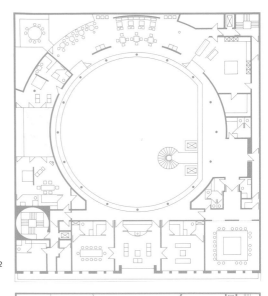

1 DIE UMLAUFENDEN
BALKONE HABEN GLAS-
BÖDEN. SIE DIENEN BEI
GROSSEN VERANSTAL-
TUNGEN IN DER HALLE
ALS EMPOREN.
2 STAFFELGESCHOSS.
3 NORMALGESCHOSS.
4 EINGANGSGESCHOSS.
1 THE CONTINUOUS
BALCONIES HAVE
GLAZED FLOORS AND
SERVE AS GALLERIES
DURING LARGE EVENTS
IN THE HALL.
2 ROOF LEVEL.
3 STANDARD LEVEL.
4 ENTRANCE LEVEL.

5

6

7

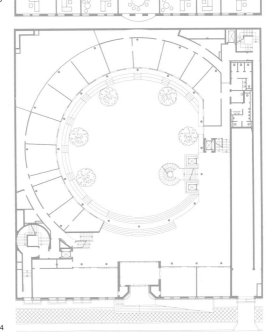

DIE KREISGEOMETRIE
PRÄGT DIE RAUMPRO-
PORTIONEN.
5 EINGANGSHALLE MIT
EMPFANG.
6 BESPRECHUNGSZONE.
7 ERSCHLIESSUNGSFLUR.
8 KONFERENZRAUM.
THE CIRCULAR GEO-
METRY CHARACTERIZES
THE SPATIAL PROPOR-
TIONS.
5 ENTRANCE HALL
AND RECEPTION.
6 CONFERENCE AREA.
7 CIRCULATION
CORRIDOR.
8 CONFERENCE ROOM.

8

1 VOM ERHÖHTEN
EINGANGSNIVEAU SENKT
SICH DIE ZYLINDRISCHE HAL-
LE AMPHITHEATRALISCH AB
UND GEWINNT DEN CHARAK-
TER EINES GROSSZÜGIGEN
EMPFANGS- UND VERAN-
STALTUNGSRAUMES.
2 DIE LINSENFÖRMIGE
DACHKONSTRUKTION AUS
STAHL MIT 30 METERN
DURCHMESSER SCHWEBT AM
BAUKRAN HÄNGEND EIN.
3 DAS FILIGRANE DACH
WIRD DURCH DIE KONSTRUK-
TIVE UNTERSPANNUNG MIT
STAHLSEILEN MÖGLICH.

1 STARTING FROM THE
ELEVATED ENTRANCE LEVEL,
THE CYLINDRICAL HALL
SINKS LIKE AN AMPHI-
THEATRE, GENERATING THE
IMPRESSION OF A SPLENDID
RECEPTION AND FUNCTION
HALL.
2 THE LENS-LIKE STEEL
ROOF CONSTRUCTION WITH
A 30 METER DIAMETER IS
BROUGHT INTO POSITION
BY CRANE.
3 THE DELICATE ROOF IS
MADE POSSIBLE BY A
TENSILE CABLE CONSTRUC-
TION.

2

3

1

1

1 DIE RAHMENLOSEN GLAS-
STUFEN DER SPIRALTREPPE SIND
DREIPUNKTGELAGERT.

2 DIE JEWEILS EIN GESCHOSS HOHE
WENDELUNG DER SPIRALTREPPE
KRAGT FREI AUS, OHNE KONSTRUK-
TIVE VERBINDUNG ZWISCHEN INNEN-
UND AUSSENWANGE.

3+4 DREIVIERTEL ALLER RÄUME
SIND ZUM ZYLINDRISCHEN
„WINTERGÄRTEN" ORIENTIERT MIT
GESCHOSSHOHER VERGLASUNG.

1 FRAMELESS GLASS STEPS OF THE
SPIRAL STAIRCASE ARE SUPPORTED
AT THREE POINTS.

2 EVERY STAIRCASE FLIGHT IS
CANTILEVERED, WITHOUT
CONSTRUCTIVE CONNECTIONS
BETWEEN THE EXTERNAL AND
INTERNAL STRINGER.

3+4 THREE QUARTERS OF THE
ROOMS ARE ORIENTATED TOWARDS
THE CYLINDRICAL"WINTER GARDEN"
AND HAVE FLOOR TO CEILING
GLAZED WALLS.

2

3

4

BEI DREI GESCHLOSSENEN
AUSSENFRONTEN MUSS DAS
TAGESLICHT ÜBER DAS DACH
DURCH VERTIKALE LUFT-
RÄUME INS INNERE GEFÜHRT
WERDEN.
1 DIE „VIRTUELLE ELLIP-
SOIDE" VON JESUS RAFAEL
SOTO VERDEUTLICHT DIE
VERTIKALE RAUMDURCH-
DRINGUNG.
2 DIE KANTINE IM STAFFEL-
GESCHOSS IST DURCH GLAS-
WÄNDE ABGETRENNT.
3 BESPRECHUNGSINSELN IN
DEN ANDEREN GESCHOSSEN
SCHWEBEN ALS PLATT-
FORMEN FREI IN DER HALLE.
DUE TO THREE SOLID EX-
TERIOR WALLS, DAYLIGHT
HAS TO BE INTRODUCED INTO
THE BUILDING THROUGH
VERTICAL LIGHT SHOOTS.
1 THE „VIRTUELLE ELLIP-
SOIDE" BY JESUS RAFAEL
SOTO, EMPHASIZES THE
VERTICAL PENETRATION OF
THE SPACE.
2 THE CANTEEN ON THE
ROOF LEVEL IS DIVIDED BY
GLASS WALLS.
3 CONFERENCE AREAS HOVER
AS PLATFORMS IN THE VOID
OF THE HALL.

1

2

3

1 WARTEZONE IM OBER-
STEN KONFERENZGESCHOSS.
2 DER KAMIN AUS
ROHEM WALZSTAHL IN DER
ENFILADE DER REPRÄSEN-
TATIVEN EMPFANGS- UND
KONFERENZRÄUME IM
STAFFELGESCHOSS.
1 WAITING AREAS ON THE
UPPER CONFERENCE LEVEL.
2 THE RAW STEEL FIRE
PLACE SITS AMONGST THE
PRESTIGIOUS RECEPTION
AND CONFERENCE ROOMS
ON THE ROOF LEVEL.

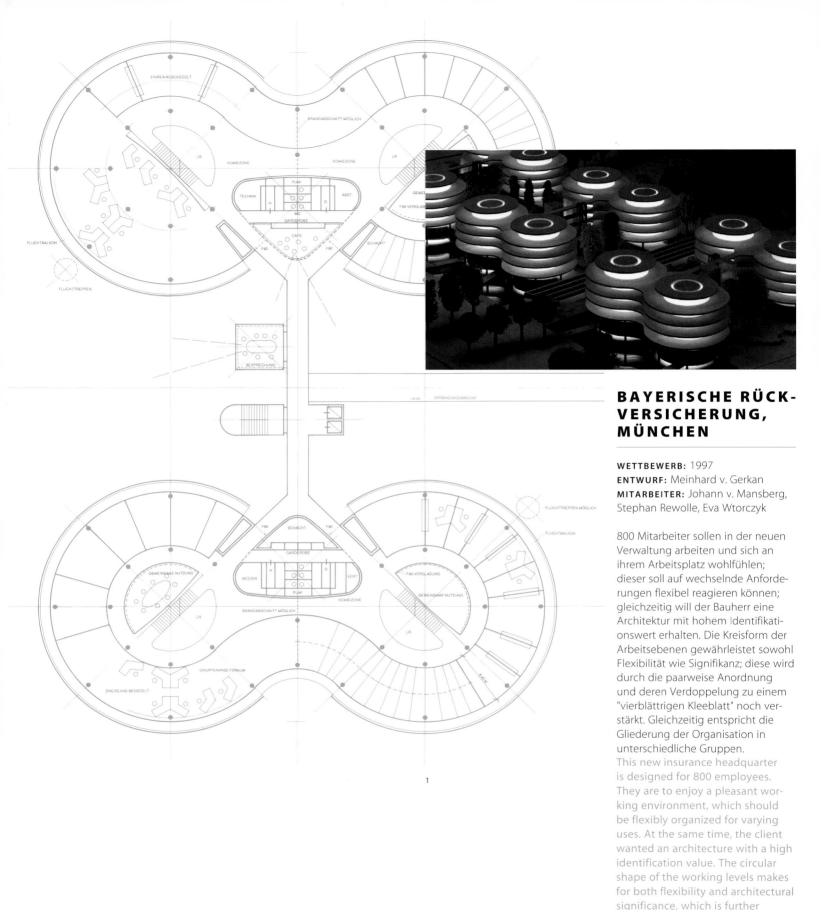

Diagram labels (floor plan):

EINREIHIG BESIEDELT · BRANDABSCHNITT MÖGLICH · LR · KOMBIZONE · KOMBIZONE · LR · PUMI · TECHNIK · H · D · ABST. · WC · GEMEI... · F90-VERGLAS... · GARDEROBE · CAFE · F90 · F90 · SCHACHT · FLUCHTBALKON · FLUCHTTREPPEN · BESPRECHUNG · +6.40 · VERBINDUNGSBRÜCKE · FLUCHTTREPPEN MÖGLICH · FLUCHTBALKON · F90 · SCHACHT · F90 · GARDEROBE · GEMEINSAME NUTZUNG · MEDIEN · VERT · F90-VERGLASUNG · PUMI · KOMBIZONE · GEMEINSAME NUTZUNG · LR · BRANDABSCHNITT MÖGLICH · LR · GRUPPENARBEITSRAUM · ZWEIREIHIG BESIEDELT

1

BAYERISCHE RÜCK-VERSICHERUNG, MÜNCHEN

WETTBEWERB: 1997
ENTWURF: Meinhard v. Gerkan
MITARBEITER: Johann v. Mansberg, Stephan Rewolle, Eva Wtorczyk

800 Mitarbeiter sollen in der neuen Verwaltung arbeiten und sich an ihrem Arbeitsplatz wohlfühlen; dieser soll auf wechselnde Anforderungen flexibel reagieren können; gleichzeitig will der Bauherr eine Architektur mit hohem Identifikationswert erhalten. Die Kreisform der Arbeitsebenen gewährleistet sowohl Flexibilität wie Signifikanz; diese wird durch die paarweise Anordnung und deren Verdoppelung zu einem "vierblättrigen Kleeblatt" noch verstärkt. Gleichzeitig entspricht die Gliederung der Organisation in unterschiedliche Gruppen.

This new insurance headquarter is designed for 800 employees. They are to enjoy a pleasant working environment, which should be flexibly organized for varying uses. At the same time, the client wanted an architecture with a high identification value. The circular shape of the working levels makes for both flexibility and architectural significance, which is further enhanced by the pairing of these floors and then doubling them to create 'four-leaved clover'. This arrangement also corresponds to the four-part corporate organization.

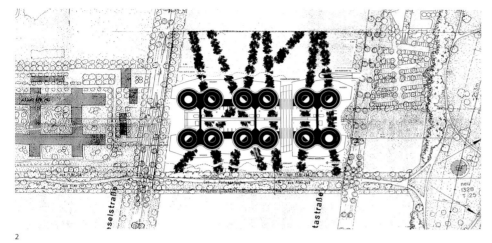

2

3

4

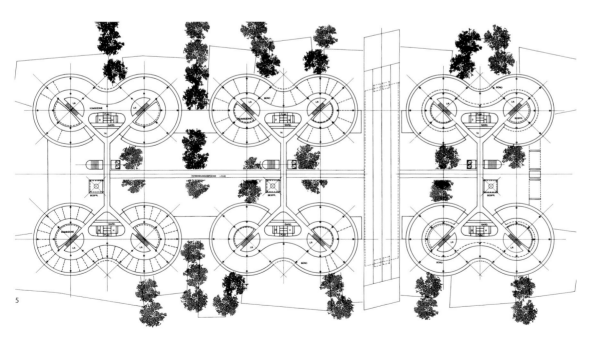

5

1 GRUNDRISS EINER
ORGANISATIONSEINHEIT.
2 LAGEPLAN.
3 BLICK IN DEN FREIRAUM
ZWISCHEN DEN „TRULLIS".
4 EINGANGSANSICHT.
5 NORMALGESCHOSS.
1 PLAN OF
ORGANISATIONAL UNIT.
2 SITE PLAN.
3 VIEW INTO THE
LANDSCAPED AREA
BETWEEN THE "TRULLIS".
4 ENTRANCE ELEVATION.
5 STANDARD LEVEL.

TELEKOM-
ZENTRALE, SUHL

WETTBEWERB: 1992 - 1. Preis
ENTWURF: Meinhard v. Gerkan
mit Jens Bothe, Kai Richter,
Hadi Teherani
2. ENTWURF: 1993
Meinhard v. Gerkan, Joachim Zais
MITARBEITER: Andreas Reich,
Stephan Dürr, Ulf Düsterhöft,
Horst-Werner Warias,
Gabriele Wysocki, Petra Weidmann,
Thomas Böhm
FREIRAUMPLANUNG: Wehberg,
Eppinger, Schmidtke + Partner
BAUHERR: DeTe Immobilien / Koblenz
BAUZEIT: 1995 - 1997
BGF: 18.477 m²
BRI: 59.276 m³

Die Realisierung des Wettbewerbser-
folges erwies sich als überaus schwie-
rig, weil das Programm sich während
der Bearbeitungszeit mehrfach, teils
radikal, änderte und reduziert wurde.
Selbst noch während der Bauzeit
entfielen das geplante oberste Geschoß und die Kantine.
Für das gesamte Gebäude wurde eine
kammartige, sich nach Süden hin
öffnende, orthogonale Baustruktur
entwickelt, die mit einem zweiten,
ringförmigen Baukörper überlagert
wird. Dieser überragt den „Kamm"
um ein Geschoß und bildet so eine
dominierende Form, die dem Bau
seine eigene Identität verleiht. Er ist
einbündig mit zum Zentrum hin
orientierten Fluren organisiert.
In der Überlagerung beider Struktu-
ren entsteht eine Sonderform, eine
knapp bemessene zweigeschossige

1 DIE EMPFANGS-
GESTE DES EINGANGS.
2 DIE NACH BAUBE-
GINN IN HÖHE UND
LÄNGE GESTUTZTEN
RIEGEL DES „KAMM"-
GEBÄUDES.

1 THE WELCOMING
GESTURE OF THE
ENTRANCE.
2 THE BARS OF THE
"COMB" BUILDING,
SHORTENED AFTER
CONSTRUCTION START.

1 AUSGLEICHSTREP-
PE EINES NEBEN-
TREPPENHAUSES.
2+3 ELEMENTARE
GEOMETRIE DER
BAUKÖRPER UND DIE
WELLBLECHSTRUKTUR
DER FASSADEN
BESTIMMEN DIE
ERSCHEINUNG DES
KOMPLEXES.
1 SERVICE STAIR OF
A SECONDARY
STAIRCASE.
2+3 THE CLEAR
BUILDING GEOMETRY
AND THE CORRUGATED
IRON FACADE
STRUCTURE
CHARACTERIZE THE
APPEARANCE OF THE
COMPLEX.

1

2

Verteilerhalle, von der aus die Erschließung des gesamten Gebäudes erfolgt. Selbst diese für den Gesamtkomplex äußerst bescheidene Fläche wurde nur unter der Bedingung bewilligt, daß die gesamten Verteilerflächen nicht mehr als 20 % der Bruttogrundrißfläche betrugen. In der unmittelbaren Nähe der Verteilerhalle liegen die kundenbezogenen Abteilungen des Betriebsgebäudes, so daß diese direkt vom Haupteingang erreicht werden können, ohne daß man nicht-öffentliche Bereiche kreuzen muß.

Konstruktiv handelt es sich bei diesem Gebäude um eine Stahlbeton-Skelettkonstruktion mit aussteifenden Kernen und Scheiben. Die erdberührten Wände der Untergeschosse wurden in Ortbeton mit einer Vormauerung aus Betonstein hergestellt. Die Fassade der Obergeschosse ist als hinterlüftete Aluminium-Wellblechkonstruktion mit durchlaufenden Leichtmetall-Fensterbändern ausgebildet.

The realization of the competition winning project has proved problematic, due to the program being repeatedly altered and reduced during the conception phase. Even during the construction period the proposed upper-most floor and the canteen were removed.

A comb-like orthogonal structure opening up towards the south has been proposed as the main structure. This comb building is overlapped with a circular form, which exceeds the eaves height by one level, presenting a dominant element, which renders a clear identity to the complex. The standard plan offices are orientated towards the centre.

The overlapping of both structures results in a specific form, a reduced multi-level circulation hall, which serves the whole building. Even this area, modest in its dimension in comparison to the overall complex, had only been approved under the precondition, that the

total circulation area would be less than 20 % of the gross floor space. The customer service department which neighbours the circulation hall, can be reached directly from the main entrance without entering private areas.

The building structure is a reinforced concrete frame supported by stiffening cores. Basement walls are constructed from in-situ concrete and a facing layer of reconstituted stone. The facade of the upper levels is cladded with an open joint corrugated metal construction and continuous aluminium windows.

3

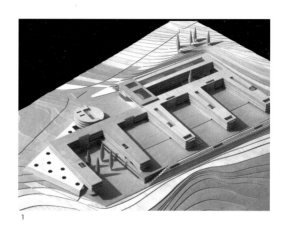

1

2

1 DER WETTBEWERBS-
ENTWURF IM MODELL.
2 DIE REALISIERTE
LÖSUNG NACH MEHRFA-
CHER ÄNDERUNG DES
PROGRAMMS UND
DRASTISCHER REDUZIE-
RUNG DES VOLUMENS.
3 REGELGESCHOSS.
4 AUS DER ÜBER-
SCHNEIDUNG VON
KREISFIGUR UND GERA-
DEM BAUKÖRPERRIEGEL
VERBLIEB EINE MINIA-
TUR-EINGANGSHALLE.

1 MODEL OF COMPETI-
TION DESIGN.
2 THE BUILT SOLUTION
AFTER NUMEROUS
PROGRAM ALTERATIONS
AND DRASTIC REDUCTION
IN VOLUME.
3 STANDARD LEVEL.
4 A MINIATURE
ENTRANCE HALL
REMAINS FROM
THE INTERSECTION
OF A CIRCULAR
AND A LINEAR
BUILDING FORM.

3

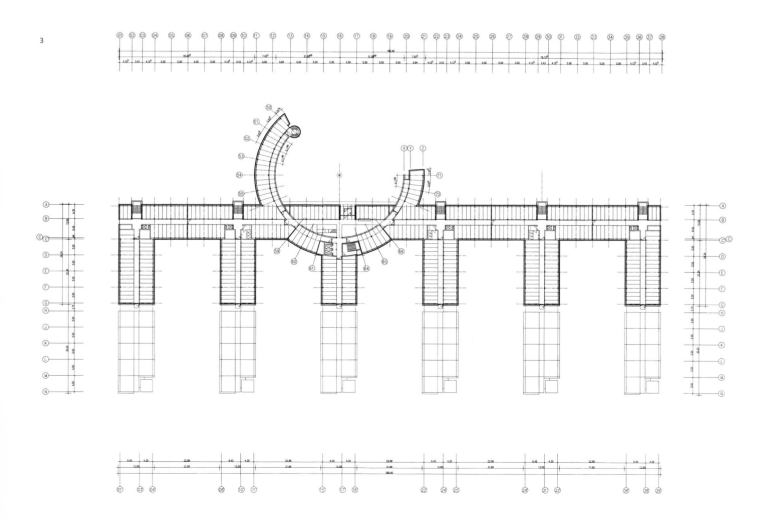

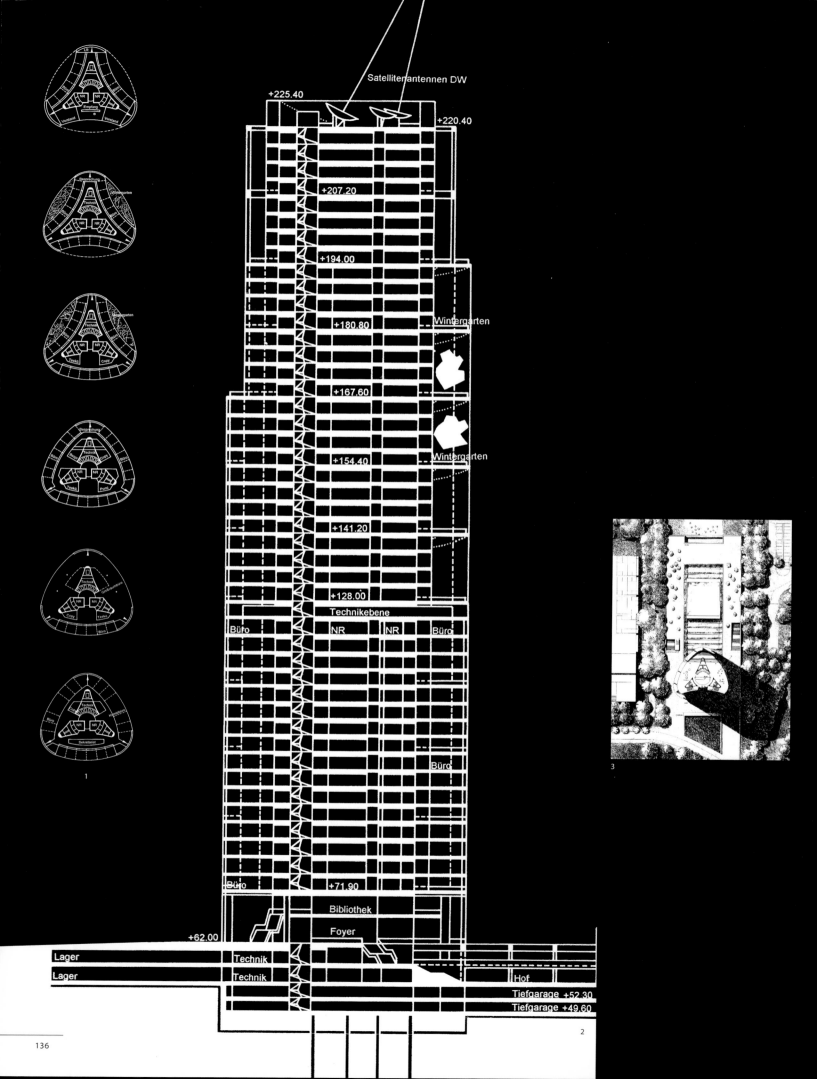

Satellitenantennen DW

+225.40

+220.40

+207.20

+194.00

+180.80   Wintergarten

+167.60

+154.40   Wintergarten

+141.20

+128.00

Technikebene

Büro   NR   NR   Büro

Büro

+71.90

Bibliothek

Foyer

+62.00

Lager   Technik

Lager   Technik   Hof

Tiefgarage +52.30

Tiefgarage +49.60

1

2

3

GENERALDIREKTION DEUTSCHE POST AG, BONN

WETTBEWERB: 1998
ENTWURF: Meinhard v. Gerkan
mit Sigrid Müller
MITARBEITER: Klaus Lenz,
Elke Hoffmeister, Bettina Groß

Der Neubau sieht sich als Teil eines
städtebaulichen Ensembles, das
aus dem Abgeordnetenhochhaus
(E. Eiermann) und den niedrigen
Schürmann-Bauten innerhalb des
Rheinauenparks besteht. Im Kontrast
zum kantigen „langen Eugen" bekommt das neue Hochhaus eine
weich schwingende, gekurvte Kon-
tur, die zugleich eine sehr flexible
Grundrißausbildung zwischen Ein-
bund und Kombibüro bietet. Der Ge-
bäudesockel soll dagegen durch
Anpassung an die Topografie zum
Bestandteil des Parks werden; der
schützenswerte Baumbestand bleibt
vollständig erhalten. Der neu ent-
wickelte Grundrißtyp erlaubt, noch
während der Planungsphase die Entscheidung für eine bestimmte Büro-
struktur offenzuhalten.

The building is designed as part of
an urban ensemble, consisting
of the high-rise building for MPs (E.
Eiermann) and the low-rise "Schürmann Units" within the park along
the River Rhine. In contrast to the
sharp-profiled "Langer Eugen"
building, the new tower has a
smooth, curved contour, which offers a flexible plan for standard and
combined offices uses. The plinth
should adapt to the topography
and become part of the park; the
trees worth preserving are maintained. The newly developed type
of plan allows a delayed decision
regarding the detailed office structure until the execution phase.

GENEALOGIE DES
GRUNDRISSES.
SCHNITT.
LAGEPLAN.
ANSICHT.
GENEALOGY OF
PLAN.
SECTION.
SITE PLAN.

TELEKOM-ZENTRALE, HOLZHAUSER STRASSE, BERLIN

ENTWURF: Meinhard v. Gerkan, Joachim Zais; 1993
MITARBEITER: Vera Warneke, Susanne Schröder, Jürgen Stodtko, Gabriele Wysocki, Petra Staack, Stephan Schütz, Doris Schäffler, Dieter Rösinger, Ursula Köper, Stefan Schwappach, Angelika Schneider
BAUHERR: DeTe Immobilien
BAUZEIT: 1995 - 1998
BGF: 34.000 m²
BRI: 128.505 m³

Das Gebäude dient als eine neue Niederlassung für die Betreuung von Privat- oder Geschäftskunden und ist für etwa 1000 Mitarbeiter ausgelegt. Es dient als zentraler Anlaufpunkt für Kunden im Bereich Berlin-Nord. Das bauliche Konzept besteht aus fünf parallel stehenden, sich wegen der Grundstückssituation verkürzenden Bürotrakten von je sechs Geschossen. Diese sind durch eine „Magistrale" miteinander verbunden. Dieses einbündige „Rückgrat" prägt das Innere des Gebäudes; es wird durch die Verbindung der beiden unteren, am stärksten vom Publikum frequentierten Geschosse über eine Galerie betont. Ein Kopfbau liegt zur Holzhauser Straße und markiert durch Gestaltung und Geschossigkeit die Eingangssituation, die zur U-Bahnstation hin orientiert ist. In diesem Bauteil ist für die Beschäftigten der Telekom ein Bildungszentrum vorgesehen. Eine Kantine für die Mitarbeiter ist als eingeschossiger Bauteil im Innenhof eingerichtet.

The building serves as a new branch office for private and commercial customers of the Berlin-North region and is designed for 1,000 employees. The proposal consists of five parallel, six-storey office blocks, with their length following the site boundary; they are linked by a "magistrale". The standard office plan characterizes the interior: it is emphasized by a gallery, connecting the two lowest levels, which are primarily used by customers. The head building is situated on Holzhauser Straße, its design and scale defining the entrance area, which is orientated towards the subway station. An educational centre for Telekom employees is intended in this section. The canteen for employees is proposed as a one-storey unit in the inner court-yard.

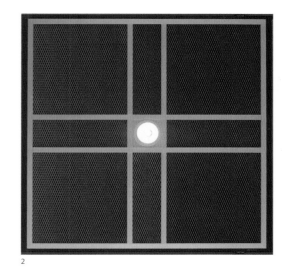

2

1 EINGANGSHALLE.
2 STRUKTUR DER ABGEHÄNGTEN DECKE IN STRECKMETALL.
1 ENTRANCE HALL.
2 STRUCTURE OF SUSPENDED METAL CEILING.

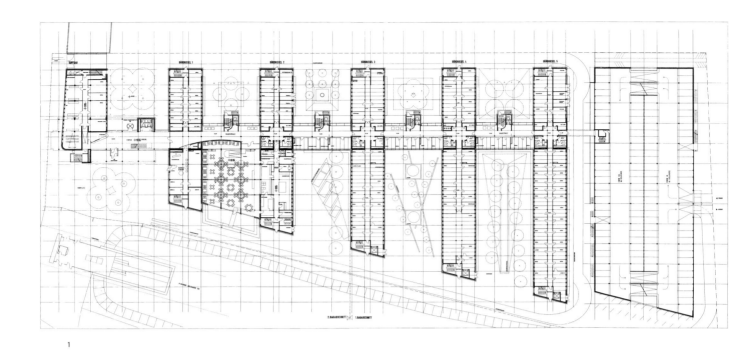

1

2

3

1 ERDGESCHOSS.
2 DIE KAMM-
STRUKTUR DER
ANLAGE AUS DER
VOGELPERSPEKTIVE.
3 KOPFGEBÄUDE
AN DER HOLZ-
HAUSER STRASSE.
4 BLICK IN DEN
TIEFEN HOF.

1 GROUND LEVEL.
2 AERIAL VIEW OF
THE DEVELOPMENT'S
COMB STRUCTURE.
3 HEAD BUILDING
ON HOLZHAUSER
STRASSE.
4 VIEW INTO THE
DEEPEST COURT
YARD.

4

1

1

1 FLURTRENNWAND
ZUR ANGRENZENDEN
KANTINE.
2 EMPFANGSTRESEN.
3 SPEISERAUM
DER KANTINE.
4 BESPRECHUNGS-
RAUM.
1 SEPARATING WALL
BETWEEN CORRIDOR
AND CANTEEN.
2 RECEPTION DESK.
3 DINNING HALL.
4 CONFERENCE
ROOM.

2

3

4

GESTALTUNG DER
FLURZONE IM
DREIBÜNDIGEN
KOPFBAU MITTELS
HOLZVERTÄFELUNG.
WOODEN CLADDED
CORRIDORS IN THE
HEAD BUILDING.

DIE TRENNWÄNDE
ZU DEN ARBEITS-
RÄUMEN SIND MIT
BEWEGLICHEN
LAMELLEN AUS-
GESTATTET. DIE
RÄUME LASSEN SICH
OPTISCH ÖFFNEN
UND SCHLIESSEN.
THE SEPARATING
WALLS OF OFFICES
ARE FITTED WITH
MOVABLE LOUVERS.
THE ROOMS CAN BE
OPTICALLY OPENED
AND CLOSED.

BERTRANDT AG TECHNOLOGIE-ZENTRUM, EHNINGEN

WETTBEWERB: 1998 - 3. Preis
ENTWURF: Meinhard v. Gerkan
mit Philipp Kamps
MITARBEITER: Elke Hoffmeister

Eine Industrieanlage erfordert eine klare Organisation, in klare Bauformen umgesetzt, und die Zukunftsfähigkeit der Gesamtanlage. Das wird durch eine systematisch aufgebaute Abfolge vom einladenden Vorplatz über die repräsentative Eingangshalle bis in die Werkstätten in einer großen Mittelhalle erreicht. Auf beiden Seiten lagern sich die Bürozonen an, die so mit der Fertigung optisch verbunden sind. Das Erscheinungsbild der flexibel organisierbaren Halle wird wesentlich durch den modularen Aufbau der tragenden Dachelemente mit integrierter Technik und Lichtlenkung bestimmt.

An industrial site needs clear organisation which must be translated into a clear built form which will result in future effectivity in use. This is achieved here by the systematic organisation of space; an inviting forecourt, through the representative entry hall and up to the workshop areas placed in a large central hall. Office zones run along both sides and are visually connected to the production area. The overall image generated by the flexible central hall is one of clarity with clearly modulated roof elements and fully integrated technical and lightning arrangements.

1

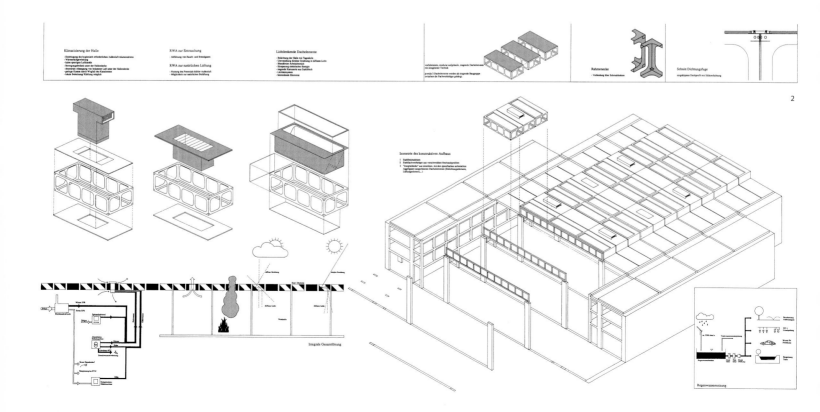

2

1 LAGEPLAN.
2 FÜGUNG DER
BAUELEMENTE UND
DER TECHNIK.
3 GESAMTKOMPLEX
IM MODELL VON DER
ZUGANGSSEITE.
4 BAUSTRUKTUR.

1 SITE PLAN.
2 ALLOCATION OF
BUILDING ELEMENTS
AND PLANT.
3 MODEL OF OVERALL
COMPLEX, VIEWED FROM
ENTRANCE.
4 BUILDING STRUCTURE.

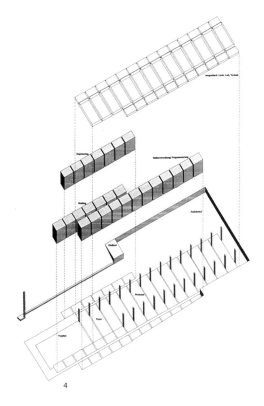

4

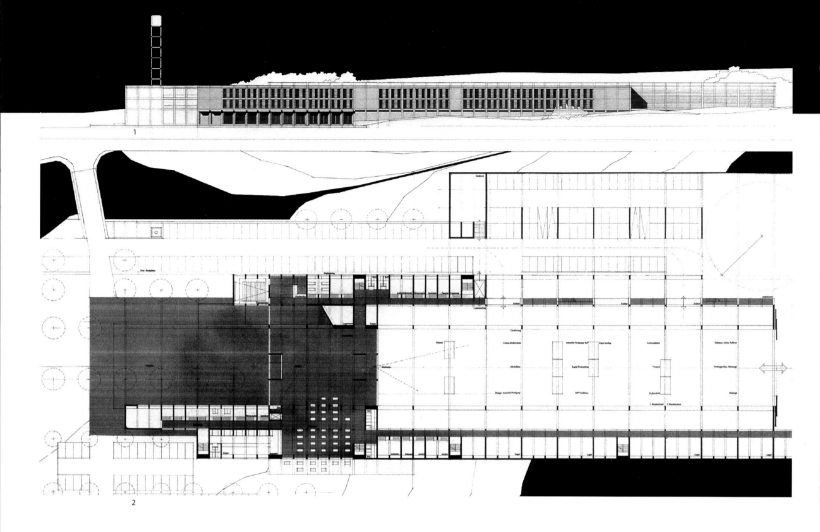

1

2

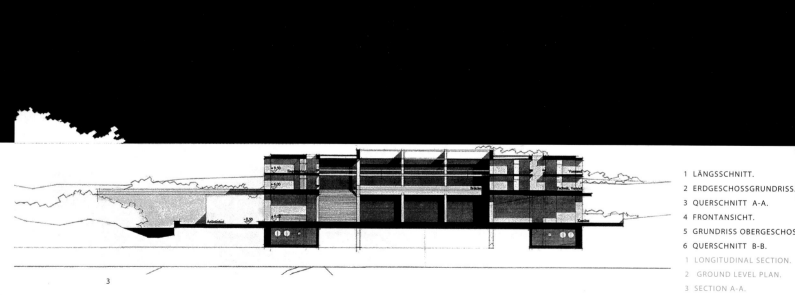

3

1 LÄNGSSCHNITT.

2 ERDGESCHOSSGRUNDRISS.

3 QUERSCHNITT A-A.

4 FRONTANSICHT.

5 GRUNDRISS OBERGESCHOS

6 QUERSCHNITT B-B.

1 LONGITUDINAL SECTION.

2 GROUND LEVEL PLAN.

3 SECTION A-A.

4 FRONT ELEVATION.

5 PLAN UPPER LEVEL.

6 SECTION B-B.

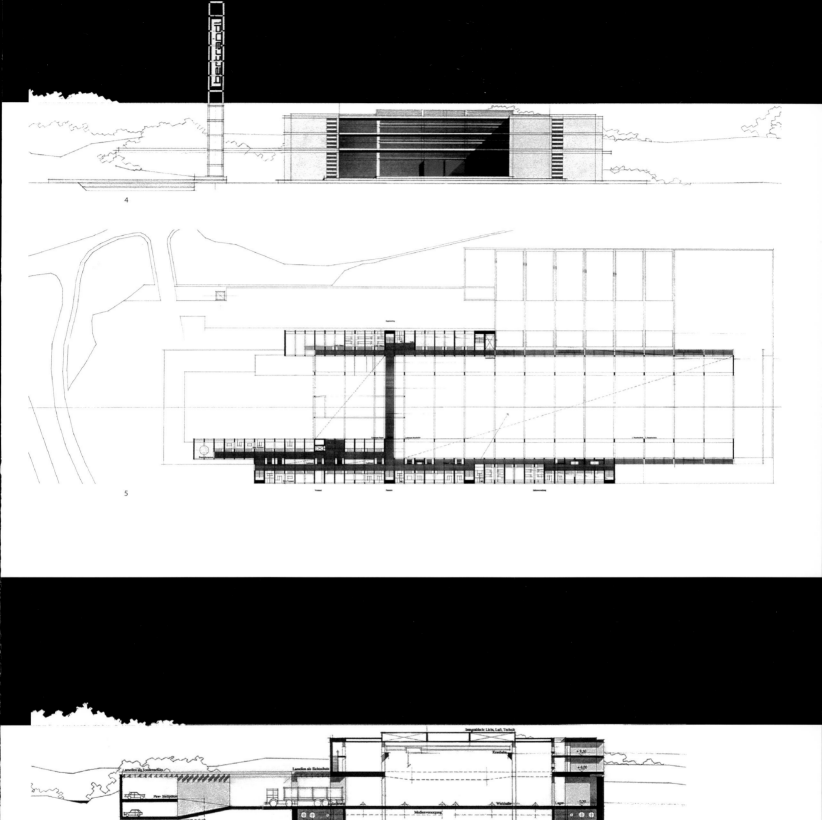

4

5

6

MESSE UND KONSUM

EXHIBITION AND CONSUMERISM

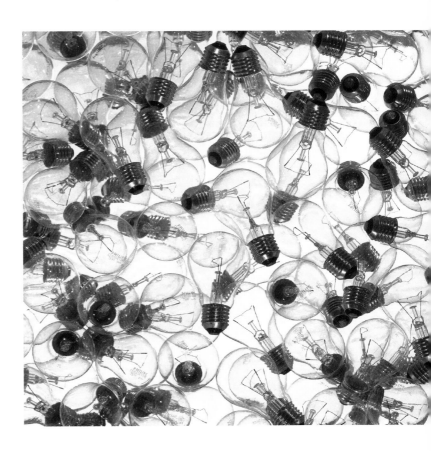

1

PHILIPS MESSESTAND

WETTBEWERB: 1998 - 1.Preis
ENTWURF: Meinhard v. Gerkan
mit Wolfgang Haux
und Magdalene Weiß
MITARBEITER: Peter Radomski
BAUHERR: Philips Licht, Hamburg
BAUZEIT: Jan. - April 1999
BGF: 450 m²
BRI: 1.072 m³

Idee

Jede Ausstellung ist ein Jahrmarkt, architektonische Aufgeregtheiten und Ausstellungsinszenierungen überbieten sich in Vielgestaltigkeit und Reizüberflutung. Deshalb soll der 2-geschossige Pavillon der Philips Licht AG als Messestand ein kontemplatives Gegenstück darstellen. Durch seine Geschlossenheit nach außen macht er das Messepublikum neugierig und bietet dem eintretenden Standbesucher innen offene Ausstellungsbereiche. Die Aufmerksamkeit des Betrachters wird ungestört auf die Exponate gelenkt. Die Erscheinung des Pavillons ist strukturell einfach und sinnfällig, reduziert auf wenige Materialien und präzise im Detail. Sein unverwechselbares Erscheinungsbild wird dafür sorgen, daß der Philips-Messestand

über die kurzlebige Ausstellung hinaus dem Besucher dauerhaft in Erinnerung bleiben wird.

Bausystem

Der Pavillon wird aus einem modularen Bausystem mit wenigen unterschiedlichen Elementen zusammengefügt. Diesem elementierten System liegt ein räumliches Rastermaß von 3,00 m in x-, y- und z-Achsen zugrunde. Die Primärstruktur besteht aus einem Pfosten-Riegel-System und wird in Stahlbau gefertigt. Biegesteife Verbindungsknoten sorgen für die notwendige Aussteifung. Die Sekundärstruktur bilden Ausfachungen, die austauschbar sind. Sie können nach Anforderung und geplanter Rauminszenierung aus offenen oder geschlossenen, aus transparenten oder transluzenten, aus selbstleuchtenden oder beleuchteten Elementen bestehen. Als Symbol für die Firma Philips, die als eine der ersten Firmen die Glühbirne entwickelt hat und heute weltweit führend in der Lampenproduktion ist, werden die Wände und Raumteiler aus angehäuften Philips-Lampen (klar) hergestellt, gehalten durch eine Stahl-Rahmen-Konstruktion mit 2 Sicherheits-Glasscheiben. Bei der Präsentation auf der Hannover-Messe 1999 waren in den Wänden insgesamt 110.000 Glühlampen eingefüllt.

Concept

Every exhibition is a fair, architectural excitement and enacted presentations exceed one another in variety with an incessant flood of stimuli. Contrary to this, the two-storey "Philips Licht AG" pavilion is intended to be a contemplative counterpart. The external closure arouses the public's curiosity and offers open spaces for the visitor internally. The attention of the viewer is exclusively drawn to the exhibits. The appearance of the pavilion is structurally simple and clear, reduced to a few materials, precise in detail. Its unmistakable appearance will ensure, that the Philips exhibition stand will be remembered beyond the short exhibition period.

Construction system

The pavilion is constructed from a modular system with limited elements. The elementary system is based on a grid dimension of 3,00 m in the x-, y- and z-axis. The primary structure consists of a frame system, bending stiff joints providing the required support. The secondary structure are of exchangeable infills. According to the spatial design, these infills can be made from open or closed, transparent or translucent, self-illuminating or illuminated elements. As a symbol for the Philips firm, which was one of the first to deve-

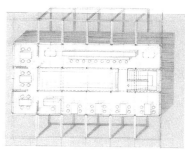

2

lop light-bulbs and is presently world-wide market leader, walls and separating elements are made from stacked Philips-bulbs (clear), sandwiched between two safety glass panes with a steel frame. During the presentation on the Hanover Fair in 1999, the walls were filled with a total of 110,000 light-bulbs.

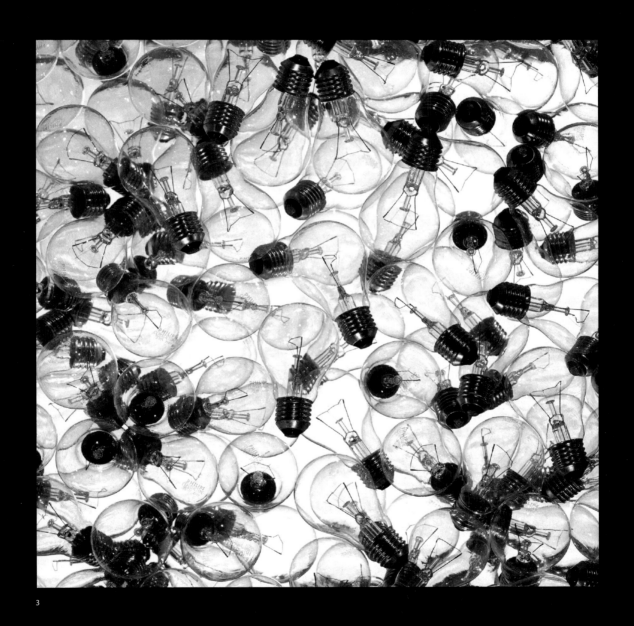

3

1

2

1+2 OBERGESCHOSS
MIT OFFENEM LUFT-
RAUM ZWISCHEN
DEN EBENEN.
3 HAUPTZUGANG IM
HAUPTGESCHOSS.
1+2 UPPER LEVEL
WITH VOID SPACE
BETWEEN THE FLOORS.
3 MAIN LEVEL
ENTRANCE.

1

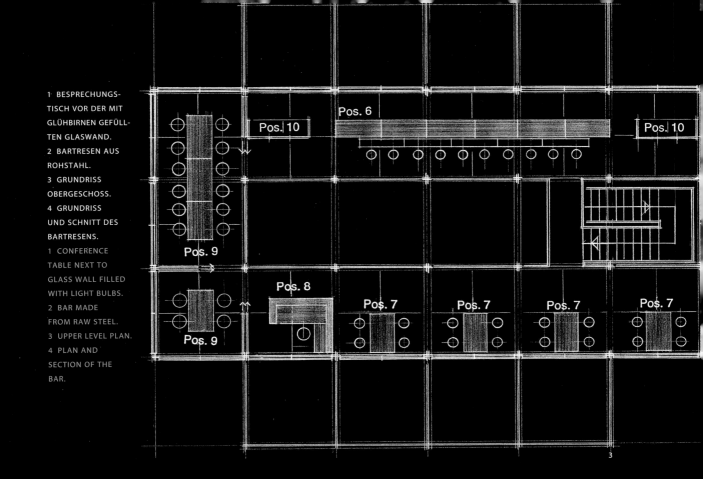

1 BESPRECHUNGS-
TISCH VOR DER MIT
GLÜHBIRNEN GEFÜLL-
TEN GLASWAND.
2 BARTRESEN AUS
ROHSTAHL.
3 GRUNDRISS
OBERGESCHOSS.
4 GRUNDRISS
UND SCHNITT DES
BARTRESENS.
1 CONFERENCE
TABLE NEXT TO
GLASS WALL FILLED
WITH LIGHT BULBS.
2 BAR MADE
FROM RAW STEEL.
3 UPPER LEVEL PLAN.
4 PLAN AND
SECTION OF THE
BAR.

Pos. 6

Pos. 10

Pos. 10

Pos. 9

Pos. 9

Pos. 8

Pos. 7

Pos. 7

Pos. 7

Pos. 7

3

4

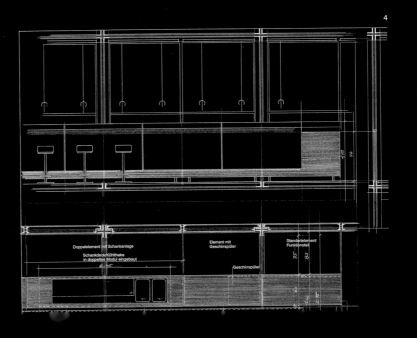

Doppelelement mit Schankanlage

Element mit
Geschirrspüler

Standartelement
Funktionsteil

Schankdeck/Kühltheke
in doppeltes Modul eingebaut

Geschirrspüler

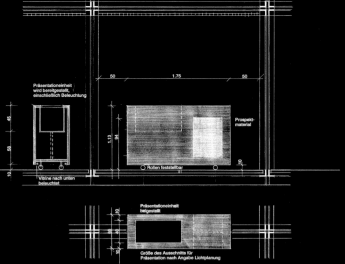

Präsentationseinheit
wird bereitgestellt,
einschließlich Beleuchtung

50   1.75   50

45

1.13   94

Prospekt-
material

58

10

○ Rollen feststellbar   ○

Vitrine nach unten
beleuchtet

10

Präsentationseinheit
beigestellt

10

Größe des Ausschnitts für
Präsentation nach Angabe Lichtplanung

1

2

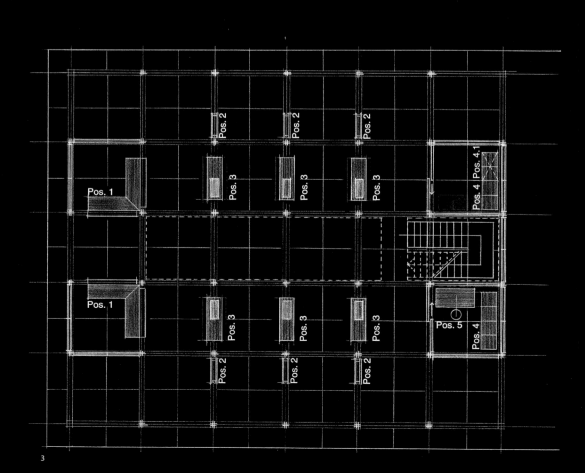

Pos. 2   Pos. 2   Pos. 2

Pos. 1   Pos. 3   Pos. 3   Pos. 3   Pos. 4   Pos. 4.1

Pos. 1   Pos. 3   Pos. 3   Pos. 3   Pos. 5   Pos. 4

Pos. 2   Pos. 2   Pos. 2

3

1+2 CONTAINER
AUF ROLLEN MIT
SCHAUVITRINE UND
PROSPEKTLAGER.
3 GRUNDRISS
HAUPTGESCHOSS.
4 SCHAUVITRINEN
AUS ROHSTAHL.
1+2 MOVABLE CON-
TAINER WITH GLASS
CABINET AND
BROCHURE STORAGE.
3 MAIN LEVEL PLAN.
4 GLASS CABINET
MADE FROM RAW
STEEL.

4

2

3

1

MESSE RIMINI

WETTBEWERB: 1997 - 1. Preis
ENTWURF: Volkwin Marg
PROJEKTLEITUNG: Stephanie Jöbsch
MITARBEITER: Hauke Huusmann,
Yasemin Erkan, Thomas Damman,
Wolfgang Schmidt, Regine Simoneit,
Helene van gen Hassend,
Maria-Chiara Breda, Susanne Bern,
Carsten Plog, Marco Vivori,
Arne Starke
KONTAKTARCHITEKT:
Clemens Kusch
STATIK: Favero & Milan, Venedig,
Schlaich, Bergermann und Partner
LANDSCHAFTSPLANUNG: Studio
Land, Mailand
BAUHERR: Ente Autonoma Fiera
BAUZEIT: 1999 - 2001
BGF: 130.134 m^2

Atrien an den Enden sowie einer überwölbten Säulenhalle als verbinddendem Zentrum. Die Dächer der Messehallen bestehen aus einer hölzernen Rautenkonstruktion, mit Stahlkreuzen verbunden und mit Unterspannseilen zur Aufnahme der Horizontalkräfte versehen.

As an exhibition centre the complex has to be flexible and meet the highest technological standards. Due to the location, its architecture has to consider the building tradition of the Ancients and the Renaissance. Based on these requirements a linear, symmetrical ensemble with a clear orientation has been proposed. An entrance hall with a Tetrapylon (a reference to the historical family towers) defines the entrance to the Exhibition Street. It is formed as a

1

Als Messe muß die Anlage flexibel und auf technisch höchstem Niveau nutzbar sein. An diesem Ort muß die Architektur auf die große Bautradition der Antike und der Renaissance eingehen. Aus beiden Vorgaben wurde ein lineares, axialsymmetrisches Ensemble mit klarer Orientierung entwickelt. Ein Eingangsbereich mit einem Tetrapylon, der an die historischen Geschlechtertürme erinnert, schafft die Vorzone zur Messe-Straße als langgestreckter Agora mit beidseitigen Kolonnaden auf gestuftem Peristyl, Brunnenhöfen und gedeckten

longitudinal Agora with colonnades on both sides on stepped Peristyl, fountains and sheltered atria at the terminating points. A columned hall with an arched roof is the focal point. The roofs of the exhibition halls are of wooden construction, linked with tensile cables, tensioned rods bearing horizontal loads.

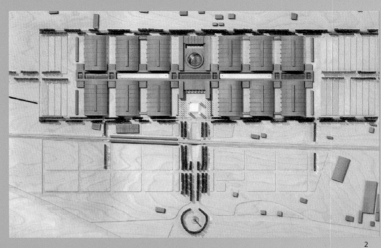

1 MESSE ENTRE
BEI NÄCHTLICHER
STIMMUNG.
2 LAGEPLAN IN DER
MODELLDARSTELLUNG.
3 INNENRAUM
EINER AUSSTELLUNGS-
HALLE MIT DER
RAUTENSTRUKTUR
DES DACHES.
1 ENTRANCE MODEL,
AT NIGHT.
2 SITE PLAN MODEL.
3 INTERIOR SPACE OF
AN EXHIBITION HALL
WITH THE RHOMBOID
ROOF STRUCTURE.

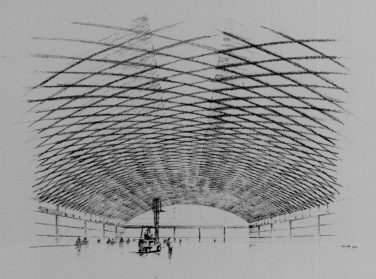

MESSE DÜSSELDORF

WETTBEWERB: 1997 - 1. Preis
ENTWURF: Volkwin Marg
MITARBEITER: Frederik Jaspert,
Marek Nowak, Olaf Drehsen,
Thomas Heuer, Christina Harenberg,
Thomas Behr
LEITUNG DER AUSFÜHRUNG:
Joachim Rind
MITARBEITER: Michael Haase,
Heiko Körner, Marek Nowak,
Simone Ripp, Stefanie Streb,
Petra Tallen, Andreas Wietheger,
Timo Holland, Stefan Menke,
Anne Werrens
STATIK: Schlaich, Bergermann
und Partner; Ing.-Büro Gehlen
LANDSCHAFTSPLANUNG:
WES und Partner
BAUHERR: Düsseldorfer
Messegesellschaft mbH
BAUZEIT: 1998 - 2000
BGF: 42.500 m²
BRI: 622.000 m³

Um die Signifikanz der Messe zu steigern, sollen zwei Eingänge zusätzlich zum heutigen, elliptischen Nordeingang neue Zeichen in der Rheinlandschaft setzen: Ein neuer Westeingang mit Europas größtem Kuppelbau für die Mehrzweckhalle in der Achse des Rheinstadions und der aufgewertete Südeingang mit dem markanten Bau des Kongreßhotels. Das weitere Wachstum der Messe wird durch eine Binnenverdichtung in Form einer von zweigeschossigen Kolonnaden gefaßten „Agora" aufgefangen. Besonders wichtig ist dabei der Kuppelbau als Sonderfall einer Messehalle mit hohem architektonischen Anspruch. Er korrespondiert mit der Tonhalle von Wilhelm Kreis als Wahrzeichen der ersten Messeanlage (1926).

In order to enhance the significance of the exhibition grounds, two entrances are added to the existing elliptical north entrance and present new symbols in the Rhine landscape: A new west entrance with Europe's largest domed structure proposed as a multi-functional hall is located in the continuation of the Rheinstadion axis, and the rejuvenated south entrance with the prominent congress hotel.

An increased interior density reduces further extension of the exhibition grounds, introducing an "agora" framed by two-level colonnades. Of special importance is the structurally daring dome form, which is unusual in exhibition halls. It corresponds to the "Tonhalle" by Wilhelm Kreis, the symbol of the first exhibition grounds (1926).

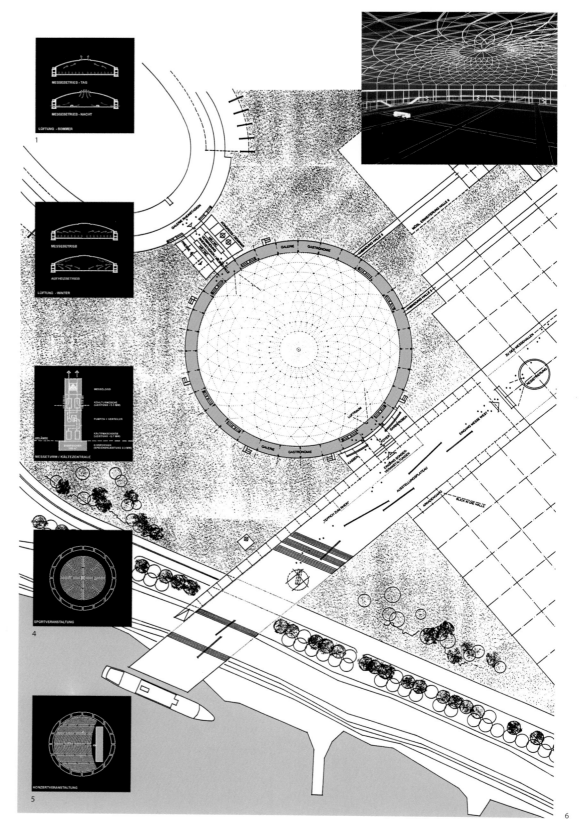

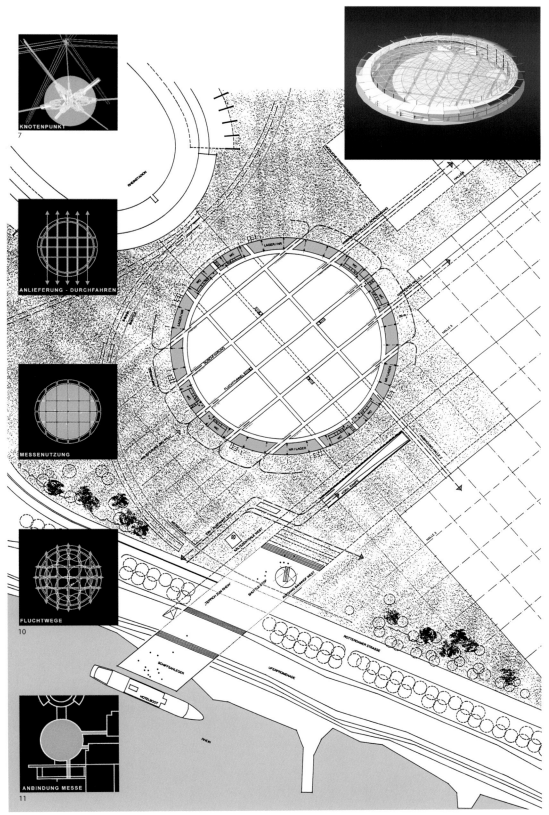

1 LÜFTUNG IM SOMMER.
2 LÜFTUNG IM WINTER.
3 MESSETURM/KÄLTEZENTRALE.
4 SPORTVERANSTALTUNG.
5 KONZERTVERANSTALTUNG.
6 GRUNDRISS OBERGESCHOSS.
7 KNOTENPUNKT.
8 ANLIEFERUNG - DURCHFAHREN.
9 MESSENUTZUNG.
10 FLUCHTWEGE.
11 ANBINDUNG DER MESSE.
12 GRUNDRISS ERDGESCHOSS.

1 VENTILATION IN SUMMER.
2 VENTILATION IN WINTER.
3 EXHIBITION TOWER /
AIR CONDITIONING .
4 SPORT EVENT.
5 MUSICAL EVENT.
6 UPPER LEVEL PLAN.
7 MEETING POINT.
8 DELIVERY / ROAD WAY.
9 EXHIBITION USE.
10 ESCAPE ROUTES.
11 TRAFFIC CONNECTION TO
EXHIBITION GROUNDS.
12 GROUND LEVEL PLAN.

1

GESCHÄFTSHAUS NEUER WALL 43, HAMBURG

GUTACHTEN: 1990
ENTWURF: Volkwin Marg
PROJEKTLEITUNG: Tim Hupe
MITARBEITER: Ahmet Alkuru, Frank Hülsmeier, Detlef Papendick, Christoph Berle, Detlef Porsch, Christel Timm-Schwarz, Arend Buchholz-Berger, Uli Rösler
BAUHERR: Andersen & Co GmbH+Co
BAUZEIT: 1994 - 1997
BGF: 7.480 m²
BRI: 35.700 m³

Als erste Gebäude mit einer Vorhangfassade wurden die Geschäftshäuser Neuer Wall 41 bis 43 von Godber Nissen 1951 bis 1958 errichtet. Der Um- und Neubau unter Mitwirkung des seinerzeitigen Architekten bietet nach den neuen städtebaulichen Leitvorstellungen einer geschlossenen Bebauung ein attraktives Laden-Kaufhaus neuen Typs, bei dem um eine Glashalle herum auf drei Galerien von unten einsehbare Läden angeboten werden.

3

2

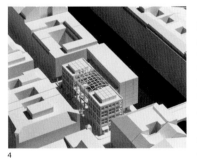

4

1+2 DIE STRASSEN-
FRONT AM
„NEUEN WALL"
- 1A ADRESSE FÜR
MODE IN HAMBURG.
LINKS: JIL SANDER
RECHTS: PETRA TEUFEL.
3 DER NEUE
BAUKÖRPER IN DER
STRASSENFLUCHT.
4 DIE SCHICHTUNG
DES NEUEN VOR
DEM ALTEN.
5 BEGEGNUNG VON
ALT UND NEU.
1+2 STREET
FACADE ONTO
"NEUER WALL" -
FIRST-RATE
ADDRESS FOR FASHI-
ON IN HAMBURG.
LEFT: JIL SANDER
RIGHT: PETRA TEUFEL.
3 THE NEW
BUILDING IN THE
STREET CONTEXT.
4 THE LAYERING
OF NEW IN
FRONT OF OLD.
5 ENCOUNTER OF
OLD AND NEW.

The first building with a curtain wall system was the commercial building Neuer Wall 41-43, built in 1951 - 1958 by Godber Nissen. The conversion and extension in cooperation with the former archi-tect, and in correspondence with the latest urban guide-lines for in-fill developments, offer an attrac-tive modern shopping zone. Transparent commercial units are located on three galleries around a glass hall.

5

FORUM KÖPENICK, BERLIN

WETTBEWERB: 1994 - 1. Preis
ENTWURF: Volkwin Marg
PROJEKTLEITUNG: Joachim Rind
MITARBEITER: Christina Harenberg,
Monika Kaesler, Franz Lensing,
Gabriele Mones, Marek Nowak,
Efstratios Sianidis, Uta-Eyke Witzel,
Robert Stüer, Thomas Behr
BAUHERR: GP Fundus Gewerbebau
und Projektierung GmbH
BAUZEIT: 1996 - 1997
BGF: 103.423 m²
BRI: 425.000 m³

Das "Forum Köpenick" bildet kein ab-
geschlossenes, eher stadtfeindliches
Einkaufszentrum, sondern eine
große, einfache Markthalle. Ihre glas-
gedeckte, langgestreckte Halle ist
Zentrum für Aktionen, Gastronomie,
fliegende Märkte, gleichzeitig bildet
sie den Zu-gang zu den Fachmärk-
ten und Läden. Nach außen hin bietet sie freie Sicht auf die
Bahnhofstraße und, nach Westen hin,
zum Wohnquartier am neu geschaf-
fenen Wuhle-Becken, das durch Auf-
stauung des Flusses entstanden ist.
Die Bauhöhe entspricht der Nachb-
arbebauung und fügt sich so in das
vorhandene urbane Gefüge ein. Der
Wohnungsbau enthält in der
geschlossenen Bebauung geförderte
Mietwohnungen; westlich des Beckens
gibt es eine dreigeschossige offene
Bauweise, dem Charakter des Viertels
entsprechend.

The Köpenick Forum does not create
the usual introverted hostile shopping centre, but is instead a simple
market hall. The long glass covered
market has created a central focus
for events, gastronomy, side stalls
whilst forming the gateway to the
more specialist markets and shops.
It offers un-inhibited views onto
Bahnhofstrasse and also to the
newly created residential area at
Wuhle Becken, which was created
by damming the main river flow.
The height of the building responds to its neighbours and thereby
complies with the existing urban
structure. The residential unit holds
whithin its compact structure sub-
sidized flats. To the west of the
new waterside development a
three storey open building reflects
the existing character of the area.

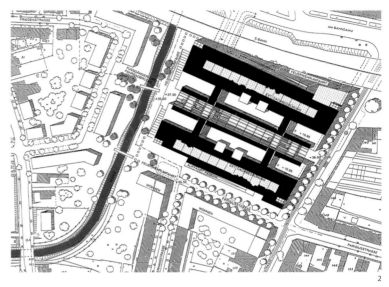

2

3

1 SEITENFRONT
DER PASSAGE.
2 LAGEPLAN.
3 HAUPTZUGANG.

1 LATERAL VIEW
OF THE ARCADE.
2 SITE PLAN.
3 MAIN ENTRANCE.

1

1

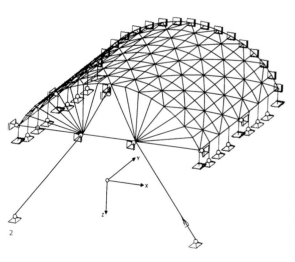

2

1 TRANSPARENTE
FAHRSTUHLANLAGE
IM ZENTRUM
DER PASSAGE.
2 STATIK DER
SEILUNTERSPANNTEN
DACHSCHALE.
3 DIE FILIGRANE
KONSTRUKTION
PRÄGT DIE GESTALT
DES TONNENDACHES.
1 TRANSPARENT
LIFT IN THE ARCADE
CENTRE.
2 STRUCTURE
OF THE CABLE
SUPPORTED ROOF
GEOMETRY.
3 THE DELICATE
CONSTRUCTION
CHARACTERIZES THE
FORM OF THE
BARREL VAULT ROOF.

3

VERKEHR

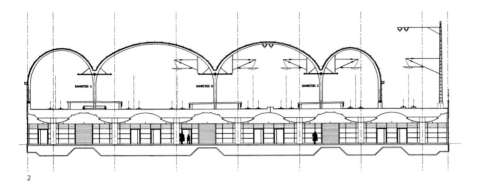

BAHNHOF BERLIN-SPANDAU

WETTBEWERB: 1993 - 3. Preis
ENTWURF: Meinhard v. Gerkan
PARTNER: Hubert Nienhoff
PROJEKTLEITUNG:
Sybille Zittlau-Kroos,
Birgit Keul-Ricke, Elisabeth Menne
MITARBEITER: Almut Schlüter,
Peter Bozic, Agnieska Preibisz,
Margret Böthig, Diane Berve,
Karl Baumgarten, Matthias Wiegelmann,
Gerd Meyer, Andreas Dierkes,
Paul Wolff, Marietta Rothe,
Kerstin Struckmeyer, Peter Schuch,
STATIK:
Schlaich, Bergermann und Partner
BAUHERR: Deutsche Bahn AG
BAUZEIT: 1996 - 1998
BGF BAHNHOFSHALLE: 4.891 m²
BGF ÜBERDACHT: 20.607 m²
BRI BAHNHOFSHALLE: 28.369 m³

Der Bahnhof Spandau ist Teil der Fernbahnstrecke Hannover-Berlin und befindet sich in unmittelbarer Nähe zum Rathaus der Stadt in Hochlage. Er wird durch eine ebenerdige Passage mit Ladenzonen und bahnspezifischen Nutzungen erschlossen. Die eigentliche Halle ist 430 m lang und vollständig mit parallel laufenden Tonnendächern gedeckt. Typologisch knüpft sie damit an historische Bahnhofshallen an, wie sie in einer Ausstellung der Deutschen Bahn AG 1996, vier Jahre nach Entstehung des Entwurfes, in Venedig zur Biennale 1996 unter dem Titel „Renaissance der Bahnhöfe" gezeigt wurden.

Während der Typus damit an die Tradition anknüpft, ist die Konstruktion der Halle eher dem 21. Jahrhundert verpflichtet. Die Tonnenkonstruktion ruht auf Längsträgern, die in der Mittelachse der Bahnsteige von Stützen im Abstand von 18 m getragen werden. In der Querachse jeder Stütze liegen der Aussteifung dienende, bogenförmige Rippen. Die Eindeckung der Tonnen erfolgte mit planen Glasscheiben, die infolge der komplizierten Geometrie der Bahnsteige je geringfügig voneinander abweichen, obwohl sie alle gleich aussehen.

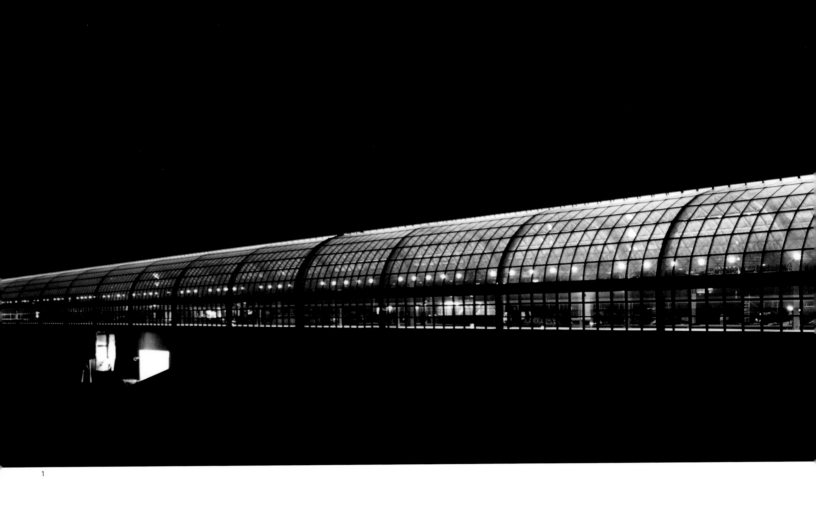

1

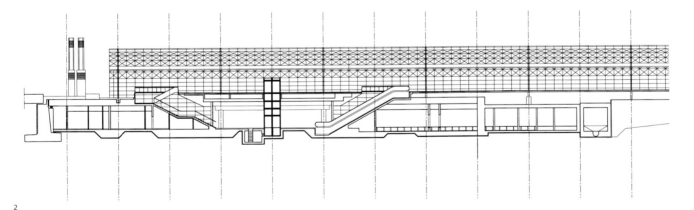

2

Die gesamte Konstruktion wird durch diagonale, unter der Dachfläche verlaufende Seile stabilisiert. Im Abstand von 3 m angeordnete Lampenausleger geben nachts Licht auf die Bahnsteigsebene und erzeugen mit nach oben gerichteten Strahlern Reflektionen in der Glastonne. Dadurch entsteht auch bei Dunkelheit ein eindrucksvolles Raumerlebnis der filigranen Stahl-Glasstruktur.

The Spandau Railway Station is part of the main-line service Hanover - Berlin and runs in an elevated position close to Spandau´s town hall. It is developed with a ground-floor arcade for shopping and railway related functions. The main hall is 430 m long and completely covered with parallel vaulted roofs. Typologically this evokes links to historic station halls, as were presented in the exhibition "Renaissance of Railway Stations" by the Deutsche Bahn AG in Venice during the Biennale in 1996 (four years after the design of this concept). While typology welcomes tradition, the construction is committed to the 21st century. The roof construction rests on longitudinal beams, supported by columns positioned at 18 m centres in the central axis of the platforms. The cross axis of each column holds curved stiffening ribs. The glass panel cladding vary slightly due to the complex geometry of the platforms, but nevertheless appear identical. The overall construction is stabilized by tensile cables, running diagonally below the roof surface. Cantilevered lights at 3 m centres illuminate the platform level at night and create reflections in the glass vault with upward beams, resulting in an impressive spatial experience of the fine steel-glass structure.

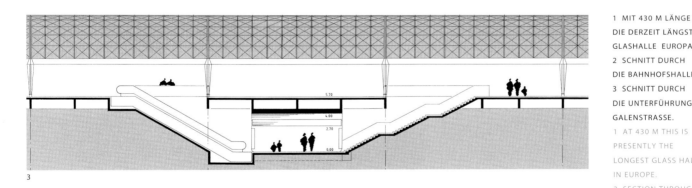

3

1 MIT 430 M LÄNGE
DIE DERZEIT LÄNGSTE
GLASHALLE EUROPAS.
2 SCHNITT DURCH
DIE BAHNHOFSHALLE.
3 SCHNITT DURCH
DIE UNTERFÜHRUNG
GALENSTRASSE.
1 AT 430 M THIS IS
PRESENTLY THE
LONGEST GLASS HALL
IN EUROPE.
2 SECTION THROUGH
THE STATION HALL.
3 SECTION THROUGH
THE UNDERPASS
GALENSTRASSE.

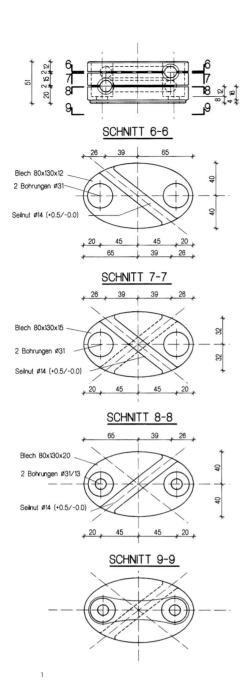

SCHNITT 6-6

SCHNITT 7-7

Blech 80x130x12
2 Bohrungen Ø31
Seilnut Ø14 (+0.5/-0.0)

SCHNITT 8-8

Blech 80x130x15
2 Bohrungen Ø31
Seilnut Ø14 (+0.5/-0.0)

SCHNITT 9-9

Blech 80x130x20
2 Bohrungen Ø31/13
Seilnut Ø14 (+0.5/-0.0)

1

1 DETAILS DER KLEMMSCHEIBEN FÜR DIE DIAGONALE SEILVERSPANNUNG. 2 AUCH DIE BAHN-STEIGAUFBAUTEN SIND IN EINER STAHL-GLAS-KONSTRUKTION AUSGEFÜHRT.

DIE KUNST-BELEUCHTUNG IST MIT ABSICHT SO DIS-PONIERT, DASS MEHRFACHE REFLE-XIONEN VON DER GLASTONNE DIE LICHTSTIMMUNG IN DER HALLE MODULIEREN.

1 CLAMPING COMPONENT DETAILS OF THE TENSILE CABLE STRUCTURE. 2 PLATFORM BUILDINGS ARE ALSO DESIGNED AS STEEL-GLASS-CONSTRUCTIONS.

THE ARTIFICIAL LIGHTING DELIBER-ATELY AIMS AT MULTIPLE REFLEC-TIONS FROM THE GLASS VAULT IN ORDER TO MODULATE THE LIGHTING ATMOSPHERE INSIDE THE HALL.

2

2

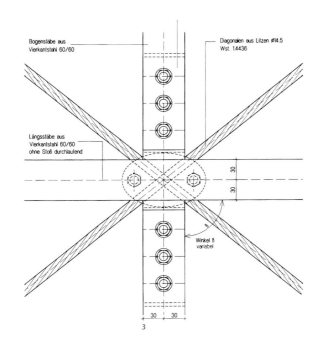

Bogenstäbe aus
Vierkantstahl 60/60

Diagonalen aus Litzen Ø14.5
Wst. 1.4436

Längsstäbe aus
Vierkantstahl 60/60
ohne Stoß durchlaufend

Winkel δ
variabel

30

30

30   30

3

Bohrung Ø11

66.5   66.5

4

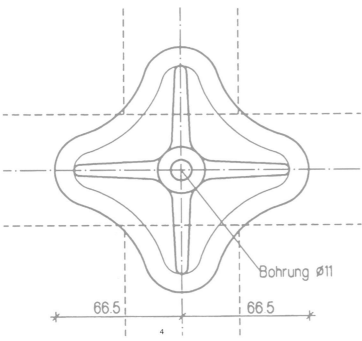

1 UNTERSICHT DES
DACHES IM DETAIL.
ALLE KNOTENPUNKTE
SIND 'GELENKIG'
AUSGEBILDET.
DAMIT PASST SICH
DAS SCHEINBAR
RECHTWINKLIGE GIT-
TER DER IN BEIDEN
RICHTUNGEN GE-
KRÜMMTEN GEOME-
TRIE EBENSO AN, WIE
ES AUF DIE SICH
VERÄNDERNDEN
KRÜMMUNGS-
RADIEN REAGIERT.
KEIN STAB DES GIT-
TERWERKES UND
KEINE GLASSCHEIBE
SIND GLEICH.
2 DAS DACH
BESTEHT AUS 12.700
VERSCHIEDENEN
GLASSCHEIBEN.
3 KNOTENPUNKT
VON UNTEN.
4 KNOTENPUNKT
VON OBEN MIT
DEM ALS GUSSTEIL
GEFERTIGTEN
ABDECKUNGSTELLER,
DER DURCH EINE
MITTIGE SCHRAUBE
GEHALTEN WIRD.

1 UNDERSIDE OF
ROOF DETAIL. ALL
NODAL POINTS ARE
FLEXIBLE. THUS THE
APPARENTLY
RECTANGULAR GRID
ADJUSTS IN BOTH
DIRECTIONS TO THE
CURVED GEOMETRY
AND REACTS TO THE
CHANGING RADIUS
OF CURVATURE.
NO GRID OR GLASS
ELEMENT IS ALIKE.
2 THE ROOF
CONSISTS OF
12,700 DIFFERENT
GLASS PANES.
3 UNDERSIDE OF
NODAL POINT.
4 NODAL POINT
FROM ABOVE WITH
CAST STEEL COVER
PLATE, FIXED BY A
CENTRAL BOLT.

1

1

2

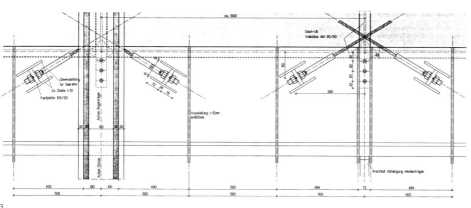

3

4

1

2

1+2 DIE IN SINUS-
WELLEN GEFORMTE
DECKE DER
BAHNHOFSHALLE
UNTER DEN
GLEISKÖRPERN IST
MIT INDIREKTER
LICHTFÜHRUNG
AUSGESTATTET, UM
DIE NIEDRIGE
RAUMHÖHE OPTISCH
ZU ERWEITERN.
3 AUFGANG ZUM
BAHNSTEIG.
4 QUERSCHNITT
DURCH
BAHNHOFS- UND
BAHNSTEIGHALLEN.

1+2 THE STATION
HALL CEILING BELOW
THE PLATFORM
LEVEL IS BASED ON A
SINUSOIDAL CURVE.
INDIRECT LIGHTING
OPTIMIZES THE
RESTRICTED CEILING
HEIGHT.
3 STAIRCASE TO
PLATFORM LEVEL.
4 CROSS SECTION
THROUGH STATION
AND PLATFORM
HALL.

3

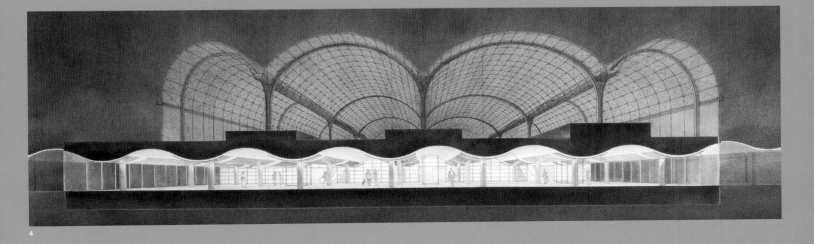

4

TRANSRAPID-STATION, SCHWERIN

GUTACHTEN: 1998
ENTWURF: Meinhard v. Gerkan
MITARBEITER: Arend Buchholz-Berger,
Oliver Christ, Justus Klement,
Michael Biwer

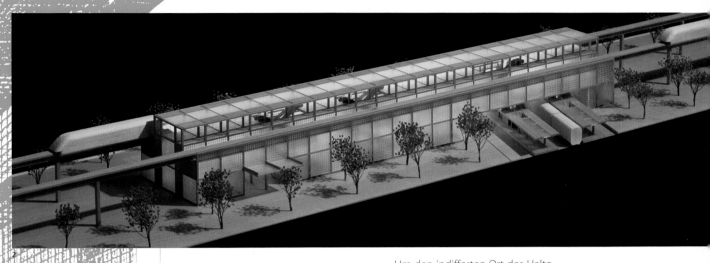

2

Um den indifferten Ort des Haltepunktes außerhalb der Stadt zu definieren, wird eine große Kreisfläche als Baumpflanzung in die Landschaft einbeschrieben. Die Station selbst überbrückt eine Bundesbahntrasse und integriert den in Hochlage liegenden Schienenweg. Im Gegensatz zum stromlinienförmigen Transrapid zeigt sich das Stationsgebäude als kristalline „Kiste" aus großräumigem Stahlbetonfachwerk, das durch Glasbausteine ausgefacht ist. In der Längsachse liegt mittig eine zweigeschossige Halle, deren Transparenz, Großräumigkeit und gute Orientierung der Innovation neuer Transporttechnik ein imposantes Raumerlebnis gegenüberstellt.

A newly planted circular arrangement of trees defines the otherwise indifferent location of the station on the outskirts of the city.
The station itself sits above train tracks and integrates the elevated Transrapid line. In contrast to the stream-lined Transrapid, the station is a crystal box supported by a long-spanning concrete structure with glass elements. A two-storey hall is centrally located on the longitudinal axis and challenges modern transport technology with its transparency, spaciousness and clear circulation.

1+2 DIE TYPOLOGIE DES ENTWURFES FOLGT DEM LEITBILD EINER SCHACHTEL, DEREN MERKMALE DENEN DES FAHRZEUGES KONTRASTIEREND GEGENÜBERSTEHEN.
3 BLICK IN DIE MITTIGE BAHNHOFSHALLE.
1+2 TYPOLOGICALLY THE DESIGN IS MODELLED ON A BOX-FORM, ITS CHARACTERISTICS CONTRASTING WITH THE TRAIN'S DYNAMIC.
3 VIEW INTO THE CENTRAL STATION HALL.

3

1

1 SÜDLICHER
ZUGANG.
2 DER HALTEPUNKT
IM NIEMANDSLAND
BEI SCHWERIN WIRD
DURCH DIE KREIS-
FIGUR EINER BAUM-
PFLANZUNG ALS
IDENTIFIZIERBARER
ORT BESTIMMT.
DAS STRUKTURELLE
GERÜST DES GEBÄU-
DES IST MIT GLAS-
BAUSTEINEN AUSGE-

FACHT, DIE EINE
INTERMISSION DES
LICHTES VON
INNEN UND AUSSEN
BEWIRKEN.
3 EINGANGS- UND
ERDGESCHOSS.
4 BAHNSTEIGEBENE
AUF + 13 M.
1 SOUTH ENTRANCE.
2 THE STATION
IN THE OPEN LAND-
SCAPE OUTSIDE
SCHWERIN IS DEFINED

BY A CIRCULAR
PLANTATION OF
TREES.
THE STRUCTURAL
BUILDING FRAME
IS INFILLED WITH
GLASS BLOCKS,
ALLOWING THE
TRANSMISSION
OF LIGHT.
3 ENTRANCE AND
GROUND LEVEL.
4 PLATFORM LEVEL
AT +13 M.

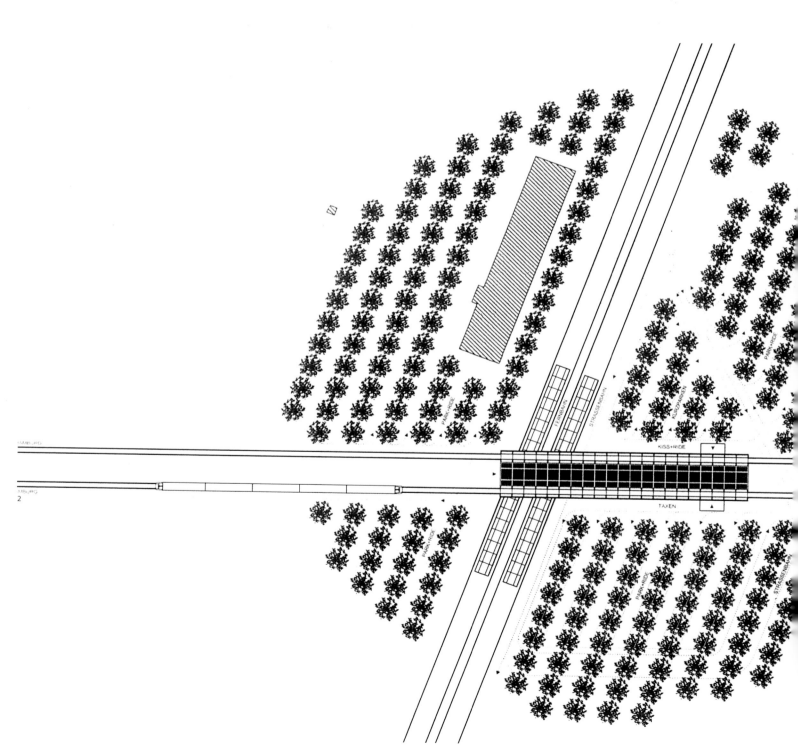

2

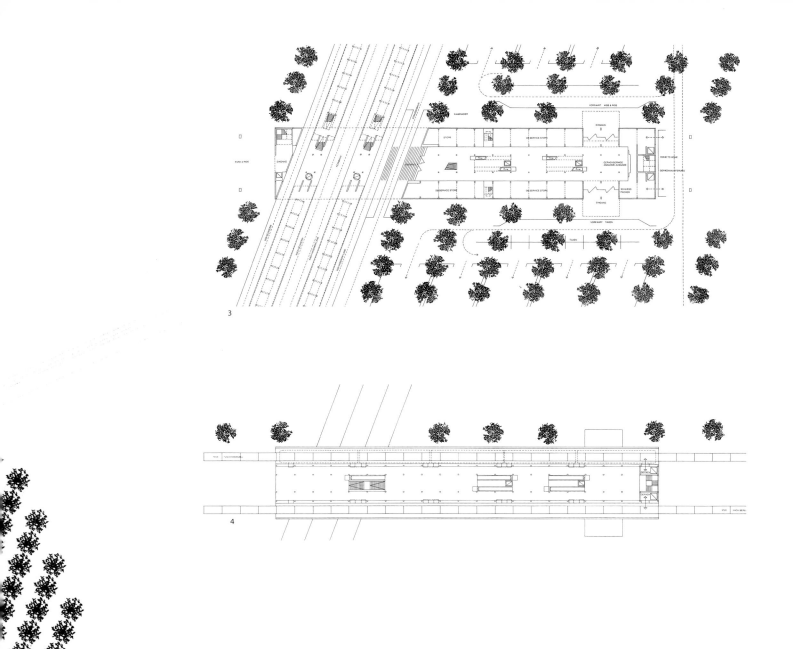

3

4

LEHRTER BAHNHOF, BERLIN

WETTBEWERB: 1993 - 1. Rang
ENTWURF: Meinhard v. Gerkan
PROJEKTPARTNER: Jürgen Hillmer
PROJEKTLEITUNG: Susanne Winter,
Klaus Hoyer, Arend Buchholz-Berger,
Hans-Joachim Glahn
MITARBEITER: Prisca Bucher,
Christel Timm-Schwarz, Gisbert v.
Stülpnagel, Andreas Ebner, Bettina
Kreuzheck, Vita Römer, Elisabeth
Mittelsdorf, Ralph Preuß, Sabine
Gressel, Stefan Bachmann,
Constantin Dumas, Michael Scholz,
Werner Schmidt, Hubertus Pieper,
Peter Karn, Thomas Weiser, Gisela
Koch, Sebastian Geiger, Peter Krüger,
Christian Kreusler, Lothar Scharpe,
Monica Sallowsky, Amra Sternberger,
Radmilla Blagovcanin, Hans
Münchhalfen, Antje Lucks, Maike
Carlsen, Claudia Gern, Saban Yazici,
Tomas Nowack, Markus Siegel, Diana
Kurscheid, Wolfgang Höhl
STATIK: Schlaich, Bergermann
und Partner; IVZ/Emsch+Berger
LICHTPLANUNG: Peter Andres
+ Conceptlicht GmbH
**TECHNISCHE GEBÄUDE-
AUSRÜSTUNG:**
Ingenieurgesellschaft Höpfner
BAUHERR: Deutsche Bahn AG
vertreten durch die DB Projekt
GmbH - Knoten Berlin
BAUZEIT: 1996 - 2005
BGF: 180.000 m²

Am Ort des historischen Lehrter Bahnhofs entsteht der wichtigste Bahnhof Deutschlands: hier kreuzen sich eine West-Ost- und eine Nord-Süd-Strecke für den ICE-Verkehr; hinzu kommen S- und U-Bahnlinien. Die Nord-Süd-Trasse verläuft 15 m unter der Erde in einem Tunnel, der Spree und Tiergarten unterquert; die West-Ost-Linie liegt in Hochlage. Deren 430 m lange Bahnsteige werden mit einer filigranen Glashalle überspannt, die zwei Gebäudescheiben durchschneidet, die den Nord-Süd-Bahnhofsteil im Stadtraum markant abbilden. Zwischen ihnen liegt die 50 m breite und 170 m lange Bahnhofshalle, die ebenfalls mit einem filigran konstruierten Tonnendach überdeckt wird. Die Halle bildet zum Stadtteil Moabit auf der einen und dem nahen Regierungsviertel auf der anderen Seite eine einladende Torsituation. Die als Dreibund ausgebildeten, 45 m hohen Gebäudescheiben überspannen die obere Bahnhofshalle brückenartig über eine Breite von 70 m; sie sind für Dienstleistungen, Büros oder Hotelnutzungen bestimmt. Die Glasdächer der Bahnhofshallen sind als Gitterschalennetz aus nahezu quadratischen, 1,2 x 1,2 m großen Netzmaschen konstruiert, die durch Seile ausgekreuzt werden. Durch das Zusammenwirken von Bögen, Längsträgern und Diagonalseilen entsteht ein schalenartiges Tragverhalten; biegesteife Rahmen im Abstand von 20 bis 30 m sorgen für die notwendige Aussteifung.

On the site of the historical "Lehrter Bahnhof", the most important train station in Germany is nearing completion: An east-west- and a north-south-link of the InterCityExpress service connect here, supported by local train links. The north-south line runs 15 m below ground level underneath the River Spree and the Tiergarten. The east-west line is elevated, its 430 m long platforms are covered by a lightweight glass structure, intersecting two bar forms, which clearly define the north-south train station in the city scope. The central hall, 50 m wide and 170 m long, is located between these bars and is also covered by a fine vaulted roof structure. The hall offers an inviting gateway between the Moabit quarter on one side and the new government quarter on the other. The 45 m high bar forms bridge the upper station hall over a 70 m width, which are intended to be used for service, offices or hotels. The station hall glass roofs are designed as tensile cable structures, using a square module of 1.2 m. The combination of vaults, beams and diagonal cables forms a shell-like structure. Lateral stiffness is provided by steel frames at 20 to 30 m intervals.

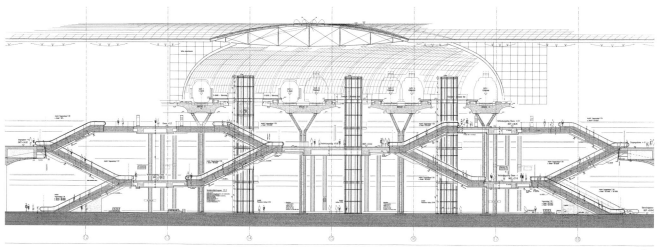

1 LÄNGSSCHNITT
DURCH DIE BAHN-
HOFSHALLE.
2 BAHNHOFSZU-
GANG VON SÜDEN.
1 LONGITUDINAL
SECTION THROUGH
STATION HALL.
2 SOUTH ENTRANCE.

2

3

1 BAUSTELLE AUS
DER LUFT IM MAI
1999.
2 ZWEI REITER-
GEBÄUDE ÜBER-
BRÜCKEN DIE OST-
WEST-BAHNHOFS-
HALLE.
3 BLICK IN DIE
HAUPTHALLE.
4 BLICK IN DIE
GEKRÜMMTE OST-
WEST-BAHNHOFS-
HALLE.

1 AERIAL VIEW OF
CONSTRUCTION SITE
IN MAY 1999.
2 TWO BUILDINGS
BARS BRIDGE THE
EAST-WEST STATION-
HALL.
3 VIEW INTO
MAINHALL.
4 VIEW INTO THE
CURVED EAST-WEST
STATION-HALL.

4

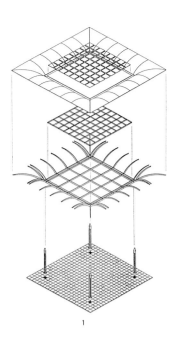

1

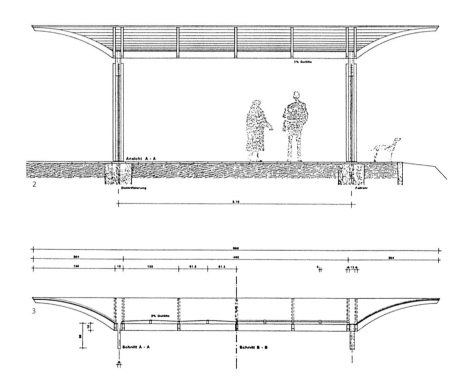

Ansicht A - A

2

Schnitt A - A   Schnitt B - B

3

4

1 ELEMENTE
DES SYSTEMS.
2 ANSICHT.
3 SCHNITT.
4 STATION IN
HANNOVER-OTZE.
5 AUSBILDUNG
DES DACHRANDES.
1 SYSTEM
ELEMENTS.
2 ELEVATION.
3 SECTION.
4 STATION IN
HANOVER-OTZE.
5 ROOF EDGE
DETAILS.

S-BAHN STATIONEN IN HANNOVER

ENTWURF: Meinhard v. Gerkan, Jürgen Hillmer; 1996
MITARBEITER: Klaus Nolting
BAUHERR: Deutsche Bahn AG
BAUZEIT: 1997 - 1998, derzeit gibt es 7 Dächer
GRUNDFLÄCHE: 9 x 9 m

Die S-Bahn-Haltestelle soll in unterschiedlichen Situationen angewendet werden können. Deshalb wurde eine quadratische Grundform gewählt, die ungerichtet ist und den Zugang von verschiedenen Seiten ermöglicht. Die Haltestelle selbst ist durch ein 9 x 9 m großes Flachdach definiert, das auf vier aufgelösten Kreuzstützen im Achsabstand von 5,10 m ruht. Das Dach wird mit einem für die Deutsche Bahn AG entwickelten Wellblech gedeckt, das einen leicht geschwungenen, „beschwingten" Kragen ergibt. Im Bereich der Stützen ist das Dach verglast. Die Beleuchtung fällt aus den in Stützenachsen angeordneten Downlights auf das darunter anzuordnende Mobiliar. Durch einen im Bereich der Blechkrempe helleren Bodenbelag wird das Licht an das Wellblech gelenkt, um auch nachts die geschwungene Form erlebbar zu machen.

The S-Bahn stop is to be used in different "scenarios". That is why the architects chose a basic square form that is undirectional and allows access from all sides. The platform area is covered by a 9x9-metre flat roof which rests on four broken-down supports, cruciform in plan, at unit-spacing intervals of 5.10 m. The roof is covered with corrugated sheet metal that was specially developed for the Deutsche Bahn corporation. This forms a slightly curved, "sprightly collar" for the station. The platform area is lit by means of downlights aligned between the roof supports. The platform edges are covered with a lighter-colour flooring so that they reflect light up to the metal-sheeting underside of the upward-curving roof edge, thus literally highlighting their "uplifting" shape at night.

FLUGHAFEN TENERIFFA

WETTBEWERB: 1997
ENTWURF: Meinhard v. Gerkan
MITARBEITER: Klaus Lenz,
Nicolai Pix, Maren Lucht

Der Entwurf stellt eine architektonische Einheit dar, die dem Flughafen von Teneriffa einen unverwechselbaren Charakter verleiht. Das Wechselspiel der konvexen Formen des Hauptterminals mit der konkaven Anordnung der Nebenterminals unterstreicht die Bedeutung des zentralen Gebäudeteils und optimiert die Stellplätze der Flugzeuge. Die Anordnung der aus Bögen und geraden Linien bestehenden Ebenen vermittelt den an- und abreisenden Fluggästen den Eindruck eines großzügig dimensionierten Raumes und einfacher Orientierbarkeit.
Die Form des Dachtragwerks der zentralen Halle ist symbolischer Ausdruck der Leichtigkeit des Fliegens. Die bautechnisch und gestalterisch einzigartigen „Segel", die sich wie großflächige Leinwände weiträumig ausbreiten, überdecken jeden der zentral gelegenen Räume und erzeugen den Eindruck einer lichtdurchfluteten Weite. Ihre Form entsteht durch das Zusammenspiel der längsgerichteten Gewölbe mit glatten, quer verlaufenden Flächen.

The design resembles an architectural unity, which lends an unmistakable character to the Tenerife airport. The interplay of the convex form of the main terminal and the concave order of the secondary terminals reinforces the significance of the central building and optimizes the aeroplane parking area. The sequence of curved and linear levels allows passengers arriving and departing the impression of a generous spatial proportion and a clear orientation.
The roof form of the main hall is a symbolic expression of the weightlessness of flying. Unique for their construction and design, the "sails" extend like large screens across the centrally located areas, creating the impression of a light-flooded expanse. The form is derived from the combination of longitudinal vaults and smooth cross-sectional surfaces.

SATELLITENTERMINAL
IM MODELL.
MODEL OF SATELLITE
TERMINAL.

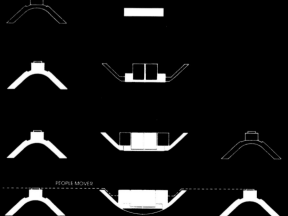

PEOPLE MOVER

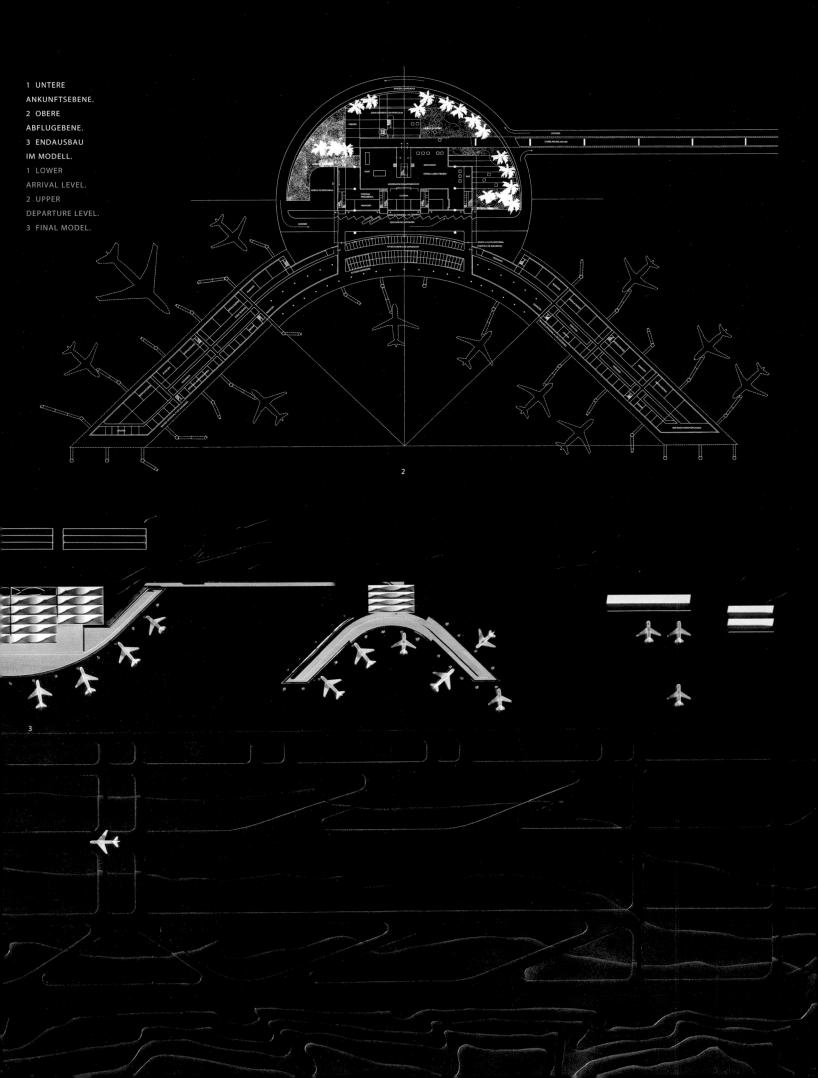

1 UNTERE
ANKUNFTSEBENE.
2 OBERE
ABFLUGEBENE.
3 ENDAUSBAU
IM MODELL.
1 LOWER
ARRIVAL LEVEL.
2 UPPER
DEPARTURE LEVEL.
3 FINAL MODEL.

2

3

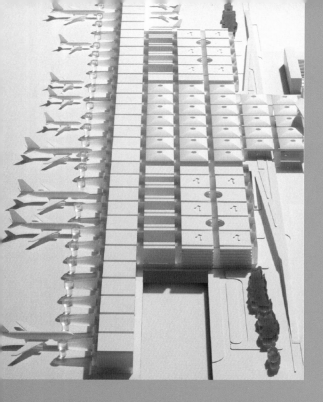

FLUGHAFEN
MÜNCHEN
TERMINAL 2

WETTBEWERB: 1998 - Ankauf
ENTWURF: Meinhard v. Gerkan
mit Klaus Lenz
MITARBEITER: Nicolai Pix, Sigrid
Müller, Ralf Schmitz, Bettina Groß,
Philipp Kamps, Eva Wtorczyk,
Anne-Kathrin Rose

Der bestehende Flughafen ist in
formaler Hinsicht eine geschlossene
Anlage, der keine weitere eigen-
willige Architektursprache hinzutre-
ten sollte. Deshalb und wegen der
Offenhaltung für zukünftige Verän-
derungen wird ein modulares
System für eine Addition von „Bausteinen" vorgeschlagen, die man
je nach Bedarf weglassen, hinzufü-
gen oder austauschen kann - eine
Ordnungsstruktur, die Wachstum und
Anpassung flexibel ermöglicht. Dieses modulare System schafft ein neu-
trales Strukturgerüst, in dem nur die
Primärfunktionen vorgegeben werden.
Der gesamte Ausbau einschließlich
Fassaden und Dachabschluß wird
nach Bedarf implantiert: ein „Baukasten", bei dem nicht die Form die
Nutzung festlegt, sondern diese sich
im Strukturgerüst „einrichtet".

Formally, the existing airport
is a self-contained complex, which
should not be extended with an
unconventional type of architecture.
Due to this and a permanent flexibility, a modular system of additional
elements has been suggested.
These can be omitted, introduced
or exchanged - a structural principle
allowing for flexible growth and
adaption. This modular system
creates a framework, in which only
primary functions are pre-defined.
The completion including facade
and roof works will be integrated in
accordance with demand: A unit
construction system, where form
does not define use, but use
implements itself in the structural
framework.

1+2 DAS MODELL
VERDEUTLICHT
DIE MODULARE
STRUKTUR DES
ENTWURFES.
3 DIE KONSTRUK-
TIVE STRUKTUR DER
MODULAREN ELE-
MENTE PRÄGT DEN
RAUMCHARAKTER
DES FLUGGASTPIERS.

1+2 THE MODEL
ILLUSTRATES THE
MODULAR
STRUCTURE OF THE
CONCEPT.
3 THE CONSTRUC-
TION OF THE MODULAR
ELEMENTS CHARAC-
TERIZES THE SPATIAL
APPEARANCE OF THE
PASSENGER PIER.

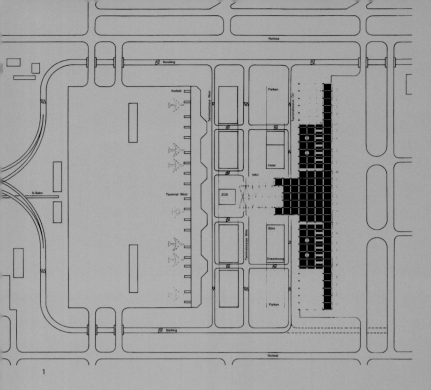

1

2

3

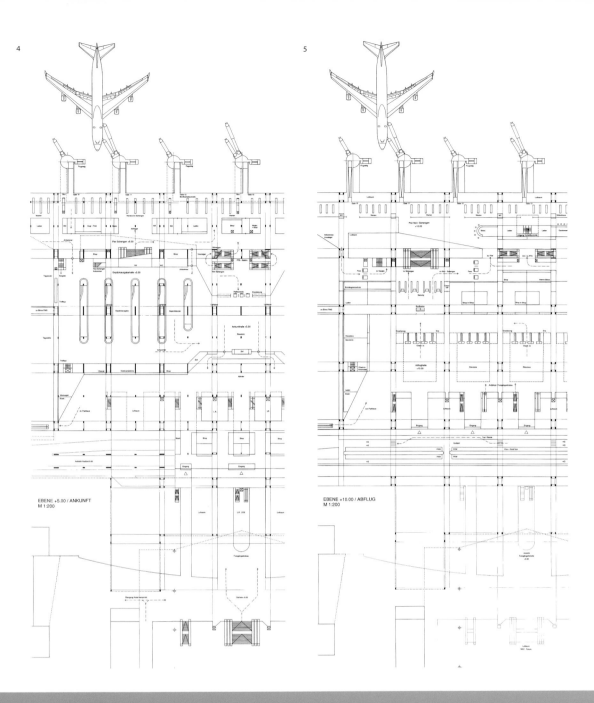

4

5

1 LAGEPLAN.
2 AUSBAUSTUFEN.
3 BLICK IN DIE AB-
FERTIGUNGSHALLE.
4 UNTERE
ANKUNFTSEBENE.
5 OBERE
ABFLUGEBENE.
6 QUERSCHNITT MIT
ANSCHLIESSENDEM
DACH DES MÜNCHEN
AIRPORT CENTER.

1 SITE PLAN.
2 COMPLETION
PHASES.
3 VIEW INTO
DEPARTURE HALL.
4 LOWER
ARRIVAL LEVEL.
5 UPPER
DEPARTURE LEVEL.
6 CROSS SECTION
WITH ADJACENT
ROOF OF MUNICH
AIRPORT CENTRE.

EBENE +5.00 / ANKUNFT
M 1:200

EBENE +10.00 / ABFLUG
M 1:200

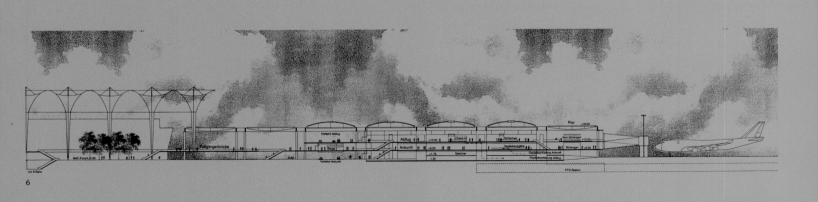

6

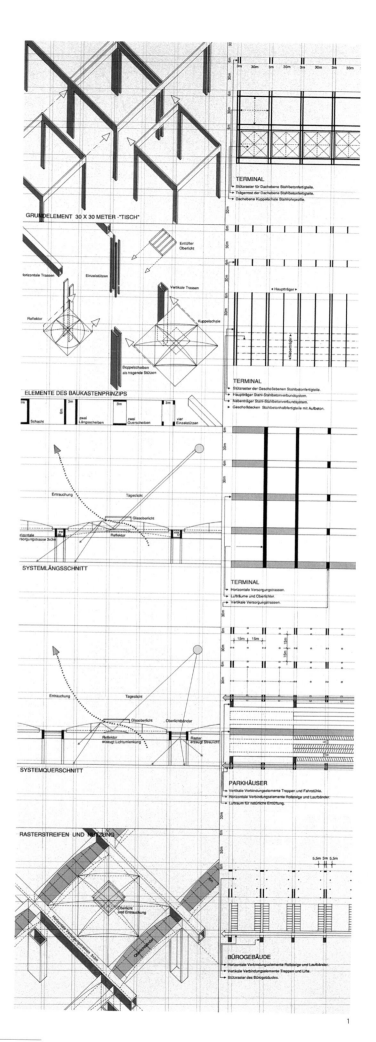

GRUNDELEMENT 30 X 30 METER -"TISCH"

Horizontale Trassen   Einzelstützen

Reflektor

Vertikale Trassen

Kuppelschale

Doppelscheiben
als tragende Stützen

ELEMENTE DES BAUKASTENPRINZIPS

1m   3m   3m   3m

6m

Schacht   zwei
Längsscheiben   zwei
Querscheiben   vier
Einzelstützen

Entrauchung   Tageslicht

Glasoberlicht

Horizontale
Versorgungstrasse 3x3m   Reflektor

SYSTEMLÄNGSSCHNITT

Entrauchung   Tageslicht

Glasoberlicht   Oberlichtbänder

Reflektor
erzeugt Lichtumlenkung   Raster
erzeugt Streulicht

SYSTEMQUERSCHNITT

RASTERSTREIFEN UND NUTZUNG

Oberlichte
und Entrauchung

Horizontale Versorgungstrasse 3x3m

3m

TERMINAL
→ Stützraster für Dachebene Stahlbetonfertigteile.
→ Trägerrost der Dachebene Stahlbetonfertigteile.
→ Dachebene Kuppelschale Stahlrohrprofile.

Entlüfter
Oberlicht

◄ Hauptträger ►

◄ Nebenträger ►

TERMINAL
→ Stützraster der Geschoßebenen Stahlbetonfertigteile.
→ Hauptträger Stahl-Stahlbetonverbundsystem.
→ Nebenträger Stahl-Stahlbetonverbundsystem.
→ Geschoßdecken Stahlbetonhalbfertigteile mit Aufbeton.

TERMINAL
→ Horizontale Versorgungstrassen.
→ Lufträume und Oberlichter.
→ Vertikale Versorgungstrassen.

15m   15m

15m

15m

PARKHÄUSER
→ Vertikale Verbindungselemente Treppen und Fahrstühle.
→ Horizontale Verbindungselemente Rollsteige und Laufbänder.
→ Luftraum für natürliche Entlüftung.

5,5m 3m 5,5m

BÜROGEBÄUDE
→ Horizontale Verbindungselemente Rollsteige und Laufbänder.
→ Vertikale Verbindungselemente Treppen und Lifte.
→ Stützraster des Bürogebäudes.

1 DARSTELLUNGEN
ZUR STRUKTURELLEN
FÜGUNG DES MODU-
LAREN SYSTEMS.
2+3 MODELLSTUDIEN
ZUR TRAGSTRUKTUR
DES DACHES.
1 ILLUSTRATIONS OF
STRUCTURAL ARRANGE-
MENT OF THE
MODULAR SYSTEM.
2+3 MODEL STUDIES
OF SUPPORTING
ROOF STRUCTURE.

1

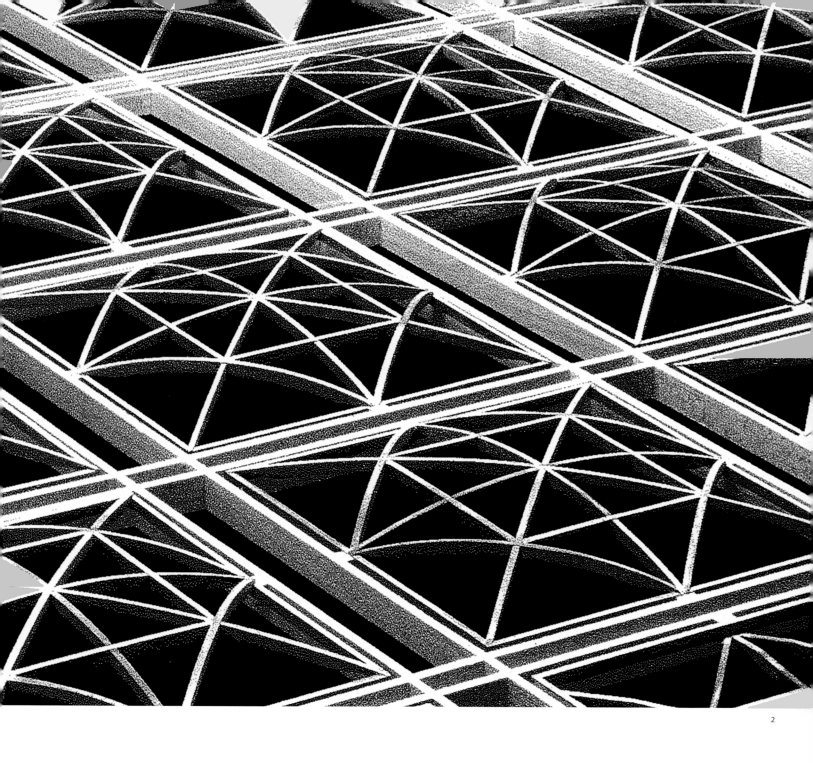

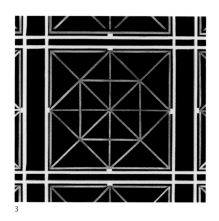

FLUGHAFEN STUTTGART TERMINAL 3

WETTBEWERB: 1998 - 1. Preis
ENTWURF: Meinhard v. Gerkan
MITARBEITER: Klaus Lenz,
Sigrid Müller, Stephan Rewolle,
Oliver Christ, Hito Ueda,
Volkmar Sievers, Otto Dorn
BAUHERR: Flughafen Stuttgart GmbH
BAUZEIT: 2000 - 2004
BGF: 53.300 m²
BRI: 384.300 m³

Baumstützen und der deichartige Gebäuderiegel sind unverwechselbare Elemente, die auch bei der Erweiterung beibehalten werden sollen. Die Begrenzung der Bauhöhe zugunsten der Luftsicherheit ließ jedoch die Fortführung der Firstlinie nicht zu. Die „Dachschirme" der einzelnen Stützen reagieren durch shedartige Staffelung auf diese Bedingung. Die gewünschte größere Gebäudetiefe wird durch einen flachen, dem Hauptbaukörper vorgelagerten Baukörper erreicht. Auf der Landseite schließt sich die Traufkante des Pultdaches zu einer einheitlichen Vorfahrtüberdachung von 260 m Länge.

Tree-like columns and the dike-formed building section are characteristic elements, which are to be maintained during the extension. The restrictive building height in favour of air safety, prohibits the continuation of the existing roof level. The "roof umbrellas" of the single columns correspond to this pre-condition with a gradual descent. The requested increased building depth is achieved by a flat bar in front of the main building. On the street side, a 260 m long entrance canopy connects to the main roof structure.

1+2 DIE VON BAUMSTÜTZEN GETRAGENEN DACHFLÄCHEN WERDEN BEI DER ERWEITERUNG SHEDARTIG ABGESTAFFELT, UM DIE LIMITIERTE BAUHÖHE ZU RESPEKTIEREN.
3 KONTINUITÄT DER DACHSTRUKTUR VON TERMINAL 1 UND 3.
4 QUERSCHNITT.
5 KONSTRUKTIVE STRUKTUR DER DACHFLÄCHE.

1+2 AFTER THE EXTENSION ROOF AREAS WILL BE SUPPORTED BY TREE-LIKE STRUCTURES AND GRADUALLY STEP DOWN IN ORDER TO RESPECT THE RESTRICTED BUILDING HEIGHT.
3 CONTINUATION OF THE ROOF STRUCTURE FROM TERMINAL 1 AND 3.
4 CROSS SECTION.
5 ROOF CONSTRUCTION.

1

3

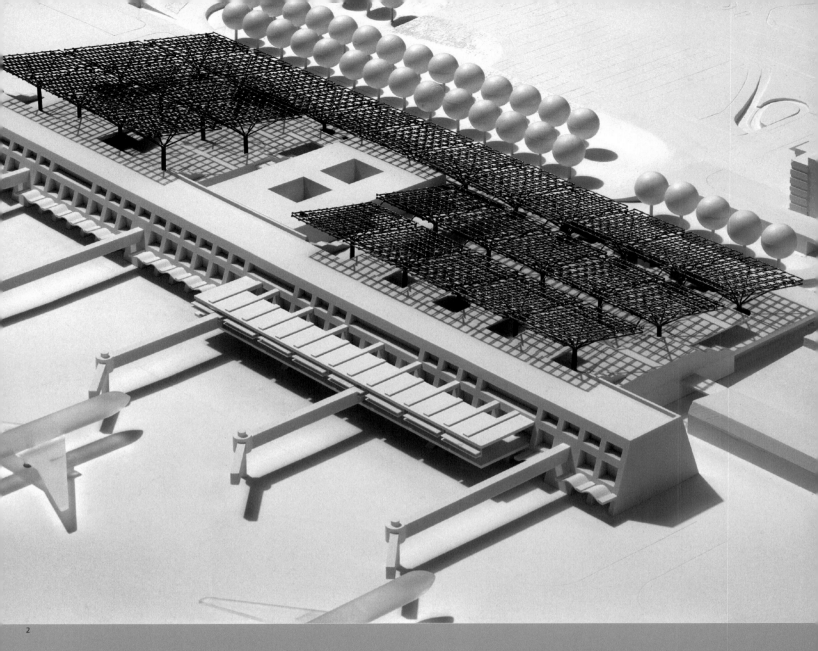

2

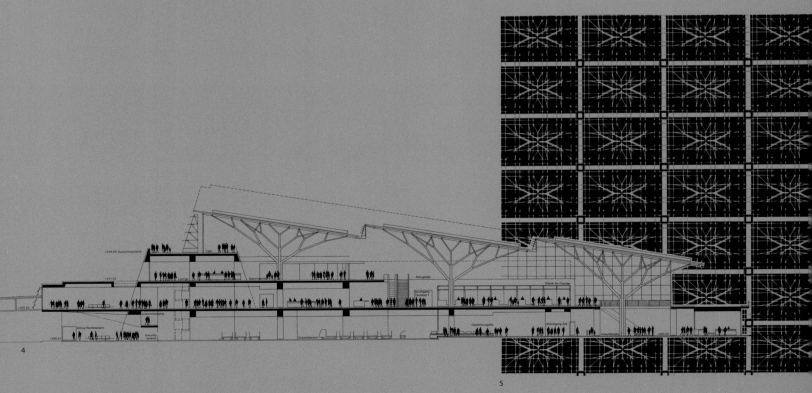

4

5

FLUGHAFEN BERLIN BRANDENBURG INTERNATIONAL

WETTBEWERB: 1998 - 1. Preis
ENTWURF: Meinhard v. Gerkan,
Hubert Nienhoff, Joachim Zais mit
Hans-Joachim Paap
MITARBEITER: Alexander Buchhofer,
Carsten Borucki, Christian Eling,
Stefan Friedrichs, Marc Gatzweiler,
Anne Harnischfeger, Sven-Eric Korff,
Jörn Orthmann, Nicolas Pomränke,
Cornelia Thamm, Olaf Timm,
Monika van Vught, Gabriele Wisocky

2

Das Konzept basiert auf der Erkenntnis, daß ein Flughafen immer „Prozeß" und niemals „Zustand" ist. Deswegen galt es, einen robusten Rahmen für Erweiterungen in der Zukunft zu entwickeln, der zugleich genügend Freiraum läßt für die Vielfalt des Einzelnen, um auf diese Weise ein Gesamtkonzept über viele Jahre zu bewahren. Wachstum und Veränderung haben einen gleich hohen Stellenwert gegenüber einem funktionsfähigen Erstzustand. Das Konzept des neuen Flughafens für die deutsche Hauptstadt sieht eine Mittelachse des parallelen Start- und Landebahnsystems in Ost-West-Richtung als „Rückgrat" der Anlage vor. Sie ordnet die Haupterschließungselemente. Die Organisation von An- und Abflug findet in einem Zentralterminal mit einer zweiten, vorgelagerten Pier statt. Als Verbindung ist eine Passagierbrücke vorgesehen, unter der die Flugzeuge hindurchfahren - diese Attraktion, eine Weltneuheit, wird zum Wahrzeichen

des neuen Flughafens: während man auf Rollsteigen zum Abflug fährt, hat man bereits den Blick auf das Rollfeld.
Ein modulares System setzt den gesamten Komplex aus Segmenten zusammen, die je nach Erfordernis hinzugefügt werden können. Das Hauptterminal ist in zwei Ebenen geteilt, so daß auf der Landseite eine Trennung von Ankunft und Abflug erfolgt. Das Abfluggeschoß als Hauptebene ist als großzügige, lichtdurchflutete Halle konzipiert, die mit einer filigranen Stahl-Glas-Konstruktion überspannt wird. Auf der Landseite sind, seitlich flankierend, Parkhäuser vorgesehen, die über wettergeschützte Wege und Rollsteige mit dem Terminal verbunden sind. Das unmittelbare Vorfeld der Vorfahrt ist jedoch als Grünfläche gestaltet. Zusätzlich werden in der ersten Ausbaustufe ebenerdige Parkplätze in Terminalnähe angeboten, die mit einen Bus-Shuttle bedient werden.

The concept is based on the recognition that an airport must be perceived as a "process" and never a fixed state. For this reason it was necessary to create a robust frame for future extensions which would simultaneously leave enough space for the freedom of the individual, whilst maintaining a general strategy into the future. Growth and variation are of equal importance as a fully functioning initial solution. Conceptually the new airport designed for the German capital establishes a middle axis for the parallel start and landing strips orientated East-West, as a major "spine" element within the new facility. This defines the main circulation elements.
The organisation of arrival and departure lounges takes place in a centralized terminal with a second "off-shore" pier. A passenger bridge forms the connection under which aeroplanes taxi. Being a novel structure, the bridge is the

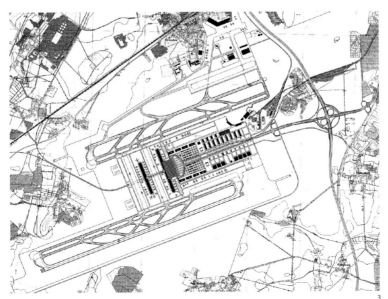

1 DER SKYWALK
VERBINDET DEN
HAUPTTERMINAL
MIT DEM SATELLITEN.
2 GENERALAUSBAU
IM MODELL.
3 GENERALAUSBAU-
PLAN.
1 THE SKYWALK
LINKS THE MAIN
TERMINAL WITH THE
SATELLITS.
2 MODEL OF GENE-
RAL INTERIOR WORK.
3 PLAN OF GENERAL
INTERIOR WORK.

1

3

1

most distinctive element of the
new airport. When taking the travel-
ator to the departure area one
already has a view onto the runway.
A modular system, created from
segments which can be added on
demand, embraces the whole
complex. The main terminal is subdivided into two levels so that on
the land side a seperation of arriv-
als and departures is achieved. The
departure area forming the main
level has been created as a generous light filled hall which is to be
covered by a filigree steel-glass-
structure. On the land side flanking
multi-storey car parks are planned
which are to be connected to the
terminal with sheltered walkways
and travelators. The immediate
forefield to the apron is designated
as a green area. The first phase parking spaces located at street level
are in close proximity to the terminal and served by a shuttle bus
link.

2

1 VORFAHRT
UNTER DEM AUS-
KRAGENDEN DACH.
2 DER SKYWALK
ÜBERBRÜCKT MIT
300 M SPANNWEITE
DAS VORFELD UND
DIE ROLLWEGE DER
FLUGZEUGE.
3 ABFLUGHALLE MIT
BLICK AUFS VORFELD.
1 DROP-OFF ZONE
BENEATH THE CANTI-
LEVERED CANOPY.
2 THE SKYWALK
BRIDGES THE
APRON AND THE
RUNWAYS WITH
ITS 300 M SPAN.
3 DEPARTURE HALL
WITH VIEW
ONTO THE APRON.

3

1

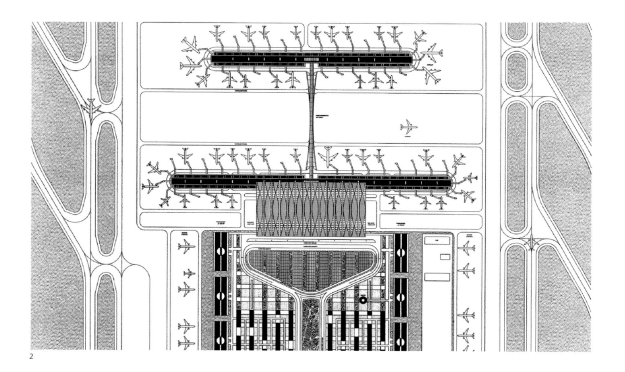

2

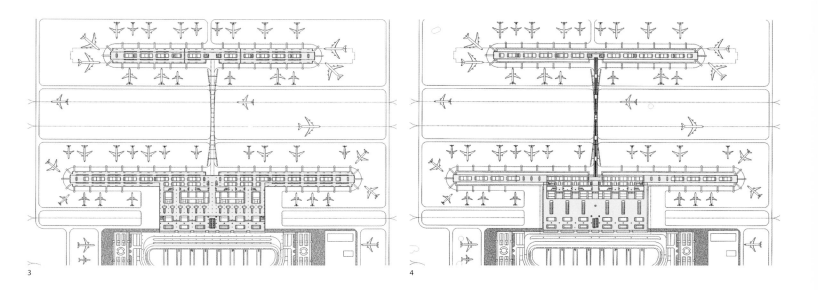

3

4

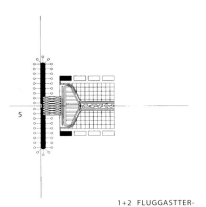

5

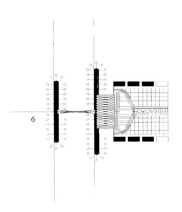

6

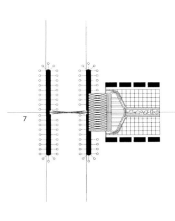

7

1+2 FLUGGASTTER-
MINAL IN DER ZWEI-
TEN AUSBAUSTUFE.
DIE VORFAHRT WIRD
SEITLICH VON PARK-
HÄUSERN FLANKIERT.
3 UNTERE
ANKUNFTSEBENE.
4 OBERE
ABFLUGEBENE.
5-7 AUSBAUSTUFEN.
1+2 SECOND
COMPLETION PHASE
OF THE PASSENGER
TERMINAL. THE
DROP-OFF ZONE IS
FLANKED BY MULTI-
STOREY CAR PARKS.
3 LOWER
ARRIVAL LEVEL.
4 UPPER
DEPARTURE LEVEL.
5-7 COMPLETION
PHASES.

1

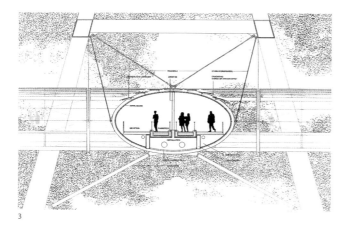

2

3

1 LÄNGSSCHNITT.
2+3 DER SKYWALK
HÄNGT ALS GLAS-
RÖHRE IN EINER
GROSSEN BOGEN-
KONSTRUKTION.
4 DER BLICK VOM
SKYWALK AUF DAS
VORFELD ENTSCHÄ-
DIGT FÜR DEN
LANGEN WEG ÜBER
ROLLSTEIGE ZUM
SATELLITEN. EINE
WELTNEUHEIT IM
GEGENSATZ ZU DEN
ÜBLICHEN TUNNEL-
VERBINDUNGEN.

1 LONGITUDINAL
SECTION.
2+3 THE SKYWALK
IS SUSPENDED AS
A GLASS TUBE IN
A LARGE ARCHED
STRUCTURE.
4 THE VIEW FROM
THE SKYWALK COM-
PENSATES FOR LONG
DISTANCES VIA TRAV-
ELATORS TO THE
SATELLITE.
A WORLD FIRST IN
CONTRAST TO THE
STANDARD TUNNEL
CONNECTION.

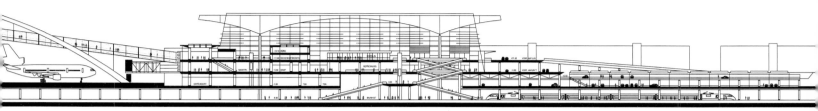

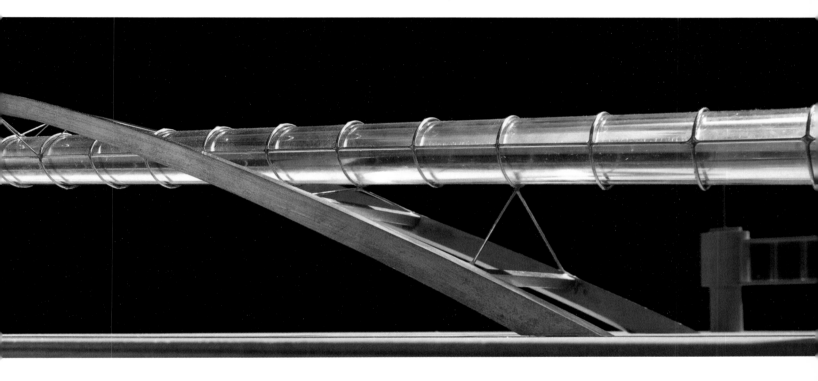

4

1

FALTBRÜCKE KIEL-HÖRN

GUTACHTEN: 1994
ENTWURF: Volkwin Marg mit
Jörg Schlaich
MITARBEITER: Reiner Schröder,
Hito Ueda, Anne-Kathrin Rose,
Dirk Vollrath in ARGE mit Schlaich,
Bergermann und Partner,
Jan Knippers
BAUHERR: Magistrat der Stadt Kiel
BAUZEIT: 1996 - 1997
LÄNGE: 116 m, davon ca. 25 m als
Faltbrücke gebildet
BREITE: 6 m

Der ehemalige Werftstandort am
Ostufer der Hörn, unmittelbar gegenüber von Innenstadt und Hauptbahnhof, wird in einem städtebaulichen
„Jahrhundertprojekt" saniert und zu
einem neuen Quartier aus Wohnen,
Büro und Gewerbe umgenutzt. Als
Teil davon wird der Stadtteil Gaarden
mit einer beweglichen Brücke über
die Hörn an die Innenstadt angebunden. Zweifeld-Klappbrücken gehören
heute im Schiffsbau zum technischen
Standard; als Zeichen von Innovation
wirkt deren weltweit neue Weiter-
entwicklung zu einer „Dreifeld-Klappbrücke" als kunstvolles, maritimes
Zeichen für die Bürger. Architektur,
Ingenieurbau und kinetische Kunst
gehen eine neue, sinnfällige und
gleichzeitig nutzbare Verbindung ein.

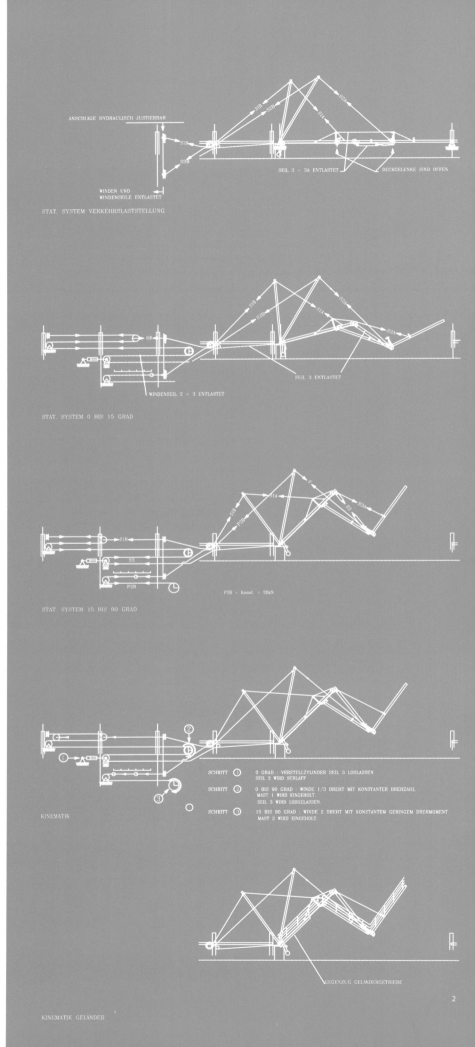

2

1 DIE BRÜCKE WIRD
AUFGEFAHREN.
2 PHASEN DES
MECHANISCH ANGE-
TRIEBENEN FALT-
VORGANGES.
3-6 DURCH FARBGE-
BUNG WIRD DIE
MECHANIK DER
EINZELNEN TEILE
SICHTBAR.

1 THE BRIDGE IS
FOLDED.
2 PHASES OF THE
MECHANICALLY
PROPELLED FOLDING
PROCESS.
3-6 COLOURING
VISUALIZES THE
MECHANICS OF
SINGLE ELEMENTS.

3

4

5

6

The former dockyard location on the eastern shore of the Hoern is set immediately opposite the city centre and the main railway station. The area will be regenerated as a "millenium project" and transformed into a new area for housing, offices and commerce. As a part of this new area Gaarden will be connected to the city centre by a new flexible bridge over the Hoern. The double element bascule or folding bridge is a common technical feature of the ship building industry. This new further development of a three element bridge creates a strong maritime inspired symbol for the citizens of the city. Architecture, Engineering and kinetic Art enter into a new, striking and simultaneously effective fusion.

1　　　　2　　　　3

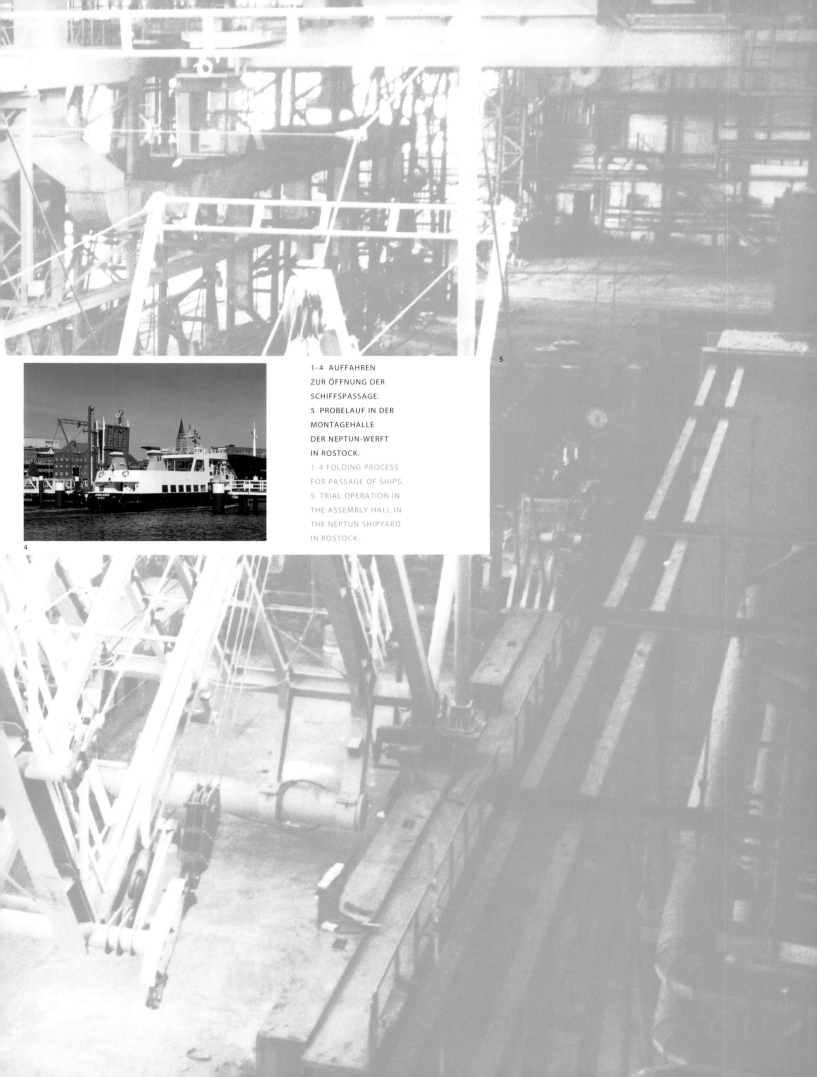

1-4 AUFFAHREN
ZUR ÖFFNUNG DER
SCHIFFSPASSAGE.
5 PROBELAUF IN DER
MONTAGEHALLE
DER NEPTUN-WERFT
IN ROSTOCK.
1-4 FOLDING PROCESS
FOR PASSAGE OF SHIPS.
5 TRIAL OPERATION IN
THE ASSEMBLY HALL IN
THE NEPTUN SHIPYARD
IN ROSTOCK.

4

5

EISENBAHN-BRÜCKE ÜBER DIE HAVEL, BERLIN-SPANDAU

ENTWURF: Jörg Schlaich mit Meinhard v. Gerkan; 1994
KONSTRUKTION: Schlaich, Bergermann und Partner
AUSFÜHRUNGSPLANUNG: Arbeitsgemeinschaft Havelbrücke Spandau
AUSFÜHRUNG DER ÜBERBAUTEN: Krupp Stahlbau Berlin GmbH
BAUHERR: Deutsche Bahn AG

BAUZEIT: 1996 - 1997
LÄNGE: 124,2 m
BREITE: 47,5 m

In Berlin-Spandau wurden im Zuge des Ausbaus der West-Ost-Verbindungen und speziell der Bundesbahnstrecke Hannover-Berlin für den ICE-Verkehr sieben Gleise über die Havel geführt. Die Planungen der Bahn sahen eine weitgehend genormte, unabhängig vom jeweiligen Ort verwendete Bogenbrücke vor, die nicht nur recht unglücklich proportioniert war, sondern auch die Stadtgestalt Spandaus empfindlich gestört hätte. Als Gegenstück wurde in intensiver Zusammenarbeit von Ingenieur und Architekt eine Eisenbahnbrücke entwickelt, die ihre Doppelschwingung durch den Verlauf an den jeweiligen Enden eingespannter Seile herleitet. Die markante Wellenform der drei stählernen Trogbrücken ergibt sich dabei aus einer dem Schnittkraftverlauf folgenden Querschnittshöhe.

Parallel to the development of East-West connections and especially with the extension of the railway link Hannover-Berlin for the InterCityExpress service, seven train tracks have been built across the River Havel. German Rail's concept was to employ a largely standardized arch bridge construction, which was badly proportioned and would have severely disturbed the urban context of Spandau. Contrary to this, an intense working co-operation between engineer and architect produced a classic suspension bridge, its form derived from a tensile cable structure mounted on both ends. The salient wave form

of the three trough bridges results
from the section height, consider-
ing the course of the static forces.

1 SECHS PARALLELE
TRÄGER SORGEN
FÜR DIE KONSTRUK-
TIVE TRENNUNG
DER BRÜCKEN.
2 DAS KONSTRUKTIVE
PRINZIP IST ENTGE-
GENGESETZT ZU EI-
NER BOGEN-BRÜCKE.
DER OBERGURT IST
ZUGBEANSPRUCHT.
DESWEGEN LIEGT DIE
GRÖSSTE HÖHE ÜBER
DEM AUFLAGER UND
NICHT IN DER MITTE
DER BRÜCKE. DAMIT
BLEIBT DER BLICK
ÜBER DEM STROM
UNGESTÖRT.

1 SIX PARALLEL
BEAMS ALLOW FOR
THE CONSTRUCTIVE
DIVISION OF
THE BRIDGE.
2 THE CONSTRUCTIVE
PRINCIPLE IS CON-
TRARY TO THAT OF
AN ARCHED BRIDGE.
THE TOP CHORD IS
TENSIONED, THERE-
FORE THE TALLEST
POINT IS HIGHER
THAN THE SUPPORT
AND NOT POSITIONED
CENTRALLY, THE
VIEW ONTO THE RIVER
REMAINS CLEAR.

1

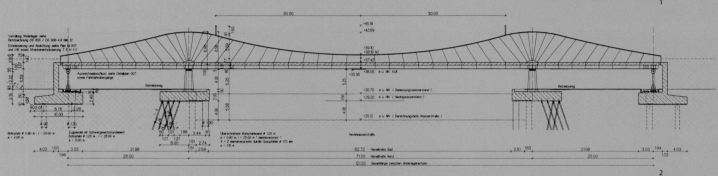

1

BRÜCKE ÜBER DIE WUBLITZ, POTSDAM

WETTBEWERB: 1997
ENTWURF: Meinhard v. Gerkan
mit Gregor Hoheisel

Aus Anlaß der Bundesgartenschau
im Jahre 2001 soll Potsdam mit dem
Umland zu einer „Kulturlandschaft
des Potsdamer Wald- und Havelseen-
gebietes" verbunden werden. Als erstes, symbolträchtiges Projekt verbindet eine Brücke über die Wublitz die
Inseln Potsdam und Töplitz.
Ein Durchlaufträger bildet mit seiner
Fachwerkkonstruktion den Brückenschlag und das mit Holzlamellen ver-
kleidete Geländer. Aus dem Wasser
aufragende Holzstelen markieren den
Weg und setzen die Baumallee mit
strukturellen Mitteln fort.
On the occasion of the Federal
Garden Show, in the year 2001,
Potsdam is to be linked with a
"cultivated landscape of the Potsdam forests and Havel lakes area".
As a first iconic project, this bridge
across the Wublitz makes the
connection between the Potsdam
and Töplitz islands.
A continuous lattice beam is used
to form both the main bridge
structure and the railing, which is
clad with wooden slats. Wooden
poles rise up out of the water,
marking the path and continuing
the tree-lined road in architectural
structure.

2

1+2 DIE LEUCHT-
STELEN DER BRÜCKE
BEGLEITEN DEN WEG
ANALOG ZU DEN
PAPPELN EINER ALLEE.
3 SCHNITT UND
ANSICHT.
1+2 THE ILLUMINATED
BRIDGE COLUMNS
FRAME THE PATH
LIKE POPLARS ON
AN AVENUE.
3 SECTION UND
ELEVATION.

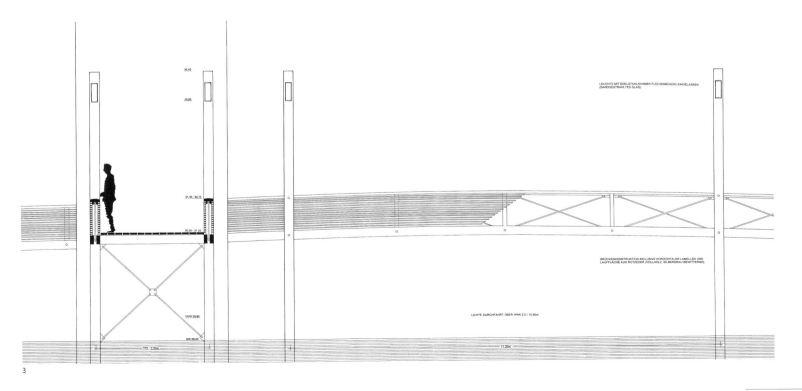

3

INNENGESTALTUNG TRANSRAPID

WETTBEWERB: 1997
ENTWURF: Meinhard v. Gerkan, Jürgen Hillmer
MITARBEITER: Renata Dipper, Stefan Bachmann, Thilo Jacobsen

Die Magnetschnellbahn steht für eine neue Technologie im Schienenverkehr. Sie muß sich durch eine adäquate, im Großen wie im Kleinen nachvollziehbare gestalterische

The magnetic railway represents a new technology for rail-bound traffic, which must be interpreted in a concise design concept, understandable at all levels of detail. Progress, speed and comfort are reflected in a few, but essential design principles, which can be summarized by the motto "unity of the whole - variety in detail". The Transrapid is conceived as a continuous, uniform entity. The dynamic image of the envelope is continued internally with a horizontal emphasis of the longitudinal window arrangement.

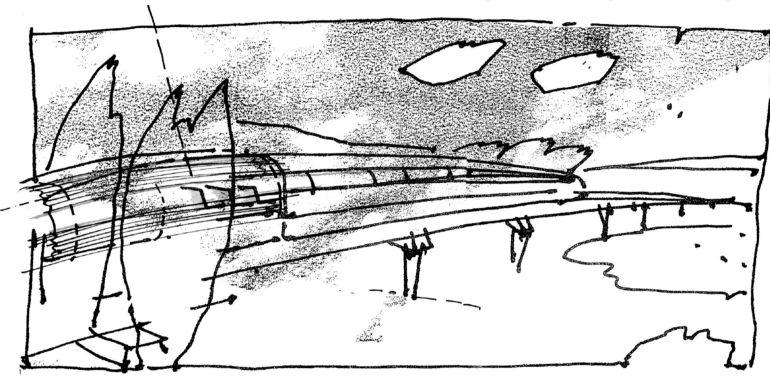

Gesamtkonzeption darstellen. Fortschritt, Schnelligkeit und Komfort spiegeln sich in wenigen, aber wesentlichen Grundsätzen der Gestaltung wider, die unter dem Schlagwort „Einheit des Ganzen - Mannigfaltigkeit des Einzelnen" gefaßt werden können. Der Transrapid wird als ein durchgängiges, formal einheitliches Ganzes gestaltet. Der dynamische Eindruck der Außenhülle setzt sich durch die horizontale Akzentuierung des durchlaufenden Fensterbandes auch im Innenraum fort. Eine lineare Gliederung der Großraum- und Gangzonen in Längsrichtung verstärkt diesen Eindruck. Natürliche Materialien wie Glas, Metall, Naturholz und Echtleder werden bevorzugt, die eine natürliche und zugleich noble Atmosphäre vermitteln sollen. Farben werden nur sparsam als Identitätskomponente eingesetzt. Natürliches und künstliches Licht unterstützen die zeitlose gestalterische Präsenz.

The linear sequence of seating and corridor areas follows this principle. Materials such as glass, metal, wood and leather are used in the detailing, which render an atmosphere both natural and elegant. Colour is scarcely used, only as a component for identification. Natural and artificial light support the timeless design.

2

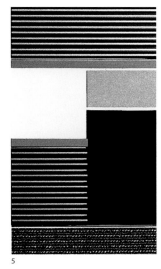

1 SKIZZE.

2 INNENRAUM-
PERSPEKTIVE.

3 GRUNDRISS.

4 LÄNGSSCHNITT.

5 MATERIAL-
COLLAGE.

6 QUERSCHNITT.

1 SKETCH.

2 PERSPECTIVE OF
THE INTERIOR.

3 PLAN.

4 LONGITUDINAL
SECTION.

5 MATERIAL
COLLAGE.

6 CROSS SECTION.

5

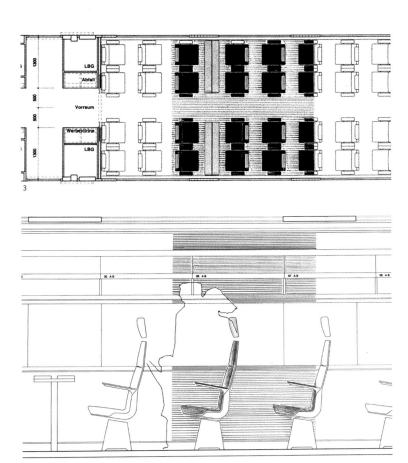

3

4

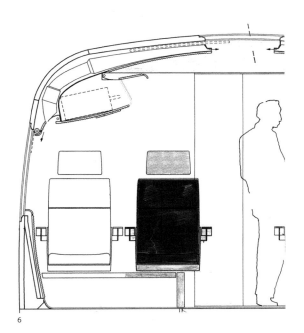

6

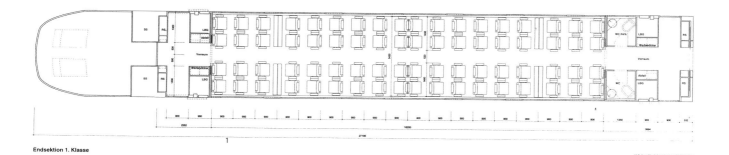

Endsektion 1. Klasse

18 Reihen / 2 + 2 Anordnung = 72 Sitzplätze

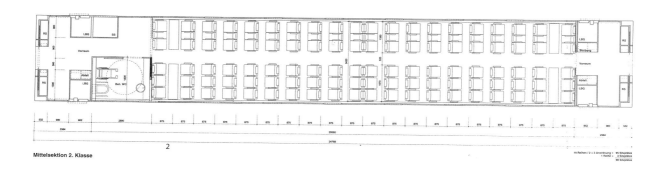

Mittelsektion 2. Klasse

19 Reihen / 2 + 3 Anordnung = 95 Sitzplätze
1 Reihe = 3 Sitzplätze
98 Sitzplätze

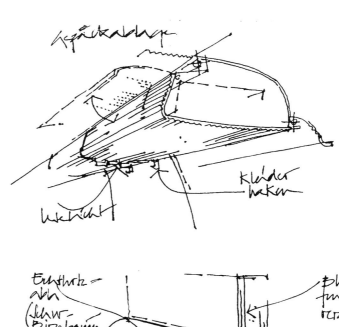

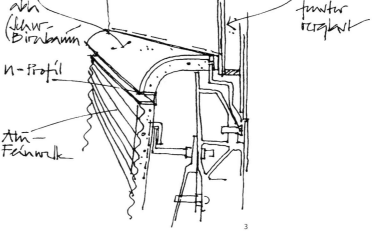

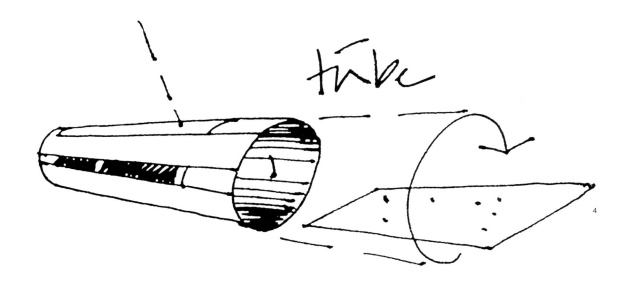

tube

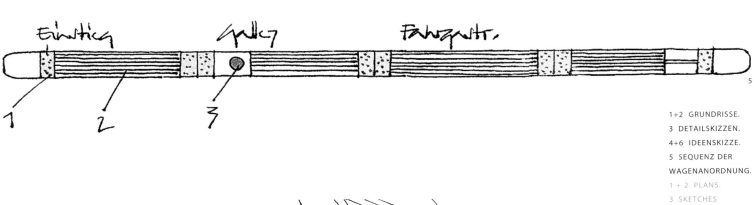

Einstieg   galley   Fahrzentr.

1

2

3

5

1+2 GRUNDRISSE.
3 DETAILSKIZZEN.
4+6 IDEENSKIZZE.
5 SEQUENZ DER
WAGENANORDNUNG.
1 + 2 PLANS.
3 SKETCHES
OF DETAILS.
4 + 6 CONCEPT
SKETCH.
5 SEQUENCE
OF CARRIAGES.

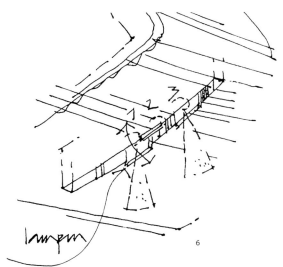

lampen

6

INTERIEUR
METROPOLITAN
EXPRESS TRAIN

WETTBEWERB: 1996 - 1. Preis
ENTWURF: Meinhard v. Gerkan, Jürgen Hillmer
PROJEKTLEITUNG: Renata Dipper, Birgit Föllmer
MITARBEITER: Susan Krause, Frank Hülsmeyer, Maja Gorges, Kristina Kaib, Bernd Stehle, Torsten Neeland
LICHTPLANUNG: Conceptlicht GmbH Helmut Angerer
BAUHERR: Deutsche Bahn AG
BAUZEIT: 1998 - 1999

Der "Metropolitan" ist ein neues Zugsystem, das eine Schnellverbindung zwischen zwei Städten mit hohem Reisekomfort und Service anbietet, mit dem Ziel, eine Alternative zum Flugzeug zu bilden. Beim Entwurf kam es also darauf an, ein eigenständiges, unverwechselbares Erscheinungsbild für den Zug zu entwickeln. Innen wie Außen sollten dabei in formaler Hinsicht als durchgängiges Ganzes ablesbar sein. Durch ein Design, das sich von vergleichbaren Produkten wie dem ICE absetzt, wurde eine eigene „Zugidentität" geschaffen:
Der "Metropolitan" ist der „silberne Zug". Der metallische Charakter der Außenhülle steht für Geschwindig- und Hochwertigkeit. Ihr dynamischer Eindruck setzt sich in der horizontalen Gliederung und Akzentuierung des durchlaufenden Fensterbandes bis in den Innenraum fort. Eine klare, lineare Gliederung der Großraum- und Gangzonen verstärkt den Eindruck.
Eine wagenbezogene Zonierung in die drei Bereiche „Office", „Club" und „Silence" bietet dem Reisenden unterschiedliche Nutzungsmöglichkeiten mit spezifischen Angeboten. Durchgängig für alle Wagen gibt es eine 3-er Bestuhlung aus zwei Sitzen auf der einen und einem auf der anderes Seite des Ganges. Alle Wagen haben das gleiche Stuhlmodell, in das ein Klapptisch sowie Schaltvor-

richtungen und Auslaßbuchsen integriert sind.

Wichtiger Bestandteil der Ausstattung ist die Verwendung natürlicher Materialien; Schichtholz, Edelstahl und Leder schaffen eine Atmosphäre des Echten und Vertrauten; zudem altern sie „würdevoller"; Kunststoffe wurden vermieden. Entsprechend ist das Farbkonzept auf die natürliche Beschaffenheit der Materialien mit ihrer je eigenen Nuancierung, Zeichnung und Textur reduziert.

Das Gepäck wird oberhalb des Fensterbandes auf einer Ablage gestaut. In diese sind zusätzlich zur indirekten Beleuchtung punktgerichtete Leseleuchten integriert.

2

The "Metropolitan" is a new train system offering a shuttle connection between two cities, with a high standard of comfort and service, aiming to be an alternative to planes. Therefore the design process concentrated on the creation of an individual identity for the train. The exterior as well as the interior should be perceivable as a stringent unit.

The design, which stands out against comparable products such as the InterCityExpress train, forms an independent "train identity". The "Metropolitan" is the "silver train". The metal character of the envelope represents speed and quality. Its dynamic impression is continued in the interior with horizontal sections and a continuous row of windows. A clear linear structure of seating and aisle zones enhances this impression.

A separation by carriages in the zones "Office", "Club" and "Silence" offers the passenger various forms of utilization with specific functions. All carriages are equipped with rows of two seats on one side and one seat on the opposite side of the aisle. The seats are identical throughout, with integrated folding tables and communication connections.

An important characteristic of the equipment is the use of natural materials: multiplex boards, stainless steel and leather creating a comfortable atmosphere; these materials also age with "grace". Plastics are avoided. Respectively, the colour concept is reduced to the natural texture and nuances of these materials.

Luggage is stored above the windows on a shelf which integrates indirect lighting and reading lamps simultaneously.

3

4

VORHERIGE SEITE: BLICK IN DEN REISEWAGEN. DIE DECKE IST MIT EDELSTAHLGEWEBE VERKLEIDET UND DIENT ALS REFLEXIONSFLÄCHE FÜR DIE INDIREKTE ALLGEMEINBELEUCHTUNG.

1 SITZSCHALEN AUS GEBOGENEN SCHICHTHOLZPLATTEN MIT SCHWEIZER BIRNE ALS DECKFURNIER. POLSTER IN SCHWARZEM LEDER.

2-4 SEITENVERKLEIDUNG AUS EDELSTAHLWELLBLECH UND BIRNBAUMHOLZ. KOFFERABLAGEN IN EDELSTAHL MIT INTEGRIERTEN LEUCHTEN.

PREVIOUS PAGE: VIEW INTO PASSENGER -CARRIAGE. THE CEILING IS CLADDED WITH STEEL MESH, WHICH DOUBLES AS A REFLECTION DEVICE FOR THE OVERALL LIGHTING CONCEPT.

1 LAMINATED SEAT STRUCTURE WITH SWISS PEAR VENEER, COVERED WITH BLACK LEATHER CUSHIONS.

2-4 SIDE PANELS CONSTRUCTED FROM CORRUGATED STEEL AND SWISS PEAR. STAINLESS STEEL SUITCASE SHELVES WITH INTEGRATED LIGHTING.

1

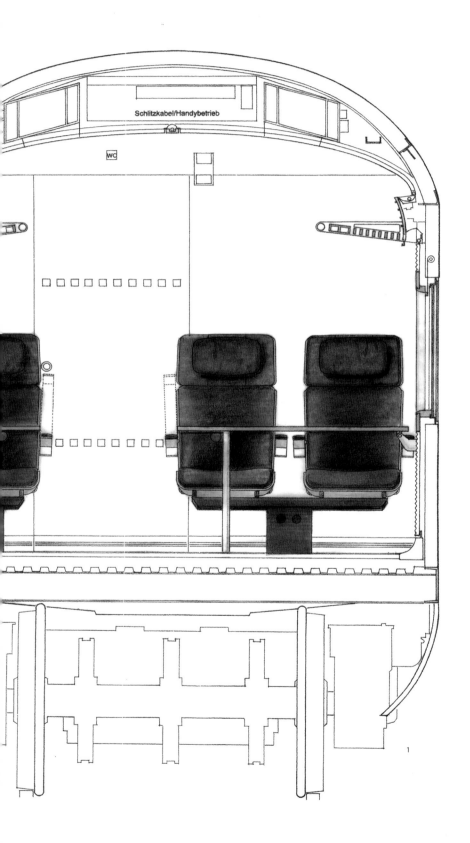

Schlitzkabel/Handybetrieb

WC

1

1 QUERSCHNITT.
2-3 KLAPPTISCH
IN EINER VIERER-
GRUPPE.
4. REISEWAGGON.
HOHENVERSTELL-
BARE KOPFKISSEN
MIT LEDERBEZUG.
1 CARRIAGE
CROSS SECTION.
2-3 FOLDING
TABLES BETWEEN
FOUR SEAT
ARRANGEMENT.
4 VERTICALLY
ADJUSTABLE
LEATHER HEAD
CUSHIONS.

2

3

4

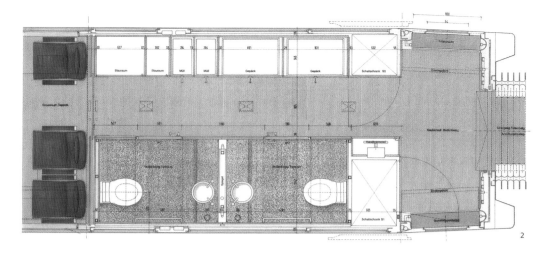

1 WAGGONEINSTIEG.
INDIREKTE TREPPEN-
BELEUCHTUNG. HALTE-
GRIFF IN EDELSTAHL.
WANDVERKLEIDUNG IN
BIRNENFURNIER MIT EDEL-
STAHLSCHIENEN ALS
KOFFERRAUMSCHUTZ.
TEILE DER VERKLEIDUNG
SIND ZUGLEICH TÜREN
ZU DAHINTERLIEGENDEN
STAUFLÄCHEN. FUSSBODEN
MIT WOLLTEPPICH.
2 GRUNDRISSAUSSCHNITT
MIT WC'S, STAUFLÄCHEN
UND ZEITSCHRIFTEN-
AUSLAGE.
3 INTERIEUR DES WC-
RAUMES. EDELSTAHL,
NATURSTEIN, SPIEGEL.
4. DURCHGANG ZWISCHEN
WC-TÜREN UND
ZEITSCHRIFTENAUSLAGE.

1 CARRIAGE ENTRANCE.
INDIRECT LIGHTING ON
STAIRS. STAINLESS STEEL
HAND-RAIL. PEAR WOOD
WALL CLADDING WITH
STAINLESS STEEL STRIPS
AS PROTECTORS.
WALL CLADDING DOUBLES
AS OPENING UNITS FOR
STORAGE. WOOLLEN
CARPET FLOOR AREA.
2 PARTIAL PLAN WITH
TOILETS, STORAGE AREA
AND NEWSPAPER
SHELVES.
3 TOILET INTERIOR:
STAINLESS STEEL, STONE
AND MIRROR.
4 PASSAGE BETWEEN
TOILET ENTRANCE AND
NEWSPAPER SHELVES.

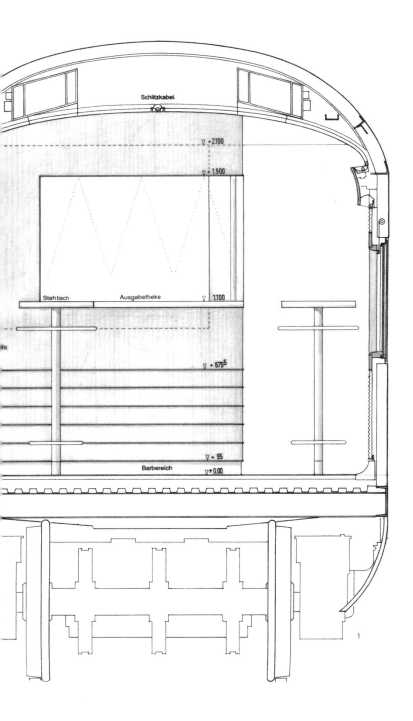

Schlitzkabel.

▽ + 2.100

▽ + 1.900

Stehtisch   Ausgabetheke   ▽ 1.100

▽ + 679.5

▽ + 95

Barbereich   ▽ ± 0.00

1

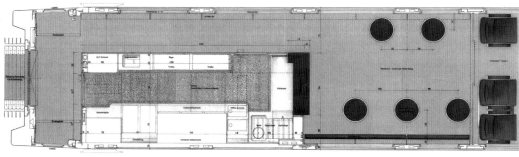

2

3

STAAT UND KOMMUNE

STATE AND COMMUNITY

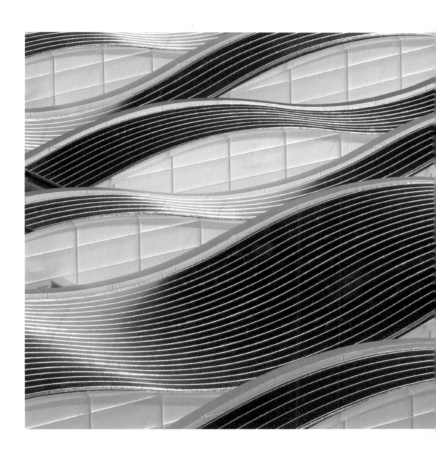

1+2 LAGEPLAN
IN MODELL UND
ZEICHNUNG.
3 DER AXIALE SICHT-
BEZUG VOM BADINH
PLATZ MIT HO CHI
MINH-MAUSOLEUM
AUF DAS "DENKMAL
FUR DIE GEFALLENEN"
WIRD SEITLICH VON
DEN KOLONNADEN
DES KONGRESSBAUS
LINKS UND DES PAR-
LAMENTSGEBAUDES
RECHTS GEFASST.

1+2 SITE PLAN IN
MODEL AND SKETCH.
3 THE AXIAL CON-
NECTION FROM BA-
DINH SQUARE WITH
HO CHI MINH MAU-
SOLEUM TOWARDS
THE MEMORIAL OF
THE FALLEN SOLDIERS,
IS FRAMED BY THE
COLONADES OF THE
CONGRESS BUILDING
ON THE LEFT AND THE
PARLIAMENT BUIL-
DING ON THE RIGHT.

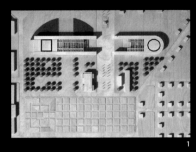

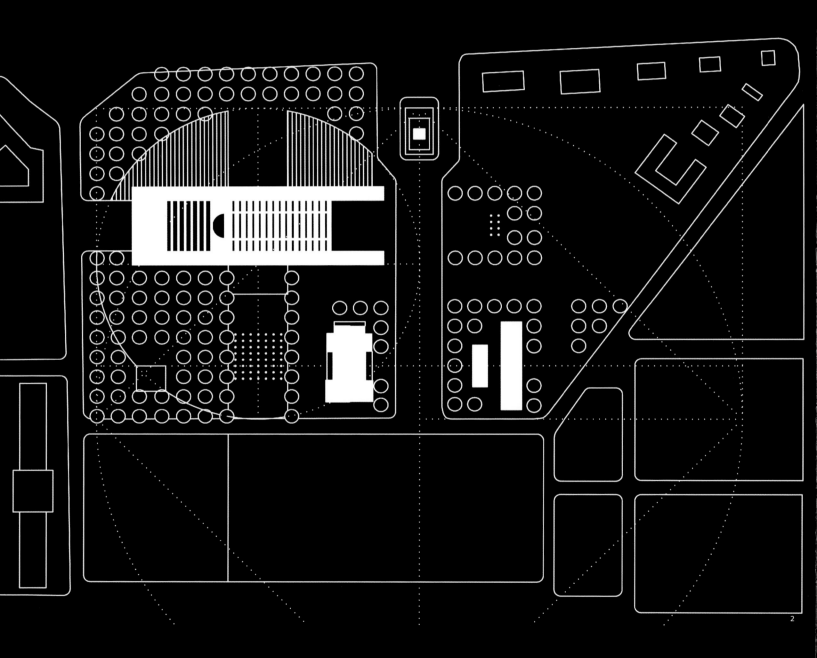

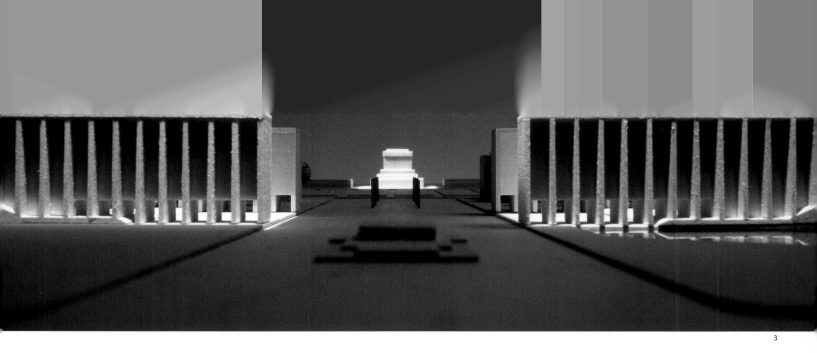

PARLAMENT UND KONGRESSZENTRUM HANOI, VIETNAM

WETTBEWERB: 1998
ENTWURF: Meinhard v. Gerkan
mit Nikolaus Goetze
MITARBEITER: Oliver Christ

Im ersten Bauabschnitt wird das Kongreßzentrum errichtet, das senkrecht zu einer Achse liegt, die auf das Mausoleum für Ho Chi Minh und das Monument der Gefallenen ausgerichtet ist. Im 2. Bauabschnitt wird die Querachse um das Parlament ergänzt. Beide Teile beziehen sich in einer großen , durch die Längsachse unterbrochenen Figur aufeinander. Zwischen den gegenüberliegenden Baukörpern entsteht so ein öffentlicher "Regierungsplatz", von dem aus beide Bauten erschlossen werden. In einer Variante wird die Lage des Parlaments im Süden des Kongreßzentrums dargestellt.

The first phase of this building, the Congress hall, will be built perpendicular to the main axis which is orientated towards the mausoleum to Ho Chi Minh and the monument to the fallen dead. In the second phase a transverse axis is to be created with the new Parliament building. Both parts relate to each other, forming a large simple figure, bisected by the longitudinal axis. An open 'parliament square' is created between opposing built forms, through which both buildings are accessible. In one variation the Parliament building was located to the south of the Congress centre.

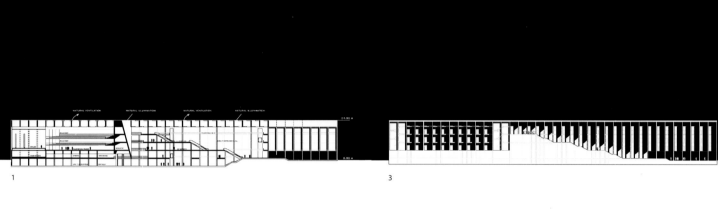

1

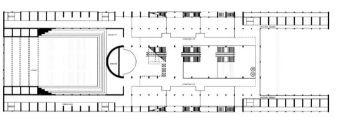

2

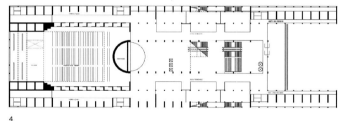

3

4

1 LÄNGSSCHNITT.   1 LONGITUDINAL

2 GRUNDRISS   SECTION.

1. RANG SAAL.   2 HALL PLAN ON

3 ANSICHT SÜD.   FIRST CIRCLE LEVEL.

4 GRUNDRISS   3 SOUTH ELEVATION.

EINGANGS-   4 HALL PLAN AT

EBENE SAAL.   ENTRANCE LEVEL.

5 LÄNGSSCHNITT.   5 LONGITUDINAL

6 GRUNDRISS   SECTION.

PARLAMENTSSAAL   6 PARLIAMENT

RANG.   HALL PLAN ON

7 ANSICHT SÜD.   CIRCLE LEVEL.

8 GRUNDRISS   7 SOUTH ELEVATION.

EINGANGSEBENE   8 PARLIAMENT PLAN

PARLAMENT.   ON ENTRANCE LEVEL.

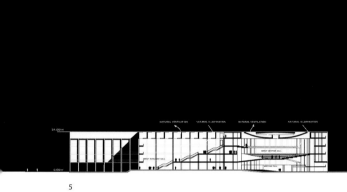

5

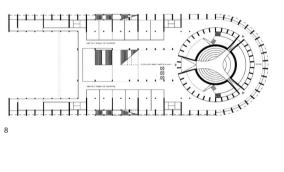

7

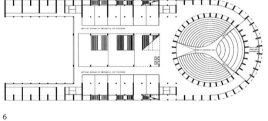

6

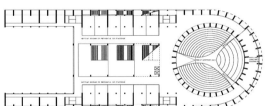

8

1

ALTERNATIVER
ENTWURF MIT LAGE
BEIDER TEILE AUF
DEM WESTLICHEN
GRUNDSTÜCK.
1 ANSICHT
SÜD-WEST.
2 GRUNDRISS
ERDGESCHOSS.
3 LAGEPLAN MIT
HO CHI MINH-
MAUSOLEUM.
ALTERNATIVE
PROPOSAL WITH
LOCATION OF BOTH
ELEMENTS ON THE
WESTERN SITE.
1 SOUTH-WEST
ELEVATION.
2 GROUND
LEVEL PLAN.
3 SITE PLAN WITH
HO CHI MINH
MAUSOLEUM.

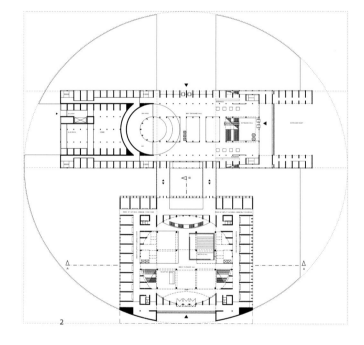

2

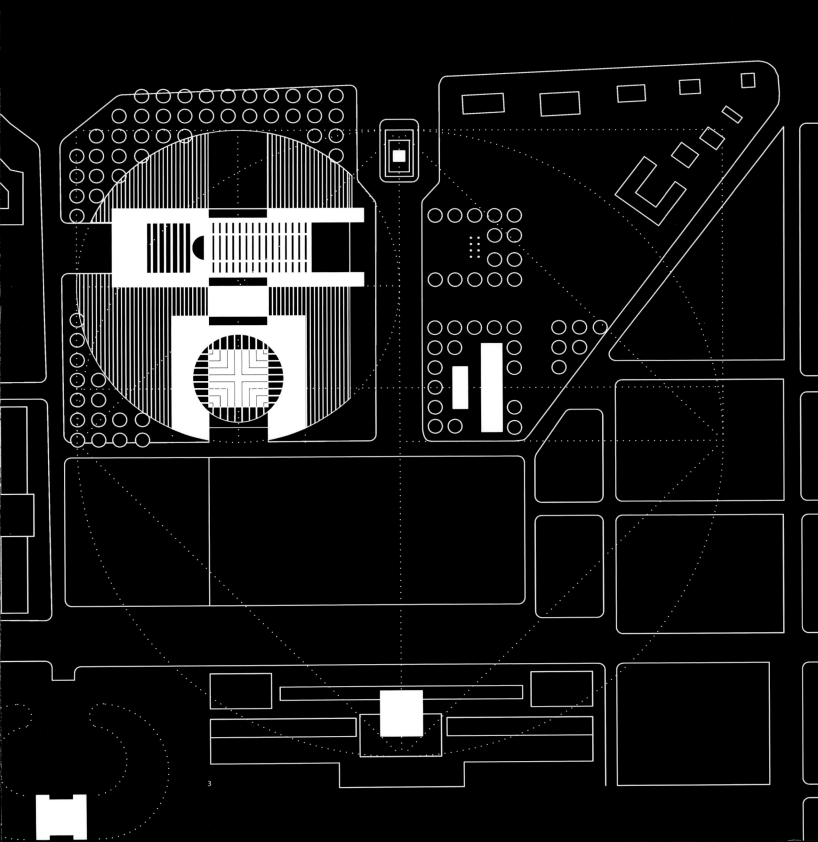

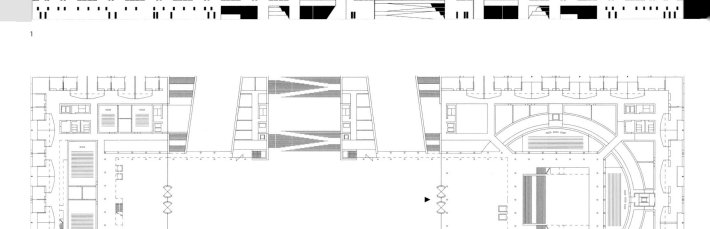

1

2

GERICHTSHOF ANTWERPEN, BELGIEN

WETTBEWERB: 1998
ENTWURF: Meinhard v. Gerkan,
Klaus Staratzke
MITARBEITER: Oliver Christ,
Pinar Gönul-Cinar

Der Entwurf muß den Widerspruch aushalten, als Gerichtsgebäude repräsentativen Charakter zu haben, aber am Rand der Innenstadt, über dem Endpunkt der Stadtautobahn, liegen zu müssen. Er reagiert auf diesen Konflikt dadurch, daß er die Einfahrt in die Stadt als „Stadttor" interpretiert, das aus einem quer zur Straße liegenden, langgestreckten Block herausgeschnitten ist. Die Blockinnenfläche wird zum urbanen Ort und dient als Erschließungsfläche, von der die zwei separaten Funktionseinheiten zugänglich sind. Der Hauptgerichtssaal tritt zur städtischen Öffentlichkeit hin durch einen gläsernen Turm in Erscheinung.

This building has to confront the essential contradiction of providing a court building with a representative character yet located on the edge of the city above the end of the city motorway route.
It responds to this difficulty by presenting a reinterpretation of the motorway entrance point to the city as a "town gateway" cut through an extruded block lying at right angles to the road. The inside face of the block becomes an urban space and serves as an access zone from which the two separate functional units can be reached. The main court room is presented to the public as a glazed tower.

1 SÜDANSICHT.
2 OBERGESCHOSS.
3 LÄNGSSCHNITT.
4 HAUPTER-
SCHLIESSUNGSEBENE.
5 MASSENMODELL.
1 SOUTH ELEVATION.
2 UPPER LEVEL.
3 LONGITUDINAL
SECTION.
4 MAIN CIRCULATION
LEVEL.
5 MASSING MODEL.

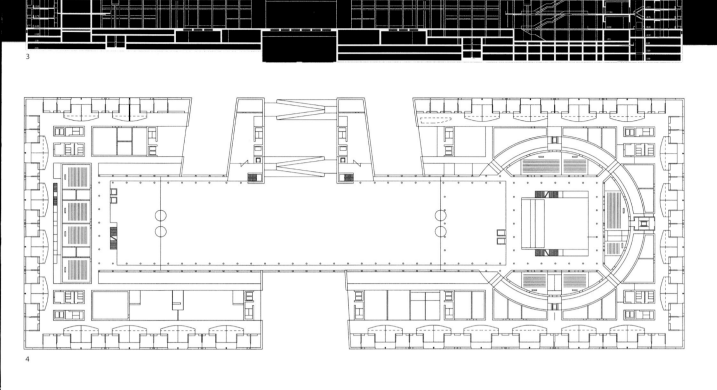

3

4

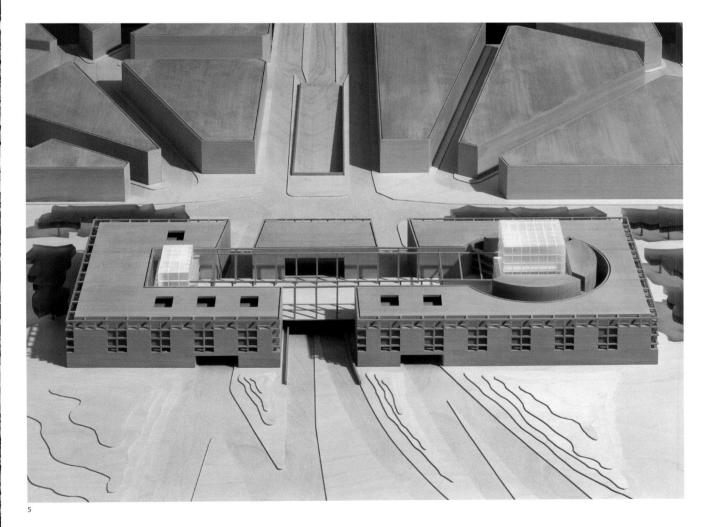

5

RATHAUS BRAMSCHE

WETTBEWERB: 1997 - 2. Preis
ENTWURF: Meinhard v. Gerkan mit Philipp Kamps

Ein historisches Gebäude, das ehemals der Unterbringung lediger Fabrikarbeiter diente, bildet das „Herz" des neuen Rathauses von Bramsche. Sein identitätstiftender Charakter wird aufgegriffen und sorgsam in die Neuplanung eingebracht. Der Anbau, wiewohl größer im Volumen als der Altbau, fügt sich daher äußerst zurückhaltend an der Rückseite an, um seinen Respekt vor dem Alten zu bezeugen. Die Art seiner architektektonischen Gestaltung zeigt jedoch auch seine Einbindung in die Gegenwart; es gibt keine historisierende Architektur, sondern das Gegenüber von Alt und Neu, aus dem ein Drittes als eigene Qualität erwächst.

Die zentrale Treppe des Gebäudes an der Hasestraße wird zum Kern der Erschließung, an die rückseitig ein glasüberdachtes kleines Bürgerforum anschließt, von dem alle öffentlichen Bereiche des Rathauses direkt zu erreichen sind. So bleibt der Altbau als Zeichen von ortstiftender Tradition, der Neubau schafft die Voraussetzungen für ein Rathaus als „Bürgerhaus".

A historic building, once used to accommodate unmarried factory workers, forms the "heart" of the new town hall of the town of Bramsche. Its former identity is used and carefully "re-worked" into the new design. Although larger in volume, the extension to the rear therefore interlocks with the old building in a way as to show respect for history. At the same time, its architectural design is evidence of the integration of past and present. There is no historicizing, but the juxtaposition of old and new, out of which grows

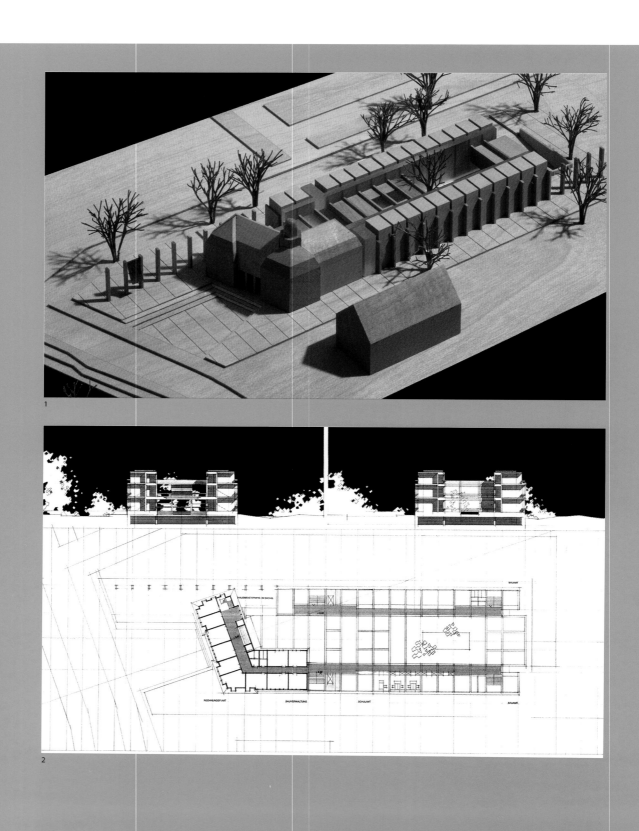

1

2

a third entity with its own individual quality. The main staircase of the building on Hasestrasse forms the access core, adjoined by a small glass-roofed civic centre at the back, from where all public areas of the town hall are directly accessible. The historic building thus remains as a symbol for the identity of place and tradition, and the new structure creates the conditions for the town hall functioning as a community centre.

1 MODELL.
2 SCHNITTE UND
OBERGESCHOSS.
3 LAGEPLAN.
4 FASSADENDETAIL.
5 LÄNGSSCHNITT
UND ERDGESCHOSS.
1 MODEL.
2 SECTIONS AND
UPPER LEVEL.
3 SITE PLAN.
4 FACADE DETAIL.
5 LONGITUDINAL
SECTION AND
GROUND LEVEL.

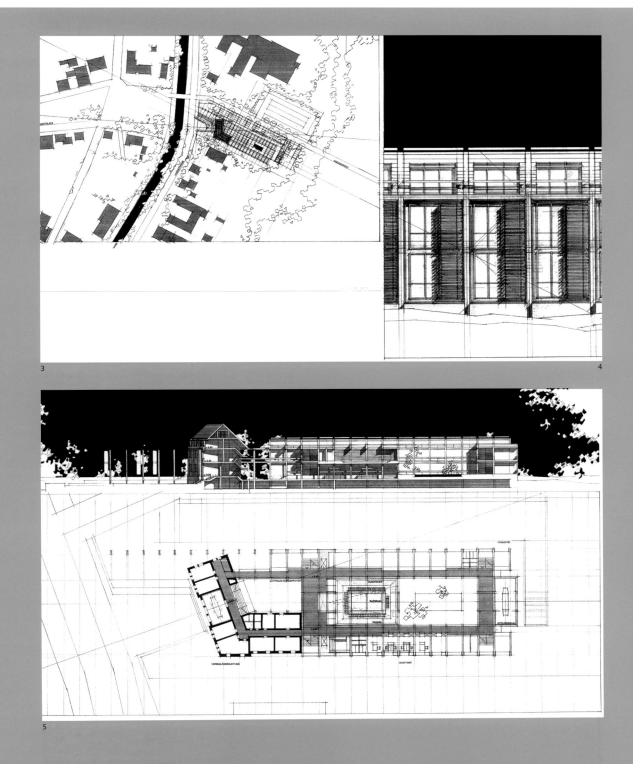

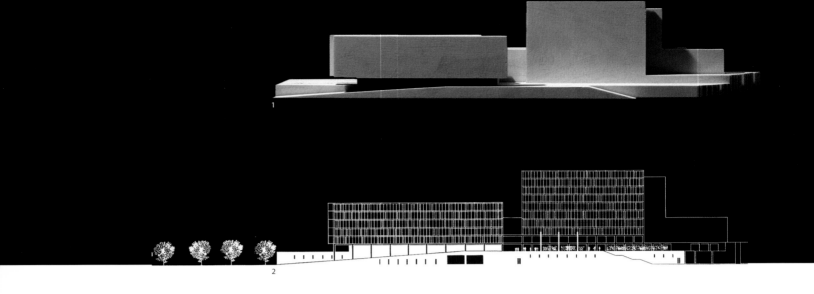

ZENTRALE POLIZEITECHNISCHE DIENSTE, DUISBURG

WETTBEWERB: 1998
ENTWURF: Meinhard v. Gerkan
MITARBEITER: Michael Biwer,
Nicolai Pix

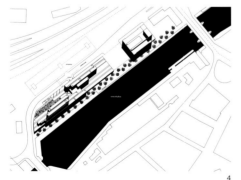

Das beengte, langgestreckte Grundstück am ehemaligen Holzhafen in Duisburg soll neben einer großen Zahl von normalen Büroarbeitsräumen einen umfangreichen und komplexen Fahrdienst aufnehmen. Dieser findet im Sockelgebäude Platz, auf dem sich die Bürotrakte stapeln. Deren große Baumasse wird sowohl horizontal im Grundriß der Büroscheiben wie vertikal in Länge und Höhe der einzelnen Trakte in einer Analogie zu geschichteten Holzstapeln oder einem Floß aus Baumstämmen im Wasser unterschiedlich dimensioniert und damit gebrochen. Durch dieses Prinzip der Schichtung und Stapelung entsteht eine außenräumliche und baukörperliche Differenzierung für ein Programm, das von seiner Nutzung her eher monoton ist.

The restricted and narrow site at the former "Holzhafen" in Duisburg is the proposed location for a large number of standard offices and additionally a comprehensive vehicle service centre. The latter is located at ground floor level, on top of which the office floors are built. As an analogy to the structure of wood piles or rafts made from treetrunks, the extensive building mass has been divided in plan horizontally and in section vertically.
The principle of stacking and layering introduces an interior and exterior variation to a building program, which in itself is functionally monotonous.

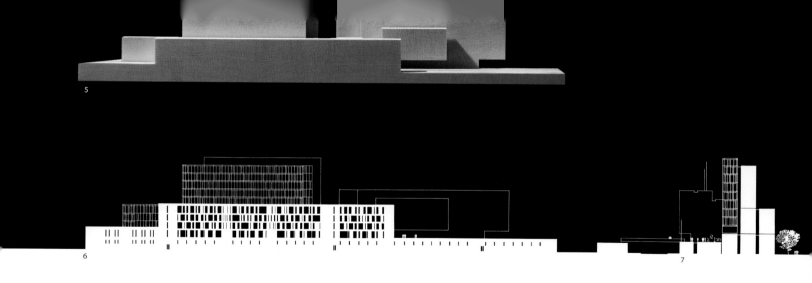

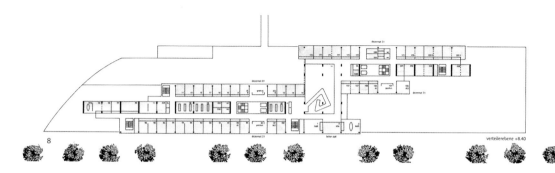

1 MODELL VON SÜDEN.
2 SÜDANSICHT.
3 DAS FLÖßEN GESCHLA-
GENEN HOLZES ALS
ENTWURFSMETAPHER
ZUM STANDORT HOLZ-
HAFEN.
4 LAGEPLAN.
5 MODELL VON NORDEN.
6 NORDANSICHT.
7 WESTANSICHT.
8 NORMALGESCHOSS.
9 FASSADENDETAIL IN
SCHNITT UND ANSICHT.

1 MODEL VIEWED FROM
THE SOUTH.
2 SOUTH ELEVATION.
3 THE STRUCTURE OF
RAFTS MADE FROM
TREE-TRUNKS. AS
ANALOGY TO THE
"HOLZHAFEN" LOCATION.
4 SITE PLAN.
5 MODEL VIEWED
FROM THE NORTH.
6 NORTH ELEVATION.
7 WEST ELEVATION.
8 PLAN OF STANDARD
FLOOR.
9 FACADE DETAIL
IN SECTION AND
ELEVATION.

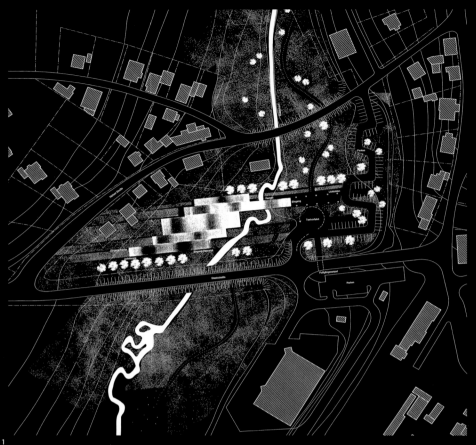

1

1 LAGEPLAN.
2+4 WETTBEWERBS-
MODELL.
3   RAUMFÜGUNG.
1 SITE PLAN.
2+4 COMPETITION
MODEL.
3 SPATIAL PROGRAM.

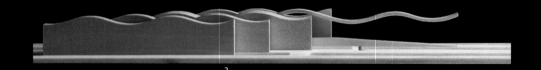

2

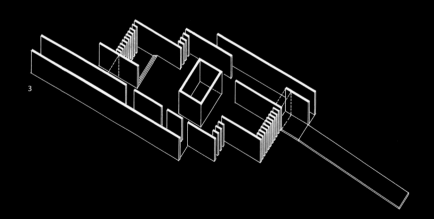

3

SPIELBANK
BAD STEBEN

WETTBEWERB: 1997 - 1. Preis
ENTWURF: Meinhard v. Gerkan mit
Anja Knobloch-Meding
MITARBEITER: Sigrid Müller,
Sona Kazemi
LEITUNG DER AUSFÜHRUNG: Anja
Knobloch-Meding, Justus Klement
MITARBEITER: Bettina Groß, Evgenia
Werner, Maja Gorges, Jessica Weber,
Marina Hoffmann
BAUHERR: Gemeinde Bad Steben
BAUZEIT: 1999 - 2001
BGF: 4.216 m²
BRI: 20.038 m³

Eine schwach geneigte Rampe führt
als empfangende Geste von Vorfahrt
und Parkplatz über den Graben des
Stebenbaches unter ein weit heraus-
gezogenes Vordach - der Eingang
als Inszenierung von etwas Beson-
derem, etwas Festlichem, das zum

Besuch einer Spielbank gehört. Der
Gestus wird aufgenommen durch
das in versetzten Bändern verlaufende wellenförmige Dach - Symbol
des Spielglücks, aber ohne dessen
wahrscheinlichen Absturz.
Die wellenförmige Dachlandschaft
gliedert und verkleinert optisch die
für den Ort ungewöhnlich große
Baukörpermasse.
Kongruent zu den Dachbändern ist
der Grundriß in parallele Raumzonen
gegliedert, die klaren Funktionen
entsprechen; jedem Baukörperband
ist eine Nutzungsart zugeordnet.
Interne Räume liegen im 1. Obergeschoß, technische im Sockelgeschoß.
Eine Spielbank in einem kleinen Ort:
selbst etwas verspielt, aber mit der
Disziplin und Konsequenz, die den
Regeln beim Spiel entsprechen.
From the drive and parking lot, a
gradually rising ramp leads across
the ditch of the Steben stream to
the entrance area underneath a
long drawn-out roof canopy - an

entrance scenario for festivity,
conveying the sense of a very
special event, manifest in a casino
building. This gesture is taken up
by the undulating roof of offset
bands - symbolic for the changing
fortunes of gambling, but without
the latter's (potential) plunge.
The undulating roofscape structures
optically reduces the size of the
building volume, unusual in this
spa town.
The ground floor organization
matches the band-structure of the
roof with parallel rows of spaces,
each row with its distinct function.
Non-public spaces are on the first
floor, technical services are in the
basement.
A casino in a small town - playful
and a bit ornate, but with the
discipline and stringency which
correspond to the rules of the
game.

1 ZUGANGSSEITE.

2 SEITENANSICHT.

3 ERDGESCHOSS.

4 OBERGESCHOSS.

5 LÄNGSSCHNITT.

6 QUERSCHNITT.

1 ENTRANCE AREA.

2 SIDE ELEVATION.

3 GROUND LEVEL.

4 UPPER LEVEL.

5 LONGITUDINAL.
SECTION.

6 CROSS SECTION.

1

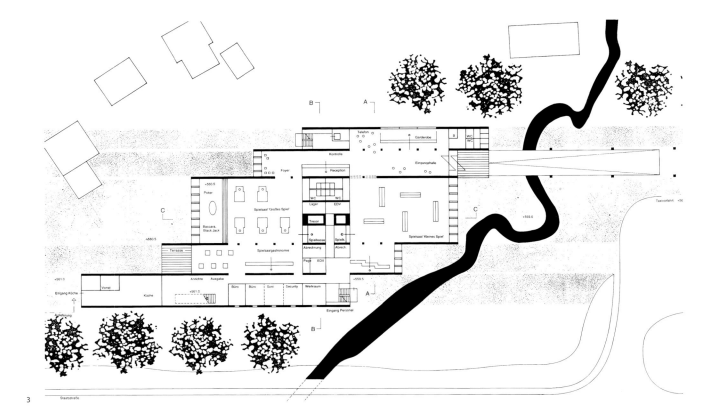

3

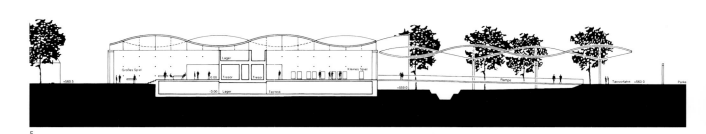

5

258

2

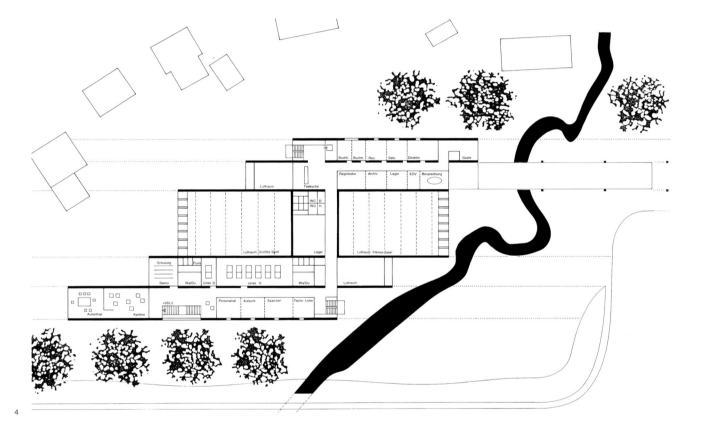

4

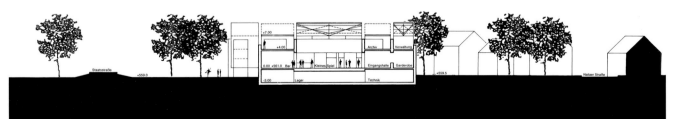

6

DIE WELLENBEWE-
GUNG DER DACH-
BÄNDER IST EINE
ANSPIELUNG AUF
DAS AUF UND AB
DES GLÜCKSSPIELS.

THE WAVE-LIKE
MOVEMENT OF THE
ROOF PROFILE IS
A REFERENCE TO
THE MIXED FORTUNES
OF GAMBLING.

HECKSCHERKLINIK, MÜNCHEN

WETTBEWERB: 1997
ENTWURF: Meinhard v. Gerkan
MITARBEITER: Klaus Lenz,
Johann v. Mansberg

Der Neubau schließt als Blockbebau-
ung an drei Seiten die vorhandenen
Straßenräume und schafft auf der
Innenseite ruhige Freiflächenzonen.
Der Baukörper selbst ist in drei „Pfle-
gehäuser" gegliedert, in denen die
Pflegestationen vertikal organisiert
sind. So werden lange Krankenhaus-
flure vermieden und für die Patien-
ten überschaubare Einheiten gebil-
det. Der rhythmischen Gliederung in
„Häuser" entspricht die bandartige
Struktur der Freibereiche, deren
Terrassierung der Belichtung der
Untergeschosse dient.

The new building encloses the existing block structure and streetscape
on three sides, creating an open
calm spatial zone on its inner face.
The body of the building is clearly
structured into three nursing units
into which the wards are arranged
vertically. This results in an avoidance
of long hospital corridors and en-
courages ease of orientation for the
patient. A rhythmic structuring into
blocks mirrors the pattern of open
spaces between which terraces serve
to illuminate the lower floor levels.

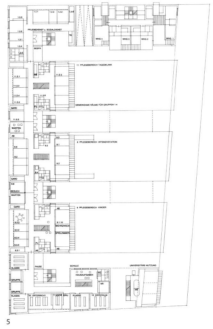

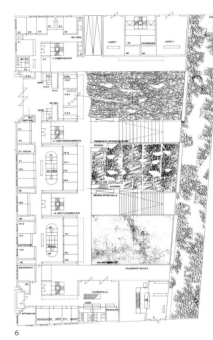

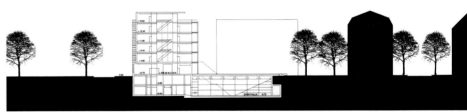

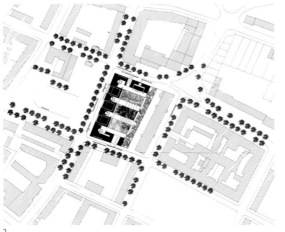

1 MASSENMODELL.

2 LAGEPLAN.

3 WESTANSICHT.

4 SÜDANSICHT.

5 OBERGESCHOSS.

6 ERDGESCHOSS.

7 QUERSCHNITT.

1 MASSING MODEL.

2 SITE PLAN.

3 WEST ELEVATION.

4 SOUTH ELEVATION.

5 UPPER LEVEL.

6 GROUND LEVEL.

7 CROSS SECTION.

KINDER- UND FRAUENKLINIK UNIVERSITÄT DRESDEN

WETTBEWERB: 1997
ENTWURF: Meinhard v. Gerkan
MITARBEITER: Johann v. Mansberg

Eine große Eiche im Innenhof der neuen Anlage strukturiert das Ensemble und gibt ihm einen Mittelpunkt. Zu ihr hin öffnet sich die Eingangshalle nach Süden, während sie zur Straße hin das Entree für die Öffentlichkeit bildet. Organisatorisch und architektonisch ist die Klinik in eine zweigeschossige Sockelzone mit den Untersuchungs- und Behandlungsräumen gegliedert und in darüberliegende dreigeschossige Betten„häuser". Sie vermitteln zwischen dem Klinikgarten und dem Elbevorland und stellen für die Patienten einen Bezug zur angrenzenden Landschaft her.

A large oak tree located in the inner courtyard of the new scheme structures the building group and creates a central point. The entrance hall opens out towards it to the south, whilst to the roadside it forms the main public entrance. Organisationally and architectonically the clinic is divided into a two storey high base with examination and treatment rooms and three storey nursing wards set above. They interpose between the clinic gardens and the banks of the river Elbe and create for the patients a reference point with the adjoining landscape.

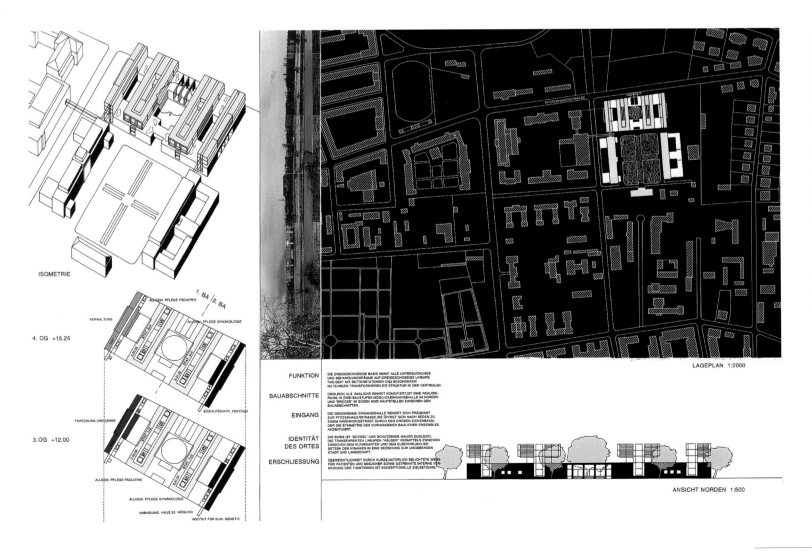

ISOMETRIE

4. OG +15.25

3. OG +12.00

VERWALTUNG

ALLGEM. PFLEGE PÄDIATRIE

1. BA / 2. BA

ALLGEM. PFLEGE GYNÄKOLOGIE

FORSCHUNG UND LEHRE

SOZIALPÄDIATR. ZENTRUM

ALLGEM. PFLEGE PÄDIATRIE

ALLGEM. PFLEGE GYNÄKOLOGIE

ANBINDUNG HAUS 25 MÖGLICH

INSTITUT FÜR KLIN. GENETIK

FUNKTION

BAUABSCHNITTE

EINGANG

IDENTITÄT DES ORTES

ERSCHLIESSUNG

LAGEPLAN 1:2000

ANSICHT NORDEN 1:500

VERTRETUNG DER BUNDESLÄNDER NIEDERSACHSEN UND SCHLESWIG-HOLSTEIN IN BERLIN

WETTBEWERB: 1997 - Ankauf
ENTWURF: Meinhard v. Gerkan mit Gregor Hoheisel
MITARBEITER: Hnin Kyaw Lat, Johannes Erdmann

Zwei Landesregierungen beschließen einen gemeinsamen Bau für ihre Landesvertretungen in der Bundeshauptstadt - das soll der Baukörper aus zwei selbständigen Trakten ausdrücken, die sich um eine gemeinsame Halle gruppieren. Diese schafft gleichzeitig das repräsentative Entrée und eine großzügige Verbindung zum Park. Das Gebäude besetzt einen städtebaulich wichtigen Punkt an der Kreuzung von Ebertstraße und Kleiner Grenzallee, der durch die Aufnahme der Baufluchten der umgebenden Bebauung betont wird. Die Wohntrakte der Minister und Gäste schweben als „Wolkenbügel" hoch über dem Park.

Two provincial governments decided to join forces in building and then sharing one new office building in the German Capital. This partnership is expressed in two building volumes: two independent wings adjoining one common hall, which doubles as a grand entrance hall and generously dimensioned passage to the park. This building occupies an important site in the urban layout, at the intersection of Ebertstrasse and Kleine Grenzallee, and aknowleges the building lines of the surrounding structures. The residential suites of ministers and guests hover above the complex as an "arch in the clouds".

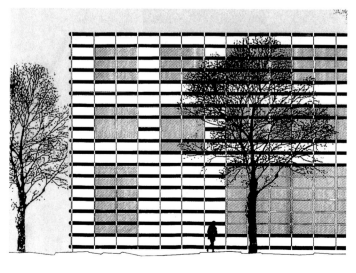

1

2
3

4

5

1 ENTWURFSSKIZZE.
2+3 FASSADEN-
DETAIL.
4 PERSPEKTIVE.
5 LAGEPLAN.
1 CONCEPTIONAL
SKETCH.
2+3 FACADE DETAIL.
4 PERSPECTIVE.
5 SITE PLAN.

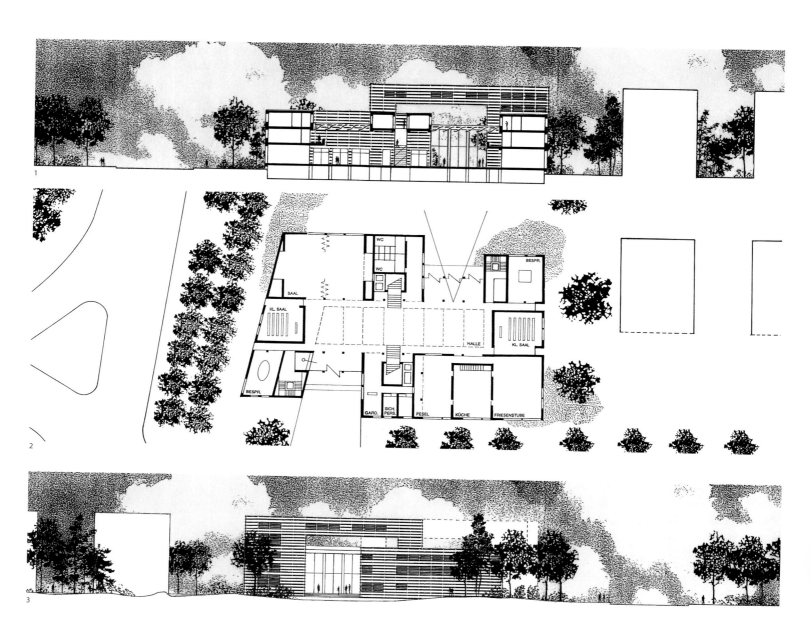

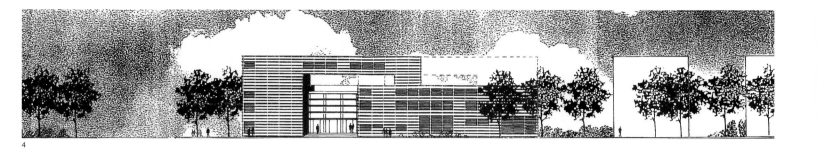

4

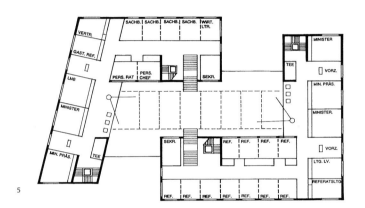

5

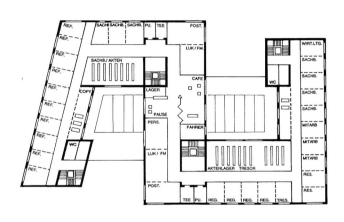

6

1 LÄNGSSCHNITT.
2 ERDGESCHOSS.
3 SÜDSEITE.
4 NORDSEITE.
5 OBERGESCHOSSE.
6 QUERSCHNITT
UND OSTSEITE.

1 LONGITUDINAL
SECTION.
2 GROUND LEVEL.
3 SOUTH SIDE.
4 NORTH SIDE.
5 UPPER LEVELS.
6 CROSS SECTION
AND EAST SIDE.

1 DER LAND-
SCHAFTSPLAN ZEIGT
DIE VERZAHNUNG
VON INNEN- UND
AUSSENRAUM.

2 3. OBERGESCHOSS,
LEITUNGSEBENE.
3 1. OBERGESCHOSS,
INNERER DIENST.
4 UNTERGESCHOSS.

5 BAUKÖRPER-
FÜGUNG IM MODELL.
6 LAGEPLAN.
1 THE LANDSCAPE
PLAN ILLUSTRATES

FILTRATION OF
INTERIOR TO
EXTERIOR SPACE.
2 THIRD LEVEL,
ADMINISTRATION

LEVEL.
3 FIRST LEVEL,
INTERNAL SERVICE.
4 BASEMENT.
5 BUILDING ARRAN-

GEMENT IN MODEL.
6 SITEPLAN.

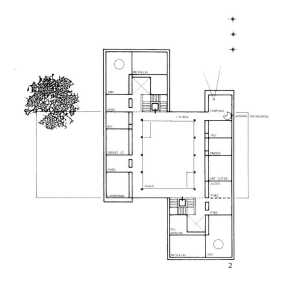

VERTRETUNG DER BUNDESLÄNDER BRANDENBURG UND MECKLENBURG-VORPOMMERN IN BERLIN

WETTBEWERB: 1998 - 1. Preis
ENTWURF: Meinhard v. Gerkan
mit Stephan Rewolle
PROJEKTLEITUNG: Stephan Rewolle
MITARBEITER: Kemal Akay,
Margret Böthig,
Antje Pfeifer, Elke Hoffmeister
BAUHERR: Land Brandenburg,
Land Mecklenburg-Vorpommern
BAUZEIT: 1999 - 2001
BGF: 4.430 m²
BRI: 19.290 m³

Zwei gleichartige, aber gegeneinander versetzte Gebäudewinkel repräsentieren die beiden Bundesländer; im Typus einer großen Stadtvilla wird die Einheit des Ganzen betont. Durch die Markierung der Ecke und ihrer Akzentuierung durch einen turmartigen Baukörper reagiert der Bau auf die städtebauliche Situation mit ihren benachbarten hohen Wohnbauten. Gemeinsame Mitte beider Landesvertretungen ist eine mehrgeschossige Halle unter einem Glasdach, um die in radialer Anordnung die Nutzungsbereiche angeordnet sind.

Two angular identical building elements are set against each other representing the two federal states. Utilising the villa form as a typus the unity of the whole is clearly stated. The building responds to the surrounding tall urban forms of the housing developments, defining and marking its corner with a tower. The middle space shared by both authorities is formed by a multi-storied atrium hall located under a glass roof around which the various offices and other uses radiate.

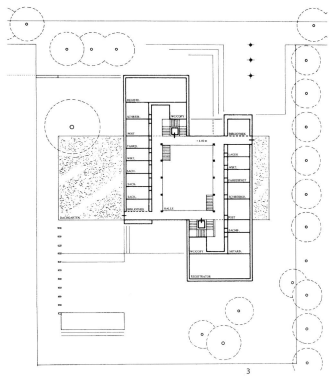

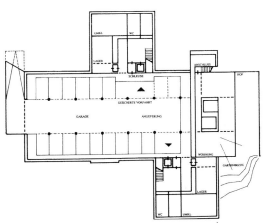

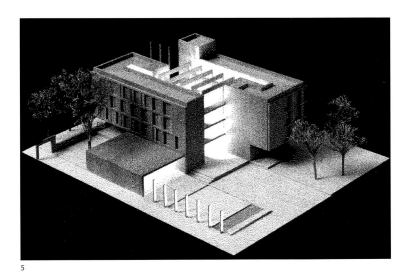

5

6

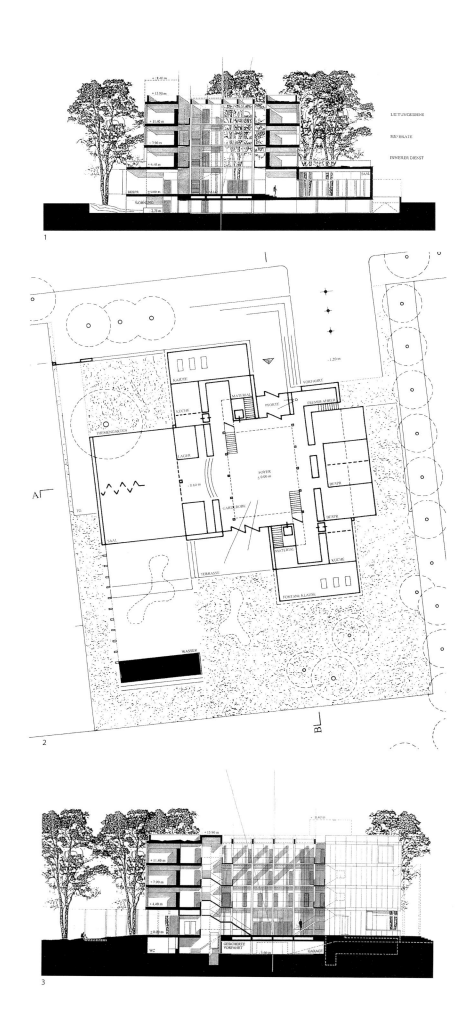

1

2

3

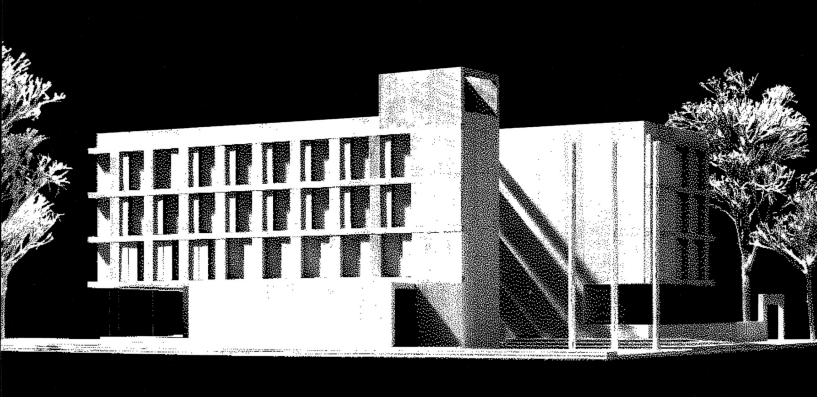

4

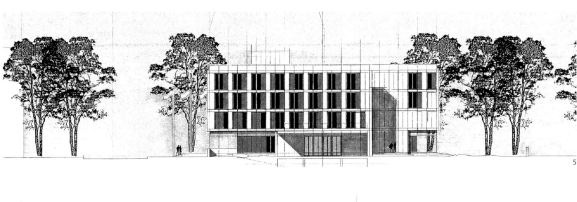

5

6

1 SCHNITT A-A.
2 ERDGESCHOSS.
3 SCHNITT B-B.
4 BAUKÖRPERLICH
BETONTE EINGANGS-
SITUATION AN DER
NORD-OST-ECKE.
5 WESTANSICHT.
6 NORDANSICHT.

1 SECTION A-A.
2 GROUND LEVEL.
3 SECTION B-B.
4 EMPHASIZED
ENTRANCE SITUATION
AT THE NORTH-EAST
CORNER.
5 WEST ELEVATION.
6 NORTH ELEVATION.

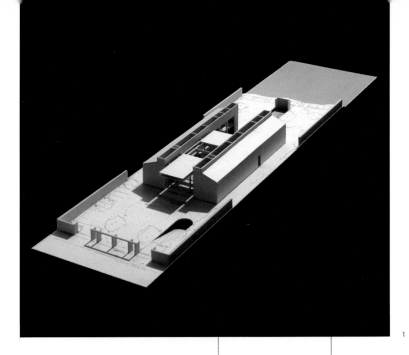

BOTSCHAFTS-RESIDENZ DER VEREINIGTEN ARABISCHEN EMIRATE, BERLIN

WETTBEWERB: 1998
ENTWURF: Meinhard v. Gerkan
mit Johann v. Mansberg

Das langgestreckte Grundstück befindet sich in hervorragender Lage direkt am Wannsee. Der Entwurf integriert die durch das Programm vorgegebene Mischung aus Repräsentation und Privatheit in einem dreischiffigen Gebäudeaufbau mit einer weitgehenden achsial symmetrischen Ordnung. Die Mittelzone schafft eine Raumsequenz, die von der Eingangshalle über einen glasgedeckten Wintergarten durch das anschließende große Speisezimmer direkte Blickbeziehung nach Süden, zum See hin offeriert. In die flankierenden seitlichen Gebäudeflügel sind in zweigeschossiger Anordnung mit teilweise durchgehenden Lufträumen die Nutzungsbereiche so organisiert, daß sich das Private vom Repräsentativen trennt, ohne die einheitliche Großzügigkeit des Ganzen zu verlieren.

The extended site is situated in a supreme location directly on lake "Wannsee". The design combines the required mix of open and private spaces in the triple-nave, almost symmetrical building. The central zone creates a spatial sequence from the entrance hall through to a conservatory and a large dining-room, offering a direct visual link to the lake in the South. Private and open areas are arranged in the parallel wings over two levels, yet separated in such a fashion, that the generous volumes are maintained.

1 MODELL.
2 LAGEPLAN UND LÄNGSSCHNITT.
3 ANSICHT NORDWEST. GRUNDRISS ERDGESCHOSS. QUERSCHNITT.
4 ANSICHT SÜDOST. GRUNDRISS OBERGESCHOSS. QUERSCHNITT.

1 MODEL.
2 SITE PLAN AND LONGITUDINAL SECTION.
3 NORTH-WEST ELEVATION. GROUND LEVEL PLAN. CROSS SECTION.
4 SOUTH-EAST ELEVATION. UPPER LEVEL PLAN. CROSS SECTION.

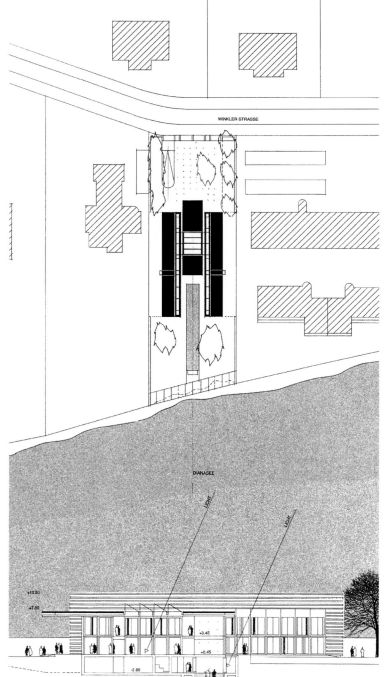

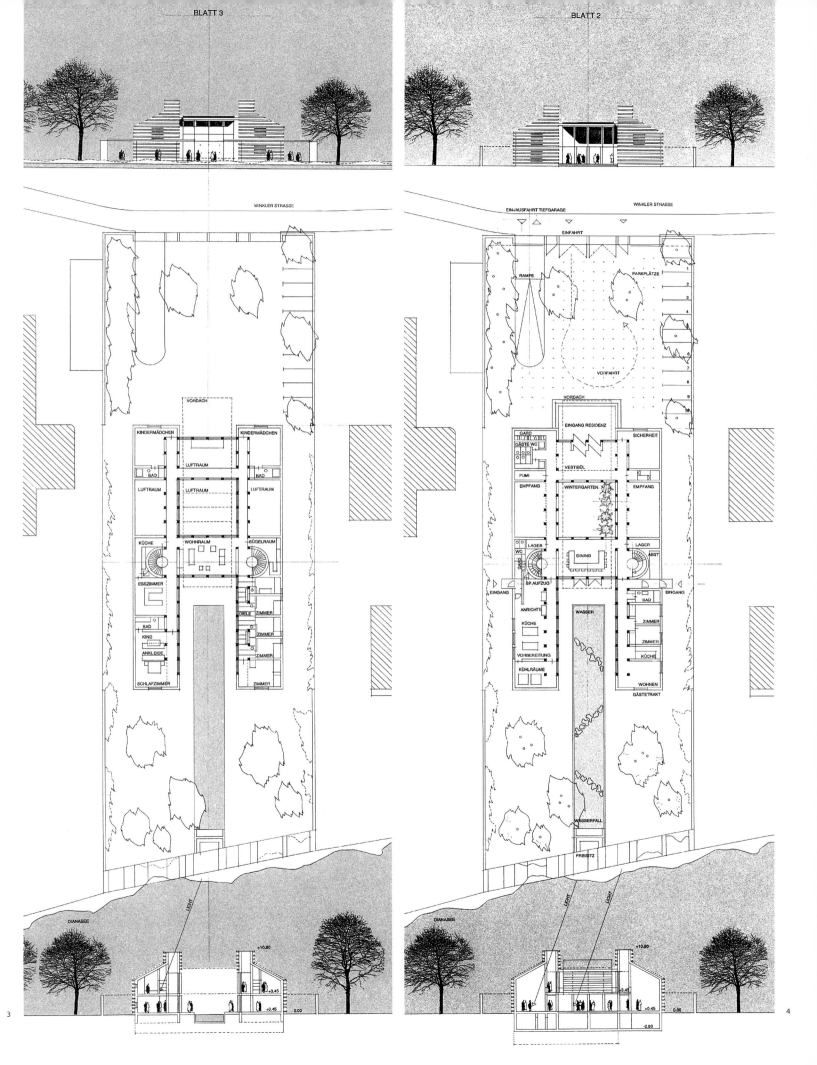

BLATT 3

BLATT 2

WINKLER STRASSE

EIN-/AUSFAHRT TIEFGARAGE   WINKLER STRASSE

EINFAHRT

RAMPE   PARKPLÄTZE

VORDACH

VORFAHRT

VORDACH

KINDERMÄDCHEN   KINDERMÄDCHEN

LUFTRAUM

BAD   BAD

LUFTRAUM   LUFTRAUM   LUFTRAUM

KÜCHE   WOHNRAUM   BÜGELRAUM

ESSZIMMER

DIELE ZIMMER

BAD   ZIMMER

KIND   ZIMMER

ANKLEIDE

SCHLAFZIMMER   ZIMMER

GARD   EINGANG RESIDENZ   SICHERHEIT
GÄSTE WC
PUMI   VESTIBÜL
EMPFANG   WINTERGARTEN   EMPFANG

WC   LAGER   LAGER   ABST
DINING
SP.AUFZUG
EINGANG   ANRICHTE   WASSER   BAD   EINGANG
ZIMMER
KÜCHE   ZIMMER
VORBEREITUNG   KÜCHE
KÜHLRÄUME   WOHNEN
GÄSTETRAKT

WASSERFALL

FREISITZ

DIANASEE   LICHT

DIANASEE   LICHT   LICHT

+10.80   +10.80

+3.45   +3.45

+0.45   0.00   +0.45   0.00

-2.80

3   4

STÄDTEBAU

URBAN DESIGN

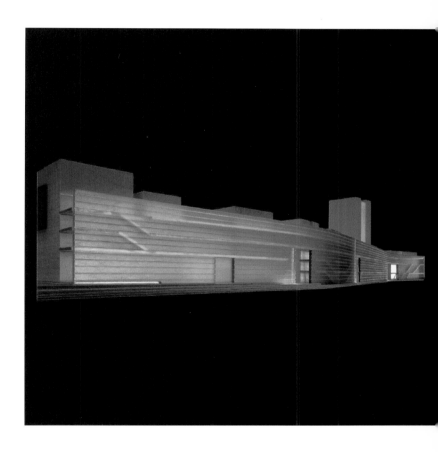

1

„BRAUEREI OTTAKRING", WIEN -STÄDTE-BAULICHE NEU-KONSTRUKTION

WETTBEWERB: 1996 - 3. Rang
ENTWURF: Meinhard v. Gerkan
mit Anja Knobloch-Meding
MITARBEITER: Sigrid Müller,
Johann v. Mansberg, Stephan Rewolle

Ziel des Entwurfes ist, dem traditionellen Ort eine neue Identität mit
charakteristischen Nutzungen zu geben. Der alte Turm dient dabei als
historischer Anknüpfungspunkt und
Wahrzeichen, das von überall her
sichtbar bleibt. Das neue Quartier

wird durch eine geschwungene, der
Straßenführung folgende Glas-Mem-
bran abgegrenzt, die aber die dahin-
ter liegenden Baukörper sichtbar läßt
und damit die Verbindung von Alt
und Neu betont. Ein zentraler Platz
vor dem Turm wird zum neuen Mittelpunkt mit Kinocenter, Volkshochschule und „Darre-Zentrum". Schließlich bildet ein „neuer Darreturm", als
scheibenartiges Hochaus, das weit-
hin sichtbare Zeichen für einen neu-
en Anfang des alten Quartiers, das
mit vielfältigen Nutzungen Anreiz
zum Flanieren und Verweilen bieten
soll.

The design intention was to give
this historic location a new identity
with dynamic new uses. The old
tower serves as a historical reference point and landmark which is

visible thoughout the area. The
new housing quarter is defined
through a glass membrane structure which follows the line of the
street, leaving the existing building
masses situated behind it visible,
and thereby enhancing the connection between old and new. A central square space in front of the
tower creates a new middle with
cinema complex, adult education
and "Darre-centre". Finally a new
"Darre-tower" forms a screen-like
skyscraper, a highly visible metaphor for a new beginning to the
old quarter with its multitude of
new uses which should encourage
further enjoyment and exploration.

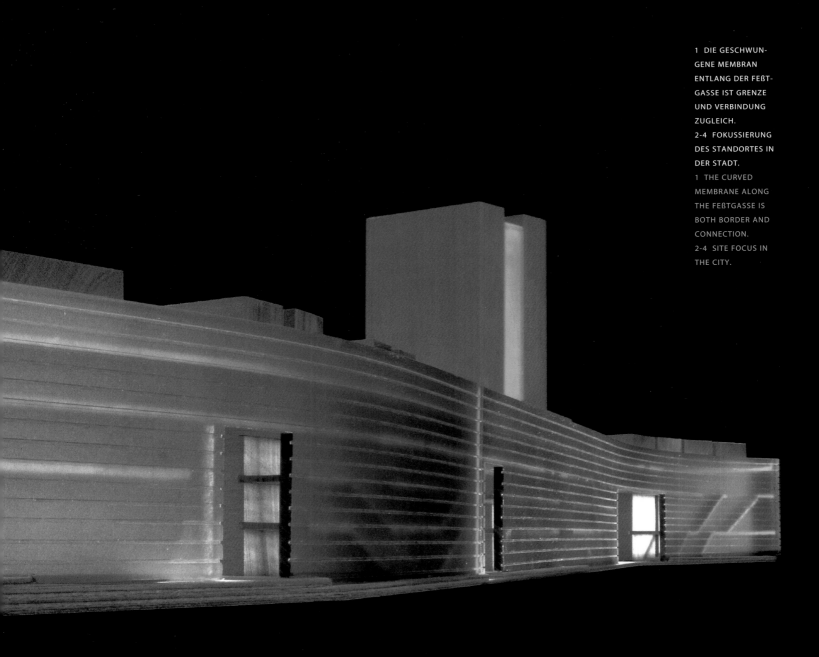

1 DIE GESCHWUN-
GENE MEMBRAN
ENTLANG DER FEßT-
GASSE IST GRENZE
UND VERBINDUNG
ZUGLEICH.
2-4 FOKUSSIERUNG
DES STANDORTES IN
DER STADT.
1 THE CURVED
MEMBRANE ALONG
THE FEßTGASSE IS
BOTH BORDER AND
CONNECTION.
2-4 SITE FOCUS IN
THE CITY.

2

3

4

1

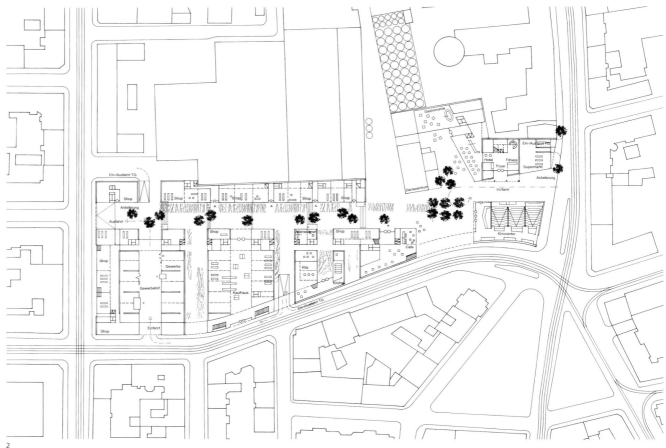

2

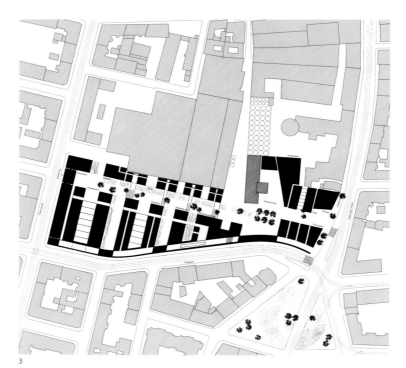

3

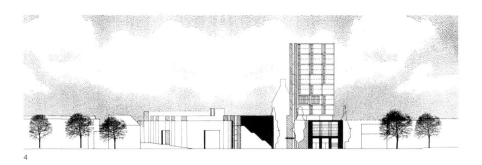

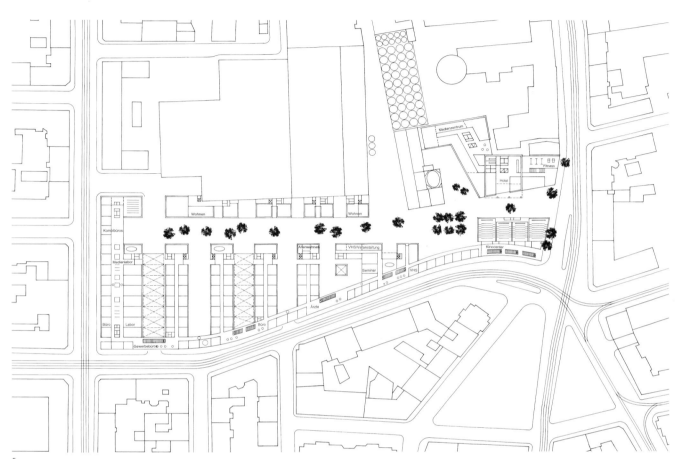

1 SÜDSEITE.

2 ERDGESCHOSS.

3 LAGEPLAN.

4 OSTSEITE.

5 OBERGESCHOSS.

6 STÄDTEBAULICHES
STRUKTURMODELL.

1 SOUTH SIDE.

2 GROUND LEVEL.

3 SITE PLAN.

4 EAST SIDE.

5 UPPER LEVEL.

6 TOWN PLANNING
MODEL.

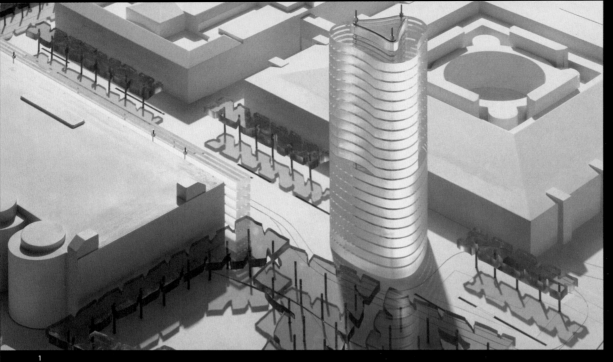

1

2

MESSEPLATZ BASEL

WETTBEWERB: 1998
ENTWURF: Meinhard v. Gerkan
MITARBEITER: Volkmar Sievers,
Brigitte Queck, Bettina Groß,
Sona Kazemi, Sigrid Müller,
Uli Heiwolt

Drei neue Gestaltungselemente sollen den Messeplatz funktional und
ästhetisch neu ordnen: Ein Hochhaus
mit geschwungener Fassade, das
als Blickfang bis auf das andere Rhein-
ufer wirkt; eine zusammenfassende
neue Gebäudeschicht vor der Halle 3
mit dem Parkhaus; und das geschwungene Wetterdach der Tram-
station. Eine einheitliche Pflasterung
der Freiraumflächen und deren Frei-
räumung von Verkehr und Mobiliar
schaffen eine neue Qualität und
Orientierung für die Messebesucher.

Three new design elements are to
redefine the open space in front of
the trade fair complex: a high-rise
with curved facade - a landmark
that can be seen from across the
Rhine, a new building "bracket" in
front of Hall 3 with the multi-storey
car-park, and the undulating roof
over the tram station. A unifying
paving of the open areas and
clearing them of traffic and street
furniture makes for the new
quality of the trade fair complex,
and better orientation for its
visitors.

1 DER NEUE
MESSETURM.
2 LAGEPLAN.
3 DIE DEM
PARKHAUS
VORGEBLENDETE
NEUE FASSADEN-
SCHICHT.
1 THE NEW
EXHIBITION TOWER.
2 SITE PLAN.
3 THE NEW FACADE
OF THE MULTI-
STOREY CAR PARK.

3

TEERHOF, BREMEN

WETTBEWERB: 1997
ENTWURF: Meinhard v. Gerkan
MITARBEITER: Charles de Picciotto, Sona Kazemi

Mit einer einfachen Typologie und unterschiedlichen Materialcharakteristiken wird auf die Situation der Insellage reagiert. Die Häuser werden giebelständig angeordnet und aufgeständert, so daß der Durchblick nach beiden Seiten erhalten bleibt. Der massiven Uferseite im Nordwesten entspricht der „harte" Betoncharakter der Bauten, die nach Südosten gerichteten Fassaden wenden sich mit filigranen Holzgittern dem neuen Platzraum zu.

This project responds to the island situation with a simple typology and distinct materials. The houses are arranged with their gable walls facing in one direction, and they are cantilevered to allow views to both sides. The massive walls along the shore on the northwest side are matched by the "hard" concrete appearance of the houses. The southwestern facades with their filigree wooden latticework face the new urban square.

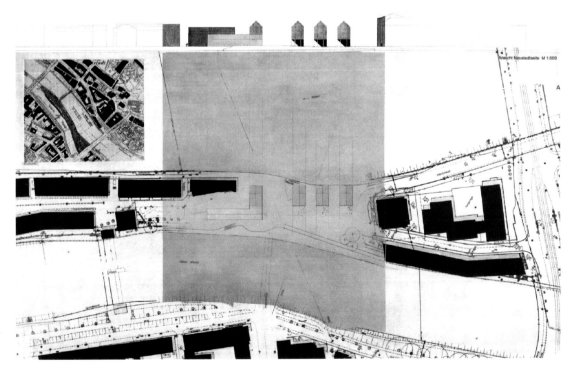

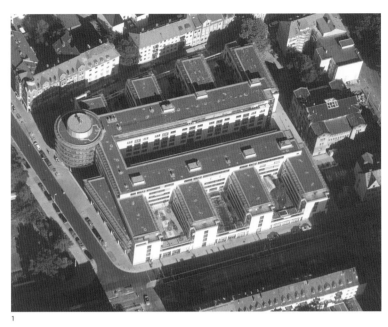

1

CALENBERGER ESPLANADE, HANNOVER

GUTACHTEN: 1991 - 1. Rang
ENTWURF: Meinhard v. Gerkan
PROJEKTPARTNER: Nikolaus Goetze
PROJEKTLEITUNG: Karen Schroeder
MITARBEITER: Martina Klostermann, Michael Haase, Jörg Steinwender, Cordula v. Graevenitz, Andreas Perlick
BAUHERR: Nileg, Niedersächsische Gesellschaft für Landesentwicklung und Wohnungsbau mbH
BAUZEIT: 1996 - 1999
BGF: 44.000 m²
BRI: 161.823 m³

Das neue Ensemble der „Calenberger Esplanade" ergänzt die Calenberger Neustadt in Hannover mit einer städtischen Nutzungsmischung von Wohnen, Büros, Läden und Arztpraxen. Es ist aus einer doppelten Kammstruktur entwickelt, deren Rücken zueinander orientiert sind und dadurch eine ruhige Wohnstraße bilden. Die hellen, intensiv begrünten Höfe öffnen sich zu den engen Straßen der Blockrandbebauung. Eine Baumallee durch die Wohnstraße hindurch bildet eine Achse zum Baudenkmal an einem Ende des Ensembles. Auf der anderen Seite, zur Calenberger Straße hin, wird der Zugang durch einen 7-geschossigen Turm und einen filigran verglasten Stahl-Glas-Erker definiert. Die Wohnstraße wird beidseitig durch hohe Arkaden begrenzt, an denen Läden und Restaurants liegen.

The new "Calenberg Esplanade" adds to the Calenberg Neustadt in Hanover with an urban mix of housing, offices, shops and surgeries. The design is based on a double comb structure with their spines positioned towards each other, generating a calm residential street-scape. The light-flooded, landscaped courtyards open up towards the narrow streets of the otherwise dense environment. An avenue of trees through the residential street forms an axis towards the monument on one end of the ensemble. Towards Calenberger Straße the entrance is defined by a seven-storey tower and a finely structured glass-steel oriel. Tall arcades with shops and restaurants frame the residential street on both sides.

2

1

2

1+2 ERSCHLIESSUNG
DER MAISONETTE-
WOHNUNGEN VON
DER ERHÖHTEN
TERRASSENEBENE
AUS. DER ZUGANG
ERFOLGT VON DER
AXIALEN GASSE
UNTER DEN LÄNGS-
GERICHTETEN
GEBÄUDERIEGELN
HINDURCH.
3 QUERSCHNITT.
4 BLICK IN DIE
AXIALE GASSE, DIE
SYMMETRISCH
AUF DEN ALTBAU
ADOLFSTRASSE 8
ORIENTIERT IST.
1+2 CIRCULATION
OF MAISONETTE
APARTMENTS FROM
THE ELEVATED
TERRACE LEVEL.
THE ENTRANCE IS
POSITIONED ALONG
THE PATH BENEATH
THE LONGITUDINAL
BAR FORMS.
3 CROSS SECTION.
4 VIEW INTO AXIAL
PATH, ORIENTATED
SYMMETRICALLY
TOWARDS THE
BUILDING,
ADOLFSTRAßE 8.

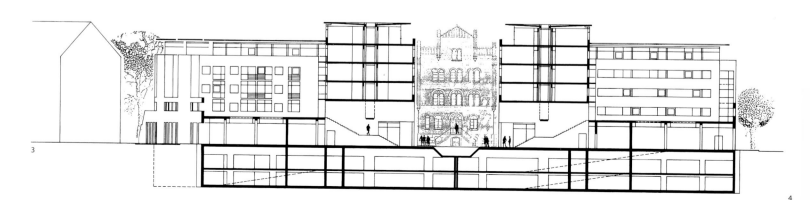

3

4

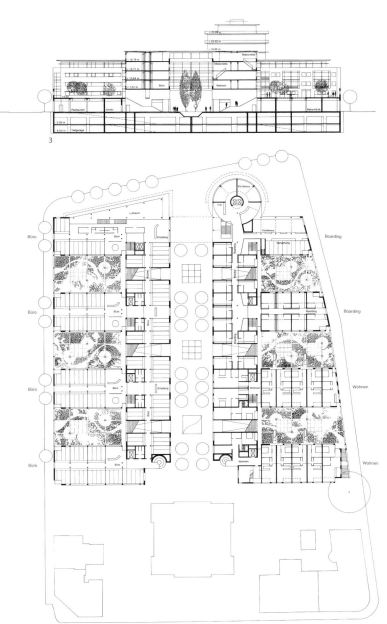

1 BEGEGNUNG
VON ALT UND NEU.
2 DIE AXIALE
GASSE MIT BLICK
NACH NORDEN.
3 QUERSCHNITT.
4 GRUNDRISS 1.
OBERGESCHOSS.
1 OLD MEETS NEW.
2 THE AXIAL PATH
TO THE NORTH.
3 CROSS SECTION.
4 FIRST LEVEL PLAN.

1

1 GEBÄUDEFRONT
ENTLANG DER HUM-
BOLDTSTRASSE.
2 TREPPENAUFGANG
ZUR TERRASSEN-
EBENE UNTER
DEM LÄNGSRIEGEL
HINDURCH.
1 FACADE ALONG
HUMBOLDTSTRASSE.
2 STAIRCASE TO
TERRACE LEVEL
THROUGH THE
LONGITUDINAL BAR.

2

1

1 DIE HAUPTFRONT
DES KOMPLEXES
AN DER CALENBER-
GER STRASSE.
2 NORMAL-
GESCHOSSGRUNDRISS
DES ZYLINDRISCHEN
BAUKÖRPERS.
3 UMLAUFENDE
GALERIEN
STRUKTURIEREN
DIE FASSADE.

1 MAIN ELEVATION
OF THE COMPLEX
ON CALENBERGER
STRASSE.
2 STANDARD
FLOOR PLAN
OF CYLINDRICAL
BUILDING.
3 SURROUNDING
GALLERIES
STRUCTURE THE
FACADE.

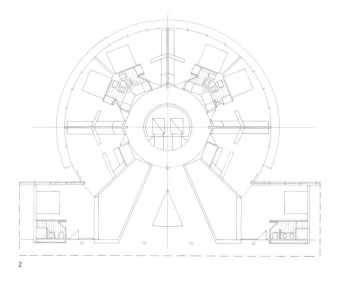

2

3

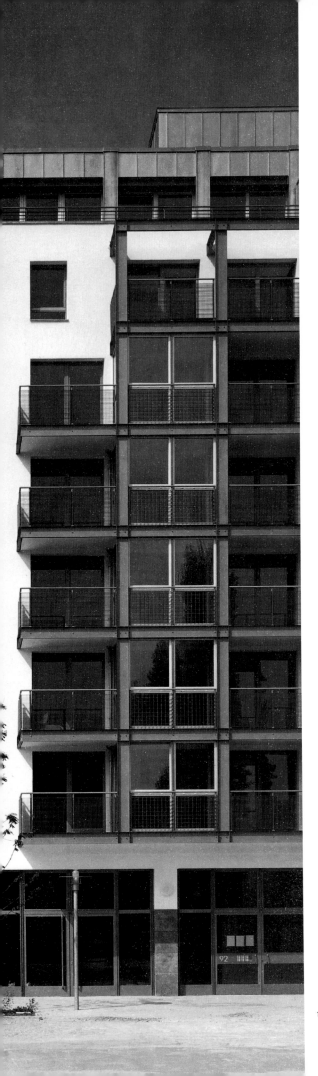

WOHNBEBAUUNG, BERLIN-FRIEDRICHSHAIN

GUTACHTEN: 1992
ENTWURF: Volkwin Marg
PROJEKTLEITUNG:
Sybille Zittlau-Kroos, Dirk Heller
MITARBEITER: Asunta Foronda,
Ivanka Perkovic, Ruth Scheurer,
Susanne Winter
BAUHERR: GSW Gemeinnützige
Siedlungs- und
Wohnungsbaugesellschaft Berlin;
Grundstücksgesellschaft
Friedenstraße Büll & Dr. Liedke
BAUZEIT: 1994 - 1997
BGF: 20.809 m²
BRI: 63.751 m³

Der soziale Wohnungsbau an der
Friedenstraße bildet den ersten
Bauabschnitt des Projektes „Forum
Friedrichshain", mit dem das Gelände
des ehemaligen „Böhmischen Brau-
hauses" städtebaulich neu geordnet
und genutzt werden soll. Ziel ist es,
den Block zwischen Friedenstraße
und Landsberger Allee zu schließen;
der winkelförmige Baukörper des
Wohnungsbaus bildet dazu den ersten Teil, der durch ein Hotel ergänzt
wird. Er ist in acht Einzelhäuser mit
zwei- oder dreispänniger Erschließung
gegliedert; ein zurückgestaffeltes
Dachgeschoß respektiert die traditio-

nelle Berliner Traufhöhe. Das Erdgeschoß einschließlich der Fläche über
der Tiefgarage wird für Läden genutzt; es ist auch in der Fassade von
den Wohngeschossen abgesetzt.
Social housing set along Frieden-
strasse forms the first element of
the "Friedrichshain Forum" project
which reorganizes the urban
design and uses which have taken
place on the former Boehmisches
Brauhaus site. The aim was to close
the block edge between Frieden-
strasse and Landsberger Allee. The
angular residential block forms the
first section which is added to with
a new hotel building. The block is
subdivided into eight individual
units each comprising two or three
span layouts, the staggering of the
attic floor is a reference to the traditional Berlin roof line. The whole
of the ground floor area above
underground car parking will be
allocated to retail use and is also
differentiated in its elevational
treatment from the residential
floors above.

1 FASSADE
ZUR BLOCKDURCH-
QUERUNG. PLASTI-
SCHE GLIEDERUNG
DURCH WINTER-
GÄRTEN, LOGGIEN
UND BALKONE.
2 LAGEPLAN.
1 FACADE
TOWARDS BLOCK
PASSAGE.
THREE-DIMENSIONAL
SEQUENCE THROUGH
CONSERVATORIES,
LOGGIAS
AND BALCONIES.
2 SITE PLAN.

1
2

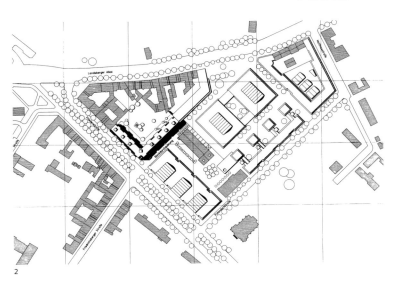

1

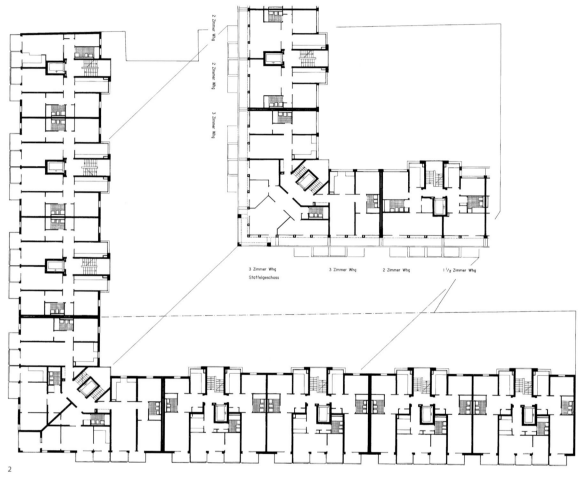

2 Zimmer Whg

2 Zimmer Whg

3 Zimmer Whg

3 Zimmer Whg
Staffelgeschoss

3 Zimmer Whg

2 Zimmer Whg

1 1/2 Zimmer Whg

2

1+3 DIE BLOCKECKE
IN DER PERSPEKTIVI-
SCHEN VISION UND
GEBAUTEN REALITÄT.
2 GRUNDRISSE NOR-
MALGESCHOSS UND
STAFFELGESCHOSS.
1+3 BLOCK CORNER
- 3D IMAGE AND
BUILT REALITY.
2 FLOOR PLANS
OF STANDARD AND
ROOF LEVEL.

„DAS STÄDTISCHE HAUS", BERLIN

WETTBEWERB: 1997
ENTWURF: Meinhard v. Gerkan
MITARBEITER: Stephan Rewolle

Die „Split-Level"-Typen mit der versetzten Fassadenfront sind stadträumlich vielfältig kombinierbar und geben dem Straßenraum Profil und Rhythmus. Im Inneren sind die Flächen vielseitig nutzbar je nach den Wohnvorstellungen der Familie; es gibt weder Flure noch ungenutzte Restflächen. Der schmale, vertikal betonte Gebäudetypus verbraucht zudem wenig Grundstücksfläche, bleibt dabei dennoch von außen klar als Einheit ablesbar. Die Gebäude sind als „Niedrigenergiehäuser" konzipiert mit einem Nutzwärmebedarf unter 70 kWh/m².

The "split-level" housing types with their staggered facades can be combined in various forms, rendering a profile and frequency to the street environment. Internally, the spaces offer a flexible use according to the living conceptions of the families, corridors and residual areas have been avoided. The narrow, vertically emphasized building type occupies little site area, but is externally nevertheless a clearly identifiable unit. The buildings are designed as "low-energy-houses" with an energy consumption of less than 70 kwh/m².

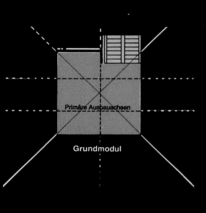

Primäre Ausbauachsen

Grundmodul

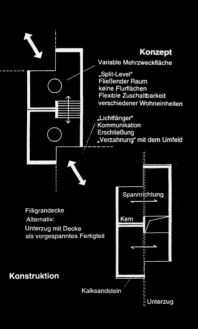

Konzept
Variable Mehrzweckfläche

„Split-Level"
Fließender Raum
keine Flurflächen
Flexible Zuschaltbarkeit
verschiedener Wohneinheiten

„Lichtfänger"
Kommunikation
Erschließung
„Verzahnung" mit dem Umfeld

Spannrichtung

Filigrandecke
Alternativ:
Unterzug mit Decke
als vorgespanntes Fertigteil

Kern

Konstruktion

Kalksandstein

Unterzug

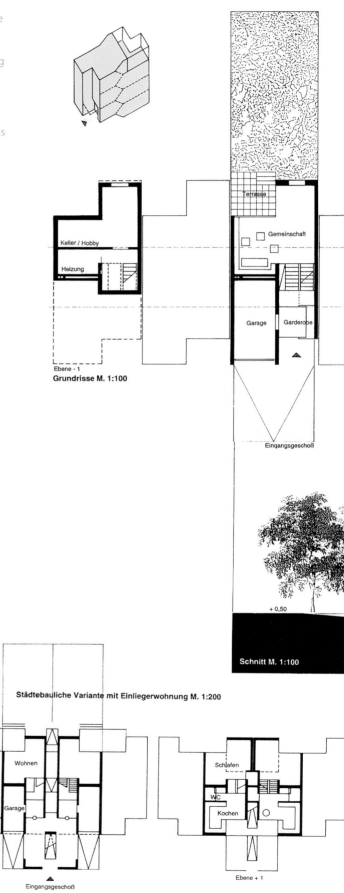

Keller / Hobby

Heizung

Terrasse

Gemeinschaft

Garage   Garderobe

Ebene - 1
Grundrisse M. 1:100

Eingangsgeschoß

+ 0,50

Schnitt M. 1:100

Städtebauliche Variante mit Einliegerwohnung M. 1:200

Wohnen

Garage

Schlafen

WC

Kochen

Eingangsgeschoß

Ebene + 1

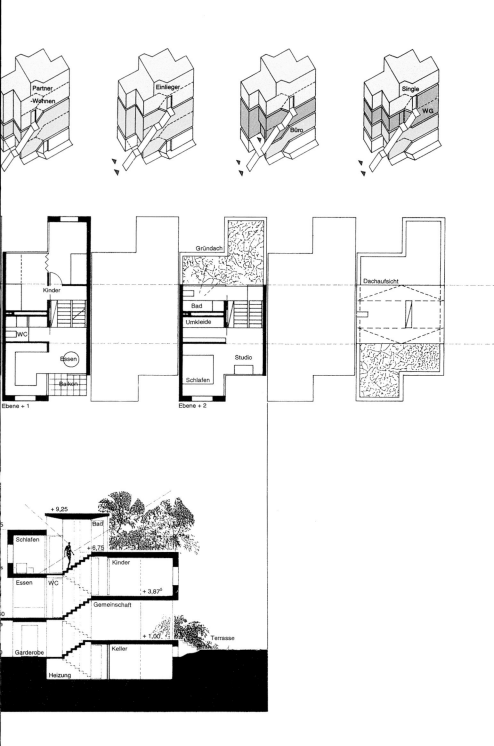

Ebene + 1

Gründach

Bad
Umkleide

Studio

Schlafen

Ebene + 2

Dachaufsicht

Partner
-Wohnen

Einlieger

Büro

Single

WG

Kinder

WC

Essen

Balkon

+ 9,25

Bad

Schlafen

+ 6,75

Kinder

Essen   WC

+ 3,87⁵

Gemeinschaft

+ 1,00

Terrasse

Garderobe

Keller

Heizung

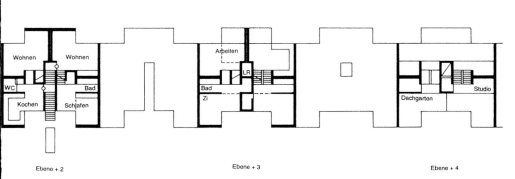

Wohnen   Wohnen

WC   Bad

Kochen   Schlafen

Ebene + 2

Arbeiten

LR

Bad
Zi

Ebene + 3

Studio

Dachgarten

Ebene + 4

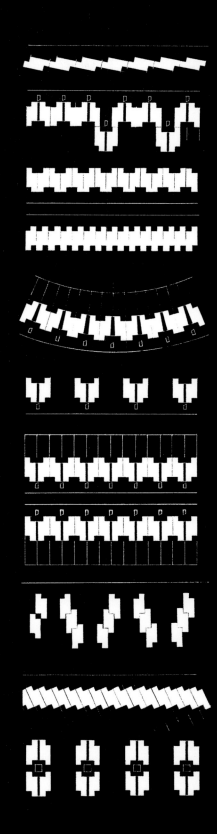

ALSTERFLEET BEBAUUNG, HAMBURG

WETTBEWERB: 1997
ENTWURF: Meinhard v. Gerkan
mit Johann v. Mansberg
MITARBEITER: Philipp Kamps,
Sigrid Müller, Michael Biwer

Die Bebauung schließt die letzte Baulücke zwischen Alster und Elbe („Fleetachse") und verläuft parallel zum Alsterwanderweg.
Deshalb wird auf die öffentlichen Nutzungen in einer Arkadenzone besonderer Wert gelegt (Antiquariate, Buchläden, Café). Gegliedert ist die geforderte Nutzung so, daß das Bürohaus zur Hauptstraße hin orientiert ist, die Wohnhäuser, die als Einzelbauten bestehen, mit ihren Grünhöfen zur ruhigeren Zone am Fleet liegen.
Alle Wohnhäuser sind als modifizierte Dreibünder aufgeteilt. Verglaste Gänge erschließen die Wohnungen, deren mittlere nur zum Fleet hin orientiert ist. Das bietet vielfältige Wohnformen zwischen Loft und Maisonnetten.

This development closes the last urban structural gap between the Alster and the Elbe along the narrow canal (Fleet) axis and runs parallel to the footpath on the Alster bank. This is why special emphasis is laid on the embankment's public use as a shopping arcade with antiques and bookshops and a cafes. The required functional spaces were arranged in such a way that the offices face the main street, and the dwellings (single units) have their garden courts on the Fleet.
All residential buildings are modified three-part structures. Glazed corridors give access to the apartments, the middle ones of which face only the Fleet. This arrangement offers various types of dwelling, from lofts to maisonnettes.

1

2

3

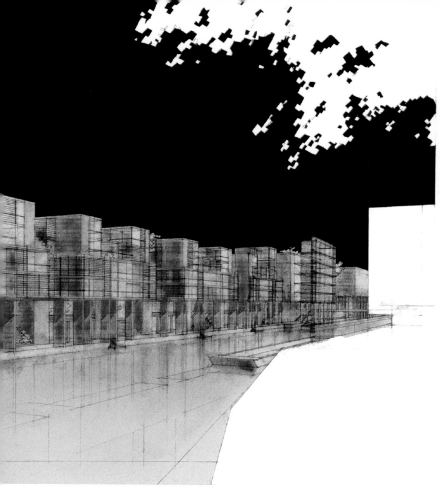

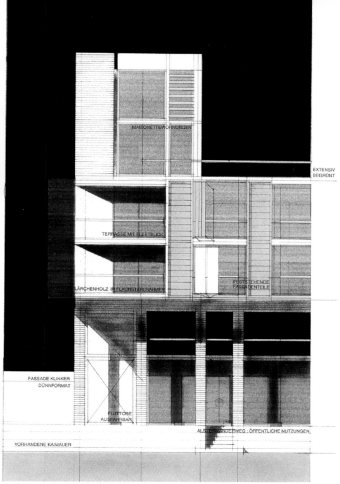

EXTENSIV BEGRÜNT

MAISONETTEWOHNUNGEN

TERRASSE MIT FLEETBLICK

LÄRCHENHOLZ IM FLACHSTAHLRAHMEN

FREISTEHENDE FASSADENTEILE

FASSADE KLINKER DÜNNFORMAT

FLUTTÖRE AUSFAHRBAR

ALSTERWANDERWEG : ÖFFENTLICHE NUTZUNGEN

VORHANDENE KAIMAUER

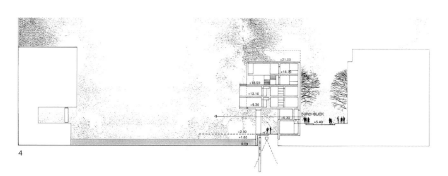

4

1 BLICK VON SÜDEN/
FASSADENDETAIL.
2 SÜDOSTANSICHT.
3 EINGANGSGESCHOß.
4 QUERSCHNITT.
5 LAGE IN DER STADT.
1 VIEW FROM THE
SOUTH / FACADE
DETAIL.
2 SOUTH-EAST
ELEVATION.
3 ENTRANCE LEVEL.
4 CROSS SECTION.
5 LOCATION IN THE
CITY CONTEXT.

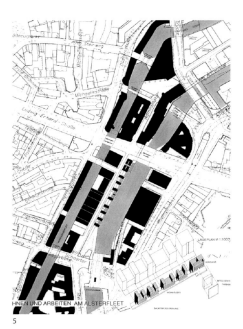

HNEN UND ARBEITEN AM ALSTERFLEET

5

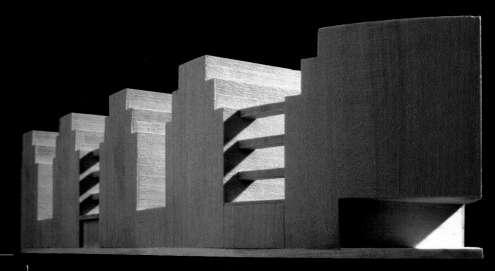

HAUS DER ARCHITEKTEN, DÜSSELDORF

WETTBEWERB: 1998
ENTWURF: Meinhard v. Gerkan
mit Nicolai Pix

Die Lage des Grundstücks parallel zum Rhein erlaubt die Assoziation eines „Architektenschiffes" - ein Symbol, das über Jahrhunderte eng mit dem Bauen verbunden ist. Es wird in der Form der geschlossenen Sockelzone angedeutet. Darüber liegen fünf „Speicherhäuser" senkrecht zum Ufer, von Höfen jeweils unterbrochen. Sie werden durch gläserne Brücken miteinander verbunden. Ihre charakteristische, identifizierbare Form erhalten sie durch die Staffelung der obersten zwei Geschosse.
The site location, parallel to the Rhine, allowed for a metaphorical design association with an "architects' ship" - a symbol that for centuries has been closely connected with building. A reference is made with a windowless base course, above which are five "warehouses", perpendicular to the waterline, and interrupted by harbour basins. The five wings are linked by bridges, each receiving its distinct form through two receding stepped floors at roof level.

1+2 MODELL.
3 ANSICHT ZOLLHOF.
4 ERDGESCHOSS.
5 REGELGESCHOSS.
6 LÄNGSSCHNITT.
1+2 MODEL.
3 ELEVATION
FROM ZOLLHOF.
4 GROUND LEVEL.
5 STANDARD LEVEL.
6 LONGITUDINAL
SECTION.

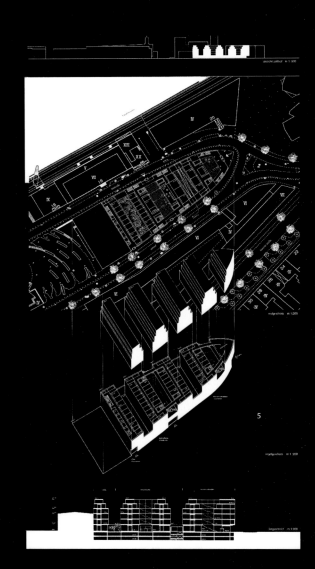

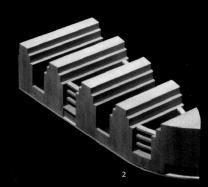

WOHN- UND GESCHÄFTSHAUS AM BENEDIKTS- PLATZ, ERFURT

WETTBEWERB: 1997
ENTWURF: Meinhard v. Gerkan mit Philipp Kamps

Zwischen Fischmarkt, Benediktsplatz und dem öffentlichen Durchgang zur ehemaligen Synagoge sollen Arkaden im Erdgeschoß vermitteln; das Wohn- und Geschäftshaus bekommt so eine Funktion als städtisches Element. Das wird durch die einfache baukörperliche Schließung der Ecke im Sinne der Heilung einer einstmals intakten Stadtstrutur betont. Vertikal gliedert sich das Gebäude in die Sockelzone in Betonwerkstein und die Hauptfassade in Sandstein mit Intarsien in Baubronze. Der gesamte Baukörper erhält ein treppenförmig abgestaffeltes Dach.

With its arcaded passage at ground floor level, this office and apartment building is to make the link between the squares of Fischmarkt and Benediktsplatz and the public passageway to the former synagogue, thus functioning as an urban design element. This idea is substantiated by means of the simple architectural closing of the corner in the sense of healing the formerly intact urban fabric. Vertically, the building is organized in layers: first the base course of cast concrete blocks, then the main fassade area in sandstone with inlays of architectural bronze. The entire building volume is covered by a stepped roof.

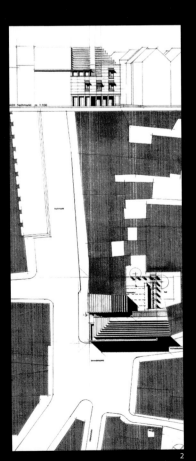

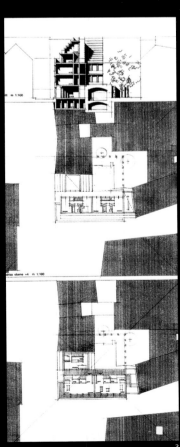

1 MODELLSTUDIE.
2 LAGEPLAN, WESTANSICHT.
3 SCHNITT, GRUNDRISSE.
4 FASSADENDETAIL.

1 MODEL STUDY.
2 SITE PLAN, WEST ELEVATION.
3 SECTION, PLANS.
4 FACADE DETAIL.

INTERIMSBEBAUUNG - EXPO 2000, HANNOVER

STUDIE: 1998
ENTWURF: Meinhard v. Gerkan, Joachim Zais
MITARBEITER: Monika van Vught, Cornelia Thamm, Gabriele Wysocki, Ulf Düsterhöft, Hilke Eustrup, Rolf Duerre, Olaf Schlüter, Thomas Dreusicke, Helge Reimer, Thomas Kehl
AUFTRAGGEBER:
Expo 2000 Hannover GmbH

Bei der Studie handelt es sich um den Nachweis einer möglichen temporären Bebauung auf den Randfeldern der EXPO-Plaza, sofern die Investoren-Bebauung nicht vollständig realisiert werden kann. In den nur für die Dauer der Ausstellung zu errichtenden Gebäuden sollen EXPO-Funktionen untergebracht werden. Vorgeschlagen wird für diesen Fall ein „Strukturgerüst" aus Stahl mit großer Flexibilität in der Grundrißausbildung. Die zweigeschossige Bebauung, die sich um Höfe gruppiert, erhält „Türme", die die vorgesehene Bauhöhe aus dem Bebauungsplan von etwa 18 m erreicht und somit die räumlichen Proportionen wahrt. An ihnen können zum Beispiel Transparente mit dem EXPO-Logo installiert werden. Das „Strukturgerüst" basiert auf einem in Grundriß und Höhenentwicklung gleichen Achsmaß. Die Höfe können mit einer leichten Stahlkonstruktion überspannt werden und bilden so stützenfreie, etwa 9 m hohe Hallenbereiche für verschiedenste Nutzungen. Treppen an den Eckpunkten und Aufzüge an den Außenbereichen sichern die vertikale Erschließung. In offenen Bereichen zu den Höfen entstehen zur Plaza hin Kolonnaden. Das gesamte Stahltragsystem ist als sichtbar verzinkte Konstruktion vorgesehen, die Fassaden werden witterungsbeständig aus genuteten Betoplanplatten oder Aluminium-Wellblech gebildet, auch die Sonnenschutzlamellen werden aus verzinktem Stahlblech gebaut.

The study acknowledges a feasibility of temporary developments in the border areas of the EXPO plaza. If the investor generated development cannot be completely realized, these buildings (erected only for the exhibition duration) should serve for EXPO functions. A structural steel framework with a highly flexible plan has been proposed. Two-story buildings are grouped around courtyards and are extended with towers, which reach the designated height of 18 m, therefore maintaining spatial proportions. EXPO flags can be mounted on these towers. The structural framework is founded upon an axial dimension identical in the horizontal and vertical extension. The courtyards can be covered with a lightweight steel construction and would offer approximately 9 m high, column-free halls for various uses. Stair cores positioned in each corner and external escalators ensure for clear vertical circulation. Colonnades are proposed for the open courtyard towards the plaza. The supporting steel structure is totally galvanized, with facades made from weatherproof "Betoplan" elements or corrugated aluminium. The sun protection louvers are also constructed from galvanized sheet steel.

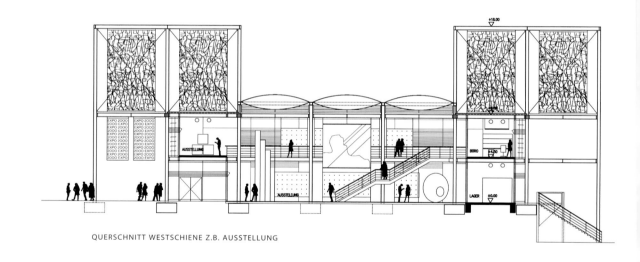

QUERSCHNITT WESTSCHIENE Z.B. AUSSTELLUNG

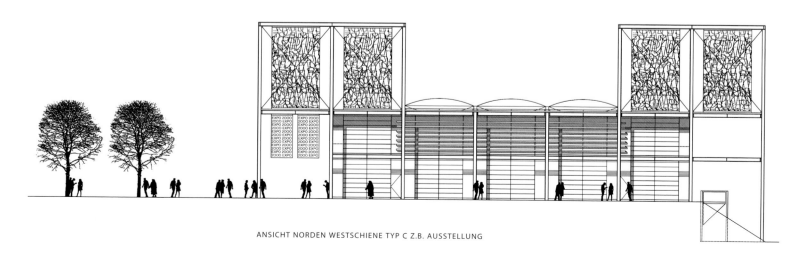

ANSICHT NORDEN WESTSCHIENE TYP C Z.B. AUSSTELLUNG

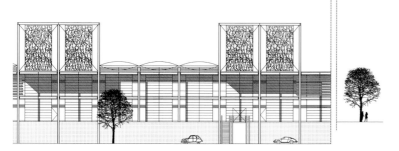

ANSICHT STRASSE WESTSCHIENE TYP E Z.B. FOOD-COURT

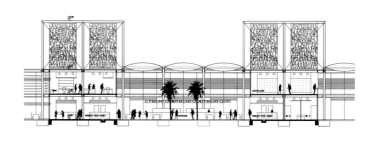

LÄNGSSCHNITT WESTSCHIENE Z.B. FOOD-COURT

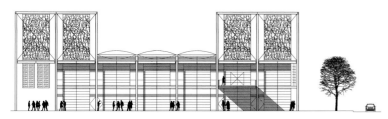

ANSICHT SÜDEN OSTSCHIENE TYP B Z.B. EINGANG OST/MERCHANDISING

LÄNGSSCHNITT OSTSCHIENE Z.B. EINGANG OST/MERCHANDISING

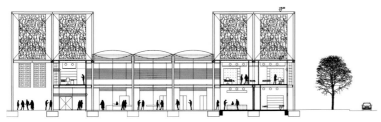

QUERSCHNITT OSTSCHIENE Z.B. EINGANG OST/MERCHANDISING

ANSICHT PLAZA OSTSCHIENE TYP A Z.B. EINGANG OST/MERCHANDISING

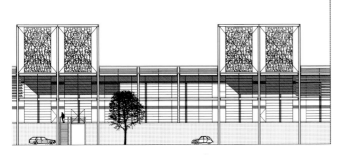

ANSICHT STRASSE WESTSCHIENE TYP D Z.B. GEFLÜGELHAUS

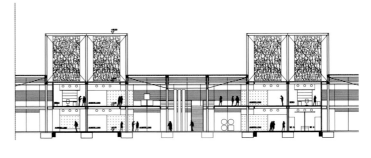

LÄNGSSCHNITT WESTSCHIENE Z.B. INTERNATIONALE ORGANISATION

QUERSCHNITT WESTSCHIENE Z.B. GEFLÜGELHAUS

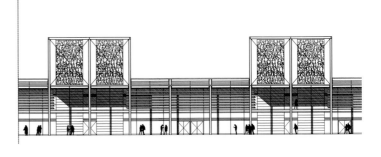

ANSICHT PLAZA WESTSCHIENE TYP A Z.B. GEFLÜGELHAUS

EXPO

TÜREN GANZGLAS
BODENSCHLIESSER

DETAIL 5   DETAIL 6

ANSICHT

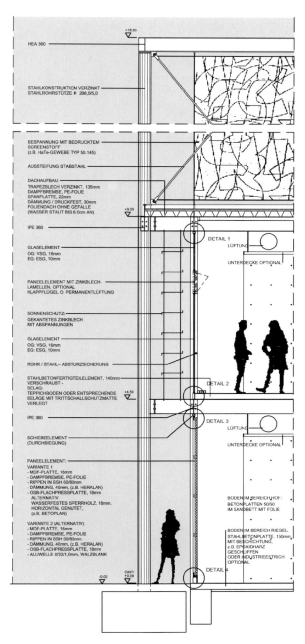

HEA 360

STAHLKONSTRUKTION VERZINKT
STAHLROHRSTÜTZE ∅ 298,5/5,0

+18.00

BESPANNUNG MIT BEDRUCKTEM
SCREENSTOFF
(z.B. HaTe-GEWEBE TYP 50.145)

AUSSTEIFUNG STABSTAHL

DACHAUFBAU:
TRAPEZBLECH VERZINKT, 135mm
DAMPFBREMSE, PE-FOLIE
SPANPLATTE, 22mm
DÄMMUNG / DRUCKFEST, 30mm
FOLIENDACH OHNE GEFÄLLE
(WASSER STAUT BIS 6.0cm AN)

IPE 360

GLASELEMENT
OG: VSG, 16mm
EG: ESG, 10mm

PANEELELEMENT MIT ZINKBLECH-
LAMELLEN, OPTIONAL
KLAPPFLÜGEL O. PERMANENTLÜFTUNG

SONNENSCHUTZ:
GEKANTETES ZINKBLECH
MIT ABSPANNUNGEN

GLASELEMENT
OG: VSG, 16mm
EG: ESG, 10mm

ROHR / STAHL- ABSTURZSICHERUNG

STAHLBETONFERTIGTEILELEMENT, 140mm
VERSCHRAUBT -
BELAG:
TEPPICHBODEN ODER ENTSPRECHENDE
BELÄGE MIT TRITTSCHALLSCHUTZMATTE
VERLEGT

IPE 360

SCHIEBEELEMENT
(DURCHBIEGUNG)

PANEELELEMENT:
VARIANTE 1
- MDF-PLATTE, 16mm
- DAMPFBREMSE, PE-FOLIE
- RIPPEN IN BSH 60/80mm
- DÄMMUNG, 40mm, (z.B. HERALAN)
- OSB-FLACHPRESSPLATTE, 18mm
  ALTERNATIV
  WASSERFESTES SPERRHOLZ, 18mm,
  HORIZONTAL GENUTET,
  (z.B. BETOPLAN)

VARIANTE 2 (ALTERNATIV)
- MDF-PLATTE, 16mm
- DAMPFBREMSE, PE-FOLIE
- RIPPEN IN BSH 60/80mm
- DÄMMUNG, 40mm, (z.B. HERALAN)
- OSB-FLACHPRESSPLATTE, 18mm
- ALUWELLE 6/32/1,0mm, WALZBLANK

+9.00

DETAIL 1
LÜFTUNG

UNTERDECKE OPTIONAL

DETAIL 2

+4.50

DETAIL 3
LÜFTUNG

UNTERDECKE OPTIONAL

BODEN IM BEREICH HOF:
BETONPLATTEN 50/50
IM SANDBETT MIT FOLIE

BODEN IM BEREICH RIEGEL:
STAHLBETONPLATTE, 150mm,
MIT BESCHICHTUNG,
z.B. EPOXIDHARZ
GESCHLIFFEN
ODER INDUSTRIEESTRICH
OPTIONAL

DETAIL 4

OKFF
+0.08

-0.02

SCHNITT

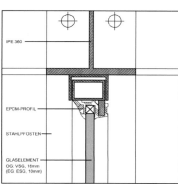

IPE 360

EPDM-PROFIL

STAHLPFOSTEN

GLASELEMENT
OG: VSG, 16mm
(EG: ESG, 10mm)

KOPFPUNKT FASSADE OG

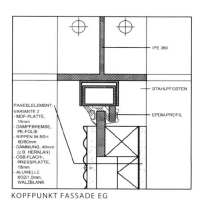

IPE 360

STAHLPFOSTEN

PANEELELEMENT:
VARIANTE 2
- MDF-PLATTE,
  19mm
- DAMPFBREMSE,
  PE-FOLIE
- RIPPEN IN BSH
  60/80mm
- DÄMMUNG, 40mm,
  (z.B. HERALAN)
- OSB-FLACH-
  PRESSPLATTE,
  18mm
- ALUWELLE
  6/32/1,0mm,
  WALZBLANK

EPDM-PROFIL

KOPFPUNKT FASSADE EG

GLASELEMENT
OG: VSG, 16mm
(EG: ESG, 10mm)

STAHLPFOSTEN

EPDM-PROFIL

BELAG:
TEPPICHBODEN O.
ENTSPR. BELÄGE
M. TRITTSCHALL-
SCHUTZMATTE
VERLEGT

STAHLBETON-
FERTIGTEIL-
ELEMENT, 140mm,
VERSCHRAUBT

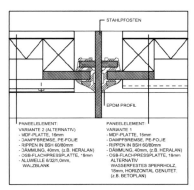

FUSSPUNKT FASSADE OG

PANEELELEMENT:
VARIANTE 1
- MDF-PLATTE,
  16mm
- DAMPFBREMSE,
  PE-FOLIE
- RIPPEN IN BSH
  60/80mm
- DÄMMUNG, 40mm,
  (z.B. HERALAN)
- OSB-FLACH-
  PRESSPLATTE,
  18mm, ALTERN.
  WASSERFESTES
  SPERRHOLZ,
  18mm, HORIZONT.
  GENUTET,
  (z.B. BETOPLAN)

STAHLBETON-
PLATTE, 150mm,
MIT BESCHICHT.,
z.B. EPOXIDHARZ
GESCHLIFFEN O.
INDUSTRIEESTR.
OPTIONAL

EPDM-PROFIL

STAHLPFOSTEN

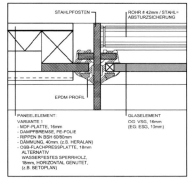

FUSSPUNKT FASSADE EG

STAHLPFOSTEN

EPDM PROFIL

PANEELELEMENT:
VARIANTE 2 (ALTERNATIV)
- MDF-PLATTE, 16mm
- DAMPFBREMSE, PE-FOLIE
- RIPPEN IN BSH 60/80mm
- DÄMMUNG, 40mm, (z.B. HERALAN)
- OSB-FLACHPRESSPLATTE, 18mm
- ALUWELLE 6/32/1,0mm,
  WALZBLANK

PANEELELEMENT:
VARIANTE 1
- MDF-PLATTE, 16mm
- DAMPFBREMSE, PE-FOLIE
- RIPPEN IN BSH 60/80mm
- DÄMMUNG, 40mm, (z.B. HERALAN)
- OSB-FLACHPRESSPLATTE, 18mm
  ALTERNATIV
  WASSERFESTES SPERRHOLZ,
  18mm, HORIZONTAL GENUTET,
  (z.B. BETOPLAN)

HORIZ.-SCHNITT PFOSTEN OG

STAHLPFOSTEN

ROHR ∅ 42mm / STAHL=
ABSTURZSICHERUNG

EPDM PROFIL

PANEELELEMENT:
VARIANTE 1
- MDF-PLATTE, 16mm
- DAMPFBREMSE, PE-FOLIE
- RIPPEN IN BSH 60/80mm
- DÄMMUNG, 40mm, (z.B. HERALAN)
- OSB-FLACHPRESSPLATTE, 18mm
  ALTERNATIV
  WASSERFESTES SPERRHOLZ,
  18mm, HORIZONTAL GENUTET,
  (z.B. BETOPLAN)

GLASELEMENT
OG: VSG, 16mm
(EG: ESG, 10mm)

HORIZ.-SCHNITT PFOSTEN EG

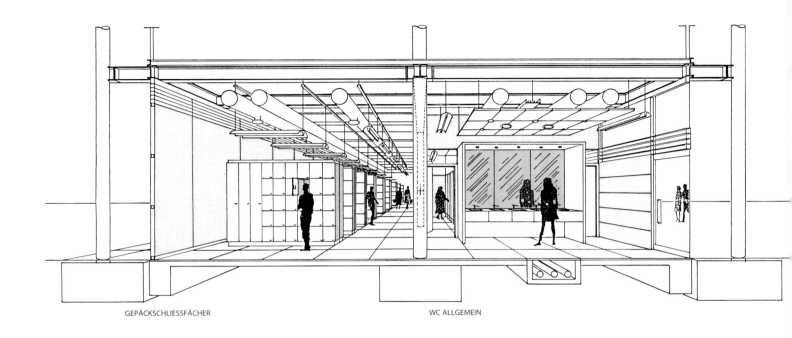

GEPÄCKSCHLIESSFÄCHER   WC ALLGEMEIN

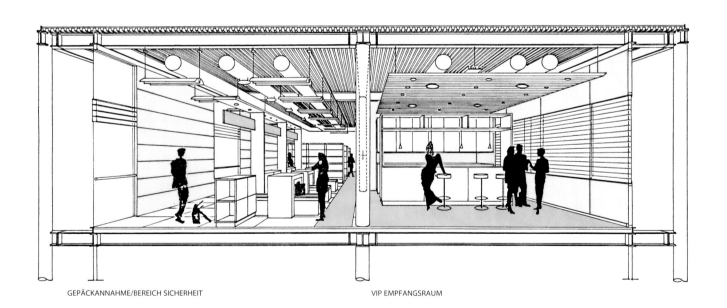

GEPÄCKANNAHME/BEREICH SICHERHEIT   VIP EMPFANGSRAUM

VARIANTE „GEFLÜGELHAUS" GRUNDRISS OG

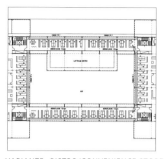

VARIANTE „BISTRO/CONVENIENCE STORE"
GRUNDRISS OG

VARIANTE „FOOD-COURT" GRUNDRISS OG

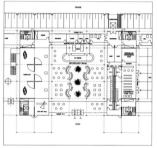

VARIANTE „GEFLÜGELHAUS" GRUNDRISS EG

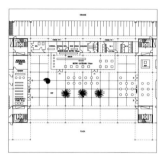

VARIANTE „BISTRO/CONVENIENCE STORE"
GRUNDRISS EG

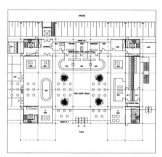

VARIANTE „FOOD-COURT" GRUNDRISS EG.

VARIANTE „AUSSTELLUNG" GRUNDRISS OG

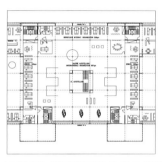

VARIANTE „INTERNATIONALE ORGANISATION"
GRUNDRISS OG

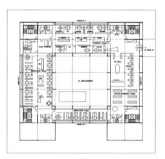

VARIANTE „EINGANG OST/MERCHANDISING"
GRUNDRISS OG

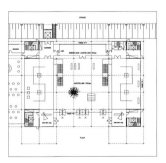

VARIANTE „AUSSTELLUNG" GRUNDRISS EG

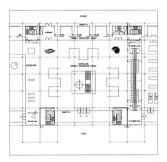

VARIANTE „INTERNATIONALE ORGANISATION"
GRUNDRISS EG

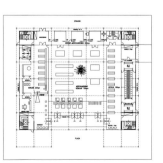

VARIANTE „EINGANG OST/MERCHANDISING"
GRUNDRISS EG

GRUNDRISS

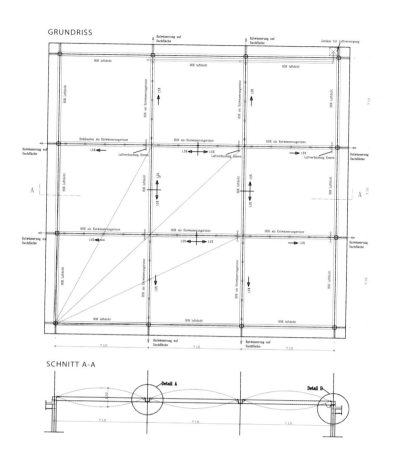

Entwässerung auf Dachfläche   Entwässerung auf Dachfläche   Gebläse für Luftversorgung

HOK luftdicht   HOK luftdicht   HOK luftdicht

Hohlkasten als Entwässerungsrinne   HOK als Entwässerungsrinne   HOK als Entwässerungsrinne

Entwässerung auf Dachfläche

Luftverbindung Kissen   Luftverbindung Kissen   Luftverbindung Kissen

HOK als Entwässerungsrinne   HOK als Entwässerungsrinne   HOK als Entwässerungsrinne

Entwässerung auf Dachfläche

HOK luftdicht   HOK luftdicht   HOK luftdicht

Entwässerung auf Dachfläche   Entwässerung auf Dachfläche

7.10   7.10   7.10

SCHNITT A-A

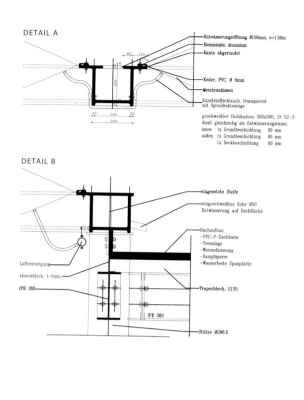

Detail A   Detail B

7.10   7.10   7.10

DETAIL A

Entwässerungsöffnung Ø150mm, e=1.50m
Klemmleiste, Aluminium
Kante abgerundet
Keder, PVC, Ø 8mm
Membrankissen
Kunststoffschlauch, transparent mit Spiraldrahteinlage

geschweißter Hohlkasten 300x300, St 52-3
dient gleichzeitig als Entwässerungsrinne,
innen   1x Grundbeschichtung   80 æm
außen   1x Grundbeschichtung   80 æm
   1x Deckbeschichtung   80 æm

DETAIL B

eingesetzte Steife
eingeschweißtes Rohr Ø50
Entwässerung auf Dachfläche

Dachaufbau:
– PVC-P-Dachbahn
– Trennlage
– Wärmedämmung
– Dampfsperre
– Wasserfeste Spanplatte

Luftversorgung
Abdeckblech, t=5mm
IPE 360
Trapezblech, E135
IPE 360
Stütze Ø298.5

PROFILVARIANTEN DER STAHLTRAGKONSTRUKTION - TRÄGERANSCHLÜSSE AN STÜTZEN

VARIANTE A

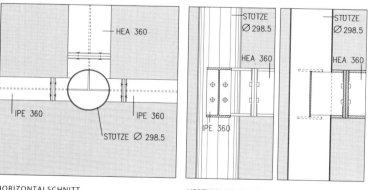

HEA 360
IPE 360
IPE 360
STÜTZE Ø 298.5
STÜTZE Ø 298.5
STÜTZE Ø 298.5
HEA 360
HEA 360
IPE 360

HORIZONTALSCHNITT   VERTIKALSCHNITTE

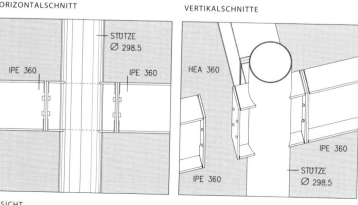

STÜTZE Ø 298.5
IPE 360
IPE 360
HEA 360
IPE 360
IPE 360
STÜTZE Ø 298.5

ANSICHT   ISOMETRIE

VARIANTE B

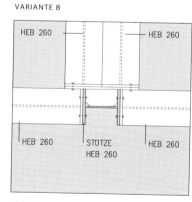

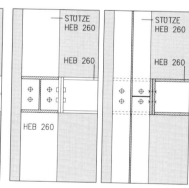

HEB 260
HEB 260
STÜTZE HEB 260
STÜTZE HEB 260
HEB 260
HEB 260
HEB 260
HEB 260
STÜTZE HEB 260

HORIZONTALSCHNITT   VERTIKALSCHNITTE

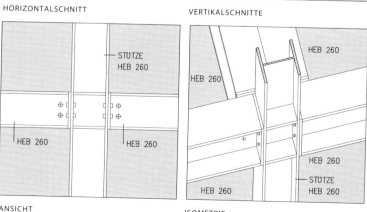

STÜTZE HEB 260
HEB 260
HEB 260
HEB 260
HEB 260
HEB 260
HEB 260
HEB 260
STÜTZE HEB 260

ANSICHT   ISOMETRIE

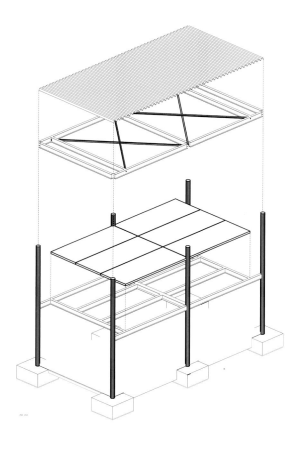

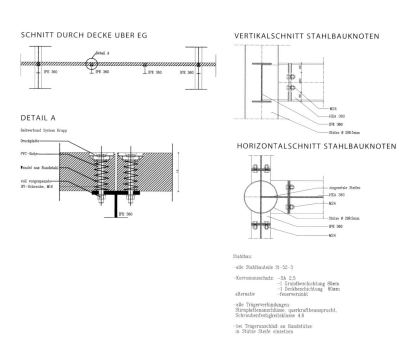

SCHNITT DURCH DECKE ÜBER EG

IPE 360   IPE 360   IPE 360   IPE 360

DETAIL A

Reibverbund System Krupp
Druckplatte
PVC-Rohr
Wendel aus Rundstahl
voll vorgespannte
HV-Schraube, M16

IPE 360

VERTIKALSCHNITT STAHLBAUKNOTEN

M24
HEA 360
IPE 360
Stütze Ø 298.5mm

HORIZONTALSCHNITT STAHLBAUKNOTEN

eingesetzte Steifen
HEA 360
M24
Stütze Ø 298.5mm
IPE 360
M24

Stahlbau:

-alle Stahlbauteile St-52-3

-Korrosionsschutz: –SA 2,5
                   –1 Grundbeschichtung 80æm
                   –1 Deckbeschichtung 80æm
alternativ   –feuerverzinkt

-alle Trägerverbindungen:
Stirnplattenanschlüsse, querkraftbeansprucht,
Schraubenfestigkeitsklasse 4.6

-bei Trägeranschluß an Randstütze:
in Stütze Steife einsetzen

FASSADENELEMENTE - AUSSEN   FASSADENELEMENTE - INNEN   ELEMENTE DER ERSCHLIESSUNG

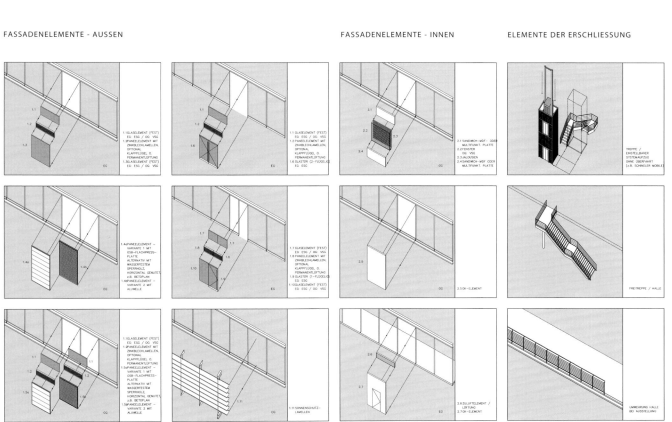

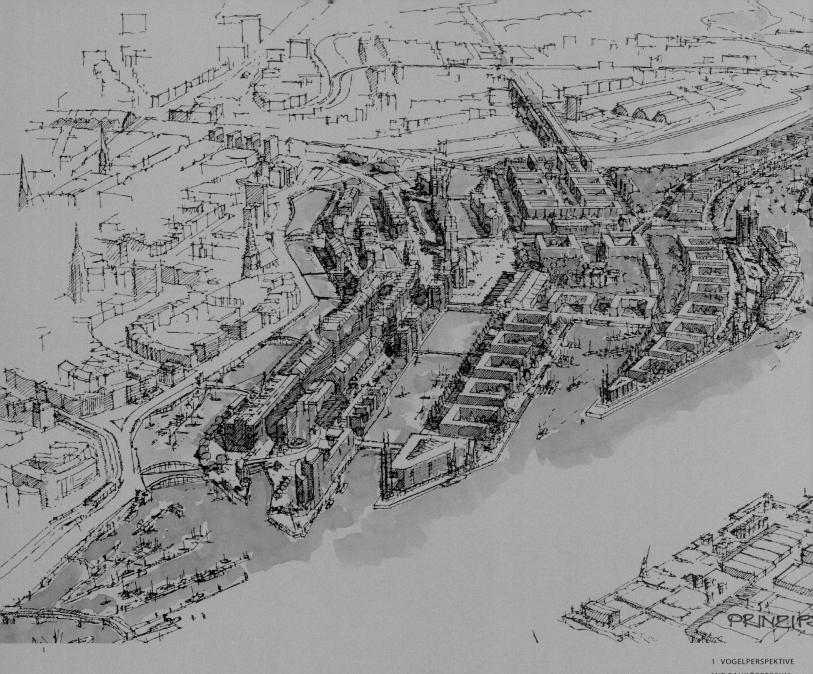

1

PRINZIP

1 VOGELPERSPEKTIVE
MIT BAUKÖRPERSYM-
BOLEN.
2 LUFTBILD DES
HAFENAREALS,
STAND 1996.
1 AERIAL
PERSPECTIVE WITH
BUILDING SYMBOLS.
2 AERIAL
PHOTOGRAPH OF
THE HARBOUR AREA,
1996.

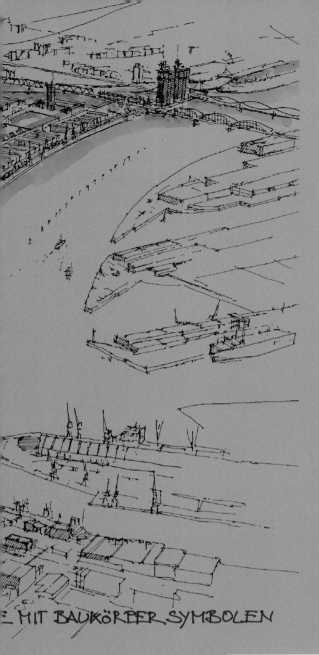

E MIT BAUKÖRPER SYMBOLEN

"HAFENCITY", HAMBURG

STUDIE: 1997
ENTWURF: Volkwin Marg
BEARBEITUNG: RWTH Aachen,
Fakultät für Architektur,
Lehrstuhl für Stadtbereichsplanung
AUFTRAGGEBER: Gesellschaft für
Hafen- und Standortentwicklung GHS

Nach der Wende mit der Öffnung
von NATO und EU zum Osten wird
das traditionelle Hinterland Hamburgs
mit einem wirtschaftlichen Potential
von 150 Millionen Menschen in zu-
nehmendem Maße wieder erschlossen - eine große wirtschaftliche
Chance. Das erfordert mehr Flächen
für metropolitane Dienstleistungen
als in der Innenstadt vorhanden sind.
Im Zuge der fortschreitenden Um-
strukturierung des Hafens wird deshalb ein Teil davon mit einer optimalen Lage zur Innenstadt, angrenzend
an die historische Speicherstadt, als
neue "Hafen - City" ausgewiesen und
in dem Gutachten modellhaft in verschiedenen Alternativen mit Nutzungen versehen.

After the re-unification and the
opening of NATO and the EU towards the East, the traditional
hinterland of Hamburg with the
economical potential of its 150 million population is being re-devel-
oped - a remarkable economic opportunity. This process requires
more area for metropolitan services
than is available in the city centre.
In the course of the advancing
re-structuring of the harbour,
an area in close proximity to the
inner city and the neighbouring
historical "Speicherstadt" is defined
as the new "Harbour City" and
presented with various uses in a
feasibility study.

2

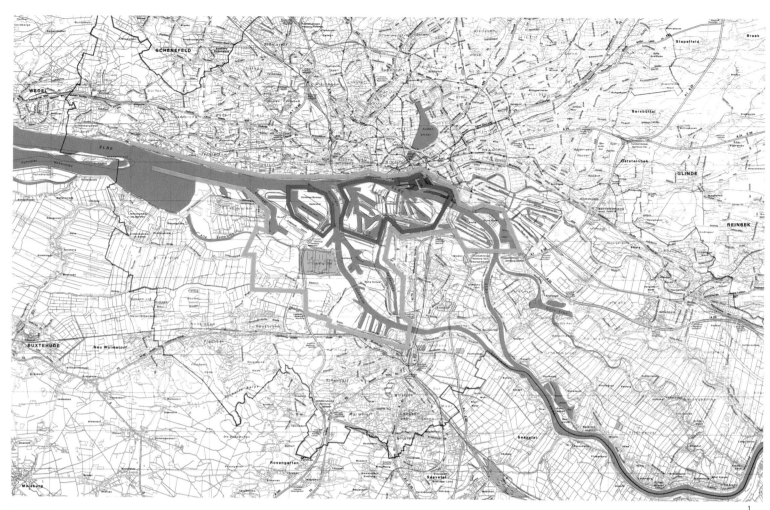

1 ENGERES
UND WEITERES
PLANUNGSGEBIET.
2 BAUSTRUKTUR
1996.
3 STRUKTUR DER
NEUBEBAUUNG.

1 FOCAL AND
SURROUNDING
PLANNING AREA.
2 EXISTING
BUILDING
STRUCTURE 1996.
3 STRUCTURE
OF PROPOSED
BUILDINGS.

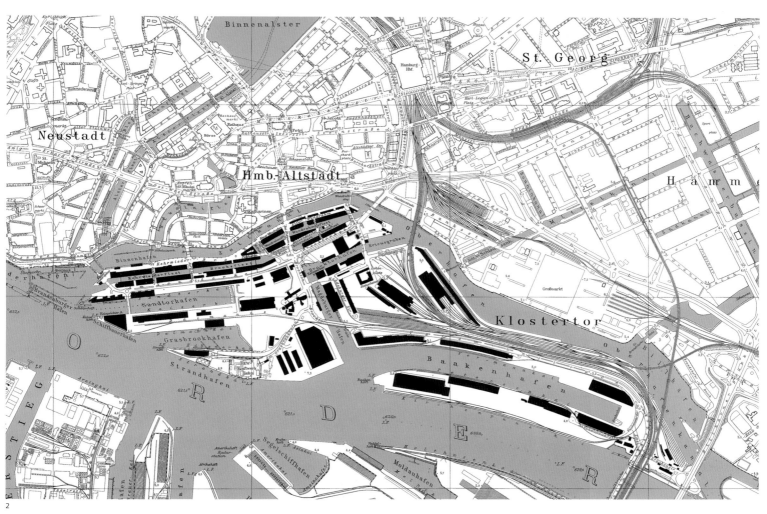

2

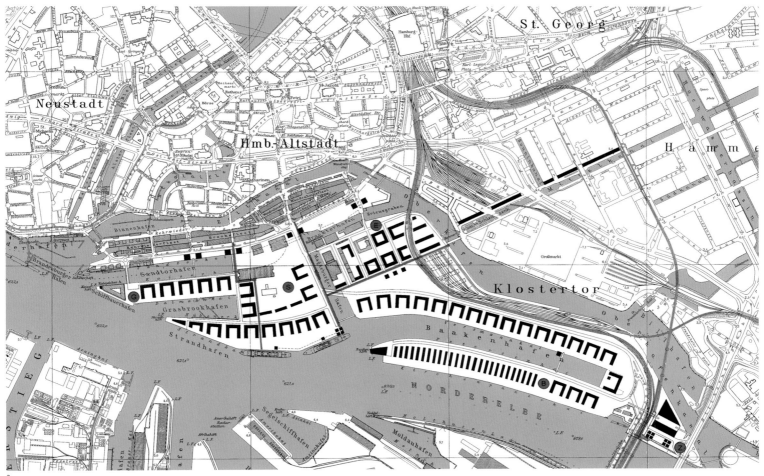

3

LÄRMSCHUTZ-WAND IN REGENSBURG

WETTBEWERB: 1998 - Ankauf
ENTWURF: Meinhard v. Gerkan
mit Sona Kazemi

Ein imaginäres Quadrat von 1000 m Kantenlänge spannt sich als Kunstkonzept über das Areal von Burgweintig; eine Viererteilung ergibt vier Quartiere mit unterschiedlichem Charakter:
– Grünraum
– dörfliche Struktur

– parzelliertes Wohngebiet
– Blockrandbebauung.
Die Lärmschutzwand ist Teil des Konzeptes; sie verläuft parallel zur Bahntrasse als Schall- und Sichtschutz. Es gibt nur zwei Oberflächenmaterialien: horizontale Holzlamellen und schmale vertikale Schlitze mit transluzentem Profilglas. Deren unterschiedlicher Abstand wirkt wie ein Barcode, der sich je nach Geschwindigkeit der Bewegung verändert. Es stellt sich ein Zeitraffereffekt ein, der Analogien zu den Mechanismen der Warenwelt erlaubt.

An imaginary one-million-square-metre quadrangle is the artistic concept which overlays the area of Burgweintig. Partitioning this area into four equal squares makes four quarters with a distinct character each:
– green areas,
– village-type structure,
– residential district with parcelled lots,
– perimeter block development.
The noise barrier wall is part of the overall concept. It runs along the railway line and is both noise barrier and screen. The barrier uses only two surface materials:

horizontal wooden slats and translucent textured glass in narrow vertical slit openings.
These are arranged at varying intervals and produce a "bar-code" of changing aspect, depending on the speed of passage, thus creating a time-lapse effect which allows to draw analogies to the mechanisms of commercial worlds.

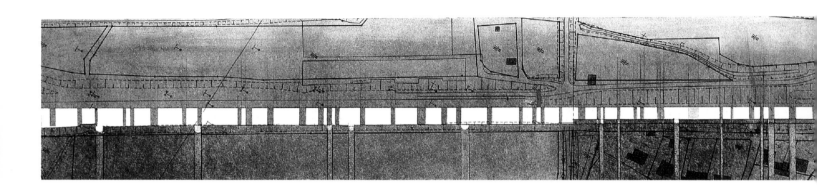

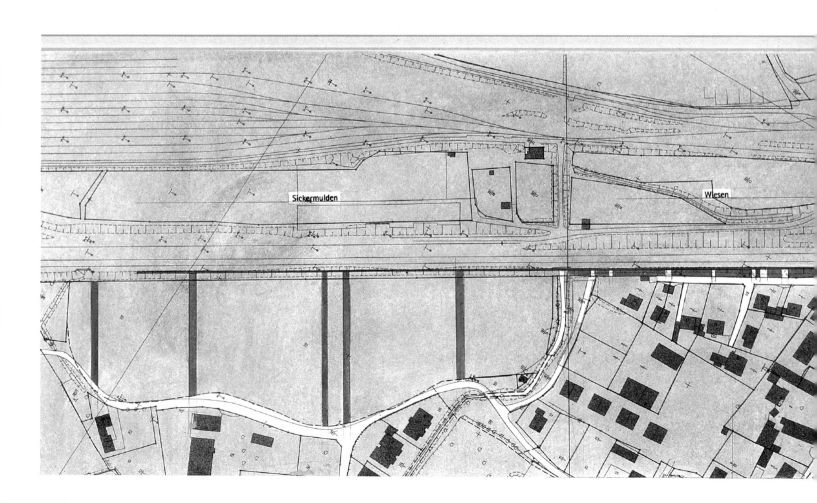

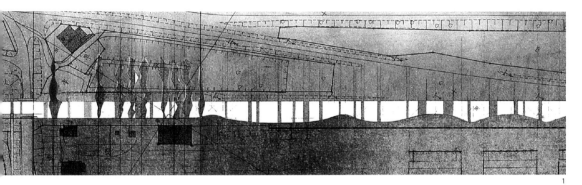

1 SEQUENZEN
ENTLANG DER WAND.
2 LAGEPLAN MIT
FREIFLÄCHEN-
GESTALTUNG.
1 PLAN SEQUENCE
ALONG THE BARRIER.
2 SITE PLAN WITH
SURROUNDING OPEN
AREAS.

1

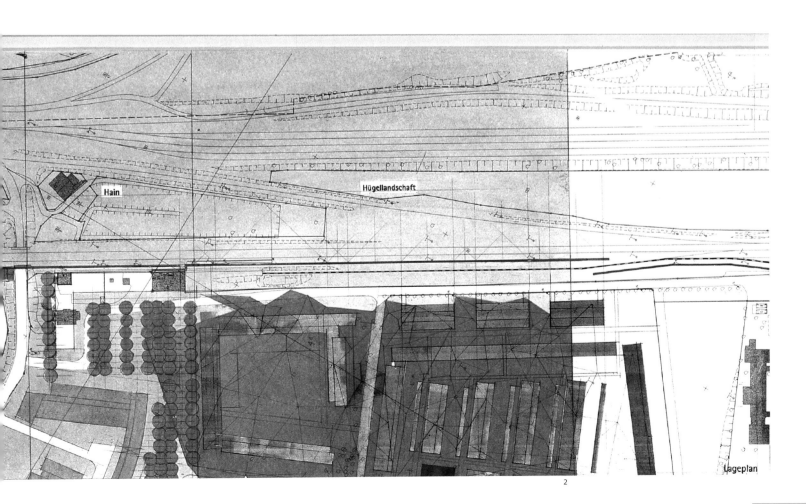

Hain

Hügellandschaft

Lageplan

2

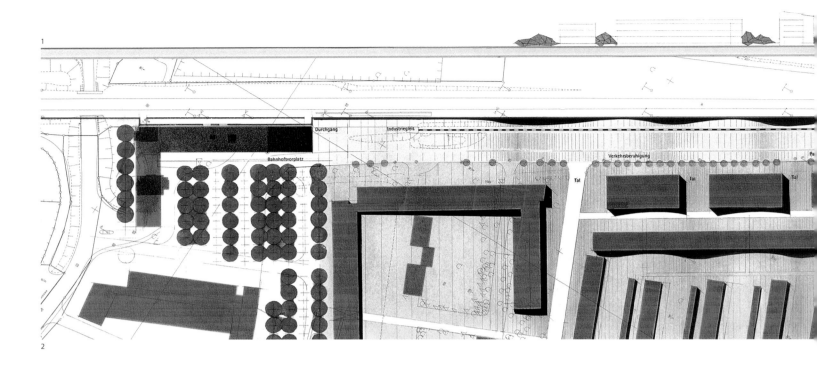

1 SCHNITT.	1 SECTION.
2 FREIFLÄCHEN-KONZEPT ENTLANG DER WAND.	2 OPEN AREA CONCEPT ALONG THE BARRIER.
3 SICKERMULDE.	3 SEEPAGE CANAL.
4 WIESEN.	4 MEADOWS.
5 HAIN.	5 GROVE.
6 HÜGELLANDSCHAFT.	6 HILLSCAPE.
7 ANSICHT LÄRM-ABGEWANDTE SEITE.	7 ELEVATION FROM PROTECTED AREA.
8 LÄRMZUGEWAND-TE SEITE.	8 STREET SIDE ELE-VATION.
9 DETAILPUNKTE.	9 DETAILS.

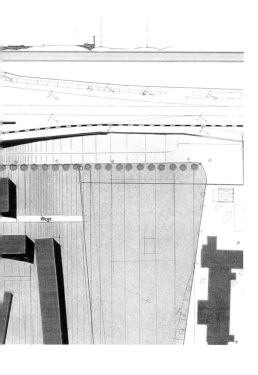

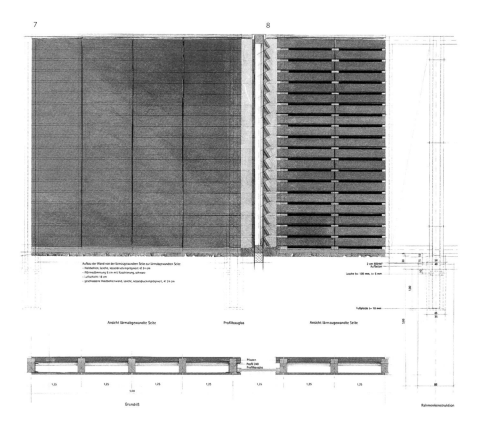

Ansicht lärmabgewandte Seite   Profilbauglas   Ansicht lärmzugewandte Seite

Grundriß   Rahmenkonstruktion

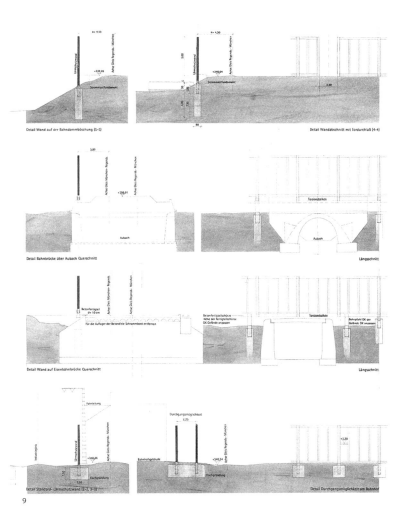

Detail Wand auf der Bahndammböschung (5-5)   Detail Wandabschnitt mit Tordurchlaß (4-4)

Detail Bahnbrücke über Aubach Querschnitt   Längsschnitt

Detail Wand auf Eisenbahnbrücke Querschnitt   Längsschnitt

Detail Standard- Lärmschutzwand (2-2, 3-3)   Detail Durchgangsmöglichkeit am Bahnhof

ORTSZENTRUM SCHÖNEICHE

ENTWURF: Volkwin Marg; 1995
PROJEKTLEITUNG: Martin Bleckmann
MITARBEITER: Jutta Hartmann-Pohl,
Franz Lensing, Olaf Drehsen,
Monika Kaesler
STATIK: Ing.-Büro Kempen
HAUSTECHNIK: HL-Technik
FREIANLAGEN: WES und Partner
BAUHERR: DSR Immobilien
BAUZEIT: 1996 - 1997
BGF: 6.350 m²
BRI: 23.600 m³

Schöneiche bei Berlin ist eine klein-
städtische Waldsiedlung mit offener,
durch ein- bis zweigeschossige Einzelhäuser geprägter Bebauung, markanten Alleen und viel Grünflächen.
Eine bauliche Mitte als Identifikationspunkt des Ortes fehlte bislang. Nach
einem Bebauungsplan der Gemeinde wurde deren südlicher Teil mit
dem vorgegebenen Fußweg in
Nord-Süd-Richtung und in zwei- bis
dreigeschossiger Bebauung realisiert.
Das Projekt gliedert sich in zwei Hälften aus je vier Einzelbaukörpern. Die
beiden Hälften umschließen Gartenhöfe auf der + 1- Ebene, während
erdgeschossig Läden unterschiedlicher Größe angeboten werden. Die
Höfe bilden die Erschließungsebene
für die Wohnungen. Den Läden zu
Straße und Platz hin vorgelagert ist
eine Arkadenreihe, die zusammen
mit stählernen Pergolen über den
Parkplätzen und der Ausstattung
der Gartenhöfe mit Sitzstufen und
Bepflanzung öffentlichkeitsbezoge-
ne, städtische Elemente bilden, die
den Charakter des Ortes als
„Zentrum"unterstützen.

Schöneiche, close to Berlin, is a
small-scale estate set in a forest
with an open housing development
comprising of one- and two-storey
buildings, prominent avenues and
large green areas. So far, a built
focal point as a central orientation
for the town was missing. According
to the local building plan, a southern
centre with the requested foot-path
in a north-south direction and two-
and three-storey houses has been
completed. The project is split in
two halves consisting of four single
buildings. Both sections enclose
gardens on level + 1, while shops
of various scales are offered on
ground-floor level. The garden
areas serve as circulation to the
apartments. Towards street and
square, an arcade sits in front of
the commercial units and forms a
public urban element together
with steel arbours stretching across
the parking area. This combined
with the landscaped gardens with
integral seating and plant arrangements, serves to reinforce the
character of the location as a
"centre".

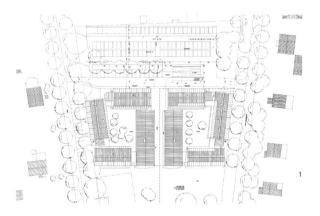

1

2

1 LAGEPLAN.
2 SCHAUBILD
GESAMTKOMPLEX.
3 FASSADEN-
GLIEDERUNG DES
ATTIKAGESCHOSSES.
1 SITE PLAN.
2 SCHEME OF
OVERALL COMPLEX.
3 FACADE
STRUCTURE FOR
THE ROOF LEVEL.

3

1

2

1 ERSCHLIESSUNG
DER WOHNUNGEN
ÜBER EINEN
LAUBENGANG IM
DACHGESCHOSS.
2+3 VON SÜDEN
GESEHEN. ARKADEN
BEGLEITEN DIE
MITTELACHSE.
4 DER WESTLICHE
BLOCK VON
NORD-WESTEN.

1 CIRCULATION TO
THE APARTMENTS
VIA AN EXTERNAL
CORRIDOR ON THE
ROOF LEVEL
2+3 VIEW FROM THE
SOUTH. ARCADES
FOLLOW THE CEN-
TRAL AXIS.
4 THE WESTERN
BLOCK VIEWED FROM
THE NORTH-WEST.

3

4

RESTAURIERUNG UND INTERIEUR

RESTORATION AND INTERIOR DESIGN

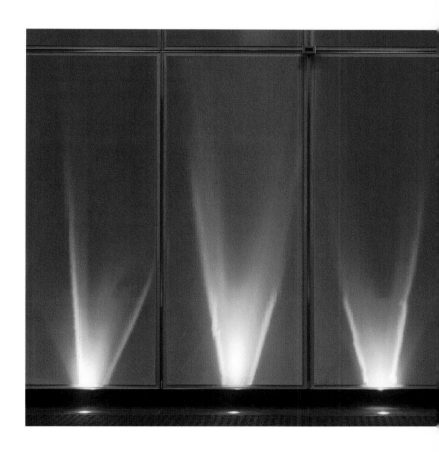

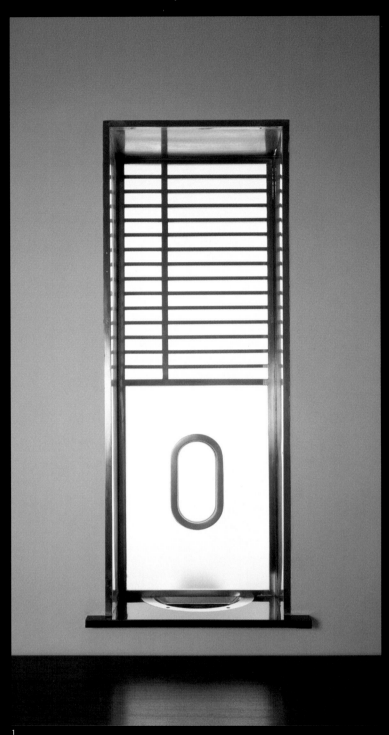

1

RESTAURIERUNG DES THALIA THEATERS, HAMBURG

ENTWURF: Klaus Staratzke
PROJEKTLEITUNG: Dagmar Winter
MITARBEITER: Maja Gorges
BAUHERR: Thalia Theater
BAUZEIT: Juni - Okt. 1997

Das Theater wurde 1912 von Georg Kallmorgen erbaut und nach der teilweisen Zerstörung im Krieg von seinem Sohn Werner 1960 modernisiert. Die unterschiedlichen Handschriften, in denen sich unterschiedliche Architekturepochen widerspiegeln, sollten sorgfältig in Abstimmung mit dem Denkmalschutz restauriert werden. So wurden die Kassenhalle mit den alten Mosaikböden und das Entrée mit der über zwei Geschosse reichenden Holzvertäfelung im Sinne Kallmorgen sen. aufgearbeitet. Die Umgänge aus den 60 er Jahren wurden durch die jetzt längs angeordneten Garderoben räumlich klar definiert. Das in Teilen vorhandene alte Farbkonzept aus Naturholz, Marmor und Messing wurde freigelegt, das des Sohnes aus weiß lackierten Flächen und Hölzern und dem farbigen Teppich dagegengestellt.

The theatre was built in 1912 by Georg Kallmorgen and was modernized in 1960 by his son Werner after the partial demolition during the war. The various styles, reflecting different architectural eras, had to be carefully restored in accordance with conservation requirements. Consequently, the box office hall with its ancient mosaic floor and the entrée, decorated with wooden cladding reaching over two levels, have been restored according to Kallmorgen senior. The embracing corridors from the 60s have been spatially defined by the longitudinal sequence of the cloak-rooms. The partially maintained colour scheme of wood, marble and brass has been uncovered and contrasted with Kallmorgen junior's concept of white lacquered surfaces, wood and coloured carpets.

1 THEATER-
TAGESKASSE.
2+3 EINGANGS-
FOYER NACH UND
VOR DEM UMBAU.
1 BOX OFFICE.
2+3 ENTRANCE
FOYER AFTER AND
BEFORE RENOVATION.

1

2

1 VESTIBÜL NACH
UND VOR DEM
UMBAU.
3 GARDEROBEN-
TRESEN.
4 WINDFANG.
DER UMBAU WAR
IN VIELEN TEILEN
EIN RÜCKBAU.
DER SCHÖNE
TERRAZZOBODEN
WURDE WIEDER
FREIGELEGT.
5+6 AUSLEGE-
TEPPICHE UND
GRELLE BELEUCH-
TUNG HÄTTEN
DIE ATMOSPHÄRE
GESTÖRT.
1 VESTIBULE
AFTER AND BEFORE
RENOVATION.
3 CLOAK-ROOM
DESK.
4 PORCH.
THE RENOVATION
INCLUDED THE
REMOVAL OF MANY
BUILDING ELEMENTS.
THE BEAUTIFUL TER-
RAZZO FLOOR HAS
BEEN UNCOVERED.
5+6 CARPETS AND
GLARING LIGHTING
HAS DISTURBED THE
AMBIENCE.

3

4

5

6

1

2

UMBAU UND RESTAURIERUNG HAPAG LLOYD AG AM BALLINDAMM, HAMBURG

WETTBEWERB: 1997
ENTWURF: Volkwin Marg, Klaus Staratzke
PROJEKTLEITUNG: Dagmar Winter
MITARBEITER: Kerstin Steinfatt, Maja Gorges
BAUHERR: Hapag Lloyd AG
BAUZEIT: Jan. - Juni 1997

Zum 150jährigen Jubiläum ihrer Firma wünschte sich die Hapag Lloyd AG eine Sanierung und, soweit möglich und sinnvoll, Restaurierung der repräsentativen Eingangszone des Firmensitzes, der von Fritz Höger in den Jahren 1912 - 1923 als Um- und Erweiterung eines Vorgängerbaus von Martin Haller errichtet worden war (1901-03). Unter Berücksichtigung denkmalpflegerischer Belange sollten dabei heutige funktionale und repräsentative Ansprüche einer großen Firma erfüllt werden. Die symmetrische Anlage des Entrées mit einer Raumfolge von Vor-, Quer- und Haupthalle wurde als Eingangsbereich wiederhergestellt. Auch die Glasdächer wurden freigelegt und erstanden in der alten Form mit neuer Verglasung. Die ehemalige große „Passagenhalle" für den Verkauf der Schiffspassagen nach Amerika konnte erst durch den Rückbau zahlreicher späterer Einbauten wieder freigelegt werden. Mit modernster Medientechnik ausgestattet, wurde hier ein unterteilbarer Konferenzraum eingerichtet. Alle vorhandenen Materialien wurden vorsichtig restauriert, die noch intakten Marmorböden aufgefrischt.

For its 150 year anniversary, Hapag Lloyd asked for remedial work and - where possible - restoration of the grand entrance area to its head quarters, which had been built by Fritz Höger in 1912-1923 as an extension of the original building by Martin Haller (1901-03). While respecting conservation, the modern requirements of a developing firm should be accommodated. The symmetrical design of the entrée with a sequence of foyer, small and main halls has been restored. The glazed roofs were stripped and reglazed to their original specification. The old vast "Passage Hall" for the purchase of fares to America could only be restored by the reduction of numerous built-in units.

MEIN FELD IST DIE WELT

3

It is now used as a dividable conference hall, equipped with modern computer technology. All existing materials have been carefully restored and the intact marble floors were renovated.

1 DIE TAGESLICHT-
GLASDECKE IST RE-
STAURIERT. DARÜBER
WURDE EINE NEUE
STAHL-GLAS-KON-
STRUKTION GEBAUT.
2 RESTAURIERTE
DECKENSTRUKTUREN:
VERGOLDETE
INTARSIEN AUF
HOLZMALEREI.

3 DIE RESTAURIERTE
HAUPTHALLE
MIT VESTIBÜL.
4 HAUPTHALLE VOR
DER RENOVIERUNG.
1 THE RESTORED
GLAZED SKYLIGHTS.
ABOVE, A NEW
STEEL-GLASS
CONSTRUCTION
BEEN ERECTED.

2 RESTORED CEILING
STRUCTURE: GOLD-
PLATED INLAYS ON
WOOD PAINTINGS.
3 MAIN HALL WITH
VESTIBULE AFTER
RESTORATION.
4 MAIN HALL
BEFORE RENOVATION.

4

1

2

1 JE NACH NUTZUNGSANSPRUCH LÄSST SICH DER SAAL AUCH BEI TAG VERDUNKELN, ODER MIT KUNSTLICHT BELEUCHTEN.

2 DER KONFERENZ-RAUM VOR DER RENOVIERUNG, GEKENNZEICHNET DURCH ABGEHÄNGTE DECKEN OHNE TAGESLICHT.

3 DER KONFERENZ-RAUM - DIE TAGES-LICHTDECKE IST REKONSTRUIERT.

4+5 KLEINER BESPRECHUNGSRAUM: EINMAL MIT BLICK AUF DIE ALSTER; EINMAL MIT BLICK AUF DIE PANTRY, ABGETRENNT DURCH HOLZ-GLAS-SCHIEBE-ELEMENTE.

1 ACCORDING TO USE REQUIREMENTS, THE HALL CAN BE DARKENED OR ILLUMINATED WITH ARTIFICIAL LIGHT.

2 THE CONFERENCE ROOM BEFORE RENOVATION, CHARACTERIZED BY A SUSPENDED CEILING WITH NO DAYLIGHT.

3 THE CONFERENCE ROOM WITH RECONSTRUCTED GLAZED SKYLIGHTS.

4+5 SMALL MEETING ROOM: EITHER WITH VIEWS TOWARDS THE ALSTER OR THE PANTRY, SEPARATED BY SLIDING WOOD-GLASS ELEMENTS.

3

4

5

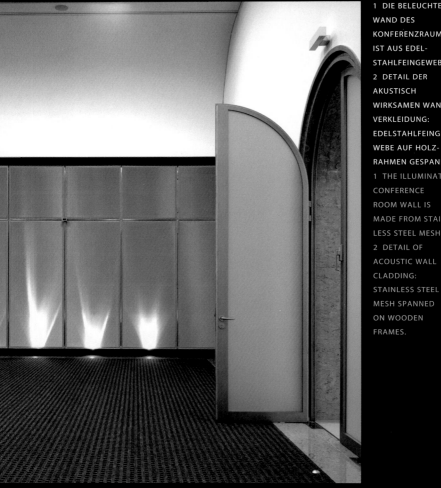

1 DIE BELEUCHTETE
WAND DES
KONFERENZRAUMES
IST AUS EDEL-
STAHLFEINGEWEBE.
2 DETAIL DER
AKUSTISCH
WIRKSAMEN WAND-
VERKLEIDUNG:
EDELSTAHLFEINGE-
WEBE AUF HOLZ-
RAHMEN GESPANNT.
1 THE ILLUMINATED
CONFERENCE
ROOM WALL IS
MADE FROM STAIN-
LESS STEEL MESH.
2 DETAIL OF
ACOUSTIC WALL
CLADDING:
STAINLESS STEEL
MESH SPANNED
ON WOODEN
FRAMES.

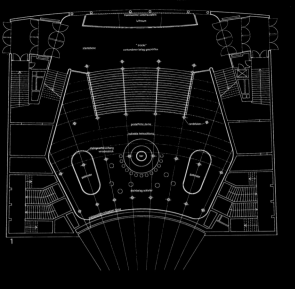

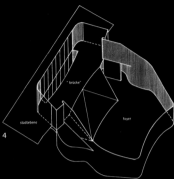

HAMBURGISCHE STAATSOPER - NEUGESTALTUNG FOYER UND GARDEROBE

WETTBEWERB: 1997 - 3. Preis
ENTWURF: Meinhard v. Gerkan
MITARBEITER: Michael Biwer, Stephan Rewolle

Foyer und Garderobe der Oper werden als wenig attraktiv empfunden und entsprechen nicht mehr heutigen Ansprüchen. Der Entwurf bestimmt die beiden getrennten Ebenen durch eine eingestellte Paraventwand als eine neue räumliche Einheit, hinter deren fließenden Wänden vorhandene Bauteile "verhüllt" werden können. Eine neue Rauminszenierung entsteht, mit einem Raumkontinuum, das unter der Erschließungstreppe hindurch den Bewegungsfluß der Funktion unterstützt und jeden Winkel nutzt.

The foyer and cloakroom of the Opera House are considered unattractive and do not meet present requirements. The design unites the two separate levels creating a new spatial harmony by introducing movable screens, which cover existing building elements. A new spatial impression is formed with a continuous volume, which enhances movement underneath the main circulation staircase and completely utilizes the available spaces.

1 EINGANGSEBENE.
2 BASEMENT.
3 SCHNITT.
4 DIE ALS „PARAVENT"
EINGESTELLTE WAND
VERBINDET BEIDE EBENEN
ZU EINEM KONTINUUM.
5 BLICK IN DIE
GARDEROBE.
1 ENTRANCE LEVEL.
2 BASEMENT.
3 SECTION.
4 MOVABLE SCREENS
CONNECT BOTH LEVELS
TO FORM A CONTINUUM.
5 VIEW INTO THE
CLOAKROOM.

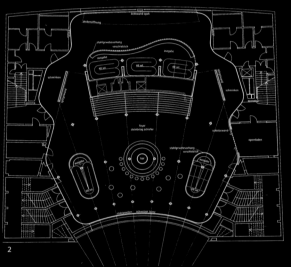

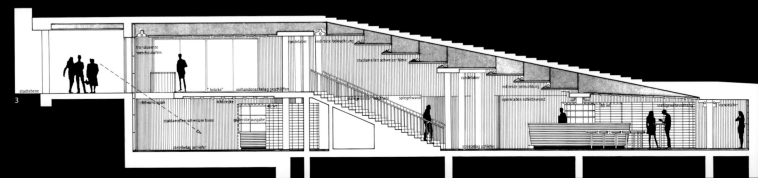

ANHANG

APPENDIX

MEINHARD VON GERKAN
PROF. DIPL.-ING. ARCHITEKT BDA

geboren am 3. Januar 1935 in Riga/Lettland.
1964 Diplom-Examen an der TU Braunschweig.
seit
1965 Freiberuflicher Architekt
zusammen mit Volkwin Marg.
1972 Berufung in die Freie Akademie
der Künste in Hamburg.
1974 Berufung an die TU Braunschweig
als ordentlicher Professor/
Lehrstuhl A für Entwerfen.
1982 Berufung in das Kuratorium der
Jürgen-Ponto-Stiftung, Frankfurt.
1965 -
1995 Mehr als 300 Preise in nationalen und
internationalen Wettbewerben, darunter
mehr als 130 1. Preise zusammen mit
Volkwin Marg. Zahlreiche Preise für vor
bildliche Bauten. Zahlreiche Veröffent-
lichungen im In- und Ausland. Zahlreiche
Preisrichter- und Gutachtertätigkeit.
1988 Gastprofessor an der Nihon
Universität, Tokio/Japan.
1993 Gastprofessor an der University
of Pretoria/Südafrika.
1995 American Institute of Architects,
Honorary Fellow, USA.
Ehrenauszeichnung der Mexikanischen
Architektenkammer.

born on 3 January 1935 in Riga/Latvia.
1964 Diploma examination at the TU
Braunschweig.
since
1965 Free lance architect together
with Volkwin Marg.
1972 Appointment to the Freie Akademie
der Künste in Hamburg.
1974 Appointment to the Technische
Universität Braunschweig as
professor/course A for design.
1982 Appointment to the board
of the Jürgen-Ponto-Foundation,
Frankfurt.
1965 –
1995 More than 300 national and
international competition prizes
incl. more than 130 1st prizes together
with Volkwin Marg. Many awards for
outstanding buildings. Many
publications in Germany and abroad.
Considerable involvement with
competition juries and reports.
1988 Guest professor at the Nihon
University, Tokyo/Japan.
1993 Guest professor at the University
of Pretoria/South Africa.
1995 American Institute of Architects,
Honorary Fellow, USA.
Honored by the Mexican
Architectural Society.

VOLKWIN MARG
PROF. DIPL.-ING. ARCHITEKT BDA

geboren am 15. Oktober 1936 in Königsberg/
Ostpreußen, aufgewachsen in Danzig.
1964 Diplom-Examen an der TU
Braunschweig.
seit
1965 Freiberuflicher Architekt mit
Meinhard v. Gerkan.
Zahlreiche Wettbewerbserfolge und
große Bauaufträge,
Vorträge und Texte zu Fragen der
Architektur, des Städtebaus und der
Kulturpolitik.
1972 Berufung in die Freie Akademie der
Künste in Hamburg.
1974 Berufung in die Deutsche Akademie für
Städtebau und Landesplanung.
1975 -
1979 Vizepräsident des Bundes Deutscher
Architekten BDA.
1979 -
1983 Präsident des BDA.
1986 Berufung an die RWTH Aachen,
Lehrstuhl für Stadtbereichsplanung und
Werklehre.
1996 Fritz-Schumacher-Preis der FVS-Stiftung.

born on 15 October 1936 in Königsberg/
Ostpreußen, childhood in Danzig.
1964 Diploma examination at the
TU Braunschweig.
since
1965 Free lance architect together with
Meinhard von Gerkan.
Many competition successes and
large projects, lectures and
manuscripts on architecture, urban
planning and political culture.
1972 Appointment to Freie Akademie der
Künste Hamburg.
1974 Appointment to Deutsche Akademie
für Städtebau und Landesplanung.
1975 -
1979 Vice President of the Bund Deutscher
Architekten BDA.
1979 -
1983 President of the Bund Deutscher
Architekten BDA.
1986 Appointment to the Chair of Town
Planning and Tradesmanship.
1996 Fritz-Schumacher-Award.

KLAUS STARATZKE
DIPL.-ING. ARCHITEKT

geboren am 12. Dezember 1937 in
Königsberg/Ostpreußen.
1963 Diplom-Examen an der TU Berlin.
1963 -
1966 Freier Mitarbeiter im
Architekturbüro Hentrich +
Petschnigg, Düsseldorf.
1968 Mitarbeit im Büro
von Gerkan und Marg.
1972 Partner im Büro
von Gerkan, Marg und Partner.

born on 12 December 1937 in
Königsberg/Ostpreußen.
1963 Diploma examination at the
TU Berlin.
1963 -
1966 Free lance work by
Architekturbüro Hentrich
+ Petschnigg, Düsseldorf.
1968 Work with von Gerkan and Marg.
1972 Partner of von Gerkan, Marg
and Partners.

UWE GRAHL
DIPL.-ING. (FH) ARCHITEKT AIV

geboren am 19. Oktober 1940 in Dresden.
1959 Maurerlehre, Gesellenbrief.
1963 Examen an der Staatlichen
      Ingenieurschule für
      Bauwesen Berlin-Hochbau.
1963 Mitarbeit im Büro
      Dipl.-Ing. Siegfried Fehr.
1969 Mitarbeit im Büro
      Dipl.-Ing. Rolf Niedballa.
seit
1974 Büro von Gerkan, Marg und Partner,
      Berlin.
seit
1990 Assoziierter Partner im Büro
      von Gerkan, Marg und Partner.
seit
1993 Partner im Büro von Gerkan, Marg
      und Partner.

born on 19 October 1940 in Dresden.
1959 Bricklayer apprentice, trade
      certificate.
1963 Examination at the
      Staatliche
      Ingenieurschule für Bauwesen
1963 Work with Büro
      Dipl.-Ing. Siegfried Fehr.
1969 Work with Büro
      Dipl.-Ing. Rolf Niedballa.
since
1974 Office von Gerkan, Marg
      and Partners, Berlin.
since
1990 Associate partner of
      von Gerkan, Marg and Partners.
since
1993 Partner of von Gerkan, Marg
      and Partners.

JOACHIM ZAIS
DIPL.-ING. ARCHITEKT BDA

geboren am 10. Dezember 1951 in
Marburg/Lahn.
1969 Tischlerlehre in Hildesheim.
1975 Examen an der FH Hildesheim mit
      Abschluß Ing. grad.
1975 Architekturstudium an der
      TU Braunschweig.
      Tätigkeit während des Studiums
      in verschiedenen Architektur-
      büros und Wettbewerbstätigkeit.
1982 Diplom an der TU Braunschweig.
1982 Tätigkeit im Büro für
      Stadtplanung Dr. Schwerdt,
      Braunschweig.
1983 –
1989 Assistententätigkeit am Institut
      für Baugestaltung A – Prof. M. v.
      Gerkan.
      Freier Mitarbeiter im Büro
      von Gerkan, Marg und Partner,
      Braunschweig,
      und eigene Tätigkeit als
      Architekt.
1989 Leitung des Büros
      von Gerkan, Marg und Partner,
      Braunschweig.
seit
1993 Partner im Büro
      von Gerkan, Marg und Partner.

born on 10 December 1951 in
Marburg/Lahn.
1969 Carpenter apprentice in
      Hildesheim.
1975 Examination Ing. grad. at the
      FH Hildesheim.
1975 Architectural studies at the
      TU Braunschweig.
      Worked during studies for
      different architects and
      on various competitions.
1982 Diploma at the TU Braunschweig.
1982 Worked in Büro für Stadtplanung
      Dr. Schwerdt, Braunschweig.
1983 –
1989 Lecturer at Institut für Bauge-
      staltung A – Prof. M. v. Gerkan.
      Free lance architect with
      von Gerkan, Marg and Partners and
      as architect on own projects.
1989 Head of office von Gerkan, Marg
      and Partners, Braunschweig.
since
1993 Partner of von Gerkan, Marg
      and Partners.

HUBERT NIENHOFF
DIPL.-ING. ARCHITEKT

geboren am 4. August 1959 in Kirchhellen/
Westfalen.
1985 Diplom-Examen an der
      RWTH Aachen.
1985 –
1987 Mitarbeit im Büro für
      Architektur und Stadtbereichsplanung
      – Ch. Mäckler, Frankfurt/Main.
1987 –
1988 Auslandsaufenthalt in den USA,
      städtebauliche Studien.
1988 –
1991 Assistent an der RWTH Aachen,
      Lehrstuhl für Stadtbereichs-
      planung und Werklehre,
      Prof. Volkwin Marg.
1988 Mitarbeit im Büro
      von Gerkan, Marg und Partner, Aachen.
seit
1993 Partner im Büro
      von Gerkan, Marg und Partner.

born on 4 August 1959 in Kirchhellen/West-
falen.
1985 Diploma examination at the
      RWTH Aachen.
1985 –
1987 Work with Büro für Architektur
      und Stadtplanung – Ch. Mäckler,
      Frankfurt/Main.
1987 –
1988 Foreign visit to USA with urban
      studies.
1988 –
1991 Lecturer at the RWTH Aachen
      Chair for Stadtbereichsplanung
      und Werklehre,
      Prof. Volkwin Marg.
1988 Work with von Gerkan, Marg
      and Partners.
since
1993 Partner of von Gerkan, Marg
      and Partners.

WOLFGANG HAUX
DIPL.-ING. ARCHITEKT BDA

geboren am 13. August 1947 in Hamburg.
1969 Architekturstudium an der
      Hochschule für Bildende Künste.
1975 Diplom-Examen.
1976 Mitarbeit im Architekturbüro
      Prof. Dieter Hoor, Steinhorst.
seit
1978 Mitarbeit im Büro
      von Gerkan, Marg und Partner,
      Hamburg.
seit
1994 Assoziierter Partner im Büro
      von Gerkan, Marg und Partner.

born on 13 August 1947 in Hamburg.
1969 Architectural Studies at
      Hochschule für Bildende Künste.
1975 Diploma Examination.
1976 Work with Architekturbüro
      Prof. Dieter Hoor, Steinhorst.
since
1978 Work with von Gerkan, Marg
      and Partners, Hamburg.
since
1994 Associate Partner with
      von Gerkan, Marg and Partners.

NIKOLAUS GOETZE
DIPL.-ING. ARCHITEKT

geboren am 25. September 1958 in Kempen.
1980 Architekturstudium an der
      RWTH Aachen.
1985 –
1986 Meisterklasse Prof. W. Holzbauer,
      Hochschule für angewandte
      Kunst, Wien.
1987 Diplom an der RWTH Aachen.
seit
1987 Mitarbeit im Büro
      von Gerkan, Marg und Partner,
      Hamburg.
1994 Assoziierter Partner im Büro
      von Gerkan, Marg und Partner.
seit
1998 Partner im Büro
      von Gerkan, Marg und Partner.

born on 25 September 1958 in Kempen.
1980 Architectural studies at
      RWTH Aachen.
1985 –
1986 Master Class Prof. W. Holzbauer
      Hochschule für angewandte
      Kunst, Wien.
1987 Diploma at the RWTH Aachen.
since
1987 Work with
      von Gerkan, Marg and Partners.
1994 Associate Partner with von
      Gerkan, Marg and Partners.
since
1998 Partner of von Gerkan, Marg
      and Partners.

JÜRGEN HILLMER
DIPL.-ING. ARCHITEKT

geboren am 26. Dezember 1959 in
Mönchengladbach.
1980 Architekturstudium an der
      Carolo-Wilhelmina in
      Braunschweig.
1988 Diplom.
1988 –
1992 Mitarbeit im Büro
      von Gerkan, Marg und Partner,
      Hamburg.
1992 –
1995 freiberuflicher Architekt in
      Haltern, Nordrhein-Westfalen.
1994 Assoziierter Partner im Büro
      von Gerkan, Marg und Partner.
seit
1998 Partner im Büro
      von Gerkan, Marg und Partner.

born on 26 December 1959 in
Mönchengladbach.
1980 Architectural studies at the
      Carolo- Wilhelmina in Braunschweig.
1988 Diploma.
1988 –
1992 Work with von Gerkan, Marg
      and Partners, Hamburg.
1992 –
1995 Free lance architect in Haltern,
      Nordrhein-Westfalen.
1994 Associate Partner with
      von Gerkan, Marg and Partners.
since
1998 Partner of von Gerkan, Marg
      and Partners.

ERFOLGE BEI WETTBEWERBEN UND GUTACHTEN

SUCCESSFUL COMPETITION ENTRIES

1. Preis/Rang
1st prize/place:

1964	1.	Sports and Conference Hall, Hamburg
	2.	Indoor and open-air swimming pool, Brunswick
1965	3.	Indoor and open-air swimming pool, SPD
	4.	Max Planck Institute, Lindau/Harz
	5.	Tax Bureau, Oldenburg
	6.	Sports Center, Diekirch/Luxemburg
	7.	Airport Berlin-Tegel
	8.	Stormarn Hall, Bad Oldesloe
1966	9.	District indoor swimming pool, Cologne
	10.	Sports Forum, University of Kiel
1970	11.	Shell AG head offices, Hamburg
	12.	District Vocational School, Bad Oldesloe
1971	13.	European Patent and Trademark Office, Munich
	14.	Multi-purpose building III, University of Hamburg
	15.	Housing Gellertstrasse, Hamburg
	16.	Shopping mall, Alstertal, Hamburg
1972	17.	ARAL AG head offices, Bochum
	18.	Schools Center, Friedrichstadt
1974	19.	Vocational Training Center G 13, Hamburg-Bergedorf
	20.	Provinzial Insurance offices, Kiel
1975	21.	Deutscher Ring, Hamburg
	22.	Airport, Munich II
1976	23.	District Administration, Recklinghausen
	24.	Airport, Moscow
	25.	Airport, Algiers
1977	26.	Parish House, Stade
	27.	Otto mail-order company, head offices extension, Hamburg
	28.	MAK head offices, Kiel
	29.	Police Station, Pankstrasse, Berlin
1978	30.	Pahlavi National Library, Tehran
	31.	Joachimsthaler Platz, Berlin
	32.	Federal German Ministry of Transportation, Bonn
1979	33.	Indoor/outdoor swimming pools, Berlin-Spandau
	34.	Indoor swimming pool for competitions, Mannheim-Herzogenried
	35.	Institute of Chemistry, University of Brunswick
	36.	Institute of Biochemistry, University of Brunswick
	37.	Vereinsbank, Hamburg
	38.	District Administration, Meppen
1980	39.	Academy of Fine Arts, Hamburg
	40.	Römerberg development Frankfurt/Main – free design
	41.	Fleetinsel development, Hamburg
	42.	Lazarus Hospital, Berlin
	43.	Trade and Vocational Training Center, Flensburg
	44.	Deutsche Lufthansa office building, Hamburg
	45.	Airport, Stuttgart
	46.	Johanneum 1 sports hall, Lübeck
1981	47.	Civic Center, Bielefeld
	48.	Kravag offices, Hamburg
	49.	Hotel Plaza, Bremen
	50.	DAL office center, Mainz
	51.	Housing complex, Bad Schwartau
	52.	Law Court, Brunswick
	53.	Refurbishment/conversion, Kiel Castle
	54.	'Komplex Rose', hospital for rheumatic diseases, Bad Meinberg

1983	55.	Gruner + Jahr publishing house, Hamburg
1984	56.	Quickborn block corner development
1985	57.	District Court, Flensburg
	58.	Museum and library, Münster
	59.	Interior restructuring, Bertelsmann, Gütersloh
1986	60.	Town Hall, Husum
	61.	Airport, Hamburg-Fuhlsbüttel
	62.	Bäckerstrasse, Halstenbek
	63.	Labor Office, Oldenburg
1988	64.	Zürich-Haus, Hamburg
	65.	Federal Ministry of Environmental Protection and Reactor Safety, Bonn
	66.	Salamander building, Berlin
	67.	Störgang, Itzehoe
	68.	EAM, Kassel
	69.	Station square, Koblenz
1989	70.	Residential Park Falkenstein, Hamburg
	71.	Carl Bertelsmann Foundation, Gütersloh
1990	72.	Music and Conference Hall, Lübeck
	73.	Deutsche Revision, Frankfurt/Main
	74.	Adult Educational Institute and Municipal library, Heilbronn
	75.	Landscaped apartment complex, Kanzleistrasse, Hamburg-Nienstedten
	76.	Technology Center, Münster
1991	77.	German-Japanese Center, Hamburg
	78.	Hansetor, Hamburg-Bahrenfeld
	79.	Shopping mall, Langenhorn Markt, Hamburg
	80.	Office complex, Am Zeppelinstein, Bad Homburg
	81.	Lenné-Passage, Frankfurt/Oder
	82.	Altmarkt Dresden, 2nd stage
1992	83.	New Trade Fair, Leipzig
	84.	Forum Neukölln, Berlin
	85.	Allee-Center, Leipzig-Grünau
	86.	Commercial building and library, Mollstrasse, Berlin
	87.	Lecture Theater Center, University of Oldenburg
	88.	Siemens Nixdorf, Service Center, Munich
	89.	District Court North, Hamburg
	90.	Apartment block, Schöne Aussicht, Hamburg
	91.	Telekom operating building, Suhl
	92.	Mare Balticum Hotel, Bansin/Usedom
1993	93.	Lehrter Train Station in Berlin
	94.	German-Japanese Center, Berlin
	95.	Office building, Bredeney, Essen
	96.	Labor Office Training Center of the Federal Republic of Germany, Schwerin
	97.	Trade Fair, Hanover, Hall 4
1994	98.	Forum Köpenick, Berlin
	99.	Gerling Insurance Corp., residential and office villas, Leipzig
	100.	Lecture Theater Center, extension of Chemnitz Technical University
	101.	Building for cooperative Norddeutsche Metall-Berufsgenossenschaft, Hanover
	102.	New Center, Berlin-Schönefeld
1995	103.	Neumarkt, Celle
	104.	Dresdner Bank, Pariser Platz, Berlin
	105.	Potsdam Center, southern site [main station Potsdam Stadt]
1996	106.	Hamburg Agency in Berlin, Palais Luisenstrasse
	107.	Civic Center, Weimar
	108.	Apartment and commercial building Deutrichshof, Leipzig
	109.	Expo 2000 Plaza, Hanover

	110.	Bucharest 2000
	111.	Altmarkt Dresden, south-western side
1997	112.	Facade design, Train Station Potsdam-Stadt
	113.	Trade Fair, Hanover, Hall 8/9
	114.	Footbridges, Expo 2000
	115.	New Station Neighborhood, Bielefeld
	116.	Media-Center Leipzig
	117.	IGA 2003 Rostock
	118.	Trade Fair, Rimini
	119.	Weserbahnhof II, Grothe Museum, Bremen
	120.	Casino, Bad Steben
	121.	Christian Pavilion, Expo 2000
	122.	Trade Fair, Düsseldorf
	123.	Builders' training yard, Berlin-Mahrzahn
1998	124.	Stuttgart Airport, terminal 3
	125.	German School and Service Housing in Beijing, China
	126.	Agency of Sachsen-Anhalt in Berlin
	127.	Agency of Brandenburg and Mecklenburg-Vorpommern in Berlin
	128.	Art Kite Museum, Detmold
	129.	Berlin-Brandenburg International Airport
	130.	Philips Convention Stand
	131.	Berlin Olympic Stadium, conversion
1999	132.	Nanning Convention & Exhibition Center, China
	133.	Schloß Hopferau
	134.	Tempodrom, Berlin
	135.	Ancona Airport, Italy

2. Preis/Rang
2nd prize/place:

1959	1.	District Administration, Niebüll
1966	2.	Jungfernstieg, Hamburg
1967	3.	Buildings for the 20th Olympic Games, Munich, project B
1968	4.	Church Center, Hamburg-Ohlsdorf
1970	5.	Schools Center, Heide-Ost
	6.	Regional Postal Directorate, Bremen
1971	7.	Regional Tax Bureau, Hamburg
	8.	Sports Forum, University of Bremen
1972	9.	Regional Administration offices, Lüneburg
1975	10.	Housing Billwerder-Allermöhe, Hamburg
	11.	Regional Department of the Interior, Kiel
1976	12.	Urban design Universität-Ost, Bremen
	13.	Administrative offices, operating area of Airport Munich II
1977	14.	Row houses and urban villas, Hamburg Bau 78
1980	15.	Gasworks, Munich
	16.	Administrative offices for Volkswagen, Wolfsburg
	17.	Town Hall, Oldenburg
	18.	Max Planck Institute for Quantum Optics, Munich
1981	19.	Institute of Chemistry, University of Brunswick
	20.	Labor Office, Kiel-Hörn
	21.	Klinikum II, Nuremberg-South
	22.	Kravag offices, Hamburg
1982	23.	Schlossparkhotel 'Orangerie', Fulda
1983	24.	Daimler Benz AG offices, Stuttgart
1984	25.	Germanisches Nationalmuseum, Nuremberg
	26.	Intermediate School and Sports Hall, Schleswig-Holstein

1985	27.	Wildlife Information Pavilion Balje
1986	28.	Post offices 1 and 3, Hamburg
	29.	Kümmellstrasse, Hamburg
	30.	Technik III, Gesamthochschule Kassel
	31.	Dockland development, Heiligenhafen
1987	32.	Telecommunications towers for German Federal postal services
	33.	Research and lecture hall building, Rudolf Virchow University Hospital, Berlin
1988	34.	Technical University Library, Berlin
	35.	Multi-story parking garage, Paderborn
	36.	New Orangery, Herten
1989	37.	Leisure swimming pool, Wyk auf Föhr
	38.	Königsgalerie, Kassel
1990	39.	VIP-Lounge, Cologne-Wahn Airport
	40.	Kehrwiederspitze-Sandtorhafen development, Hamburg
	41.	Neue Strasse, Ulm
	42.	Acropolis Museum, Athens
1991	43.	Altmarkt, Dresden
	44.	Krefeld South
	45.	Business Park, Münster docklands
	46.	Marina, Herne
	47.	Harbour Station Süderelbe, Hamburg
1992	48.	Olympia 2000, bicycle and swimming hall, Berlin
	49.	Noise Control Structures, Burgerfeld-Markt Schwaben
	50.	Cologne-Ehrenfeld urban design
1993	51.	Reichstag conversion for German Bundestag, Berlin
	52.	Building for 'Der Spiegel', Hamburg
	53.	Festival Hall, Recklinghausen
	54.	Redesign Hindenburgplatz, Münster
	55.	Nürnberger Beteiligungs AG offices
1994	56.	Erfurt-Ost, inner-urban extension
	57.	Max Planck Institute, Potsdam-Golm
1995	58.	Redevelopment of AEG-Kanis site, Essen
	59.	'Cultural area' of Peat Bath Spa Lobenstein
	60.	Fachhochschule Ingolstadt, urban design
1996	61.	Spa Hotel, Hamm
	62.	Haus Crange Training Hotel, Herne
1997	63.	Psychiatric Hospital, Kiel
	64.	Trade Fair Essen/Gruga Park
	65.	Dresden Central Bus Station
	66.	Bramsche Town Hall
	67.	Institute of Physics, Berlin Adlershof
1998	68.	Termina di Fusina, Venice

3. Preis/Rang
3rd prize/place:

1965	1.	Theater, Wolfsburg
1966	2.	Sports Hall, Bottrop
1969	3.	Engineering School, Buxtehude
1970	4.	Church Community Center, Steilshoop, Hamburg
	5.	School and Educational Center, Niebüll
1971	6.	Development of Hamburg's inner city [west]
1973	7.	Colonia Insurance offices, Hamburg, City Nord
1977	8.	Post Office Savings Bank, Hamburg, City Nord
1978	9.	Extension Alstertal shopping mall, Hamburg
	10.	City Hall, Mannheim
1979	11.	Düppel-Nord Sports Center, Free University, Berlin

1980	12.	University of Bremerhaven
1985	13.	Urban design competition, Münster
1986	14.	Bundeskunsthalle, Bonn
1987	15.	Police Headquarters, Berlin
1988	16.	Library of Technical University and Fine Arts Academy, Berlin
1989	17.	Concert Hall, Dortmund
	18.	International Maritime Court, Hamburg
	19.	Television Museum, Mainz
	20.	Deutsche Bundesbank, Frankfurt/Main
1990	21.	'Zementfabrik', Bonn
	22.	Münsterlandhalle, Münster
1992	23.	Rütgers Werke AG, Frankfurt/Main
1993	24.	Railroad station, Berlin-Spandau
	25.	Police Headquarters, Kassel
	26.	Nürnberger Insurance Company
1994	27.	Apartment and Commercial block, Kümmellstrasse/ Eppendorfer Landstrasse, Hamburg
1995	28.	New Civic Center, Scharbeutz
	29.	Trade Fair, Hanover, Hall 13
	30.	Bahrenfeld inner-urban area development
1996	31.	Gotha Main Station and station square
	32.	Nord LB bank building, Friedrichswall, Hanover
	33.	Residential Park Elbschloss, Hamburg
	34.	Housing Steinbeker Strasse, Hamburg
	35.	Central University Library, Potsdam
1997	36.	Fachhochschule Altonaer Strasse 25, Erfurt
	37.	Foyer refurbishment, State Opera, Hamburg
1998	38.	Blankenese Train Station Square, Hamburg
	39.	Münchner Tor
	40.	Technology Centre Bertrandt AG, Ehningen
1999	41.	Schwäbisch Hall, Urban Design
	42.	German Embassy in Kiev
	43.	Museum, Schloß Homburg

4. Preis/Rang
4th prize/place:

1963	1.	Civic Center, Kassel
1969	2.	Spa Center, Westerland/Sylt
	3.	Comprehensive School, Steilshoop, Hamburg
1971	4.	Federal Chancellery, Bonn
1975	5.	Extension of Town Hall, Itzehoe
1979	6.	Dahlem Sports Center, Free University, Berlin
	7.	Protestant Church Administration, Hanover
	8.	Large sports hall, Bielefeld
1981	9.	Federal Postal Department, Bonn
1983	10.	Maria-Trost Hospital , Berlin
1986	11.	Haus der Geschichte [history museum], Bonn
1987	12.	Labor Office, Flensburg
1988	13.	Schering AG offices, Berlin
1989	14.	documenta exhibition gallery, Kassel
	15.	University Library, Kiel
1993	16.	Town Hall, Halle
1994	17.	Hypo-Bank, Frankfurt/Main
	18.	mdr Middle German Broadcasting House, Leipzig
1995	19.	Office building, An der Stadtmünze, Erfurt
	20.	Federal Chancellery, Berlin
	21.	Fachhochschule Ingolstadt
1996	22.	Ferry harbour, Mukran, Rügen
	23.	Airport, Düsseldorf
	24.	mdr Middle-German Broad casting Complex, Erfurt

1997	25.	Grammar-School Waltersorfer Chaussee, Berlin

5. Preis/Rang
5th prize/place:

1966	1.	School and Sports Center, Brake
1967	2.	Open-air swimming pool, Bad Bramstedt
1980	3.	Federal Ministry of Labor and Social Affairs, Bonn
1985	4.	Library, Göttingen
1987	5.	Civic Center, Wiesloch
1989	6.	Art Museum and Town Hall extension, Wolfsburg
	7.	Extension Christian-Albrecht-University, Kiel
	8.	Zürich-Haus, Frankfurt/Main
1990	9.	Ericusspitze, Hamburg
1995	10.	MP and Regional State Department building, Mainz
	11.	Fachhochschule Ingolstadt, high-rise
1996	12.	Expo 2000, Train Station, Hanover-Laatzen
1997	13.	Elementary School Erkelenz

Ankäufe
commended

1963	1.	Residenzplatz, Würzburg
	2.	Löwenwall, Braunschweig
1965	3.	Urban design, Hamburg-Niendorf
1966	4.	New Picture Gallery, Munich
	5.	Urban design, Kiel inner city [special purchase]
1967	6.	Buildings for the 20th Olympic Games, Munich, project A
1968	7.	Schools Center, Weinheim
	8.	Apartment blocks, An der Alster/Fontenay, Hamburg
1969	9.	Comprehensive School, Mümmelmannsberg, Hamburg
1970	10.	Schools Center, Aldeby, Flensburg
	11.	Secondary School, Bargteheide1
1971	12.	Shopping mall, Hamburg-Lohbrügge
	13.	Tornesch urban design ideas1
	14.	Indoor swimming pool, Bad Oldesloe
1972	15.	Spa Gardens, Helgoland
1977	16.	Bauer publishing house, Hamburg
	17.	Axel Springer publishing house, Hamburg [special purchase]
1979	18.	Computer Center, Deutsche Bank, Hamburg
	19.	Civic Center, Neumünster
1980	20.	Valentinskamp, Hamburg, urban design
	21.	Römerberg development, Frankfurt/Main, - compulsory design
	22.	Urban villas Rauchstrasse, Berlin-Tiergarten
1981	23.	Central Post Office sorting halls, Munich
1982	24.	National Library, Frankfurt/Main
	25.	Savings Bank extension, Hamburg
1983	26.	Health Insurance Corp., Hamburg
1987	27.	Municipal Library, Münster - 2nd phase
	28.	Pfalztheater Kaiserslautern
1991	29.	Railroad stations "Rosenstein" and "Nordbahnhof", Stuttgart
	30.	State Museum of the 20th Century, Nuremberg
1992	31.	Sony, Potsdamer Platz, Berlin
1993	32.	Harness Course, Farmsen, Hamburg
	33.	Festival Complex, Recklinghausen
	34.	Hoffmannstrasse, Berlin-Treptow
	35.	Urban design Dreissigacker-South, Meiningen

1994 36. Theater of the City of Gütersloh
37. Kleist-Theater, Frankfurt/Oder
38. University Library and urban design ideas competition, Erfurt University
1995 39. Redevelopment of former Domestic and Breeding Livestock Market, Lübeck
40. Museum "Alte Kraftpost", Pirmasens [1st purchase]
41. Trade Fair and Administration Center, Bremen
42. Main Train Station, Erfurt
43. Multi-Sports Hall, Leipzig
1996 44. Prison, Gräfentonna
45. Double bridge in Fürst-Pückler-Park, Bad Muskau
46. HAB School of Architecture and Construction, Weimar
47. DVG 2000 Administration, Hanover
1997 48. Ostra-Allee, Dresden
49. Gothaer Platz, Erfurt
50. Multy-story parking garage, Trier
51. Synagogue, Dresden
52. Main Train Station, Stuttgart 21
53. Wiso, Nuremberg
54. Potsdam Train Station Quater
55. Faculty building, University of Erlangen
56. Federal Offices of Schleswig-Holstein and Lower Saxony in Berlin
1998 57. Munich Airport, Extension Terminal 2
1999 58. Tromsoe Town Hall, Norway
59. Vienna Airport

FERTIGGESTELLTE BAUTEN
COMPLETED PROJECTS

1967 • Stormann Hall, Bad Oldesloe
1969 • Max Planck Institute for Aeronomy, Lindau/Harz
W. Köhnemann House, Hamburg
1970 • Diekirch Sports Center, Luxemburg
1971 • Apartment blocks, An der Alster - Fontenay, Hamburg
1972 • Apartment block, Alstertal, Hamburg
1974 • Shell AG head offices, Hamburg
• Airport, Berlin-Tegel
1975 • ARAL AG head offices, Bochum
• Schools Center, Friedrichstadt
• Airport, Berlin-Tegel, Power Station/ Technical Services
• Airport, Berlin-Tegel, Noise Control Hangar
• Airport, Berlin-Tegel, Aircraft Maintenance Hangar
• Airport, Berlin-Tegel, Grit Store
1976 • Regional Tax Bureau, Oldenburg
• Sports Forum, University of Kiel
1977 • District Vocational School, Bad Oldesloe
• Psychiatric hospital in Rickling
1978 • Urban villas, Hamburg Bau 78
• Row houses, Hamburg Bau 78
• Airport, Berlin-Tegel, taxi station roofing
• Vocational Training Center G 13,
• Hamburg-Bergedorf
1979 • Reconstruction of the 'Fabrik', Hamburg
• Housing Kohlhöfen, Hamburg
1980 • Hanse Viertel, Hamburg
• European Patent and Trademark Office, Munich
• Taima and Sulayyil, Saudi Arabia, two new desert settlements
• Offices of the MAK, Kiel-Friedrichsort
• Institute of Biochemistry, University of Brunswick
1981 • Renaissance-Hotel Ramada, Hamburg
• House 'G', Hamburg-Blankenese
• Psychiatric hospital in Rickling, semi-open ward
1982 • Otto mail-order company, head office extension, Hamburg
• Parish House, Ritterstrasse, Stade
• 'Black box' - Schauland sales hall, Hamburg
1983 • Regional Department of the Interior, Kiel
• Home for the handicapped, Am Südring, Hamburg
• Office building, Hohe Bleichen, Hamburg
• Multi-story parking garage, Poststrasse, Hamburg
• DAL office center, Mainz
1984 • Deutsche Lufthansa office building, Hamburg
• Hillmann-Garage, Bremen
• Housing complex, Bad Schwartau
• Low-Energy House, IBA Berlin
• Urban villas, IBA Berlin
• Sports facilities, Bad Schwartau
• Police Station, Pankstrasse, Berlin
1985
• Plaza Hotel, Hillmannplatz, Bremen
• Cocoloco, bar and boutique, Hanse Viertel, Hamburg
• Psychiatric hospitals, Thetmarshof and Falkenhost in Rickling
1986 • Post Office Parking garage, Brunswick
• Reconstruction of Michaelsen Country House as a Dolls' Museum, Hamburg
• Trade and Vocational Training Center, Flensburg
• Hamburg Agency in Bonn
1987 • Apartment and office building, Grindelallee 100, Hamburg

1988 • Complex Rose, hospital for rheumatic diseases, Bad Meinberg
• Refurbishment shopping mall, Hamburger Strasse, Hamburg
• Apartment building, Saalgasse, Frankfurt/Main
1989 • District Court, Flensburg
• Housing Am Fischmarkt, Hamburg
• Glass Roof, Museum of Hamburg History, Hamburg
1990 • Elbchaussee 139, Hamburg
• Restaurant, 'Le Canard', Elbchaussee 139, Hamburg
• Telecommunications office, Post office 1, Regional Postal Directorate, Brunswick
• HEW Training Center, Hamburg
• Housing and commercial building Moorbek Rondeel, Norderstedt
• Multi-story parking garage, Hamburg-Fuhlsbüttel Airport
• Lazarus Hospital, Berlin
• Civic Center, Bielefeld
• Airport, Berlin-Tegel, crew services
1991 • Airport, Stuttgart
• Large sports hall, Flensburg
• Café Andersen - shopping mall, Hamburger Strasse, Hamburg
• Deutsche Lufthansa office building, Hamburg, 2nd stage
• Subway station, Bielefeld
• Ankara Kavaklidere Complex, Sheraton Hotel and shopping mall, Ankara
• Saar-Galerie, Saarbrücken
• City Center, Schenefeld
• Apartment and commercial building, Matzen, Buchholz
• Hillmannhaus, Bremen
• Miro Data Systems, Brunswick
1992 • von Gerkan residence, Elbchaussee 139, Hamburg
• Jumbo Shed, Deutsche Lufthansa Maintenance Hangar, Airport, Hamburg-Fuhlsbüttel
• Salamander building, Berlin
• DAL office center, Mainz, extension
• Lazarus Hospital, Berlin, refurbishment of old hospital building
• City Rail Station, Stuttgart Airport
1993 • Zürich-Haus, Hamburg
• Fleetinsel - Steigenberger Hotel, Hamburg
• Labor Office, Oldenburg
• Telecommunications office 2, Regional Postal Directorate, Hanover
• EAM, Kassel
• Airport, Berlin-Tegel, parking garage P2
• Airport, Hamburg-Fuhlsbütte
• Collegium Augustinum, Hamburg
• Airport, Stuttgart, 2nd stage
• Trade and Vocational Training Center, Flensburg, 2nd stage
1994 • Hillmann-Eck, Bremen
• Hypo-Bank, Hamburg - 'Graskeller'
• Music and Conference Hall, Lübeck
• Galeria, Duisburg
• Law Courts, Brunswick
• Deutsche Revision, Frankfurt/Main
• Bank and commercial building, Brodschrangen/Bäckerstrasse, Hamburg
• Apartment and commercial building Schaarmarkt, Hamburg
• Trade and Vocational Training Center, Flensburg, 3rd stage
• Refurbishment Law Courts, Flensburg
• Rehabilitation clinic, Trassenheide, Usedom
• Buildings for 'Premiere' TV channel, Studio Hamburg
1995 • German-Japanese Center, Hamburg
• City villa Dr. Braasch, Eberswalde
• Trade Fair, Hanover, Hall 4

1996 • New Trade Fair, Leipzig
    • Hapag-Lloyd offices, Rosenstrasse, Hamburg
    • Allee-Center, Leipzig-Grünau
1997 • Quartier 203/Atrium, Friedrich-strasse/Leipziger Strasse, Berlin
    • Dresdner Bank, Pariser Platz, Berlin
    • Dr. med. Manke consulting office
    • Star houses, Norderstedt
    • Restaurant Vau, Jägerstrasse, Berlin
    • Several platform roofs for the Deutsche Bahn AG
    • Housing complex, Friedrichshain, Berlin
    • Commercial building, Neuer Wall 43, Hamburg
    • Nordseepassage (mall), Wilhelmshaven
    • Forum Köpenick, Berlin
    • Town center of Schöneiche near Berlin
    • Gerling Insurance, Am Löwentor, Stuttgart
    • Telekom operating building, Suhl
    • Bridge across the River Hörn, Kiel
    • Restructuring/refurbishing Thalia-Theater, Hamburg
    • Restructuring Hapag Lloyd head office, Hamburg
1998 • Lecture Theatre Centre, University of Oldenburg
    • Lecture Theatre Centre, extension of Chemnitz Technical University
    • Telephone offices 3 + 5, Telekom, Berlin
    • Office building, Bredeney, Essen
    • Residence in Jurmala, Riga
    • Building for cooperative Norddeutsche Metall-Berufs-genossenschaft, Hanover
    • Railroad Station, Berlin-Spandau
    • Railroad bridge across the River Havel
    • Connecting structures for Halls 3, 4, 5 Trade Fair, Hanover
1999 • Connecting structures for Halls 5, 6, 7 Trade Fair, Hanover
    • Calenberger Esplanade, Hannover
    • Hanseatic Trade Center, Kehrwiederspitze, Hamburg
    • Metropolitan Express Train, interior
    • Philips Convention Stand
    • Hanover Trade Fair, Hall 8/9
    • Alvano House, Hamburg
    • Expo 2000 - roofing over City-Railroad Stop, Hanover
    • Civic Center, Weimar
    • Entertainment-Center, Hamburg
    • Astron Hotel, Berlin
    • New supermarkets complex, Göttingen
    • Office and commercial building, Friedrichstrasse 108/Johannisstrasse, Berlin
    • Elbkaihaus, Hamburg

Projects under construction - up until 1999

    • Foot bridges, Expo 2000
    • Dar El Beida Airport, Algiers
    • Noise Barrier, Station Spandau
    • »Lehrter Bahnhof« - central station, Berlin
    • Station 2000 - platform furnishings
    • Several (ICE-)platform roofs for the Deutsche Bahn AG
    • Dorotheen Blocks, parliamentarians offices, Berlin
    • Ku´damm Eck Hotel, Berlin
    • Labor Office Training Center of the Fed. Rep. of Germany, Schwerin
    • Altmarkt, Dresden, south-western side
    • Stuttgart Airport, extension
    • German School, Beijing
    • Trade Fair, Rimini
    • Trade Fair, Dusseldorf
    • Station square, Koblenz

    • Lenné-Passage, Frankfurt/Oder
    • Railroad bridge, Lehrter Station, Berlin
    • Casino, Bad Steben
    • Media Center, Leipzig
    • Christian Pavilion, Expo 2000
    • Agency of Brandenburg and Mecklenburg-Vorpommern in Berlin
    • Art Kite Museum, Detmold
    • Mining Archives, Clausthal-Zellerfeld

Projects at planning stage - up until 1999

    • Shopping mall, Harburger Hof
    • Development Bei St. Annen/ Holländischer Brook, Hamburg
    • Residence, Dr. Manke, Uelzen
    • Stuttgart Airport, terminal 3
    • Conversion Main Railroad Stations Kiel, Mainz, Lübeck
    • Central Bus Station, Wilhelmshaven
    • Deutrichs Hof, Leipzig
    • Agency of Sachsen-Anhalt in Berlin
    • German Trade Center, Bucharest
    • International Horticulture Exhibition, Rostock
    • Kroepcke Center, Hanover
    • Apartment House, Riga
    • Office and Commercial Building, Riga
    • Berlin Olympic Stadium, conversion
    • Berlin-Brandenburg International Airport
    • Nanning Convention & Exhibition Center, China
    • Ancona Airport, Italy

AUSZEICHNUNGEN
AWARDS

    • German Architecture Award 1977, commendation:
      Power station/technical services building Airport Berlin-Tegel

    • Gold medal of the Federal Competition Industry in Urban Design 1978:
      Airport, Berlin-Tegel

    • 'Exemplary Buildings', disctinction:
      Housing Kohlhöfen, Hamburg

    • 'Exemplary Buildings' 1978, distinction:
      Vocational training center G 13, Hamburg-Bergedorf

    • Building of the Year 1979 (AIV):
      Vocational training center G 13, Hamburg-Bergedorf

    • BDA Award Schleswig-Holstein 1979:
      Sports forum, University of Kiel

    • Architecture Award Concrete 1979, commendation:
      Sports forum, University of Kiel

    • 'Exemplary Buildings', distinction: Urban villas, Hamburg, Bau 78

    • Poroton Architects' Competition, 1st prize:
      Urban villas, Hamburg, Bau 78

    • 'Exemplary Buildings', distinction:
      Row houses, Hamburg, Bau 78

    • Poroton Architects' Competition, special prize:
      Row houses, Hamburg, Bau 78

    • BDA Award Lower Saxony 1980:
      Max Planck Institute, Lindau/Harz

    • BDA Award Bavaria 1981, commendation:
      European Patent and Trademark Office, Munich

    • International Color Design Award 1980/81, commendation:
      Airport, Berlin-Tegel

    • Building of the Year 1981 (AIV):
      Hanse Viertel, Hamburg

    • Building of the Year 1983 (AIV):
      Multi-story parking garage, Hamburg

    • Mies van der Rohe Award 1984:
      Hanse Viertel, Hamburg

    • North-German Timber Construction Award 1984:
      House 'G', Hamburg-Blankenese

    • BDA Award Schleswig-Holstein 1985:
      Marktarkaden, Bad Schwartau

    • BDA Award Schleswig-Holstein 1985:
      Regional Department of the Interior, Kiel

    • 'Exemplary Buildings' 1989, commendation:
      Grindelallee 100, Hamburg

- Mies van der Rohe Award 1990:
  Glass roof, Museum of Hamburg History,
  Hamburg

- Building of the Year 1990 (AIV):
  Elbchaussee 139, Hamburg

- BDA Award Bremen 1990:
  Hillmann-Garage, Bremen

- BDA Award Lower Saxony 1991:
  Regional Postal Directorate, Brunswick

- Deutscher Natursteinpreis 1991:
  Regional Postal Directorate, Brunswick

- German Architecture Award 1991:
  Multi-story parking garage,
  Hamburg-Fuhlsbüttel

- BDA Award
  North Rhine-Westphalia 1992,
  'Bauen für die öffentliche Hand'
  [public buildings],
  commendation:
  Civic Center, Bielefeld

- BDA Award
  North Rhine-Westphalia 1992,
  'Bauen für die öffentliche Hand'
  [public buildings],
  commendation:
  Subway station, Bielefeld

- BDA Award Berlin 1992,
  commendation:
  Salamander building, Berlin

- German Steel Construction Award 1992:
  Airport, Stuttgart

- Westhyp Architecture Award 1992,
  commendation: HEW Training Center,
  Hamburg

- Deutscher Natursteinpreis 1993,
  commendation:
  Airport, Stuttgart

- Deutscher Verzinkerpreis 1993,
  commendation:
  Zürich-Haus, Hamburg

- Deutscher Verzinkerpreis 1993,
  commendation:
  'Le Canard' bridge, Hamburg

- Building of the Year 1993 (AIV):
  Jumbo shed, Hamburg

- Deutscher Verzinkerpreis 1993:
  Multi-story parking garage,
  Hamburg-Fuhlsbüttel

- Balthasar Neumann Award 1993:
  Airport, Hamburg-Fuhlsbüttel

- Building of the Year 1994 (AIV):
  Airport, Hamburg-Fuhlsbüttel

- Prix d'Excellence 1994 –
  Finaliste Catégorie
  Immobilier d'Entreprise:
  Jumbo shed, Hamburg

- BDA Award Lower Saxony 1994,
  commendation:
  Labor Office, Oldenburg

- Peter Joseph Krahe Award 1994:
  Regional Postal Directorate, Brunswick

- Peter Joseph Krahe Award 1994:
  Miro Data Systems, Brunswick

- BDA Award Lower Saxony 1994:
  Miro Data Systems, Brunswick

- Constructec Award 1994,
  commendation:
  Miro Data Systems, Brunswick

- Deutscher Natursteinpreis 1995,
  commendation:
  Law Court, Brunswick

- Oldenburger Stadtbildpreis 1995,
  commendation:
  Labor Office, Oldenburg

- German Architecture Award 1995,
  commendation:
  Airport, Hamburg-Fuhlsbüttel

- USITT 1996, Honor Award:
  Music and Conference Hall, Lübeck

- German Steel Construction Award 1996,
  commendation:
  Airport, Hamburg-Fuhlsbüttel

- Saxony State Award for Architecture and
  Construction 1996:
  New Trade Fair, Leipzig

- Westhyp Architectural Award 1996,
  commendation:
  Bank and Commercial building,
  Brodschrangen, Hamburg

- BDA Award Hamburg 1996:
  Jumbo shed, Hamburg

- BDA Award Hamburg 1996,
  commendation:
  Airport, Hamburg-Fuhlsbüttel

- BDA Award Lower Rhine 1996,
  commendation:
  Galeria, Duisburg

- Brunel Awards 1996:
  Platform roof prototype for
  Deutsche Bahn AG

- Deutscher Natursteinpreis 1996,
  commendation:
  Hapag-Lloyd offices, Hamburg

- Design Innovations 1997,
  Red Point for high design quality:
  glass-door band, type 16058

- Design Innovations 1997,
  Red Point for high design quality:
  Platform roof prototype for
  Deutsche Bahn AG

- Deutscher Verzinkerpreis 1997:
  New Trade Fair, Leipzig

- German Architecture Award 1997,
  distinction:
  New Trade Fair, Leipzig

- Martin-Elsaesser-Plakette 1998,
  commandation: C&L Deutsche Revision

- Bathasar-Neumann Award 1998:
  Trade Fair, Hanover, Hall 4

- German Steel Construction Award 1998,
  commendation: New Trade Fair, Leipzig

- The 1998 Dupont Benedictus Awards:
  Dresdner Bank, Pariser Platz, Berlin

- The 1998 Dupont Benedictus Awards:
  Nordseepassage, Wilhelmshaven

- Deutscher Natursteinpreis 1999,
  commandation: Railroad Station, Berlin-
  Spandau

- Marble Architectural Awards 1999,
  special mention: New Trade Fair, Leipzig

- Deutscher Verzinkerpreis 1999:
  Railroad Station, Berlin-Spandau

AUSSTELLUNGEN
EXHIBITIONS

- Architecture of von Gerkan,
  Marg and Partners, BDA, Dresden 1989

- Architecture of von Gerkan, Marg and
  Partners, Weimar Bauhaus, BDA 1990

- Idea and Model -
  30 Years of Architectural Models of
  von Gekan, Marg and Partners,
  Architecture Workshop, Hamburg 1994

- Under Big Roofs, wide-tensed projects of
  von Gerkan, Marg and Partners, Berlinische
  Gallery, Berlin 1995

- Infobox Berlin:
  Lehrter Bahnhof - new central train station
  in Berlin, Berlin 1996/1997

- Building for Air Travel -
  Architecture and Design for Commercial
  Aviation: Airport Tegel, Stuttgart, Hamburg,
  Jumbo Shed,
  The Art Institute of Chicago 1996/1997
  Museum of Flight, Seattle 1997
  San Francisco International Airport 1997
  Rhein-Main International Airport,
  Frankfurt/Main 1997
  Tempelhof Airport, Berlin 1997
  Hamburg Airport 1997

- Sensing the Future -
  The Architect as Seismograph:
  New Trade Fair, Leipzig,
  Architecture Biennial, Venice 1996

- Renaissance of Railway Stations.
  The City in the 21st Century,
  22 buildings and projects of von Gerkan,
  Marg and Partners, Architecture Biennial,
  Venice 1996
  Former Dresdner Train Station in Berlin 1997
  Main Train Station, Stuttgart 1997
  Deichtor halls, Hamburg 1997
  Former Deutsche Bahn cargo hall,
  Munich 1998
  Colosseum, Essen 1999

- Building According to Nature -
  The Heirs of Palladio in Northern Europe:
  New Trade Fair, Leipzig, Museum of Hamburg
  History, Hamburg 1997

- Berlin Scrapes the Sky, DAZ, Berlin 1997

- Airports - Vision and Tradition -
  Designs for an Berlin-Brandenburg
  International Airport:
  Airport Berlin-Tegel, Stuttgart, Hamburg and
  21 student projects under Prof. M. v. Gerkan,
  IDZ, Berlin-Tempelhof Airport, Berlin 1997

- Macht und Monument: Lehrter Bahnhof,
  German Architecture Museum, Frankfurt
  1998

- The Architect as Designer: The VAU chair,
  Shoe-cleaning step stool,
  Museum of Arts and Crafts, Berlin 1998

- 2002 - 800 Years Riga, "A House for the Music", diploma designs and Music and Conference hall in Lübeck, Rigas Galerija, Riga 1998

- Bucharest 2000, German-Romanian Architectural Workshop, a project of the Jürgen-Ponto-Foundation Supervision: Meinhard von Gerkan Sala Dalles Artexpo, Bucharest 1998

- Architecture of Contemplation, Gallery Aedes East, Berlin 1998

- 100 Years Art on the Move: Conversion of the Reichstag building, Lehrter Bahnhof, Berlin Gallery Bonn, Bonn 1998

- In/From China. Art and Architecture: German School of Beijing, Asian Fine Arts Factory, Berlin 1999

- "The Christian Pavilion" on the World Exhibition EXPO 2000 Evangelic Academy, Hanover 1999

- von Gerkan, Marg and Partners - Building for the Public, Yan-Huang Art Museum, Beijing, China 1999

BÜCHER
BOOKS

- Meinhard von Gerkan Architektur 1966 – 1978 von Gerkan, Marg und Partner Stuttgart: Karl Krämer Verlag 1978 ISBN 3-7828-1438-X

- Meinhard von Gerkan Die Verantwortung des Architekten - Bedingungen für die gebaute Umwelt Stuttgart: Deutsche Verlags-Anstalt 1982 ISBN 3-421-02584-3

- Meinhard von Gerkan Architektur 1978 – 1983 von Gerkan, Marg und Partner Stuttgart: Deutsche Verlags-Anstalt 1983 ISBN 3-421-02597-5

- Meinhard von Gerkan Alltagsarchitektur Gestalt und Ungestalt Wiesbaden/Berlin: Bauerverlag 1987 ISBN 3-7625-2449-1

- Meinhard von Gerkan Architektur 1983 – 1988 von Gerkan, Marg und Partner Stuttgart: Deutsche Verlags-Anstalt 1988 ISBN 3-421-02893-1

- Meinhard von Gerkan Jürgen-Ponto-Stiftung West-Östlicher Architektenworkshop in Dresden 13. – 20. Juli 1990 Hamburg: Christians Verlag 1990 ISBN 3-7672-1121-1

- Meinhard von Gerkan Architektur 1988 – 1991 von Gerkan, Marg und Partner Stuttgart: Deutsche Verlags-Anstalt 1992 ISBN 3-421-03021-9

- Volkwin Marg Architektur in Hamburg seit 1900 Hamburg: Junius Verlag GmbH 1993 ISBN 3-88506-206-2

- Meinhard von Gerkan von Gerkan, Marg and Partners London: Academy Editions Berlin: Ernst & Sohn 1993 ISBN 1-85490-166-4

- Meinhard von Gerkan Idea and Model Idee und Modell 30 years of architectural models 30 Jahre Architekturmodelle von Gerkan, Marg und Partner Meinhard v. Gerkan unter Mitarbeit von Jan Esche und Bernd Pastuschka Berlin: Ernst & Sohn 1994 ISBN 3-433-02482-0

- Ideen, Entwürfe, Modelle Meinhard von Gerkan, gmp Die Musik- und Kongresshalle (MUK) (Ausstellungskatalog) Hg. v. Overbeck-Gesellschaft Verein von Kunstfreunden e.V., Lübeck Lübeck: 1994

- Meinhard von Gerkan Architektur im Dialog Texte zur Architekturpraxis Berlin: Ernst & Sohn 1994 ISBN 3-433-02881-8

- von Gerkan, Marg und Partner Unter großen Dächern (Ausstellungskatalog) Hg. v. Klaus-Dieter Weiß in Kooperation mit Berlinische Galerie, Landesmuseum für Moderne Kunst, Photographie und Architektur Gütersloh,Braunschweig/Wiesbaden: Bertelsmann Fachzeitschriften GmbH und Friedr. Vieweg & Sohn Verlagsgesellschaft mbH 1995 ISBN 3-528-08194-5

- C & L Deutsche Revision Bürogebäude Heddernheim Hg. v. C & L Deutsche Revision Frankfurt: 1995

- Meinhard von Gerkan Architektur 1988 – 1991 von Gerkan, Marg und Partner 2., veränderte Auflage Basel, Boston, Berlin: Birkhäuser 1995 ISBN 3-7643-5221-3

- Meinhard von Gerkan Culture Bridge Deutsch-Polnischer Ideenwettbewerb "Kulturbrücke Görlitz/Zgorzelec" Berlin: Vice Versa Verlag 1995

- architypus special von Gerkan, Marg und Partner Unter großen Dächern Hg. v. Klaus-Dieter Weiß Gütersloh, Braunschweig/Wiesbaden: Bertelsmann Fachzeitschriften GmbH und Friedr. Vieweg & Sohn Verlagsgesellschaft mbH 1995 ISBN 3-528-08113-9

- Meinhard von Gerkan Architektur 1991 – 1995 von Gerkan, Marg und Partner Basel, Boston, Berlin: Birkhäuser 1995 ISBN 3-7643-5222-1 ISBN 0-8176-5222-1

- Volkwin Marg Pilot-Projekt Aufbau Ost – Neue Messe Leipzig, Planung + Bau 1992-1995 Basel, Boston, Berlin: Birkhäuser 1996 ISBN 3-7643-5409-7

- Renaissance of Railway Stations. The City in the 21st Century (Ausstellungskatalog) Hg. v. Bund Deutscher Architekten BDA, Deutsche Bahn AG, Förderverein Deutsches Architekturzentrum DAZ in cooperation with Meinhard v. Gerkan Wiesbaden: Vieweg 1996

- Meinhard v. Gerkan von Gerkan, Marg und Partner: Architecture for Transportation, Architektur für den Verkehr Basel, Boston, Berlin: Birkhäuser 1997 ISBN 3-7643-5611-1 ISBN 0-8176-5611-1

- Volkwin Marg Neue Messe Leipzig, New Trade Fair Leipzig Basel, Boston, Berlin: Birkhäuser 1997 ISBN 3-7643-5429-1 ISBN 0-8176-5429-1

- John Zukowsky The Architecture of von Gerkan, Marg + Partners Prestel Verlag, München, New York 1997 ISBN 3-7913-1861-6

- Meinhard von Gerkan Architecture 1995 - 1997 von Gerkan, Marg und Partner Basel, Boston, Berlin: Birkhäuser 1998 ISBN 3-7643-5844-0

- Meinhard von Gerkan Möbel Furniture von Gerkan, Marg und Partner Verlag Gert Hatje, Stuttgart 1998 ISBN 3-7757-0766-2

- Von Gerkan, Marg and Partners - Building for the Public (Ausstellungskatalog) Hg. v. Yan-Huang Art Museum, Beijing: 1999

- Volkwin Marg Hall 8/9, von Gerkan, Marg + Partners Munich, London, New York 2000 ISBN 3-7913-2136-6

Abbreviations:
D for: design; P for: partner;
PL for: project leader; C for: co-worker;
Co for: in cooperation with

1965 and before

1 District Administration, Niebüll
competition, 2nd prize

2 Civic Center, Kassel
competition, 4th prize

3 Residenzplatz, Würzburg
competition, award

4 Löwenwall, Brunswick
competition, award

5 Airport, Hanover-Langenhagen
M. v. Gerkan, diploma project

6 Indoor swimming pool,
Brunswick-Gliesmarode
competition, 1st prize

7 Sports- and Conference Center,
Hamburg
competition, 1st prize

8 Jungfernstieg, Hamburg
competition, 2nd prize

9 Theater, Wolfsburg
competition, 3rd prize

10 Airport, Berlin-Tegel
competition, 1st prize
completed 1975
D: M. v. Gerkan, K. Nickels
P: K. Staratzke, K. Brauer,
R. Niedballa
C: W. Hertel, H. Herzlieb,
W. Hönnicke, M. Illig, D. Perisic,
P. Römer, G. Seule, H. Pitz,
W. Zimmer, H.-J. Roeske

11 Airport, Berlin-Tegel,
Noise Control Hangar
completed 1975
D: M. v. Gerkan
P: K. Brauer

12 Airport, Berlin-Tegel,
Power Station/Technical Services
completed 1975
D: M. v. Gerkan
P: K. Staratzke
C: W. Hönnicke, L. Gerhardt,
M. Auder, C. Grzimek, R. Henning

13 Airport, Berlin-Tegel, bridges
completed 1975
D: M. v. Gerkan
P: K. Staratzke

14 Airport, Berlin-Tegel, Freight Center
completed 1972
D: M. v. Gerkan
P: K. Staratzke
C: W. Hönnecke

15 Airport, Berlin-Tegel, Grit Store
completed 1972
D: M. v. Gerkan, K. Staratzke
P: K. Staratzke

16 Airport, Berlin-Tegel, apron areas
completed 1973
D: M. v. Gerkan
P: R. Niedballa
C: P. Römer

17 Urban design, Kiel inner city
competition, award

18 Indoor/open-air swimming pool,
Sozialdemokratische Partei
Deutschlands
competition, 1st prize

19 Stormarn Hall, Bad Oldesloe
competition, 1st prize
completed 1967
D: V. Marg with H. Schmedje,
K. Nickels

20 Diekirch Sports Center, Luxemburg
competition, 1st prize
completed 1970 and 1975
(2nd stage)
D: M. v. Gerkan
C: C. Brockstedt, C. Claudius,
S. Müllerstedt
Co: R. Störmer

21 Tax Bureau, Oldenburg
competition, 1st prize
completed 1976
D: M. v. Gerkan
C: C. Mrozek
Co: D. Patschan

22 Urban design, Hamburg-Niendorf
competition, award

1966

23 School and Sports Center, Brake
competition, 5th prize

24 Max Planck Institute for Aeronomy
in Lindau/Harz
competition, 1st prize
completed 1969
D: V. Marg
C: C. Claudius, G. Fleher
Co: R. Störmer

25 District indoor swimming pool,
Cologne
competition, 1st prize

26 Sports Hall, Bottrop
competition, 3rd prize

27 New Picture Gallery, Munich
competition, award

28 Sports Forum, University of Kiel
competition, 1st prize
completed 1976
D: V. Marg with K. Nickels
C: K. Kurzweg, G. Welm,
V. Rudolph, P. Frohne

1967

29 Open-air swimming pool,
Bad Bramstedt
competition, 5th prize

30 Buildings for the 20th Olympic
Games, Munich
competition, project A: award
project B: 2nd prize

31 University of Bremen
competition

1968

32 Schools Center, Weinheim
competition, award

33 Airport, Hamburg-Kaltenkirchen
consultancy project

34 Administrative offices, Hamburgische
Landesbank, Hamburg
competition entries, 1st place

35 Adolfinum Secondary School,
Bückeburg
competition

36 Church Center, Hamburg-Ohlsdorf
competition, 2nd prize

37 Apartment blocks, An der Alster –
Alsterufer/Fontenay, Hamburg
competition, award
completed 1971
D: V. Marg
C: C. Mrozek, P. Fischer

38 W. Köhnemann House, Hamburg
completed 1969
D: V. Marg

39 Parish Hall and Church,
Osdorfer Born
competition, 2nd prize

1969

40 Shopping mall, Hamburg-Altona
competition, award

41 Dr. Hess residence,
Hamburg-Nienstedten

42 Engineering School, Buxtehude
competition, 3rd place

43 Spa Center, Westerland/Sylt
competition, 4th prize

44 Comprehensive School, Steilshoop
competition, 4th prize

45 Comprehensive School,
Mümmelmannsberg, Hamburg
competition, award

46 Church Community Center,
Hamburg-Bergedorf
competition, second round

1970

47 Shell AG head offices, Hamburg
competition, 1st prize
completed 1974
D: V. Marg
P: E. Wiehe
PL: B. Albers
C: J. Lupp, H.-P. Harm, K. Maass,
U. Rückel, H. Stetten

48 Mobil Oil AG offices, Hamburg
competition

49 District Vocational School,
Bad Oldesloe
competition, 1st prize
completed 1977
D: V. Marg
P: E. Wiehe
C: U. Ferdinand, E. Schäfer,
D. Wingsch

50 Schools Center, Heide-Ost
competition, 2nd prize

51 Regional Postal Directorate, Bremen
competition, 2nd prize

52 Church Community Center,
Steilshoop, Hamburg
competition, 3rd prize

53 School and Educational Center, Niebüll
competition, 3rd prize

54 Redesign of Gerhard-Hauptmann-
Platz, Hamburg
consultancy project

55 Schools Center, Adelby, Flensburg
competition, award

56 Secondary School, Bargteheide
competition, award

57 Program for Berlin public
swimming pools
expertise

1971

58 Airport, Berlin-Tegel,
Aircraft Maintenance Hangar
completed 1975
D: M. v. Gerkan
P: K. Staratzke, K. Brauer,
R. Niedballa
C: R. Henning

59 Shopping mall, Hamburg-Lohbrügge
competition, award

60 Hamburg-Poppenbüttel
urban design expertise

61 Development of Hamburg's inner city
(west)
competition, 3rd prize

62 Tornesch
urban design ideas competition, award

63 Multi-purpose building III,
University of Hamburg
competition, 1st prize

64 Federal Chancellery, Bonn
competition, 4th prize

65 Cultural Center, Munich-Gasteig
competition

66 Regional Tax Bureau, Hamburg
competition, 2nd prize

67 European Patent and Trademark
Office, Munich
competition, 1st prize
completed 1980
D: V. Marg
P: A. Sack
C: H. Tomhave, H. Müller-Röwekamp,
C: Korus, F. Kessler, K. Bachmann,
H.-J. Roeske, H. Springhorn

68 Indoor swimming pool, Bad Oldesloe
competition, award

69 Sports Forum, University of Bremen
competition, 2nd prize

70 Apartment blocks,
Gellertstrasse/Bellevue, Hamburg
competition, 1st place

71 Regional Administration offices,
Lüneburg
competition, 2nd prize

72 Housing Neuwiedenthal-Nord,
Hamburg-Harburg
urban design expertise

73 Shopping mall, Alstertal, Hamburg
competition, 1st prize

74 GPD-Bremen
competition 2nd prize

1972

75   Apartment block next to shopping
     mall, Alstertal, Hamburg
     consultancy project
     completed 1972
     D: V. Marg
     C: U. Ferdinand

76   Spa Gardens, Helgoland
     competition, award

77   Regional Postal Directorate, Hamburg
     competition, 2nd prize

78   Schools Center, Friedrichstadt
     competition, 1st prize
     completed 1975
     D: V. Marg
     C: R. Wilkens, H. Wolf, A. Marg,
          C. Mrozeck, U. Rückel

79   ARAL AG head offices, Bochum
     competition, 1st prize
     completed 1975
     D: M. v. Gerkan
     P: M. Sack, R. Niedballa
     C: B. Gronemeyer, J. Busack,
          H. Stetten

80   Landscaped indoor swimming pool,
     Rebstockpark, Frankfurt/Main
     competition

1973

81   Private residence for B.,
     Hamburg-Reinbek
     design

82   Colonia Insurance AG offices,
     Hamburg
     competition, 3rd prize

83   Wilhelm-Hack-Museum,
     Ludwigshafen
     competition

84   Tegeler Hafen Apartment blocks,
     Berlin
     competition

85   Psychiatric hospital in Rickling
     completed 1977
     D: V. Marg, K. Staratzke
     C: C. Mrozeck, U. Rückel,
          D. Wingsch

1974

86   Vocational Training Center G 13,
     Hamburg-Bergedorf
     competition, 1st prize
     completed 1978
     D: M. v. Gerkan
     PL: B. Albers
     C: H.-E. Bock, W. Schäfer,
          J. Busack, M. Stroh, M. Ebeling,
          G. Göb, K. Maass

87   Hanse Viertel, Hamburg
     completed 1980
     D: V. Marg
     P: K. Staratzke
     C: B. Albers, R. Born, A. Buchholz-
          Berger, O. Dorn, H.-J. Dörr,
          W. Edler, M. Eggers,
          U. Ferdinand, R. Henning,
          B. Gronemeyer, J. Krautberger,
          A. Lucks, K. Maass,
          H. Müller-Röwekamp, D. Perisic,
          R. Seifert, P. Sembritzki

88   Cocoloco, bar and boutique,
     Hanse Viertel, Hamburg
     completed 1985
     D: K. Staratzke, O. Dorn

89   Provinzial Insurance Company
     offices, Kiel
     consultancy project, 1st place

90   Satellite city, Billwerder-Allermöhe,
     Hamburg
     consultancy project

91   Airport Munich II
     project 1 and 2: 1974,
     commissioned expertise

1975

92   Airport Munich II
     competition, 1st place

93   Housing Billwerder-Allermöhe,
     Hamburg
     competition, 2nd prize

94   Regional Department of the Interior,
     Kiel
     competition, 2nd prize
     completed 1983
     D: V. Marg
     PL: B. Albers
     C: G. Göb, W. Tegge, D. Winter

95   Town Hall of Itzehoe, extension
     competition, 4th prize

96   Housing Kohlhöfen, Hamburg
     completed 1979
     D: V. Marg
     C: J. Werner, G. Werner,
          H. Huusmann, B. Albers,
          B. Gronemeyer

97   Housing Oevelgönne, Hamburg
     design

98   Regional Government offices,
     Brunswick
     competition

99   Deutscher Ring, Hamburg
     competition, 1st prize

100 Federal Department of Health,
     Berlin-Marienfelde
     competition

101 Redevelopment Große Bleichen,
     Hamburg

1976

102 Administrative offices,
     operating area of Airport Munich II
     competition, 2nd prize

103 Faculty of Inner Security, Riyadh
     consultancy project

104 Airport, Moscow
     competition, 1st prize

105 Dar El Beida Airport, Algiers
     passenger and freight terminals
     competition, version A: 1st prize

106 Bauer publishing house, Hamburg
     competition, award

107 District Administration,
     Recklinghausen
     competition, 1st prize

108 Design of a power station
     study

109 Post Office Savings Bank, Hamburg
     competition, 3rd prize

110 Urban design, Universität Ost,
     Bremen
     competition, 2nd prize

111 Training Center of the Federal
     Fiscal Administration, Münster
     competition, second round

112 Holstentorplatz, Lübeck
     competition

113 Communications Center,
     Wiesbaden
     competition

1977

114 Airport, Berlin-Tegel,
     taxi station roofing
     completed 1978
     D: M. v. Gerkan
     P: K. Brauer
     C: M. Auder, P. Römer

115 Airport, Berlin-Tegel, crew services
     completed 1978
     D: M. v. Gerkan
     P: R. Niedballa
     C: P. Römer

116 Offices of the MAK,
     Kiel-Friedrichsort
     consultancy project, 1st place
     completed 1980
     D: M. v. Gerkan
     P: K. Staratzke
     Co: Brockstedt + Discher

117 Parish House, Ritterstrasse, Stade
     competition, 1st prize
     completed 1982
     D: V. Marg
     P: K. Staratzke
     C: E. Hamer, A. Marg, U. Rückel

118 Police Station, Panckstrasse, Berlin
     competition, 1st place
     completed 1984
     D: M. v. Gerkan
     C: M. Auder, P. Römer

119 Reconstruction of the 'Fabrik',
     Hamburg
     completed 1979
     D: V. Marg
     C: J. Busack, M. Ebeling, G. Göb,
          C. Mrozeck, G. Sievers

120 Otto mail-order company,
     head office extension, Hamburg
     competition, 1st prize
     completed 1982
     D: V. Marg
     C: M. Ebeling, B. Gronemeyer,
          J. Kleiberg, R. Seifert, J. Sefl,
          C. Timm-Schwarz

121 Hyatt Hotel, Abu Dhabi

122 Axel Springer publishing house
     competition, special award

123 Psychiatric Hospital in Rickling,
     semi-open award
     completed 1981
     D: V. Marg, K. Staratzke
     C: K. Ehlert, E. Hamer, R. Henning,
          C. Mrozeck, C. Timm-Schwarz

124 Psychiatric Hospital in Rickling,
     Thetmarshof and Falkenhorst
     completed 1985
     D: V. Marg, K. Staratzke
     C: K. Ehlert, E. Hamer, R. Henning

125 Row houses, Hamburg Bau 78
     competition, 2nd prize
     completed 1978
     D: M. v. Gerkan
     P: K. Staratzke

126 Urban villas, Hamburg Bau 78
     competition, 2nd prize
     completed 1978
     D: M. v. Gerkan
     P: H.-E. Bock

127 House 'G', Hamburg-Blankenese
     completed 1981
     D: M. v. Gerkan
     C: M. Ebeling, U. Rückel, M. Stroh

128 Taima, Saudi Arabia,
     new desert settlement
     completed 1980
     D: M. v. Gerkan
     P: K. Brauer, K. Staratzke
     C: A. Buchholz-Berger, W. Haux

129 Sulayyil, Saudi Arabia,
     new desert settlement
     completed 1980
     D: M. v. Gerkan
     P: K. Brauer, K. Staratzke
     C: A. Buchholz-Berger, W. Haux

130 Sports and leisure complex, Berlin
     study

131 Development project, Uhlandstrasse,
     Berlin
     competition

1978

132 Alstertal shopping mall, extension
     competition, 3rd prize

133 Hotel, Augsburger Platz, Berlin
     competition

134 Restaurant on former garbage depot,
     Berlin-Lübars
     competition

135 Federal German Ministry of
     Transportation, Bonn
     competition, 1st prize

136 Regional Ministry for Social Affairs
     and Nutrition, Stuttgart, Wulle area
     consultancy project

137 Institute of Chemistry, University of
     Brunswick
     competition, 1st place

138 Institute of Biochemistry,
     University of Brunswick
     consultancy project, 1st place
     completed 1980
     D: M. v. Gerkan with H.-E. Bock,
          M. Stanek

139 City Hall, Mannheim
     competition, 3rd prize

140 Superior Court of
     Justice for Berlin
     competition

141 Multi-story parking garage,
Poststrasse, Hamburg
completed 1983
D: V. Marg
P. K. Staratzke
C: R. Born, R. Henning, R. Seifert,
P. Sembritzki

142 Joachimsthaler Platz, Berlin
'Urban pavilion'
competition

143 Joachimsthaler Platz, Berlin
'Kunstwäldchen'
competition
recommended for revision

144 Joachimsthaler Platz, Berlin
'Light columns'
adopted solution

145 Pahlavi National Library, Tehran
international competition, 1st prize

146 Central Library, main dining hall and
sports facilities,
University of Oldenburg
special competition procedure

1979

147 6 urban villas, IBA Berlin
competition, selected
completed 1984
D: M. v. Gerkan
C: M. Auder, P. Römer

148 Museum, Aachen
competition

149 Home for the handicapped,
Am Südring, Hamburg
completed 1983
D: V. Marg
P: K. Brauer
C: F. Brandt, M. Mews

150 Islamic Cultural Center, Madrid
competition

151 Düppel-Nord Sports Center,
Free University, Berlin
competition, 3rd prize

152 Dahlem Sports Center,
Free University, Berlin
competition, 4th prize

153 Protestant Church Administration,
Hanover
competition, 4th prize

154 Landeszentralbank Hessen,
Frankfurt/Main
competition

155 Valentinskamp, Hamburg
urban design, competition, award

156 Indoor swimming pool
Mannheim-Herzogenried
competition, 1st prize

157 Large sports hall, Bielefeld
competition, 4th prize

158 Görlitzer Bad, Berlin-Kreuzberg
competition

159 Indoor/outdoor swimming
pools, Berlin-Spandau
competition, 1st prize

160 Computer Center, Deutsche Bank,
Hamburg
competition, award

161 Civic Center, Neumünster
competition, award

162 Parliament of North
Rhine-Westphalia, Düsseldorf
competition

163 Vereins- und Westbank, branch
Ost-West-Strasse, Hamburg
competition, 1st place

164 Emsland District Administration,
Meppen
competition, 1st prize

1980

165 Gasworks, Munich
competition, 2nd prize

166 Town Hall, am Pferdemarkt,
Oldenburg
competition, 2nd prize

167 Office building, Hohe Bleichen,
Hamburg
completed 1983
D: V. Marg, K. Staratzke
P: K. Staratzke
C: E. Braunsburger, L. Flores,
W. Haux, B. Gronemeyer,
K. Maass, A. Wolter, A. Wriedt

168 Federal Ministry of Labor and
Social Affairs, Bonn
competition, 5th prize

169 Administrative offices for
Volkswagen, Wolfsburg
competition, 2nd prize

170 Renaissance-Hotel Ramada,
Hamburg
completed 1981
D: V. Marg
P: K. Staratzke
C: A. Buchholz-Berger, O. Dorn,
B. Kiel, H. Nolden, H. Ueda

171 Colonia Insurance head office,
Cologne-Holweide
competition

172 Urban villas, Rauchstrasse,
Berlin-Tiergarten
competition, award

173 Civic Center, Bielefeld
competition, 1st prize
completed 1990
D: M. v. Gerkan
PL: M. Zimmermann
C: M. Ebeling, P. Kropp, S. Rimpf,
T. Rinne, P. Sembritzki
AOS: D. Tholotowsky, H. Schröder

174 University of Bremerhaven
competition, 3rd prize

175 Academy of Fine Arts, Hamburg
competition, 1st prize

176 Residential project for the
Friedrichstadt neighborhood, Berlin
competition

177 Trade and Vocational Training
Center, Flensburg
competition, 1st prize
completed: 1st construction stage
1986, 2nd stage 1993, 3rd stage 1994
D: M. v. Gerkan
P: K. Staratzke
C: H.-E. Bock, M. Stanek, K. Krause

178 Lazarus Hospital, Berlin
competition, 1st prize
completed 1990
D: M. v. Gerkan
PL: P. Römer
C: J. Zais

179 Lazarus Hospital, Berlin
Refurbishment of old hospital
building,
completed 1992
D: M. v. Gerkan
C: P. Römer, J. Zais

180 Airport, Stuttgart
competition, 1st prize
completed 1990
D: M. v. Gerkan, K. Brauer
P: K. Staratzke
C: A. Buchholz-Berger, M. Dittmer,
O. Dorn, M. Ebeling, E. Grimmer,
G. Hagemeister, R. Henning,
B. Kiel, A. Lucks, M. Mews,
H.-H. Möller, D. Perisic,
K.-H. Petersen, U. Pörksen,
S. Rimpf, H. Thimian,
C. Timm-Schwarz, T. Tran-Viet,
H. Ueda

181 Römerberg development,
Frankfurt/Main
competition, free design: 1st prize;
compulsory design: award

182 Fleetinsel development, Hamburg
competition, 1st prize

183 Fleetinsel – Steigenberger Hotel,
Hamburg
competition, 1st prize
completed 1993
D: V. Marg with W. Haux
C: A. Böke, J. Krugmann,
H. Ladewig, R. Preuss, B. Sinnwell

184 Large sports hall, Flensburg
competition, 1st prize
completed 1991
D: M. v. Gerkan with M. Stanek
P: K. Staratzke
C: K. Krause

185 Deutsche Lufthansa office building,
Hamburg
competition, 1st prize
completed
1st stage 1984; 2nd stage 1991
D: M. v. Gerkan, K. Brauer
P: K. Staratzke
C: M. Ebeling, B. Gronemeyer,
K. Maass, M. Mews, H.-H. Möller

186 Indoor leisure swimming pool, Kiel
competition

187 Max Planck Institute for Quantum
Optics, Munich
competition, 2nd prize

188 Sports facilities, Bad Schwartau
completed 1984
D: M. v. Gerkan, K. Brauer
C: M. Ebeling, W. Haux, H.-H- Möller,
T. Tran-Viet

189 Town Hall, Norderstedt
competition

190 Johanneum sports hall, Lübeck
competition, 1st prize

1981

191 Johanneum sports hall, Lübeck
consultancy project

192 Kravag offices, Hamburg
competition, 2nd prize

193 Kiel-Hörn
urban development expertise

194 Fontenay, Hamburg
urban design expertise

195 Hotel, Lisbon
onsultancy project

196 Housing Abudja, Nigeria
planning study

197 Nigerian Bank of Commerce
and Industry, head offices, Abudja
preliminary design

198 Municipal Library, Gütersloh
competition

199 Refurbishment/conversion, Kiel Castle
competition, 1st place

200 Law Court, Brunswick
consultancy project, 1st place
completed 1994
D: M. v. Gerkan with H.-E. Bock,
M. Stanek, A. Buchholz-Berger
P: J. Zais
C: B. Kreykenbohm, H.-W. Warias,
M. Skrabal, G. Wysocki

201 DAL office center, Mainz
competition, 1st place
completed 1983/1992
D: M. v. Gerkan with J. Friedemann,
G. Tjarks
PL: A. Sack
C: R. Henning, U. Rückel

202 Housing complex, Bad Schwartau
competition, 1st prize

203 Apartment and commercial building,
Marktarkaden, Bad Schwartau
completed 1984
D: M. v. Gerkan with
J. Friedemann, G. Tjarks

204 'Black Box' – Schauland sales hall,
Hamburg
completed 1982
D: V. Marg, K. Staratzke
C: O. Dorn

205 Low-Energy House, IBA Berlin
competition, chosen for building
completed 1984
D: M. v. Gerkan
C: M. Auder, P. Römer

206 Apartment building, Saalgasse,
Frankfurt/Main
completed 1988
D: M. v. Gerkan with J. Friedemann

207 Hotel Plaza, Hillmannplatz, Bremen
competition, 1st prize
completed 1985
D: M. v. Gerkan
P: K. Brauer, K. Staratzke
C: A. Buchholz-Berger, H. Nolden,
H. Schmees, T. Tran-Viet

208 Klinikum II, Nuremberg-South
competition, 2nd prize

209 Rama Tower Hotel, Bangkok
design

210 Leisure park, Heiligenhafen
consultancy project

211 Institute of Chemistry,
University of Brunswick
competition, 2nd place

212 Connecting bridge between two
office buildings, Hamburg
case study

213 Federal Postal Department, Bonn
competition, 4th prize

214 Komplex Rose, hospital
for rheumatic diseases,
Bad Meinberg
competition, 1st prize
completed 1988
D: M. v. Gerkan
P: K. Brauer
C: P. Römer, H.-R. Franke, H. Ritzki,
B. Dziewonska, M. Stanek

215 Central Post Office sorting halls,
Munich
competition, award

216 Sheraton Hotel, Berlin
design

1982

217 International Maritime Court, Hamburg
case study

218 Stadtmarkt, Fulda
case study

219 Stollwerk-Passage, Cologne
design consultancy

220 Schlossparkhotel 'Orangerie', Fulda
competition, 2nd prize

221 Apartment and office building
Grindelallee 100, Hamburg
completed 1987
D: M. v. Gerkan with K. Staratzke
C: B. Fleckenstein, P. Sembritzki,
H. Sylvester

222 Telecommunications office,
Post Office 1, Regional Postal
Directorate, Brunswick
completed 1990
D: M. v. Gerkan
PL: B. Albers
C: K. Maass, A Lucks, M. Ebeling,
K. Lübbert, M. Mews, S. Pieper
G. Tjarks, J. Friedemann

223 National Library, Frankfurt/Main
competition, award

224 State and University Library,
Göttingen
consultancy project

225 Inner city redevelopment,
Niederes Tor, Villingen
consultancy project

226 Heimann Pickup wholesale store
design

227 Parking concept, Celle
consultancy project

228 Neumarkt redevelopment, Celle
design

229 Viktoria Insurance AG, Berlin
consultancy project

230 Savings Bank extension, Hamburg
competition, commendation

231 Daimler Benz AG offices, Stuttgart
competition 2nd prize

232 Hillmannquartier, Bremen
design

1983

233 Subway Station, Bielefeld
completed 1991
D: M. v. Gerkan with H.-H. Möller

234 Hillmann-Garage, Bremen
completed 1984
D: M. v. Gerkan
P: K. Staratzke
C: P. Sembritzki, K. Lübbert

235 Refurbishment shopping mall,
Hamburger Strasse, Hamburg
consultancy project,
completed 1988
D: V. Marg, K. Staratzke
C: B. Fleckenstein, B. Gronemeyer,
S. Peters, A. Lucks, H. Sylvester

236 Maria-Trost Hospital, Berlin
competition, 4th prize

237 Health Insurance Corp., Hamburg
competition, award

238 Gruner + Jahr publishing house,
Hamburg
competition, 1st prize

239 Housing Am Fischmarkt, Hamburg
completed 1989
D: V. Marg
C: M. Mews, W. Haux

240 Collegium Augustinum, Hamburg
completed 1993
D: V. Marg
P: K. Staratzke
C: K. Lübbert, B. Fleckenstein,
M. Dittmer, B. Gronemeyer,
D. Winter, K. Heckel

1984

241 P.O. Parking Garage, Brunswick
completed 1986
D: M. v. Gerkan
PL: B. Albers
C: K. Maass, A. Lucks

242 Tourist information system,
Hamburg
case study

243 Housing Fontenay, Hamburg
competition, 1st prize

244 Quickborn block corner development
competition, 1st prize

245 Film center, Esplanade, Berlin
competition

246 Germanisches Nationalmuseum,
Nuremberg
competition, 2nd prize

247 Ankara Kavaklidere Complex,
Sheraton Hotel and shopping mall
completed 1991
D: V. Marg, K. Brauer
C: K. Lübbert, W. Haux, D. Heller,
Y. Erkan, R. Preuss, D. Jungk,
T. Bieling

248 Kunstmuseum der Stadt Bonn
competition

249 Intermediate school and sports hall,
Schleswig-Holstein
competition, 2nd prize

1985

250 Various furniture designs
D: M. v. Gerkan
C: V. Sievers

251 District Court, Flensburg
competition, 1st prize
completed 1989/1991
D: V. Marg
P: K. Brauer
C: B. Fleckenstein, C. Boesen,
W. Haux, K. Lübbert,
S. Schliebitz, S. Pieper

252 Post offices 1 and 3, Hamburg
competition, 2nd prize

253 Wildlife Information Pavilion, Balje
competition, 2nd prize

254 Reconstruction of Michaelsen
Country House as a dolls' museum,
Hamburg
completed 1985
D (1923): K. Schneider
D (1985): V. Marg, K. Lübbert,
V. Rudolph

255 Library, Göttingen
competition, 5th prize

256 Münster
urban design competition,
3rd prize

257 City Library, Münster
competition, 1st prize group

258 Bauforum, Hamburg

259 Interior structuring of Bertelsmann
publishing house, Gütersloh
consultancy project

260 Pyongyang International Airport,
North Korea
projects A and D

1986

261 VIP State Pavilion, Pyongyang International Airport, North Korea
design

262 Labor Office, Oldenburg
competition, 1st prize
completed 1993
D: V. Marg

P: K. Staratzke
C: H. Huusmann, W. Haux, Y. Erkan,
P. Zacharias, C. Kreusler,
M. Ebeling, C. Papanikolaou

263 Bäckerstrasse, Halstenbek,
competition, a 3rd prize

264 Hamburg Agency in Bonn
completed 1986
D: V. Marg, K. Staratzke
C: P. Römer

265 Town Hall, Husum
competition, 1st prize

266 Kümmellstrasse, Hamburg
competition, 2nd prize

267 Concert hall for Lübeck
competition

268 Elbchaussee 139, Hamburg
gmp - Bureau
completed 1990
D: M. v. Gerkan
C: J. Kierig, P. Sembritzki,
S. v. Gerkan, V. Sievers

269 Elbchaussee 139 – Le Canard
completed 1990
D: M. v. Gerkan
C: J. Kierig, V. Sievers

270 Elbchaussee 139, von Gerkan
residence, Hamburg
completed 1992
D: M. v. Gerkan
C: J. Kierig, V. Sievers, S. v. Gerkan

271 Telecommunications Office 2,
Regional
Postal Directorate, Hanover
completed 1994
D: M. v. Gerkan with K. Staratzke
P: J. Zais
C: G. Feldmeyer, J. Groth, S. Schütz,
K. Pollex, T. Schreiber

272 Sparkassenpassage, Linz, Austria
design project

273 Deutsche Lufthansa Training and
Computer Center, Frankfurt/Main
competition
D: M. v. Gerkan
C: J. Zais, H. Potthoff

274 Museumsinsel, Hamburg
competition, designs 1 and 2

275 AMK trade fair halls, Berlin
competition

276 Bundeskunsthalle Bonn
competition, 3rd prize

277 Haus der Geschichte, Bonn,
competition, 4th prize

278 Seca factory and offices, Hamburg
competition

279 Free University, Witten/Herdecke
urban design study

280 Jumbo Shed, Deutsche Lufthansa
maintenance hangar, Airport Hamburg
project study

281 Airport, Hamburg-Fuhlsbüttel
competition, 1st prize
completed 1993
D: M. v. Gerkan with K. Brauer

C: A. Alkuru, T. Bieling, R. Dipper,
R. Franke, S. v. Gerkan, J. Hillmer,
K. Hoyer, F. Merkel, M. Mews,
T. Rinne, U. Schürmann,
C. Timm-Schwarz, P. Autzen,
K.-H. Follert, W. Gust, T. Hinz,
G. v. Stülpnagel

282　National Theater, Tokyo
international competition,
top 30 entries

283　Technik III, Gesamthochschule Kassel
competition, 2nd prize

284　Police Headquarters, Berlin
competition, 3rd prize

1987

285　Municipal Library, Münster
competition, 2nd phase, award

286　Hillmannhaus, Bremen
completed 1989
D: M. v. Gerkan and K. Staratzke
C: D. Papendick, B. Gronemeyer,
S. Dexling, A. Szablowski

287　Civic Center, Wiesloch
competition, 5th prize

288　Research and lecture hall building,
Rudolf Virchow University Hospital,
Berlin
competition, 2nd prize

289　Biocenter, Frankfurt/Main
competition

290　HEW Training Center, Hamburg
completed 1990
D: V. Marg
C: H. Huusmann, P. Zacharias,
M. Ebeling, C. Kreusler

291　BMW Customer Center, Munich
design study

292　'Kleines Haus' Brunswick
competition

293　Kleiner Schlossplatz, Stuttgart
consultancy project

294　Dockland development, Heiligenhafen
competition, 2nd prize

295　Birds' house
design for TV guide 'Hörzu'
D: M. v. Gerkan

296　Pfalztheater, Kaiserslautern
competition, award

297　Labor Office, Flensburg
competition, 4th prize

298　Telecommunications towers for
German Federal postal services
competition, 2nd prize

299　Löhrhof, Recklinghausen
design

300　Housing and commercial building
Moorbek Rondeel, Norderstedt,
completed 1990
D: M. v. Gerkan with J. Zais,
U. Hassels
C: B. Kreykenbohm, A. Schwemer

1988

301　Saar-Galerie, Saarbrücken
consultancy project
completed 1991
D: V. Marg
C: H. Akyol, C. Hoffmann,
H. Nienhoff, J. Rind,
M. Bleckmann, B. Bergfeld,
R. Dorn, J. Hartmann-Pohl

302　Speicherstadt
[dockland warehouse city], Hamburg,
expertise

303　Federal Ministry of Environmental
Protection and Reactor Safety, Bonn
competition, 1st prize
final planning stopped

304　Library of Technical University and
Fine Arts Academy, Berlin
competition, 3 rd prize

305　'Star Site', Birmingham,
International Business Exchange
consultancy project

306　EAM, Kassel
competition, 1st prize
completed 1993
D: V. Marg, T. Bieling
Co: Bieling + Bieling

307　Zürich-Haus, Hamburg
competition, 1st prize
completed 1993
D: V. Marg with N. Goetze
P: K. Staratzke
C: M. Mews, A Lucks, S. Lohre,
T. Haupt

308　Salamander building, Berlin
competition, 1st place
completed 1992
D: V. Marg
C: J. Rind, M. Bleckmann,
P. Römer, S. Zittlau-Kroos

309　Schering AG offices, Berlin
competition, 4th prize

310　German History Museum, Berlin
competition

311　Deutsches Luftfahrtmuseum,
Munich-Oberschleißheim
competition

312　Station square, Koblenz
competition, 1st prize
at planning stage

313　Multi-story parking garage,
Paderborn
competition, 2nd prize

314　Bank and commercial building
Brodschrangen/Bäckerstrasse,
Hamburg
study
completed 1994
D: V. Marg, K. Staratzke with
S. Krause
C: D. Winter, C. Hegel,
J. Kalkbrenner, K. Bonk,
S. Dexling, P. Sembritzki

315　New Orangery, Herten
competition, 2nd prize

316　Störgang, Itzehoe
competition, 1st prize

317　City Center, Hamburg-Schenefeld
completed 1991
D: V. Marg, K. Staratzke
PL: B. Gronemeyer, A. Leuschner
C: K.-H. Behrendt, S. Bohl,
G. Feldmeyer, U. Gänsicke,
T. Grotzeck, K. Dorn

318　Galeria, Duisburg
completed 1994
D: M. v. Gerkan, K. Staratzke,
O. Dorn
C: M. Stanek, K. Krause, C. Zeis,
T. Grotzeck, J. Brandenburg,
H. Ladewig, E. Höhler

1989

319　Jumbo Shed, Deutsche Lufthansa
Maintenance Hangar 7, Hamburg
completed 1992
D: M. v. Gerkan, K. Brauer
P: K. Staratzke
PL: M. Stanek, R. Nienhoff
C: M. Engel, C. Schönherr,
D. Winter, W. Gust, G. Maaß

320　Deutsche Lufthansa Workshops,
Hamburg
completed 1992
D: M. v. Gerkan
Co: Pysall, Stahrenberg & Partner
Krämer
P: K. Staratzke

321　Lufthansa Dock Store,
Airport, Hamburg-Fuhlsbüttel, design

322　Multi-story parking garage,
Hamburg-Fuhlsbüttel Airport
completed 1990
D: M. v. Gerkan
PL: K. Brauer
C: K. Hoyer, U. Pörksen

323　Leisure swimming pool, Wyk auf Föhr
competition, 2nd prize

324　Deutsche Bundesbank, Frankfurt/Main
competition, 3rd prize

325　International Maritime Court, Hamburg
competition, 3rd prize

326　Hertie Center Altona, Hamburg
consultancy project

327　Apartment and commercial building
Matzen, Buchholz
completed 1991
D: M. Zimmermann with H. Peter
C: A. Perlick, K.-H. Schneider-Kropp,
C. Richarz, V. Sievers

328　Savings Bank, Stuttgart
competition

329　Apartment and commercial building
Schaarmarkt, Hamburg
completed 1994
D: V. Marg
C: H. Huusmann, D. Hillmer,
Y. Erkan

330　Residential Park Falkenstein,
Hamburg
competition, 1st prize

331　Art Museum and town hall extension,
Wolfsburg
competition, 5th prize

332　Sternhäuser, Norderstedt
completed 1997
D: M. v. Gerkan, J. Zais, U. Hassels
C: U. Wiblishauser, V. Warneke,
D. Engeler, T. Böhm

333　documenta exhibition gallery, Kassel
competition, 4th prize

334　Glass roof, Museum of Hamburg
History, Hamburg
completed 1989
D: V. Marg with J. Schlaich
C: K. Lübbert
Co: J. Schlaich

335　International Forum, Tokyo
competition

336　Concert Hall, Dortmund
competition, 3rd prize

337　Extension 'Städtische Union', Celle
competition, 2nd prize

338　Carl Bertelsmann Foundation,
Gütersloh
competition, 1st prize
completed 1991
D: V. Marg
PL: H. Schröder,
M. Zimmermann
C: H. Akyol, S. Jöbsch

339　Network Operating Station of
Preussen-Electra, Hanover
consultancy project

340　Railroad Station, Norderstedt-Mitte
competition

341　Television Museum, Mainz
competition, 3rd prize

342　VIP Lounge, Airport, Cologne-Wahn
competition, 2nd prize

343　Airport, Paderborn
competition

344　Bank and office center at Stuttgart
Main Station
competition

345　City Rail Station, Stuttgart Airport
completed 1992
D: K. Staratzke
C: D. Perisic, B. Kiel

346　Library,
Christian-Albrecht-University, Kiel
competition, 4th prize

347　Extension
Christian-Albrecht-University, Kiel
competition, 5th prize

348　Zürich-Haus, Frankfurt/Main
competition, 5th prize

349　Königsgalerie, Kassel
competition, 2nd prize

350　Harburger Hof, Hamburg
at planning stage

1990

351　Berlin-Tegel Airport,
parking garage P2
completed 1993
D: M. v. Gerkan
P: R. Niedballa
C: P. Römer

352 Deutscher Ring, extension of office
building, Hamburg
consultancy project

353 Deichtor + Ericusspitze, Hamburg
competition, 5th prize

354 Kehrwiederspitze – Sandtorhafen
development, Hamburg
competition, 2nd prize

355 Office building, Mittelweg, Hamburg
competition

356 Deutsche Revision, Frankfurt/Main
competition, 1st prize
completed 1994
D: M. v. Gerkan
P: K. Staratzke
PL: A. Buchholz-Berger
C: M. Stanek, K. Krause,
     G. Hagemeister,
     J. Kaufhold, K. Maass,
     B. Meyer, M. Engel,
     M. Hoffmann, E. Grimmer

357 Neuer Wall 43, Hamburg,
Commercial Building
completed 1997
D: V. Marg
PL: T. Hupe
C: A. Alkuru, F. Hülsmeier,
     D. Papendick, C. Berle,
     D. Porsch, C. Timm-Schwarz,
     A. Buchholz-Berger, U. Rösler

358 Music and Conference Hall, Lübeck
competition, 1st prize
completed 1994
D: M. v. Gerkan with C. Weinmann
PL: T. Rinne, W. Haux
C: V. Sievers, M. Klostermann,
     B. Groß, C. Kreusler,
     K.-H. Behrendt, P. Kropp

359 Hypo-Bank, Hamburg – 'Graskeller'
completed 1994
D: V. Marg
PL: W. Haux
C: J. Kalkbrenner, B. Staber,
     R. Schmitz, K. Steinfatt

360 Landscaped apartment complex,
Kanzleistrasse, Hamburg-Nienstedten
competition, 1st prize

361 Technology Center, Münster
competition, 1st prize

362 Acropolis Museum, Athens
competition, 2nd prize group

363 Grosse Elbstrasse/
Carsten-Rehder-Strasse, Hamburg
design project

364 Münsterlandhalle, Münster
competition, 3rd prize

365 Hotel, Palace au Lac, Lugano
design

366 'Zementfabrik', Bonn
competition, 3rd prize

367 Neue Strasse, Ulm
competition, 2nd prize

368 Main Station, Duisburg
consultancy project

369 Miro Data Systems, Brunswick
completed 1991
D: M. v. Gerkan
PL: U. Hassels, J. Zais
C: W. Gebhardt, U. Kittel, H. Timpe

370 Adult Educational Institute and
Municipal Library, Heilbronn
competition, 1st prize
planning stopped

371 Airport Center,
Airport, Hamburg-Fuhlsbüttel
case study

372 Aero-City, Stuttgart Airport
case study

373 Office center, Neuss-Hammfeld
case study

374 Subway station, Mönckebergstrasse,
Hamburg
completed 1991
D: V. Marg

375 Hillmann-Eck, Bremen
completed 1994
D: M. v. Gerkan, K. Staratzke, K. Voß
C: D. Porsch

376 Bertelsmann Press Building, Berlin
competition

1991

377 Atrium Friedrichstrasse, Berlin
consultancy project
completed 1997
D: V. Marg
PL: C. Hoffmann
C: B. Dieckmann, S. Djahanschah,
     T. Naujack, E. Witzel,
     H. v. g. Hassend, S. Küppers,
     S. Ripp, S. Schindlbeck

378 Max Planck Institute for
Microbial Ecology, Bremen
competition

379 Café Andersen, Hamburger Strasse,
Hamburg
completed 1991
D: M. v. Gerkan
P: K. Staratzke
C: P. Sembritzki, O. Brück

380 Garden City on the Rhine, Speyer
consultancy and structural study

381 German-Japanese Center, Hamburg
competition, 1st prize
completed 1995
D: M. v. Gerkan
P: K. Staratzke
PL: R. Niehoff, K. Voß
C: A. Lucks, A. Perlick,
     K. Rohrmann, K. Dorn, H. Eustrup

382 Kaufmännische Krankenkassen,
Hanover
competition, award

383 Office and commercial building,
Friedrichstrasse 108, Berlin
consultancy project
completed 1999
D: V. Marg
PL: C. Hoffmann, C. Hasskamp
C: F. Lensing, C. Dost

384 Railroad stations 'Rosenstein',
'Nordbahnhof', Stuttgart
competition, award

385 Stuttgart Airport, Tower
competition

386 Development Elbe embankment,
Dresden
consultancy project

387 Business park in Brunswick
project study

388 BeWoGe Housing, Otto-Suhr-Allee,
Berlin
competition

389 Nordseepassage, Wilhelmshaven
completed 1997
D: M. v. Gerkan
P: K. Staratzke
PL: V. Sievers, G. Gullotta
C: K. Falke, K. Heckel, M. Helmin,
     M. Lucht, H. Münchhalfen,
     D. Papendick, J. Rieger, K. Ritzke,
     M. Sallowsky, R. Schmitz

390 European Trade Center, Brunswick
competition

391 Shopping mall, Langenhorn-Markt,
Hamburg
competition, 1st prize

392 Lenné-Passage, Frankfurt/Oder
competition, 1st place
under construction

393 Hansetor, Hamburg-Bahrenfeld
competition, 1st prize

394 Calenberger Esplanade, Hanover
competition, 1st place
completed 1999
D: M. v. Gerkan
P: N. Goetze
PL: K. Schroeder,
C: M. Klostermann, M. Haase,
     T. Rinne, J. Steinwender,
     C. v. Graevenitz, A. Perlick

395 Krefeld South II
urban design competition, 2nd prize

396 Altmarkt Dresden
competition, 1st prize

397 State Museum of the 20th Century,
Nuremberg
competition, award

398 Business Park, Münster docklands
consultancy project, 2nd prize

399 Salamander building, Peterstrasse/
Thomaskirchhof, Leipzig
consultancy project

400 Marina, Herne
competition, 2nd prize

401 Office towers, Frankfurt/Main
consultancy project

402 Office complex, Am Zeppelinstein,
Bad Homburg
competition, 1st prize

403 Süllbergterrassen,
Hamburg-Blankenese
competition

404 Neighborhood center,
Connewitzer Kreuz, Leipzig
consultancy project

405 Bei St. Annen/Holländischer Brook
development, Hamburg
at planning stage

406 HHLA office building, Burchardkai,
Hamburg
consultancy project

407 Harbour station, Süderelbe, Hamburg
competition, 2nd prize

408 New Trade Fair, Leipzig
international competition, 1st place
completed 1996
D: V. Marg with H. Nienhoff
C: gmp team Leipzig

1992

409 Adult Educational Institute, Koblenz
planning stopped

410 Elbkaihaus, Hamburg
completed 1999
D: V. Marg
P: K. Staratzke
PL: S. Krause, A. Juppien
C: E. Hoffmeister, I. v. Hülst,
     G. Venschott, D. Winter,
     M. Ziemons

411 Housing Fontenay Allee, Hamburg
design

412 Operational Center, Stuttgart Airport
competition

413 Rütgers Werke AG, Frankfurt/Main
competition, 3rd prize

414 EBL Office complex, Leipzig
preliminary design

415 World Trade Center, Berlin
competition

416 Spreebogen, Berlin
competition

417 Further Training Center,
Herne-Sodingen
competition, award

418 Cinema and shopping mall,
Harburg-Carré, Hamburg-Harburg
planning stopped

419 Housing Friedrichshain, Berlin,
consultancy project
completed 1998
D: V. Marg
PL: S. Zittlau-Kroos, D. Heller
C: A. Foronda, I. Perkovic,
     R. Scheurer, S. Winter

420 Forum Neukölln, Berlin
competition, 1st prize

421 Allee-Center, Leipzig-Grünau
competition, 1st prize
completed 1996
D: V. Marg
PL: K. Staratzke, W. Haux
C: B. Albers, K. Akay, H. Akyol,
     K.-H. Behrendt, E. Grimmer,
     M. Hoffmann, A. Lucks, K. Maass,
     R. Preuß, H. Reusch, J. Rind,
     K. Steinfatt, H. v. Szada,
     L. Weinmann

422 Telekom operating building, Suhl
competition, 1st prize,
completed 1997
D: M. v. Gerkan with Bothe, Richter,
Teherani 1992
D: M. v. Gerkan with J. Zais 1993
C: A. Reich, S. Dürr, U. Düsterhöft,
H.-W. Warias, G. Wysocki,
P. Weidmann, T. Böhm

423 Siemens-Nixdorf Service
Center, Berliner Strasse, Munich
competition, 1st place

424 Afrika-Haus, Hamburg
planning stopped

425 Mare Balticum Hotel, Bansin/Usedom
competition, 1st prize
planning stopped

426 Commercial building and library,
Mollstrasse, Berlin
competition, 1st prize

427 Lecture Theatre Centre,
University of Oldenburg
competition, 1st prize
completed 1997
D: M. v. Gerkan with K. Lenz
C: K.-H. Behrendt, B. Groß,
S. Krause, B. Kottsieper,
J. Reichert, D. Winter

428 District Court North, Hamburg
competition, 1st prize
planning stopped

429 Astoria Maritim Hotel, Leipzig
planning stopped

430 Apartment block, Schöne Aussicht,
Hamburg
competition, 1st prize

431 Quartier Stadtsparkasse,
development, Dresden
consultancy project, 2nd place

432 Domhof Municipal Theater,
Osnabrück
competition

433 Emergency hospital,
Dresden-Neustadt
competition

434 Sony, Potsdamer Platz, Berlin
competition, award

435 Daimler Benz AG,
Potsdamer Platz, Berlin
competition

436 Olympia 2000, bicylce and
swimming hall, Berlin
competition, 2nd prize

437 Ku'damm Eck Hotel, Berlin
under construction

438 Museum Türkenkaserne, Munich
competition

439 Cologne-Ehrenfeld urban design
competition, 2nd prize

440 Grundthalplatz, apartment block 10,
Schwerin
competition

441 Noise control structures,
Burgerfeld-Markt Schwaben
competition, 2nd prize

442 Prison, Hamburg-Billwerder
competition

443 Kongresshotel,
Mannheim-Rosengarten
competition

444 Rehabilitation Clinic, Trassenheide,
Usedom
consultancy project,
completed 1994
D: M. v. Gerkan with P. Römer
C: S. Zittlau-Kroos, R. Wolff, T. Herr,
K. Baumgarten, H. Borgwardt,
B. Galetto

445 Hapag-Lloyd offices, Rosenstrasse,
Hamburg
consultancy project
completed 1996
D: V. Marg
P: K. Staratzke
PL: S. Jöbsch
C: S. Winter, R. Preuss, K. Hoyer,
W. Schmidt, H. Schöttler

446 Shopping mall, DSN-Terrain
and office building,
Stationsstraat/Honigmannstraat,
Heerlen
consulting project

1993
447 Buildings for 'Premiere' TV channel,
Studio Hamburg
completed 1994
D: K. Staratzke
C: K. Duncker, S. Krause,
B. Gronemeyer, E. Werner

448 Hanseatic Trade Center,
Kehrwiederspitze, stage IV,
Hamburg
completed 1999
D: V. Marg
P: K. Staratzke
PL: H. Akyol,
C: A. Alkuru, K.-H. Behrendt,
R. Dipper, K. Dorn, R. Giesecke,
B. Gronemeyer, M. Lucht,
T. Polakowski, C. Plog, U. Rösler,
B. Schöll, E. Werner

449 Office building, Bredeney, Essen
competition, 1st prize
completed 1998
D: M. v. Gerkan
PL: W. Gebhardt
C: H. Gietmann, S. Kramer, R. Born,
W. Höhl, C. Kreusler, T. Neeland,
C. Papanikolaou, D. Papendick,
C. Plog, H. Reusch, H. v. Szada

450 Main Park, Würzburg
project study

451 Labor Office Training Center of the
Federal Republic of Germany,
Schwerin
competition, 1st prize,
under construction

452 Police Headquarters, Kassel
competition, 3rd prize

453 Nürnberger Beteiligungs AG offices
competition, 2nd prize

454 Trabrennbahn, Farmsen, Hamburg
competition, award

455 Festival Hall, Recklinghausen
competition, 2nd prize

456 Hoffmannstrasse, Berlin-Treptow,
competition, award

457 Marienburg project, Nijmegen
competition

458 Dreissigacker-South urban design,
Meinigen, Thuringia
competition, award

459 Secondary school, Crivitz
competition

460 Reichstag conversion for German
Bundestag, Berlin
competition, 2nd prize group

461 City villa Dr. Braasch, Eberswalde
completed 1995
D: M. v. Gerkan
PL: P. Römer
C: R. Wolff, S. Derendinger

462 Lehrter Bahnhof - Central Station,
Berlin
competition, 1st prize
under construction

463 Railroad bridge, Lehrter Bahnhof
at planning stage

464 Luisenstadt – Heinrich-Heine-Strasse,
Berlin
competition, award

465 Redesign Hindenburgplatz, Münster
competition, 2nd prize

466 Museum Grothe, Bremerhaven
study project

467 Building for 'Der Spiegel', Hamburg
competition, 2nd prize

468 German-Japanese Center, Berlin
competition, 1st prize

469 Dortmunder Union Brewery
competition

470 Telephone offices 3 + 5,
Telekom Berlin
completed 1998
D: M. v. Gerkan with J. Zais
PL: J. Zais
C: V. Warnecke, S. Schröder,
S. Stodtko, G. Wysocki, P. Staak,
S. Schütz, D. Schäffler
D. Rösinger, U. Köper,
S. Schwappach, A. Schneider

471 Max-Planck-Gesellschaft,
Marstallplatz, Munich
competition

472 Blankenese Railroad Station, Hamburg
urban design project

473 Railway Station, Berlin-Spandau
competition, 3rd prize
completed 1998
D: M. v. Gerkan
P: H. Nienhoff
PL: S. Zittlau-Kroos, B. Keul-Ricke,
E. Menne
C: A. Schlüter, P. Bozic, A. Prebisz,
M. Böthig, D. Berve,
K. Baumgarten, M. Wiegelmann,
G. Meyer, A. Dierkes, P. Wolf,
M. Rothe, K. Struckmeyer,

P. Schuch, M. Stanek,
W. Gebhardt, J. Kalkbrenner,
B. Claasen, R. Lauer, B. Töpper
Co: Schlaich, Bergermann und
Partner

474 Railroad bridge across the Havel,
Spandau Railway Station
completed 1998
D: M. v. Gerkan with J. Schlaich

475 Noise barrier, Train Station, Spandau
under construction

476 Spreeinsel, Berlin
competition

477 Neuriem-Mitte, Munich
urban design competition

478 Institute for Discrete Mathematics,
Lennéstrasse, Bonn
competition, 4th prize

479 Erfurt-Ost, inner-urban extension
competition, 2nd prize

480 Footbridge, Holstenhafen, Lübeck
3 designs

481 Concert Hall, Kopenhagen
competition

482 Two Federal Department and
Deutsche Telekom Mobilfunk
buildings, Bonn-Beuel
consultancy project

483 Urban design "Stuttgart 21"
design project

484 Rosenstein Train Station, Stuttgart
study project

485 Trade Fair, Hanover, Hall 4
competition, 1st prize
completed 1995
D: V. Marg
P: K. Staratzke
C: T. Hinz, M. Ziemons, D. Vollrath,
H. Ueda, B. Schöll, U. Rösler,
K.-H. Behrendt, I. Pentland,
R. Schröder, S. Winter, U. Heiwolt
Co: J. Schlaich

486 Telekom Training Academy,
Klein-Machnow near Berlin
urban design project

487 Speicherblock X, Hamburg
at planning stage

488 Georgsplatz, Dresden
competition

489 Webergasse, Dresden
competition

490 Apartment and Commercial building,
Deutrichshof, Leipzig
consultancy project, 1st place

491 Town Hall, Garbsen
competition

1994
492 EBL housing, Leipzig
planning stopped

493 Theater of the City of Gütersloh
competition, award

494 Housing Dovenfleet, Hamburg
consultancy project

495 Lecture Theatre Centre, extension of
Chemnitz Technical University
competition, 1st prize
completed 1998
D: M. v. Gerkan
PL: D. Heller, A. Lapp
C: A. Juppien, K. Maass, R. Schmitz,
M. Watenphul

496 Extension University of Dresden
competition

497 Institute of Chemistry,
University of Leipzig
competition, award

498 Stadtzentrum, Berlin-Schönefeld
competition, 1st place

499 Kleist Theater, Frankfurt/Oder
competition, award

500 Bridge over the Hörn, Kiel
consultancy project
completed 1997
D: V. Marg with J. Schlaich
C: R. Schröder, H. Ueda, A.-K. Rose,
D. Vollrath
Co: Schlaich, Bergmann und Partner,
J. Knippers

501 Main Train Station, Leipzig
consultancy project

502 Forum Köpenick, Berlin
competition, 1st prize,
completed 1997
D: V. Marg
PL: J. Rind
C: C. Harenberg, M. Kaesler,
F. Lensing, G. Mones, M. Nowak,
E. Sianidis, E. Witzel, R. Stüer,
T. Behr

503 Federal Chancellery, Berlin
competition, 4th prize

504 Gerling Insurance Corp.,
residential and office villas, Leipzig
competition, 1st prize
planning pending

505 Hypo-Bank, Frankfurt/Main
competition, 4th prize

506 Cardiff Bay Opera
competition

507 Tivoli Cinema, Berlin
planning stopped

508 Werdener Strasse, Düsseldorf
competition

509 Northern Wallhalbinsel develpment,
Lübeck
competition

510 Business park on Robotron site,
Sömmerda
consultancy project

511 mdr Middle-German Broadcasting
House, Leipzig
competition, 4th prize

512 Holzhafen, Hamburg-Altona
competition

513 Apartment and Commercial block,
Eppendorfer Landstrasse, Hamburg
competition, 3rd prize

514 Max-Planck-Institute, Potsdam-Golm
competition, 2nd prize

515 Building for cooperative
Norddeutsche
Metall-Berufsgenossenschaft,
Hanover
competition, 1st prize,
completed 1998
D: M. v. Gerkan
PL: W. Gebhardt
C: J. Kaufhold, A. Bartkowiak,
C. Plog, B. Gronemeyer,
M. Gorges, R. Giesecke,
R. Blagovcanin, I. v. Hülst,
L. Nachtigäller, C. Weitemeier

516 Train Station, Charlottenburg,
Berlin
study

517 Standardized platform roofs in:
Saalfeld, Marktredwitz, Hof,
Westerland, Wilhelmshaven, Merzig,
Kaiserslautern, Trudering, Bottrop,
Eglharting, Wittenberg, Lübben,
Mainz, Salzwedel, Ehlershausen,
Bitterfeld, Bamberg, Lübbenau, Ulm,
Freiburg, Frankfurt/M., Hamburg
Railway Station, Hamburg Dammtor,
Hagen, Treuchtlingen, Fürstenwalde,
Angermünde, Velgast
and 40 at planning stage
completed 1998/1999
D: M. v. Gerkan, J. Hillmer
PL: I. Gull
C: S. Bern, R. Dipper, B. Föllmer,
M. Foudehi, M. Helmin,
D. Hünerbein, I. v. Holtz,
K. Nolting, A.-B. Springer, D. Tieu,
P. Wedemann

518 Eastern Altstadtring, Dresden
competition

519 Berliner Platz, Heilbronn
consultancy project

520 Promotion Park, Bremen
competition

521 Gerlinghaus Am Löwentor, Stuttgart
comission
completed 1997
D: M. v. Gerkan with N. Goetze
PL: T. Grotzeck
C: C. Berle, K. Burmester, T. Haupt,
E. Werner

522 Hauni AG Technical Center, Hamburg
planning pending

523 Helsinki Main Train Station
competition

524 Federal President's Office, Berlin
competition

525 Library of Zwickau Technical
University
competition

526 Dorotheen Blocks,
parliamentarians' offices, Berlin
under construction

527 Yokohama Harbour area
international competition

528 Redevelopment of AEG-Kanis
site in Essen
competition, 2nd prize

529 Tiergarten Tunnel, Berlin
consultancy project
under construction

530 Development on Bahnhofstrasse,
Erfurt
abandoned

531 Office building at the Stadtmünze,
Erfurt
competition, 4th prize

532 University Library and urban design
ideas competition, Erfurt University
competition, award

533 Airport, Zürich-Kloten
study

534 Main Train Station, Stuttgart 21
consultancy project

1995

535 Urban design Munich 21
design study

536 Main Railway Station, Munich 21
design project

537 Apartment and commercial building,
Gerling Insurance Corp., Cologne
competition

538 C+L Deutsche Revision Wibera,
Düsseldorf

539 Extension Städtisches Museum im
Simeonstift, Trier
competition

540 Dresdner Bank, Pariser Platz, Berlin
competition, 1st place
completed 1997
D: M. v. Gerkan
PL: V. Sievers
C: C. Abt, K. Dwertmann, P. Kropp,
B. Queck, W. Schmidt

541 Redevelopment of former Domestic
and Breeding Livestock Market,
Lübeck
competition, award

542 High-Tech Center,
Potsdam-Babelsberg
competition

543 Neumarkt, Celle
competition, 1st prize

544 Waterways and Shipping Board
East, Magdeburg
competition

545 Extension Town Hall, Berlin-Treptow
competition

546 Elementary school, Munich
competition

547 Shopping mall, Berlin-Marzahn
study

548 Landwehrkanal Bridge, Berlin
under construction

549 Paper terminal, Pohl & Co, Kiel
study

550 Main Train Station, Erfurt
competition, award

551 Museum 'Alte Kraftpost', Pirmasens
competition, 1st award

552 New Civic Center, Scharbeutz
competition, 3rd prize

553 'Cultural area' of Peat Bath Spa,
Lobenstein
competition, 2nd prize

554 Trade Fair and Administration Center,
Bremen
competition, award

555 National Museum of Korea
competition

556 Police Headquarters, Frankfurt/Main
competition

557 Trade Fair, Hanover, Hall 13
competition, 3rd prize

558 New Forestry Teaching building,
Dresden Technical University,
Tharandt
competition

559 District Court, Brandenburg
competition

560 Hospital extension in Friedrichshain,
Berlin
competition

561 University Hospital 2000, Jena
competition

562 Prison Kempten, Bavaria
competition

563 Potsdam Center – southern site
(main station Potsdam-Stadt)
competition, 1st prize

564 Town Center of Bahrenfeld,
Hamburg
competition, 3rd prize

565 Apartment and business building
with Markt-Galerie shopping mall,
Leipzig
competition

566 Fachhochschule Rheinbach
competition

567 Multi-sports hall, Leipzig
competition, 4th prize

568 DSR Deutsche Seereederei,
Christinenhafen, Rostock
planning abandoned

569 Stadthafen Rostock
study

570 Fachhochschule Ingolstadt
competition,
urban design: 2nd prize
architecture: 5th prize

571 Parkstrasse roof cover,
Wilhelmshaven
study

572 MP and Regional State Department
buildings, Mainz
competition, 5th prize

573 Warnow-Passage, Rostock
consultancy project

574 Federal Labor Court, Erfurt
competition

575 Harare International Airport,
Zimbabwe
study

576 Extension Klinikum Buch, Berlin
competition

577 New supermarkets complex,
Göttingen
completed 1999
D: V. Marg, J. Zais
C: O. Schlüter, H.-W. Warias,
U. Düsterhöft, J. Ortmann,
C. Thamm, G. Wysocki,
H. Reimer, M. Geilenberg

578 Urban design Stuttgarter Platz,
Berlin
consultancy project

579 Institute for Chemistry, Humboldt
University, Berlin
competition

580 Espenhain, Leipzig
competition

581 Main Railway Station, Saarbrücken 21
consultancy project

582 Conference and Civic Center with
hotel, Bochum
study

583 Gotha Main Station and station
square
competition, 3rd prize

584 Dr. med. Manke consulting office,
Uelzen
completed 1997
D: V. Marg, J. Zais
PL: J. Zais
C: D. Engeler, P. Staak, R. Duerre

585 Expo 2000 Railway Station,
Hanover-Laatzen
competition, 5th prize

586 Museo del Prado, Madrid
competition

587 Living at Iseplatz, Hamburg
competition

588 Town Center of Schöneiche
near Berlin
completed 1997
D: V. Marg
PL: M. Bleckmann
C: J. Hartmann-Pohl, F. Lensing,
O. Drehsen, F. Jaspert, M. Kaesler

589 ICE 2.2 – train interior design
study and prototype

590 Railroad station of the future
at design stage

591 Holocaust Memorial,
Berlin-Grunewald
design

1996

592 VIth Architecture Biennial,
Venice Exhibition "Renaissance
of Railway Stations.
The City in the 20th Century."
D. M. v. Gerkan
C: D. Schäffler, S. Schütz,
H. Tieben
conceptual system and design

593 Secondary school, Veits-Höchheim
competition

594 Expo 2000 – roofing over
City-Railroad Stop, Hanover
completed 1998
D: M. v. Gerkan, J. Hillmer
C: K. Nolting

595 Prison, Gräfentonna
competition

596 HAB School of Architecture and
Construction, Weimar
competition, award

597 Civic Center, Weimar
competition, 1st prize
completed 1999
D(1996): M. v. Gerkan with
P. Kamps
D(1997): M. v. Gerkan with
D. Schäffler and S. Schütz
PL: D. Schäffler, S. Schütz
C: K. Akay, M. Wiegelmann,
H. Reimund, M. Böthig,
A. Pfeifer, P. Bozic,
J. Erdmann, P. Pfleiderer

598 Residential Park Elbschloss,
Hamburg
competition, 3rd prize

599 Urban design Bucharest 2000
competition, 1st prize

600 Hamburg Agency,
Palais Luisenstrasse, Berlin
competition, 1st prize

601 Double bridge in Fürst-Pückler-Park,
Bad Muskau
competition, award

602 German Foreign Office in Berlin
competition

603 mdr Middle-German Broadcasting
Complex, Erfurt
competition, 4th prize

604 Broadcasting House, Thuringia
competition, award

605 New urban district,
'Layenhof/Münchwald', Mainz
competition

606 Commercial building in Riga/Latvia
design
at planning stage

607 Jurmala residence, Riga
completed 1998
D: M. v. Gerkan
PL: O. Dorn
C: J. v. Mansberg, J. Brauner

608 Nord LB Bank building, Friedrichswall,
Hanover,
competition, 3rd prize

609 Urban design Frankfurt/Main 21
consultancy project

610 Main Railway Station,
Frankfurt/Main 21
study project

611 Station 2000 – platform furnishings
under construction

612 Old railroad operating plant, Goslar
conceptual study 'locomotive depot'

613 Veterinary Faculty, Leipzig
competition, award

614 Metropolitan Express-Train
completed 1999
D: M. v. Gerkan, J. Hillmer
PL: R. Dipper, B. Föllmer,
C: S. Krause, F. Hülsmeier,
M. Gorges, K. Kaib, B. Stehle,
T. Neeland

615 Johannesburg Airport, SA
study

616 Housing Berlin-Lichterfelde
competition

617 Seating for regional trains,
Deutsche Bahn AG
study

618 Ferry harbour, Mukran, Rügen
competition, 4th prize

619 Urban neighborhood center around
Spandau Train Station, Berlin
consultancy project

620 Expo 2000 Plaza, Hanover
competition, 1st prize

621 Expo 2000 Plaza, Hanover
development study

622 Restaurant Vau,
Jägerstrasse, Berlin
completed 1997
D: M. v. Gerkan with
D. Schäffler, S. Schütz
C: G. Hoheisel

623 Main Railway Station, Bottrop
competition

624 Administration building, Am Wall,
Göttingen
preliminary design

625 Extension of Hellerau Garden City
competition

626 DVG 2000 Administration,
Hanover
competition, award

627 Main Railway Station, Darmstadt
competition

628 Spa Hotel, Hamm
competition, 2nd prize

629 Satellite apron west,
Munich Airport
consultancy project

630 Schlossplatz, Berlin
study

631 Central University Library, Potsdam
competition, 3rd prize

632 Main Train Station, Lübeck
under construction

633 Tax Office, Schwarzenberg
competition

634 Transrapid Main Station, Hamburg
consultancy project

635 Haus Crange Training Hotel, Herne
IBA-competition, 2nd prize

636 Prison, Wulkow
competition

637 Fachhochschule Wismar
competition

638 Government buildings, Potsdam
competition

639 Private Residence, Alvano House
completed 1999
D: M. v. Gerkan, N. Goetze
PL: T. Haupt
C: G. Nunneman, N. Löffler

640 Housing Steinbeker Strasse,
Hamburg
competition, 3rd prize

641 Landesfinanz-Rechenzentrum,
Dresden
competition

642 Regional Parliament of Thuringia
competition

643 Station square, Kiel
preliminary design

644 Expo 2000 - 6 footbridges, Hanover
competition, 1st prize
completed 1999
D: V. Marg with J. Schlaich
PL: G. Gullotta
C: K. Reinhardt, B. Föllmer,
A.-K. Rose, T. Polakowski,
M. Carlsen, S. Jöbsch, M. Ziemons

645 Housing and Commercial building,
Altmarkt, Dresden
competition, 1st prize,
under construction

646 Charlottenburg urban design, Berlin
competition

647 Central Bus Station, Oldenburger
Stern
competition, 2nd round

648 Urban design, Ottakring Brewery,
Vienna
competition, 1st place

649 Apartments, Am Stadtgarten,
Böblingen
competition

650 Orthopedic Rehabilitation Hospital,
Baden-Baden
competition

651 Urban design, Ostra-Allee, Dresden
competition, award

652 New building
for State Insurance of Swabia,
Augsburg
competition

653 Gothaer Platz,
Erfurt
competition, award

654 Fachhochschule Erfurt
competition, 3rd prize,
award

655 Main Train Station, Kiel
under construction

656 Airport, Düsseldorf
competition - 4th prize

657 Technical University of Ilmenau
competition

658 Expo 2000 Plaza, Hanover
urban design masterplan

659 State Insurance head offices,
Hamburg
competition, award

660 Airport, Zürich-Kloten
competition, 1st place

661 Prison, Dresden
competition

662 Psychiatric hospital, Kiel
competition, 2nd prize

663 Trade Fair, Hanover, Hall 8/9
competition, 1st prize,
completed 1999
D: V. Marg with J. Schlaich and
S. Jöbsch
PL: T. Hinz, M. Ziemons
C: A. Alkuru, M. Holtschmidt,
K. Maass, S. Nixdorf,
T. Schuster, A. Vollstedt

664 Conversion of Block D,
dockland ware house city,
Hamburg
consultancy project

665 Media-Center, Leipzig
competition

666 Deutrichs Hof, Leipzig
competition, 1st prize

1997

667 Thalia-Theater, Hamburg
restructuring/refurbishing
completed 1997
D: K. Staratzke
PL: D. Winter
C: M. Gorges

668 Bridge across the Wublitz
competition

669 Main Railway Station, Mainz
under construction

670 Railway Station,
Limburg an der Lahn
competition

671 Builders' training yard,
Berlin-Mahrzahn
competition, 2nd prize

672 Ford Research Center, Aachen
consultancy project

673 Office and Commercial building,
Am Kröpcke, Hanover
consultancy project
at planning stage

674 Shopping mall, Areal Kühne
study

675 Potsdam Center, facade design
competition, 1st prize

676 Foyer refurbishment, State Opera,
Hamburg
competition, 3rd prize

677 Main Train Station Neighborhood
redevelopment, Bielefeld
competition, 1st prize

678 Aiport, Kopenhagen
consultancy project

679 Dresdner Bank skyscraper,
Frankfurt/Main
competition

680 Ryck Bridge, Greifswald
consultancy project

681 Expo 2000, German Pavilion, Hanover
competition

682 Apartment and commercial building,
Erfurt
competition

683 Faculty building,
University of Erlangen
competition

684 Multi-story parking garage, Trier
competition, award

685 Museum of Fine Arts, Leipzig
competition

686 New teaching building,
Fachhochschule Weihenstephan
competition

687 Pediatric and Gynecology Unit,
University Hospital, Dresden
competition

688 Connecting structures for Halls 3, 4,
5, 6, 7 Trade Fair, Hanover
consultancy project
completed 1998
D: V. Marg
PL: D. Vollrath
C: T. Hinz, S. Hoffmann,
M. Holtschmidt, B. Kottsieper,
S. Nixdorf, U. Nibler

689 EVENT-Center, Essen
consultancy project

690 Living and Working on the Alsterfleet,
Hamburg
competition

691 House Manke, Uelzen
preliminary design
under construction

692 Main Railway Station, Stuttgart 21
competition, award

693 Entertainment Center,
Friedrich-Ebert-Damm, Hamburg
completed 1999
D: V. Marg, N. Goetze
PL: M. Bechtold, R. Schröder
C: C. Berle, T. Haupt, M. Carlsen
Co: Schild Architekten + Ingenieure

694 Synagogue, Dresden
competition, award

695 Renovation, Hapag Lloyd,
Ballindamm, Hamburg
completed 1997
D: V. Marg, K. Staratzke
PL: D. Winter
C: K. Steinfatt, M. Gorges

696 Kassel Service Centre
competition

697 Potsdam Railway Station Quarter
competition, award

698 Old Airfield, Karlsruhe
competition

699 Town Hall, Saulgau
competition

700 Goree Memorial, Dakar, Senegal
competition

701 Federal Offices of Schleswig-Holstein
and Lower Saxony in Berlin
competition, award

702 Horumersiel Clinic
competition

703 The Urban House, Berlin
competition

704 Bayerische Rückversicherung,
Munich
competition

705 Trade Fair Rimini
competition, 1st prize
under construction

706 Chemnitz Industrial Museum
competition

707 IGA 2003 Rostock
competition, 1st prize
at planning stage

708 Grammar-School
Waltersorfer Chaussee, Berlin
competition, 4th prize

709 Bad Steben Casino
competition, 1st prize
under construction

710 Trade Fair Düsseldorf
competition, 1st prize
under construction

711 Dresden Central Bus Station
competition, 2nd prize

712 Leipzig University - Humanities Faculty
competition

713 Constantini Museum Buenos Aires
competition

714 Transrapid, Interior Design
competition

715 Parish Centre, Johnsallee, Hamburg
competition

716 Bramsche Town Hall
competition, 2nd prize

717 Stuttgart Airport, Extension
under construction

718 Bremen, Teerhof
competition

719 Weserbahnhof II, Grothe Museum
Bremen
competition, 1st prize

720 Christian Pavilion, Expo 2000, Hanover
competition, 1st prize
under construction

721 Linz Main Station
competition

722 Heckscher Klinik, Munich
competition

723 Design Hotel, Hamburg
competition

724 Elementary School Erkelenz
competition, 5th prize

725 Greifswald Bridge
consultancy project

726 Regensburg Burgweiting
competition, award

727 Stuttgart Airport, Terminal 3
competition, 1st prize
at planning stage

728 Basle Exhibition Grounds
competition

729 Elementary School Hanselmannstraße,
Munich
competition

730 Police Headquarters,
Technical Services, Duisburg
competition

731 St. Afra Grammar-School, Meißen
competition

732 Central Track Areas, Munich
competition

733 Institute of Physics, Berlin Adlershof
competition, 2nd prize

734 Deutsche Post AG Bonn
competition, award

735 Department of the Environment,
Dessau
competition

736 Federal Offices of Brandenburg and
Mecklenburg-Vorpommern in Berlin
competition, 1st prize
under construction

737 Berlin Brandenburg International
Airport
competition, 1st prize
at planning stage

738 United Arab Emirates Residency, Berlin
consultancy project

739 United Arab Emirates Embassy, Berlin
consultancy project

740 Astron Hotel, Landsberger Allee,
Berlin
study
completed 1999
D: V. Marg
PL: B. Lautz
C: D. Heller, K.-H. Behrendt,
F. Möhler, J. Kaufhold, D. Rösinger

1998

741 Institute of Architects, Düsseldorf
competition

742 German School and Service Housing
in Beijing
competition, 1st prize
under construction

743 Germany Industry Centre, Bucharest
planning stopped

744 Leipziger Platz Berlin
competition

745 International Congress Centre and
Assembly Building Hanoi/Vietnam
competition

746 Technology Centre Bertrandt AG,
Ehningen
competition, 3rd prize

747 Passau "New Centre"
consultancy project

748 Federal Office of Sachsen-Anhalt, Berlin
competition, 1st prize

749 Sparkasse Bremen
consultancy project

750 Munich Airport, Extension Terminal 2
competition, award

751 Trade Fair Amman, Jordan
consultancy project

752 Caesar Foundation, Bonn
competition

753 Music Theatre, Graz
competition

754 Federal Office of Hessen in Berlin
competition

755 C & A Site, Wilhelmshaven
consultancy project

756 Termina de Fusina, Venice
competition, 2nd prize

757 Transrapid Station, Schwerin
competition

758 Bremen Rhodarium
competition

759 Würzburg Sports Center
competition

760 School, Vienna
competition

761 Donau Museum, Linz
competition

762 Entertainment Center Bielefeld
competition, award

763 Bozen University
competition

764 Law Courts, Antwerpen
competition

765 Criminal Law Courts, Würzburg
competition

766 College Refectory HTWK, Leipzig
competition

767 Administration for the Public Finance Chamber, Berlin
competition

768 College Refectory, Regensburg
competition

769 Hotel Joachimstaler Platz, Berlin
consultancy project

770 Art Kite Museum, Detmold
competition, 1st prize
under construction

771 Philips Convention Stand
competition, 1st prize
completed 1999
D: M. v. Gerkan with W. Haux and
     M. Weiß
C: P. Radomski

772 Airport Johannesburg
study

773 Ulm Library
competition

774 Trade Fair Shanghai
consultancy project

775 Egyptian Embassy in Berlin
competition

776 Jahreszeitenverlag, Hamburg
consultancy project

777 Vocational Training School, Plattling
competition

778 Blankenese Train Station Square, Hamburg
competition, 3rd prize

779 Residential Development Alsteral, Hamburg
consultancy project

780 DB-Pavillon, Expo 2000, Hanover
study

781 Domplatte, Cologne
study

782 Concert Hall, Brügge
competition

783 Villa Marta Extension, Riga

784 Apartment House for the firm "Vincents", Riga

785 Office Building for the firm "Vincents", Riga

786 Congress Center, Rome
competition

787 Future TV Station Beirut
consultancy project

788 Vienna Library
competition

789 Monument O'Connel-Street, Dublin
competition

790 Housing and Festival Quarter 54, Wismar
study

791 Bochum Bridges
competition

792 BASF Social Centre, Berlin

793 Library with Computer Centre and Administration, Berlin Adlersdorf
competition

794 Trade Fair Padua, Italy
competition

795 Prager Straße Urban Design, Dresden
competition

796 Museum, Göteburg
competition

797 Public Library Erbacher Hof, Schweinfurt
competition

798 New Trade Fair, Friedrichshafen
competition

799 Neue Straße Ulm
competition

800 Münchner Tor
competition, 3rd prize

801 Mining Archives, Clausthal-Zellerfeld
under construction

802 Stuttgart Schloßplatz
competition

803 Quarter 115, Berlin-Mitte
consultancy project

804 Federal Department of the Environment, Oppenheim
competition

805 Development Concept Wieck/Eidena
study

806 Regis Detention Centre
competition

807 Therapeutic Bath, Bad Kissingen
competition

808 Berlin Olympic Stadium, conversion
competition, 1st prize
at planning stage

1999

809 Renovation of Salzburg Main Station
consultancy project

810 Renovation Innsbruck Main Station
consultancy project

811 Schwäbisch Hall, urban design
competition, 3rd prize

812 Trade Fair Shenzhen
competition

813 Elbufer Dresden
consultancy project

814 German Embassy in Kiev
competition, 3rd prize

815 Tromsoe Town Hall, Norway
competition, award

816 Ku'damm 229, Berlin
consultancy project

817 Schloßpassage Brandenburg
consultancy project

818 Vienna Airport
competition, 2nd prize

819 Bridges Expo 2001, Switzerland
competition

820 Telekom, Bonn
competition

821 Thermal Wind Power Station, Expo 2000, Hanover

822 Library 21, Stuttgart
competition

823 Ludwigspassage Bamberg
study

824 Biosphäre / Buga 2001, Potsdam
competition

825 Stuttgart Airport, Central Area
study

826 Diekirch Sports Center, Luxembourg
study

827 Museum, Schloß Homburg
competition, 3rd prize

828 Erfurt Authorities Centre
competition

829 Urban Villas Hamburg-Nienstedten

830 Benetton, Hamburg
study

831 Schirmdächer Expo 2000, Hanover
consultancy project

832 Denzlingen Community Centre
competition

833 Depesche Verlag, Geesthacht
study

834 Residential Building "Schiötz", Reinbek
at planning stage

835 Residential and Commercial Premises, Tacheles, Berlin
competition

836 Convention & Exhibition Center, Nanning International, China
competition, 1st prize
at planning stage

837 Tempodrom, Berlin
competition, 1st prize
at planning stage

838 Shopping Centre Rothenburgsort, Hamburg
study

839 Residential Buildings Nonnenstraße, Leipzig
study

840 Paderborn Airport
consultancy project

841 Trade Fair Hamburg
consultancy project

842 Ancona Airport
competition, 1st prize
at planning stage

843 Dresden University
competition

844 World of Sports "Adidas", Herzogenaurach
competition

845 Schloß Hopferau
competition, 1st prize

846 Sports Hall Extension, Flensburg
at planning stage

847 Maininsel, Schweinfurt
competition

848 Audi, Neckarsulm
study

849 Landshut Detention Centre
competition, award

850 Production Hall STN Atlas, Hamburg
study